*English Radicals
and the
American Revolution*

# English Radicals
# and the
# American Revolution

*by* Colin Bonwick

*The University of North Carolina Press*
*Chapel Hill*

Library of Congress Cataloging in Publication Data

*Bonwick, Colin.*
  *English radicals and the American Revolution.*

  *Bibliography: p.*
  *Includes index.*
  *1. Radicalism—Great Britain—History.*
*2. Great Britain—Intellectual life—18th century.*
*3. United States—History—Revolution, 1775–1783—Influence.*
*I. Title.*
*HN400.R3B66*          *322.4'4'0942*          *76-12641*
*ISBN 0-8078-1277-3*

*For Mary*

# Contents

# Acknowledgments

It is a pleasure to thank those many individuals and institutions who have given me much assistance with the preparation of this study.

I wish to thank the Twenty Seven Foundation for financing a visit to the United States in 1971 and the Higher Degree and Research Committee of the University of Keele for its support over many years. I also wish to thank the late Olive Lloyd Baker and Messrs. Josiah Wedgwood and Sons Ltd. for permission to quote from the Hardwicke Manuscripts and Wedgwood Papers respectively, the American Philosophical Society, Boston University Library, Historical Society of Pennsylvania, Houghton Library, Harvard University, and Yale University Libraries for permission to consult and quote from manuscripts; also the staffs of the many other libraries and record offices in Britain and the United States whose names appear in my bibliography for their substantial assistance in using the collections in their care. Quotations from the Adams Papers are from the microfilm edition, by permission of the Massachusetts Historical Society.

In particular, I would like to express my gratitude to Professors Donald C. Gordon of the University of Maryland and E. James Ferguson, now of the City University of New York, for guidance at an early stage; Dr. J. R. Pole of Churchill College, Cambridge, and Dr. John A. Woods of the University of Leeds for their help and advice at several crucial points; Dr. D. O. Thomas of the University College of Wales, Aberystwyth, for help in relation to Richard Price; Thomas R. Adams and the staff of the John Carter Brown Library and John Creasey of Dr. Williams's Library for making my visits to their libraries both valuable and congenial; and John Dann of the William L. Clements Library, University of Michigan, for providing not only photocopied material but scholarly advice to accompany it. I would also like to express my great thanks to Professors Ian R. Christie of University College, London, and Aubrey C. Land, now of the University of Georgia, for their advice at several critical stages and their comments on a draft of this book. Marie Bryan has done much typing and has been of great assistance in the preparation of this book.

Most of all, I wish to thank my wife for her constant help and scholarly advice over many years.

# Introduction

The second half of the eighteenth century was politically turbulent on both sides of the Atlantic. In America the rising maturity of colonial society led, after 1763, to increasingly bitter conflicts with Great Britain. At first the disputes were contained within the boundaries of an imperial framework; later they led to war, the assertion of a separate American sovereignty, and the foundation of a new and independent republic. Despite independence, the issues that lay at the heart of the conflict with Britain remained to be settled within an exclusively American structure, and though considerable progress was made, the issues were not resolved before the end of the century. During the same years in England, men were increasingly uneasy over the manner in which their political system was operating; they were horrified by what they regarded as its endemic corruption and suspected that it was being manipulated toward objectives that were anathema to the principles of traditional English constitutionalism. The outcome was an upsurge of radicalism. Initially the demands for reform came largely (though not exclusively) from the middle ranks of society, but during the 1790s another section of the community, the artisans, entered a continuous engagement in politics for the first time.

Simultaneous development of these two movements—revolution in America and radicalism in England—invites the observer to ask whether an integral relationship subsisted between them. Many contemporaries had no doubt: the perversion of English politics and the attack on colonial liberty were part and parcel of an empirewide disease infecting its entire fabric. Some recent historians have denied the connection and insisted that their only true unity rested in their contemporaneity. Yet the question lingers on. That part of its answer which is to be found in the history of the United States has been explored in recent years by Caroline Robbins, Bernard Bailyn, Pauline Maier, Gordon Wood, and others, and no further examination is needed here. The other must be sought in the domestic history of England. Such an inquiry demands consideration of the changing configuration of radicalism and discussion of its relationship to the American Revolution as both a war of independence and an experiment in government. Though the two forms often reciprocated with one another, it is possible and useful to examine them separately. Thus an analysis can be divided into two broad and overlapping themes: the problem of redefining the relationship between Britain and America, and the international role of America as an "asylum of liberty." Such a distinction is all the more desirable since the Revolution presented itself to the radicals in two distinct modes. As a war of independence it posed a direct problem that demanded an immediate solution; as an experiment it offered an analogue for their aspirations. But first the growth of radicalism must be set in its English context.

England at the accession of George III was a notably stable community. Though open to criticism on several counts (of the brutalization of many of its poor, for example), its fabric was sturdy and its members confident and secure—especially in comparison with the conditions of fifty and more years earlier. Part of the explanation for this stability rests in the fact that the shock waves of industrialization and urbanization had still to hurl their greatest strength against it; much lay in the earlier achievements of its statesmen, notably Sir Robert Walpole, and particularly in their success in inducing "a sense of common identity in those who wielded economic, social, and political power."[1] As a political society the country functioned from two principal centers, one at Westminster and the other in the local community. Since agriculture was still the most important source of the nation's wealth, power appropriately resided firmly in the hands of the landed aristocracy. Others were not excluded, especially at the local level of the county and borough, but generally speaking, politics was dominated by the great families, and patronage was the lubricant they applied to ensure that its machinery operated to their satisfaction. One other feature of mid-eighteenth-century society demands special attention. The church-by-law-established formed a second pillar in the diarchy of the constitution. Its bishops sat in the House of Lords, its parish clergy cooperated with village squires, and its courts superintended wide areas of moral and family law. In the secular realm its duty was to promote and enforce conformity to the prevailing social and political establishment, and in this it had enjoyed considerable success in recent decades; the flexibility of its theology and the latitudinarianism of its bishops had contributed significantly to the reduction of those religious tensions that so grievously bedeviled the previous century. Though the church was clearly the junior partner, its importance should not be overlooked.

All this was not achieved without cost. Stability begat inertia without accommodating all sections of English society. At the base, the deference of the lower orders to their social superiors frequently was grudging, and their reluctant subordination led to a constant undercurrent of turbulence, violence, and protest.[2] One particular interest group, the Protestant Dissenters, resented the discrimination directed against them in the alleged interest of the state—a resentment aggravated by their knowledge that they were loyal upholders of the Hanoverian settlement. Others, who were members of the broader political nation outside Westminster and Whitehall, found many aspects of the system obnoxious. These were men and women who were well educated, well informed, and often possessed of considerable local influence; they expected to be consulted and to enjoy a modest influence in national affairs, if only at second remove or by exercising a negative. Some, indeed, could be incorporated fairly well into the system: the country gentry were represented in Parliament (though less so than in the past), and the House of Commons functioned as the "grand inquest of the nation." Many, less easy to satisfy, condemned contemporary political practices on both empirical and moral grounds and, more important, because they believed that the fundamental principles of English constitutionalism were being perverted. Of these objectors, a few were residual Tories who sometimes held latent Jacobite sentiments. Most stood at the other end of the political spectrum; although the term is anachronistic, they can be conveniently labeled as radicals.[3]

After lying virtually dormant for many years, English radicalism revived so vigorously during the 1760s that within ten years three distinct types had emerged. Two were original creations and though they were not immediately visible during the age of the American Revolution they were to have long and influential careers. Jeremy Bentham was formulating the basis of what developed into utilitarianism in his *Fragment on Government*, first published in 1776. In the same year, but across the Atlantic, Thomas Paine was taking his first public steps toward a theory of society based on pure and self-justifying natural rights; fifteen years later he developed and recast it in his brilliantly iconoclastic *Rights of Man*, which provided much of the intellectual groundwork for an explicitly working-class political movement. The third element in English radicalism was the "commonwealth" or "Real Whig" tradition, which incorporated as a dependency the doctrine of the ancient constitution.

Perhaps a fourth radical group should be added to the three already mentioned: the Wilkite movement of the 1760s and early 1770s. In certain respects it provided a bridge between the commonwealth tradition and the artisan radicals of the 1790s. John Wilkes has been described as one of the founders of a mass radical movement in Britain because he extended his influence beyond the immediate confines of the cities of London and Westminster and aroused the political interest of many thousands of artisans who previously had been considered to be outside the political nation.[4] The activities of the Wilkites certainly marked a new departure in the political conduct of the lower orders—one which presaged the more systematic agitation of the closing decade of the century— but it was the social fabric of Wilkite radicalism, not its program, that was noteworthy. Although the first formal demands for reform were launched by Wilkes's associates in the City, the intellectual content of their agitation was far from original; in all essentials it enunciated the traditional principles of radicalism and can be treated as an offshoot of commonwealth radicalism, albeit a distinctive one. As for Wilkes's personal claim to be regarded as a radical, perhaps the best that can be said on such an uncertain subject is that he probably was sincere in his declarations of libertarian principles but almost invariably permitted considerations of personal interest to take precedence.

Of the three principal branches, one can be discounted immediately and the others fall into a natural sequence for discussion. Benthamite radicalism had to wait several decades before entering its prime; it can be safely ignored during the eighteenth century. Similarly, the Painite "new" or "artisan" radicalism flowered only in the 1790s, though there had been earlier hints of what was to come; consideration of this new, advanced radicalism can be postponed until after discussion of the "Commonwealthmen." For it was with the old or moderate radicals of the commonwealth tradition that the main line of English radicalism was to be discovered during the age of the American Revolution.

Intellectually, Commonwealthmen were a less tightly knit group than either of the others. Most, though not all, traced their ideological ancestry back to the troubles of the previous century; and in particular they regarded the Glorious Revolution as the vindication of English liberty and constitutionalism. Herein lay deep irony since the great oligarchs of grand Whiggery also applauded the Revolution—though chiefly because it gave political sanctity to their exercise of authority. What had happened was that the ranks of Whiggery had divided into grand Whigs who directed the country and its affairs and Real Whigs who diligently preserved the traditions of radicalism as best they could. In this latter endeavor there was a close correspondence between the goals of Commonwealthmen and the political aspirations of Protestant Dissenters to obtain relief from discrimination based on confessional criteria—so much so that commonwealth ideologues were also frequently nonconformist propagandists, and Dissenters were frequently radical in their politics. This congruence of active dissent and commonwealth radicalism is clearly demonstrated in the persons of leading old radicals. Thomas Hollis, Thomas Brand Hollis, and Capel Lofft were nonconformist laymen, and Richard Price and Joseph Priestley were dissenting ministers, for example, though Granville Sharp, Christopher Wyvill, John Cartwright, and John Jebb were either practicing or lapsed Anglicans. In another respect there was an even closer correspondence. Virtually all radicals belonged to the middle ranks of society, and the fact was evident in their politics. Their theories of natural rights demanded respect for two central principles: liberty and equality. Of these two ideals, they were devoted to the principle of liberty and embarrassed by some of the implications that flowed from the concept of equality. If a clear span divided Jebb's hotheaded demands for universal suffrage from Wyvill's shrewd caution, none went as far as the artisan ideologues of the 1790s. For this reason it is also appropriate to regard the old or commonwealth radicals as moderates.

When the American Revolution came, radical sympathy for the patriot cause was related coherently to both ideological principle and immediate circumstance. Since commonwealth axioms were explicitly universal in their relevance, it may be presumed that Real Whigs would have been concerned for the fate of American liberty on grounds of high principle alone; certainly they displayed an intense interest in libertarian causes elsewhere. Yet their sympathy was more specific and much richer than it was for other causes. In part the radicals were responding to a crisis that impinged on them directly as fellow members of the same society. For a most fundamental premise supporting their evaluation of the imperial crisis was their conviction that Englishmen and Americans belonged to a single community: not just the global community in which men of all countries were united, but a particular Anglo-American community whose members shared a cultural and spiritual affinity as well as a network of economic and (before the war) political institutions. It followed, in the opinion of Commonwealthmen, that English as well as American liberty was at risk.

Even this does not complete the explanation since another factor gave a distinctive cast to radical understanding. Unusually close connections with America and its inhabitants greatly heightened Real Whigs' perceptions and sharpened their appreciation of the issues at stake. They knew many Americans intimately—sometimes through direct personal friendship, more commonly by correspondence—and were well-read in the descriptive literature of colonial history and the pamphlet propaganda of the imperial dispute. Their consequent wide knowledge of, and high regard for, American society powerfully colored their interpretation of the Revolution.

The nature of this understanding was neither simple nor static. In general its topography followed that of the Revolution itself: radicals were concerned with both the dispute that culminated in separation and the experiment in government that formed a central element in fulfilling America's role as an asylum of liberty. In the first case they were concerned primarily for the vindication of liberty in America; in the second for the fate of liberty at home. But this is an oversimplification. At all times Commonwealthmen were so solicitous for the welfare of their American friends that the point scarcely requires further exposition. Likewise, they appreciated that any contribution to the advancement of liberty elsewhere was dependent on the successful defense of liberty in America. And their responses to the imperial crisis were influenced by the premises of their own ideology and their concern for the security of the asylum. At this point, however, it is necessary to point to a paradox in radical attitudes. Though they offered strong support for the colonists before the war, steadfast sympathy during it, and warm encouragement afterward, Commonwealthmen remained sturdily indifferent to two of the central elements in the Revolutionary experience: they resisted independence and rejected republicanism!

Of the two aspects of the American Revolution, it is logically as well as chronologically convenient to examine the imperial crisis first. For twenty years after the conclusion of the Seven Years' or French and Indian War in 1763, the question of the proper relationship between Britain and America was an inescapable issue in imperial politics. In retrospect, the dispute that may be said to have originated with the Revenue Act of 1764 appears to have moved ineluctably through the Boston Tea Party, the skirmish at Lexington and Cornwallis's surrender at Yorktown, to the final apotheosis of American independence. Radicals neither accepted the inevitability of this logic nor wished its fulfillment. Like most of their fellow Englishmen they ardently hoped to preserve the imperial connection, though unlike them their primary concerns were for political and cultural rather than strategic or commercial considerations. Beyond this, however, they diverged from the orthodox majority. Commonwealthmen appreciated that colonial society was remarkably sophisticated and understood as a matter of prudence as well as principle that the connection with Britain was dependent on the voluntary consent of the American people. Thus, while sharing colonial suspicions of a conspiracy to suppress American liberty, they strained every nerve to find some form of accommodation before the war. Similarly, though they accepted the moral legitimacy as well as the political expediency of resorting to force in 1775, radicals continued the search for a means of reconciliation long after any dispassionate spectator would have concluded that their cause was hopeless; only the facts of war persuaded them of the inevitability of separation. Once they had been induced to concede the point, however, they welcomed the vindication of American independence.

Their reasons for this change are instructive. Commonwealthmen were, of course, delighted at the prospects it offered for the new nation. But they also believed that the successful preservation of American liberty would have implications for communities far beyond the frontiers of the United States, including, in particular, their own country. And they were not alone in this belief.

American convictions that the defense of their liberty was pertinent to the prosperity of English liberty had been firmly established before the war. Universalist claims were common currency and remained an important component of public ideology for many years. Such evangelical pretensions operated at several levels but centered on the concept of America as an asylum of liberty. Many patriots would have agreed with Mercy Warren that they had been summoned to "the post Alloted us by the Great Director of the Theatre of the Universe" but if, as Abigail Adams remarked, "the cause of liberty is the cause of all mankind," their obligations could be discharged in many ways.[5] At the highest and most general level, Benjamin Rush believed "that the very existence of *freedom* upon our globe, was involved in the issue of the contest in favour of the United States."[6] As an asylum of liberty, America could offer a haven of refuge for the victims of oppression, though (as the revolutionaries appreciated) this was a contribution of limited value. They could, however, offer a service of far broader significance. Once they had decided to seek independence, Americans enjoyed the rare opportunity to formulate their own institutions of government. Their primary concern was for their own situation, but they also expected their work to be of interest to the world at large. As Thomas Jefferson claimed in 1788, "We can surely boast of having set the world a beautiful example of a government reformed by reason alone without bloodshed."[7] In spite of difficulties and disappointments, the revolutionaries remained confident that they were contributing to the promotion of human progress. They were convinced that in consequence of their own actions the "rights of Mankind, the priviledges [sic] of the people, and the true principles of liberty" were better understood throughout Europe, that the flames kindled in 1776 had "spread over too much of the globe to be extinguished by the feeble engines of despotism," and that if it did justice to itself the United States would be "the workshop of liberty to the Civilized World."[8]

Such claims were audacious and require rigorous examination. They have often seemed at variance with the social and economic forces discernible beneath the political surface, and for that reason frequently have been discounted. On occasion, no doubt, they were the protestations of men whistling to keep up their spirits in times of danger; sometimes they were no more than the propaganda of diplomats and recruiting sergeants. They were also the private views of men of distinction. Inquiries into their authors' integrity are largely a matter for historians of American domestic affairs, but it is also appropriate to examine the responses of those for whom the Revolution was intended to be exemplary. The opinions of English radicals were especially pertinent in this context since many patriots believed that their actions were particularly relevant to the defense of English as well as American freedom. James Otis insisted in 1768 that the colonial cause was "the cause of the whole British empire," and his view was reinforced shortly before the outbreak of war when John Dickinson declared that "England must be saved in *America*."[9] In the event the messianic claims fell on welcoming ears.

The nature of radical reactions changed over the years in response to differing needs and circumstances but were always enthusiastic. During the early stages of the imperial dispute, Commonwealthmen became gravely alarmed at the apparent direction of official policy and concluded that ministers were systematically conspiring to impose tyranny on the country. When they looked from the disputes surrounding John Wilkes in Middlesex to the simultaneous train of events in New England they were convinced of the existence of a single transatlantic crisis; liberty, they believed, was in peril throughout the empire, and Britain's fate was enmeshed with that of the colonies. Thus it was vital that America should survive as a haven in which the victims of oppression could seek refuge.

Other considerations reinforced this belief. Radical ideology was strongly directed by a strain of millenarianism. Both theological cosmology and secular philosophy suggested the possibility of human progress; they also made it plain that improvement was dependent on high moral conduct. When seen in this light, the challenge to English liberty and, still more, the disasters of the American war were interpreted as divine retribution for the corruption and depravity of contemporary British life. Once more it was essential that the American asylum should flourish, though in this respect more as a demonstration of the general viability of a liberal society and a step toward the advancement of human happiness.

As an experiment in government, the asylum of liberty also offered a model for emulation by other countries. Here the Commonwealthmen carefully discriminated in their selection of what was pertinent to their own circumstances and dismissal of what was not. They were well aware of the differences between English and American society and appreciated that common theoretical problems might require somewhat different empirical solutions in each country. Nevertheless, their urgently felt need for pragmatic evidence to sustain their essentially moral and theoretical principles and their belief that there was sufficient congruence between the American experience and their own persuaded them of the underlying relevance of the American model to English reform. Thus, while on the one hand it would be absurd to demand that radicals should incorporate United States constitutionalism into their own system lock, stock, and barrel, on the other it does not follow that the American example had negligible or no importance in the growth of English radicalism. Yet it would be pointless to inquire how correctly they comprehended the nature of the Revolution and is more fruitful to examine their perception and to explore the question of its value to their needs—all the more, since both the model and the radical uses of it changed considerably during the course of time.

Though the nature of the American model (and radical perceptions of it) changed in time, its example always was liberal by comparison with contemporary English practice. Initially, the Pennsylvania government of 1776 offered an especially advanced pattern of American government. After the war, however, its effect on radicals was diminished, first by the personal influence of John Adams while he was American minister in London and later by the example of the federal Constitution of 1787. Simultaneously, another development was of special interest to those many Commonwealthmen who were also religious nonconformists. During the Revolution several states dismantled or modified their apparatus of confessional discrimination; the eighteenth-century climax of this process came with the enactment of Jefferson's Virginia Statute for Religious Freedom in 1786. As they watched, Dissenters were sharply aware of the contrast with their own situation and were profoundly excited by it. For many years they had argued for relief on abstract grounds; now at last they could cite empirical evidence for their contention that the security of the secular state was more likely to be strengthened than endangered by repeal of discriminatory legislation.

A dramatic extension of English radicalism took place during the last decade of the century. For the first time a body of artisans became permanently engaged in the debates of English politics. Though they were even less successful than the Real Whigs in achieving their objectives in their own generation, their presence was very important. Their social status was not the only feature that distinguished these new radicals from the old. Pressed by the appalling circumstances of industrialization and stimulated by events in France, they constructed an ideology that was in certain respects far more advanced and much more offensive to the orthodox controllers of political power. One immediately evident characteristic was that though its rhetoric was nominally as universalist as that of the Commonwealthmen, it actually was markedly more insular. The new radicals were far more involved with immediate issues and less likely to seek encouragement from elsewhere. Most noticeable was a shift of emphasis toward an explicitly class-based ideology; it suggested that a major faultline had developed in the structure of English radicalism. The memory of America played a lesser role in artisan thought than in the programs of Commonwealthmen, but it could on occasion be deployed to devastating effect in support of an egalitarian platform. The second part of

Paine's *Rights of Man* was explicitly rooted in his American experience.

The appearance of a class-oriented, egalitarian movement created an embarrassing problem for moderate radicals. To their left was the social challenge of the artisans and the excesses of the French Revolution, and to their right the reactionary policies of the Pitt administration. They needed a model that would demonstrate the continuing viability of incremental reform. Such an example was ready at hand.

*English Radicals
and the
American Revolution*

# I

## English Radicals

In the age of the American Revolution the main line of English radicalism ran with those who stood in the commonwealth tradition.[1] Though clearly a minority in a conservative nation, they were neither a small squadron of obscure and pedantic theoreticians nor a totally uniform group. Rather, these moderate radicals were a heterogeneous body of men and women, several of whom were prominent figures in the intellectual life of the country. Among their many interests, they believed it the duty of all men to formulate and hold political opinions, especially in times of crisis, and they argued that statesmen had no right to exclude the people from knowledge of political affairs.[2]

The radicals' understanding of the two grand themes of the American Revolution—the war of independence and the experiment in government—was rooted in a complex network of social attitudes, spiritual values, intellectual principles, and ideological requirements. Most radicals belonged to those middle ranks of society who formed a broader political nation outside the aristocratic circles of national authority. As individuals they often participated in a wide range of reform activities, though for analytical convenience they can be roughly brigaded into those whose first concern was with parliamentary reform, and those, being religious Dissenters, who were primarily interested in securing relief from discriminatory legislation directed against them. Such clarity of definition is less possible when discussing their arguments. To suggest that their rhetoric expressed a systematic political philosophy would be misleading; the term "ideology" better describes their corpus of ethical values, political principles, and empirical programs. Of its many components, two are worth particular note. As inheritors of a long political tradition and beneficiaries of somewhat more recent social stability, radicals had great hopes for human progress. Yet they were poised at a crucial stage in ideological development since all around them they observed evidence of moral decay and political corruption. They were sharply aware of this anomaly and anxiously sought to resolve it. And though the radicals' deployment of their ideology in public debate often made it appear insular, in reality its application was universal. In particular, radical understanding was sensitive to libertarian issues beyond the shores of England and was willing to perceive relevance in the experience of other countries.

Excluded from the central arena of national politics by a self-denying ordinance that prevented them from making the easy compromises necessary to conform to the practices of church and state, radicals operated as a pressure group whose object was the promotion of constitutional integrity. Their recurrent argument was that the vital principles of the constitution had been so extensively corrupted that the government was in imminent danger of degenerating into tyranny; they constantly reiterated that if English liberty was to survive, immediate action was essential. They took part in many campaigns. During the second half of the eighteenth century they were involved in Wilkite agitation in London and elsewhere, the associated counties movement for parliamentary reform which began in 1779 and faded away after 1785, the more advanced recommendations of the Westminster Sub-Committee of 1780, the Society for Constitutional Information (founded in the same year), and the moderate reform movement of the 1790s. In ecclesiastical politics the radicals took part in the so-called "Feathers Tavern" petition of 1771–72 to secure for Anglican clergy relief from the obligation to subscribe to the Trinitarian Articles of Religion, the request for similar relief for dissenting clergy and schoolmasters, and the campaigns to obtain repeal of the Test and Corporation Acts in 1787, 1789, and 1790.[3] Beyond all was the cause of the American colonists.

Nor should the importance of their actions be denigrated. In objective terms, the radicals' only victory was modest—they secured relief for nonconformist ministers and schoolmasters in 1779—and success on that occasion was largely the consequence of external factors not of their making. But they set themselves tasks of a far higher order than, for example, the Quakers did when they obtained exemption from the requirement to take oaths and register their children with the ecclesiastical parish. For their programs were concerned with the central structure of English political society, and at the very least their rhetoric compelled a deeper discussion of many fundamental issues.

In some respects radicals formed a diverse gathering of men and women. Many were Dissenters, some were Anglicans; a number were landowners, most were professional men. Though many either lived permanently in London or visited the capital regularly, centers of radicalism flourished in many parts of the provinces. But if there was neither total correspondence nor symmetry in their background and social status any more than in their opinions, the bonds of unity, common interest, and similarity of outlook were sufficient to consider them as a single group. Also there was a complex network of connections among the great majority which, although it lacked the single center of a spider's web, was still very tightly knit.[4]

Before examining their social standing and the nature of their ideology, a number of radicals must be discussed individually. Although they shared a common ideology, there were so many that, for purposes of description, they should be broken down into different groups. A rough-and-ready criterion can be fashioned out of the two great causes that agitated them: parliamentary reform and the repeal of discriminatory legislation directed against Dissenters. It is essential to note, however, that this categorization is neither entirely consistent nor mutually exclusive; many radicals were actively involved in both causes.

Parliamentary reform attracted the attention of almost all radicals. Some of the most active were Christopher Wyvill, John Cartwright, Granville Sharp, John Jebb, and Thomas Brand Hollis.

Among them they spanned the gamut from moderate to advanced within the limits of their own form of radicalism.

Most cautious and most shrewd among the reformers was Christopher Wyvill. A liberal clergyman of the established church, his theological views were all but Unitarian. After the failure in 1772 of the "Feathers" petition he decided to remain a member of the church but abandoned the active practice of his ministry. At about the same time he inherited through his wife's family lands which established him as one of the leading gentry in the North Riding of Yorkshire; the independence given by his income and social status enabled Wyvill to devote his attention to political affairs. A man of complete integrity, clear vision, and political intuition, he was the guiding force behind the associated counties movement that promoted parliamentary reform from 1779 to 1785.[5] Thereafter he remained active though less prominent in the cause of reform; he also worked for the repeal of discriminatory legislation against Dissenters. As a tactician, he exploited the newspapers for propaganda purposes, understood the importance of cooperating with the great parliamentarians while remaining independent, and accepted the need for compromise. If Wyvill was unable to achieve success, no one could.

Few men played leading roles in the agitation of the nineteenth century as well as that of eighteenth; Major John Cartwright achieved this distinction.[6] A member of an old Nottinghamshire family that had lost much of its estate during the Civil War, he nevertheless owned substantial landed property and had connections with the aristocracy of his neighborhood; having originally intended to make a career in the navy, he had resigned his commission shortly before the American Revolution and taken up farming and reform politics. Though active in the associated counties movement, Cartwright's principal contribution to eighteenth-century reform was as a propagandist. His first reform tract, *Take Your Choice!* (published in 1776), advocated universal manhood suffrage and proposed one of the most advanced programs of its day: one which anticipated the Chartists by more than fifty years. In 1780 he played an important part in founding the most significant organ of its generation for the dissemination of radical opinion, the Society for Constitutional Information. Pertinacious in spirit rather than original or adaptable in mind, he continued to advocate parliamentary reform until his death in 1824; in his last years his views became markedly more extreme.

The breadth of interest among the reformers is illustrated to a remarkable degree by the career of Granville Sharp. A member of a distinguished clerical family, Sharp was highly unusual among the radicals for remaining a devout and orthodox member of the Church of England; biblical interpretation was always the principal intellectual focus of his life. John Adams, who met Sharp while Adams was American minister in London after the Revolution, aptly remarked that "the grandson of the famous Archbishop Sharp [was] very amiable & benevolent in his dispositions, and a voluminous writer, but as Zealously attached to Episcopacy & the Athanasian Creed as he is to civil and religious Liberty—a mixture which in this Country is not common."[7] Sharp's theological devotion led him into a multitude of humanitarian campaigns and particularly into the crusade against slavery; his greatest triumph (perhaps the greatest success of any reformer in his generation) came in 1772 with Lord Mansfield's decision in Somerset's Case that slavery was an institution unknown in English law. He became interested in parliamentary reform during the American Revolution and was much respected as the author of a number of tracts advocating considerably more radical reform than that proposed by Wyvill, including his own distinctive institution of "frank-pledge." He was also active in the associated counties agitation, providing material for his brother James, who sat on the London Common Council, and any others who wished to use it.

An extreme wing of commonwealth radicalism existed in the persons of Thomas Hollis, Thomas Brand Hollis, and John Jebb. Both Hollises came from dissenting stock and were said to be republicans. A retiring man, Thomas Hollis owned estates in Dorset but, disgusted by the bribery and other corrupt practices endemic in eighteenth-century politics, he rejected several suggestions that he should enter Parliament. Instead he published and distributed throughout the world books on liberty; he arranged for the republication of many of the classic texts of the previous century, and through these works he influenced the course of English radicalism in his own day. Brand Hollis was less circumspect. Although unrelated, he had inherited Thomas Hollis's estates and wealth in 1774 and used it to obtain election for the rotten borough of Hindon at the general election of that year. Later, however, he was unseated on petition and sentenced to six months' imprisonment and a fine for bribery; he was able partially to restore his reputation by his association with Jebb and the Society for Constitutional Information. In the early 1790s he associated with Thomas Paine and as a Dissenter participated in the campaign for repeal of the Test and Corporation Acts; always he was more of a lieutenant than a leader.[8]

John Jebb, who collaborated with Brand Hollis as a member of the subcommittee of the Westminster Committee for parliamentary reform in 1780 which advocated universal manhood suffrage, came from an Anglican family. As a theological liberal he was active in the movement to abolish clerical subscription, but when it failed he resigned his preferments and, with great reluctance, his Cambridge fellowship. Lacking an independent income, Jebb might have entered nonconformist orders; instead he took up medicine and practiced as a London physician. His arrival in the metropolis came at an opportune moment for he had been interested in politics for some time. He became active in the Middlesex reform movement as well as Westminster agitation and collaborated with Cartwright in founding the Society for Constitutional Information; the extremity of his views and his reputation for hotheadedness somewhat diminished his influence. Unfortunately, he died in 1786.[9] His wife Ann was also an active radical.

Many others were actively concerned with political reform. James Burgh, a dissenting schoolmaster of Newington Green, provided the radicals with a contemporary text when he published his most influential book *Political Disquisitions* shortly before his death in 1775. Catharine Macaulay, a brilliant woman who had many intellectual admirers including Thomas Hollis, published a six-volume history of England as a rebuttal to the famous *History* by David Hume. Though useful as a reference work for radicals, it failed to supplant its conservative rival in the public mind; her various political pamphlets probably were more influential. Thomas Day was a devotee of Rousseau's educational theories and author of a celebrated didactic children's book *Sandford and Merton*; he was also an active political writer and for a time was one of the leading members and authors of the Society for Constitutional Information. Radicals were rare in Parliament, but

David Hartley was notable as an enthusiastic reformer in the House of Commons; unfortunately his prolixity and eccentricity severely reduced his effectiveness. Matthew Robinson-Morris, Baron Rokeby, also sat in the Commons, but published his tracts from retirement. Charles Lennox, duke of Richmond, was an unlikely figure to be included among the radicals, as were Viscount Mahon, later Earl Stanhope, and Willoughby Bertie, earl of Abingdon; all enjoyed a reputation for radicalism in the upper House. The bench of bishops was traditionally conservative, but Jonathan Shipley, bishop of St. Asaph, was known for his liberal beliefs, and the consecration of Richard Watson as bishop of Llandaff in 1782 added a distinctive touch of political heterodoxy to the Lords, as he had earlier been active in the reform movement in Cambridgeshire.[10]

The second great cause, the relief of Dissenters, was narrower in objective and attracted the attention of a much more homogeneous group. Nevertheless, as has already been shown, Nonconformists were not concerned exclusively with their own sectarian interests but were also active in political reform. Some were laymen, others were ministers; few became as unorthodox as David Williams, who opened a deistic chapel near Cavendish Square and later became a French citizen. Andrew Kippis served for forty-two years as a Presbyterian minister in Westminster, but achieved greater fame as a journalist and biographer; his greatest enterprise was the *Biographia Britannica*. Many other London and provincial ministers offered overt or tacit support to the cause of reform. Of all the black regiment of nonconformist clergy two men stand out: Richard Price and Joseph Priestley. Both had wide intellectual interests—Price published a number of tracts on demography, finance, and insurance, and Priestley acquired a distinguished reputation as an experimental scientist—but they were particularly notable as advanced theologians. Price was an Arian and Priestley a Socinian, and their theological principles ensured that they could never be popular in a generally orthodox society. Their politics only exacerbated public hostility toward them. Price was a gentle person and a poor preacher, but his political views were clear and forceful and his tracts sometimes provoked vigorous reprisals by those who disagreed with them. Already unpopular because of his liberalism during the American war, his approval of the French

Revolution aroused an intense furor, from the full consequences of which he was probably saved only by his death in 1791.[11]

If anything, Priestley aroused even more antipathy. His radical views in theology and politics might have been tolerated by his fellow citizens, but unfortunately Priestley was an abrasive and indiscreet publicist in circumstances that called for considerable delicacy and tactical subtlety. In particular, his polemical writings in support of relief for Dissenters could all too easily be construed as leading to an immediate root-and-branch attack on the established church. Priestley's sympathy for the French Revolution increased his unpopularity to such an extent that he felt himself in danger of prosecution for sedition or treason; ultimately he decided that voluntary emigration to the United States in 1794 was preferable to the possibility of enforced transportation to Botany Bay. Even in America, Priestley's political views sometimes made his life stormy, but the closing years of his life were ones of happiness.

Dissenting radicalism was strong in London but by no means confined to the metropolis. The greatest Baptist polemicist, Robert Robinson, lived in Cambridge. Unlike the Presbyterian ministers, Robinson was a poor, self-educated man. He was active both in the parliamentary reform movement and in the campaign for Dissenters' relief; his literary style was vigorous and earthy, sometimes bawdy, and often offensive. In the west another Baptist, the Calvinist Caleb Evans, was prominent in Bristol as minister of the Broadmead Chapel, and Joshua Toulmin represented the Unitarian strain of Baptist theology in Taunton. Other Dissenters further afield included Micaiah Towgood in Exeter, Newcome Cappe in York, William Turner in Wakefield, George Walker in Nottingham, and James Murray (by origin a Scottish Presbyterian) who had a chapel in Newcastle-upon-Tyne. Without doubt the outstanding dissenting minister in the Midlands was Priestley, who was minister to the New Meeting in Birmingham from 1780 until the church and state riots of 1791 forced him to retreat to London. Among laymen the brilliant potter and entrepreneur Josiah Wedgwood lived in Staffordshire but maintained close contact with an extensive coterie of metropolitan friends, particularly through his partner Thomas Bentley. If activists like Wyvill, Cartwright, Price, and Priestley provided leadership, these were some of the men who gave support from the ranks.

One last group remains to be mentioned: the liberal Anglicans. Some have already been discussed, for leadership of the parliamentary reform movement was largely in the hands of members of the church, whether active or lapsed. They were beneficed clergy who wished to preach a rational, virtually Unitarian religion, though the Articles of Religion were Trinitarian, partly Calvinist, and included traces of Catholicism. The failure of the Feathers petition brought the ambivalence of their position to a head. Some, like Wyvill, remained only formally within the church; others, like Jebb, left it entirely. Still others, notably Archdeacon Francis Blackburne, the intellectual patriarch of Anglican liberalism in the late eighteenth century, retained their preferments and continued as active ministers. A few made the complete passage from the church to the dissenting ministry. In this respect, Theophilus Lindsey was a key figure.[12] He abandoned a promising ecclesiastical career to open the first overtly Unitarian chapel in London in April 1774. A mild, diffident, and studious man, he preferred to concentrate on his duties as a minister rather than become involved in politics, but his Essex Street chapel became one of the principal meeting places for radicals in London, and he maintained an extensive correspondence with his out-of-town friends until his death in 1808. Men such as Lindsey and his friend John Disney provided an intellectual and spiritual link between the advanced parties of the church and Dissent. With Wyvill, Jebb, and others, they helped strengthen the connection between theological and political radicalism; even men like Lindsey who were cautiously inactive contributed an ingredient of cohesiveness to the agitation for reform. Their unity was further encouraged by their similarity of social status.

Almost all old radicals were gentlemen. The duke of Richmond was an aristocrat, and Robert Robinson had been a barber's boy; the majority came from the middle ranks of English society. Some, such as Wyvill, the Hollises, and Cartwright, were landed gentry. Others were professional men, like Jebb, or ministers of religion, like Price and Priestley. Many, like Sharp, enjoyed the freedom bestowed by a private income or financial support from friends and relatives. As members of the middle ranks, they were among the beneficiaries of the stability so successfully achieved under the direction of the great oligarchs. They respected the rights of property and the gradations of a hierarchical society, manifested little hostility toward those who stood above them socially, and in return expected deference from those who stood beneath. A few, such as Sharp whose family entertained the king, had connections with those in authority; some, like Price, became intimate friends of the more liberal members of the aristocracy; and Cartwright was suitably deferential toward his neighbor the Duke of Portland.[13] A number enjoyed influence in their local communities, but this was insufficiently satisfying. Well educated, well informed, and articulate, they were members of that broad political nation outside Westminster and Whitehall that expected to be consulted and to enjoy influence in national affairs. Their right to this influence was conceded implicitly by North's government when it subsidized the distribution of pamphlets during the American Revolution.

Yet they were also a group of self-selected outsiders. Unlike most of their social peers, they declined to accommodate themselves to the terms offered by the establishment of church and state as the price to be paid for security. In politics they insisted on the application of principle rather than formal but empty homage; they described the patronage that oiled the machinery of state as corruption. It was ironic that the great Whig families traced the origins of their authority to the same fountain as that to which the radicals traced their own ideology—the Glorious Revolution of 1688—for these men maintained the political system because it confirmed their power. In another sense, they were internal aliens. Like the land, trade, or the church, Dissent was one of the "interests" of the nation, and by reason of ancient memories going back to the seventeenth-century civil wars the establishment excluded Dissenters from equal rights. Within the church, liberal Anglicans resented their obligation to subscribe to the Articles of Religion. While most of their fellow subjects accepted the rules of society in return for receiving its advantages, radicals refused to take the tempting and easy path of nominal conformity. Instead they reluctantly preferred exclusion from the main halls of the community as the price of intellectual and spiritual independence.

Independence of mind brought its own paradoxes. A libertarian philosophy such as theirs, with its emphasis on liberty, the ultimate sovereignty of the people, and freedom of conscience, implicitly articulated a program to meet the aspirations of those who were close to power but excluded from exercising it. Yet the concept of class was unimportant in politics before 1815 as far as the middle orders were concerned. Few of their constituents responded to the radical call, preferring deference instead. Nor was this the only difficulty. While they advanced principles that were inherently antiaristocratic (and dangerously subversive of the proper deference of the lower orders), the moderate radicals had no desire to dismantle the hierarchical structure that made English society stable and its middle- and upper-class citizens secure. They failed to attack aristocratic power with the vigor that intellectual logic might be thought to have required and they refused to develop the egalitarian elements of their theories; perhaps their persistent criticism of executive corruption in Parliament sublimated their latent antagonism. Rather, they wished to promote and implement a libertarian ideology without destroying that social stability from which they benefited. In short, they looked for reform rather than revolution.[14]

Before discussing the content of Real Whig ideology, it is important to realize that only superficially were the radicals nationalistic and inward-looking. Their commonwealth tradition was strongly and distinctively English, their analysis was based on English experience, and they worked out the implications of their theories largely in terms of the defects and needs of their own country. Nevertheless, they were not insular. A substratum of classical learning lay beneath their theory, and their concern for liberty in England partly flowed from their observation of events elsewhere.

Radicals visualized their actions on the wide field of human affairs as well as in the local context of their own society. Men such as Sharp, Price, and Priestley regarded themselves as citizens of the world, not merely as subjects of their own country, and believed that their principles were of universal application. Their attitude was strengthened by their acceptance of a moral obligation to see themselves in this light; as Sharp argued, "Under the glorious Dispensation of the Gospel, we are absolutely bound to consider ourselves as Citizens of the World; that every Man whatever, without any partial distinction of Nation, Distance or Complexion, must necessarily be esteemed our Neighbour, and our Brother;

and that we are absolutely bound in Christian Duty to entertain a Disposition towards all Mankind as charitable and benevolent, at least as that which was required of the Jews, under the law, towards their national Brethren."[15] A sense of community with all men was inherent in radical theory of government, and there was no inherent conflict between domestic and universal concerns. As Brand Hollis declared, "The love of general freedom and the Universal welfare of mankind is ... not inconsistent with the truest regard for one's own country."[16]

Commonwealth ideology was already well articulated by the beginning of George III's reign. Some components, notably the theory of natural rights and the doctrine of the ancient constitution of the Anglo-Saxons, dated from before the seventeenth century; the traces of egalitarianism and early suggestions of a felicific calculus had a hint of the future about them. Many ingredients, including its central core, were derived from the great debates of the civil wars; and the political analysis of men such as James Harrington, John Milton, Algernon Sydney, and somewhat later John Locke remained the foundation stone for most radicals even if they felt compelled to modify some constituents. Nevertheless, there was no single corpus of commonwealth orthodoxy to which all radicals were obliged to subscribe; instead, they shared a number of general principles but disagreed as to their relative importance and the manner of their application. Moreover, though most moderate radicals attached great spiritual and intellectual importance to their seventeenth-century inheritance, a few (notably Sharp) to whom it was of negligible significance or even offensive can be incorporated into the group because they accepted other major tenets and cooperated closely with those who were more conventional. Thus commonwealth ideology comprised not a logically integrated system but an amalgam of moral principles and political ideals that gave philosophical purpose to the state and provided a set of normative values through which fundamental beliefs could be articulated in specific situations.[17]

In one respect all moderate radicals were united. Though many had extensive interests in the natural sciences, philanthropy, or other activities, religion dominated and controlled their minds. All radicals assigned supremacy to theology as the sovereign discipline among intellectual pursuits and to religious principles as the ultimate standard by which to judge human conduct. Much of the ferocity that characterized the debates of the previous century had dissipated, but sufficient fire remained in religious controversy to keep it vigorously alive, and many radicals were active participants. In a period that claimed to be an age of reason it was appropriate that most, though not all, were members of the liberal and advanced parties of their respective churches. Religious belief did more than dictate their actions as members of a particular interest group, as it did with Anglican clergy seeking relief from subscription and Dissenters in their campaign to obtain repeal of discriminatory legislation. It suffused their entire understanding of political morality and behavior and nourished their conceptualization of social and governmental processes; in particular it heightened their sense of the political importance of the individual and diminished their sensitivity toward possible differences among the interests of various social groups.

Accordingly, radical ideology began with a philosophy founded on the premise that the universe was a logically coherent entity and man a rational creature within it. Thus, although Price and Priestley disputed as to whether man possessed free will (Price argued that man could perceive objective standards and was master of his own moral fate, whereas Priestley was a necessitarian), they agreed on his capacity for reason.[18] Commonwealthmen were not, however, shackled to a narrowly mechanistic cosmology. They saw the hand of God behind the operation of the universe, believed that Providence played a crucial if imprecise role in the affairs of mankind, and viewed the conduct of human society in the context of Divine judgment; following from this theological cosmology they believed that men's actions ought to be assessed in relation to moral criteria and that society was invested with spiritual and ethical qualities (whether good or bad). Since the principles on which their political theory was based were essentially moral, they ardently desired to promote the creation of a society that was fundamentally virtuous. This moral system naturally deeply colored their view of English politics and, in due course, their response to the American Revolution.

When Real Whigs came to consider the political structure of society, they based their theory on two interconnected foundations: the concepts of natural rights and political contract as the only authority for legitimate government. But theoretical postulates were insufficient; they insisted on the importance of validation by empirical evidence whenever possible. Accordingly the radicals constantly searched for historical and contemporary examples that could either fortify or modify their intellectual system and had little doubt that they would be vindicated by such exercises. In doing this, they made frequent reference to one particular model, the putative Anglo-Saxon or ancient constitution which, they believed, had enshrined and expressed their two basic principles before its destruction at the time of the Norman Conquest. A more detailed picture of the theory can be constructed from the letters, sermons, and tracts of those who were later to formulate a radical response to the Americans' claims on behalf of their Revolution. The reader must remember, however, that it will be a composite description and that not all radicals accepted every detail.

Natural rights theory was inherent in all their argumentation. The degree to which the concept influenced Sharp's political thought is apparent from the title of a tract he published in 1774: *A Declaration of the People's Natural Right to a Share in the Legislature: Which is a Fundamental Principle of the British Constitution of State*. In the text he contended that British subjects were free by the law of nature and were equally entitled to enjoy the corpus of rights that flowed from the natural order of the universe. Watson believed that the rights of men were founded in nature and existed antecedent to and independent of civil society, and Wyvill reprinted with evident approval the resolution of the Cambridge Constitutional Society in 1783 "That in our opinion, every individual of mankind is born with a natural right to Life, Liberty and Property."[19] The principle of natural unalienable right was part of the substructure of Price's first important political pamphlet, *Observations of the Nature of Civil Liberty*; it was so fundamental that he took it for granted and felt no need to elaborate. Much the same can be said about the theoretical foundations of Cartwright's political arguments. He told a correspondent, "I do not allow political rectitude to be according to every man's judgment, but to be defined by the laws of God and nature."[20]

Natural rights theory was articulated through the two broad principles of liberty and equality. The two principles were closely intertwined and each interacted on the other, but in some ways the radicals were unhappy and embarrassed when dealing with the concept of equality and had little difficulty in assigning primacy to the principle of liberty. On the latter, they were agreed that, in Price's words, "There is not a word in the whole compass of language which expresses so much of what is important and excellent. It is in every view of it, a blessing truly sacred and invaluable."[21] Liberty was a possession essentially different from an estate or chattels that were readily disposable for, as Wyvill put it, the love of liberty was an inherent passion of the human mind which neither art nor force nor any human authority could wholly eradicate. Man's right to liberty was axiomatic and could not be proved by charters, custom, or statute law, though these could be based on liberty and exemplify it in action. Thus Cartwright denied that the liberty embodied in the English constitution was derived from Magna Carta; it was inherent, original, and unalienable and could be forfeited only by crimes that made the perpetrator dangerous to society. Even the child of a slave was freeborn according to the law of nature.[22]

Radicals classified the concept of liberty into several categories. Priestley's general division into political and civil liberty was widely employed; political liberty was the power which members of society reserved to themselves "*of arriving at the public offices*, or at least *of having votes in the nomination of those who fill them*," while civil liberty was that power over their own actions which members of a state reserved to themselves and which their officers must not infringe.[23] David Williams accepted this broad division, but shrewdly pointed out that the evidence of the recent past suggested that civil liberty could exist without political liberty; since 1714, Britain's civil liberties had been improved, while her political liberties had been almost annihilated.[24] Most also acknowledged religious freedom as a third form of liberty. This was a matter of profound concern for the radicals as many were Dissenters. It tended to overlap both political and civil liberty, but commonly was treated as distinct from civil liberty, which in turn was often held to include political liberty.

Price analyzed the nature of liberty at greatest length. In general, he suggested, to be free was to be guided by one's own will, and to be guided by another man's will was to be in a condition of servitude; there could not be an excess of liberty. He identified four, rather than the customary two or three, types of liberty: physical, moral, religious, and political. Physical liberty was the principle of self-determination that gave man control over his own actions instead of reducing them to being the effect of an outside cause; otherwise, he argued, man would be a mere machine, incapable of merit and demerit. Moral liberty was the power to act in accordance with one's own sense of right and wrong in all circumstances; without it man was wicked, detestable, and subject to the tyranny of lust. Religious liberty was the power of enjoying one's own form of religion without interference and of making decisions on religious truth and conduct by one's own conscience instead of by the decisions of others. Civil liberty consisted of "the power of a Civil Society or State to govern itself by its own discretion; or by laws of its own making without being subject to any foreign discretion or to the imposition of any extraneous will or power"; without religious and civil liberty man was "a poor and abject animal, without rights, without property, and without a conscience, bending his neck to the yoke, and crouching to the will of every silly creature who has the insolence to pretend authority over him."[25] Not all radicals accepted Price's philosophical analysis of the nature of the human will, but as a generalized discussion of liberty in its political context it commanded broad assent.

Equality was the counterpart of liberty, but here the radicals found themselves on more difficult ground, especially when they tried to relate theoretical concepts to the practical problems of reform politics. Cartwright believed that all men were equal, since they had been made from the same mold, and that no distinctions should be made among them; he also vigorously attacked hereditary principles in *Take Your Choice!* The Society for Constitutional Information published radical tracts that made clear the commitment of its members to natural equality among all men, and the same principle was implicit in the radicals' extensive discussion of the nature of liberty and the role and functions of government. A logical extension of this theory would seem to have been the promulgation of a program leading to social equality. None of the radicals accepted this consequence of their principles, for in this respect at least they were at one with the society in which they lived. They respected property rights and accepted the normality of a stratified society; when the lines of conflict were drawn in terms of rank, they were found on the side of their own. In discussing the equality of man, they meant equality of rights and an idealized, theoretical model, not the Yorkshire miner, the Devonshire cowman, or the felon about to be hanged at Tyburn. As Joseph Towers, one of the more advanced of them, remarked, "The doctrine of an equality of property has not been propagated by any of the societies of the friends of liberty in Great Britain"; other radicals' views were similar to those of Major Cartwright when he commented in 1793, "With regard to levellers or persons aiming at an equal division of property, such men can only exist among the most abandoned and the most stupid."[26] The poor received sympathy and charity, but were expected to reconcile themselves to their status in life.

These social attitudes implied for many radicals that theoretical equality and the defense of liberty were fully compatible with discriminatory voting rights. In spite of their belief that representation was central to any system of libertarian government they often relied on property qualifications as being essential for political stability and the welfare of the community. Burgh argued that property owners should have more votes than those without, Priestley recommended a graduated franchise, and though rejecting any correlation between possession of property and a disinterested concern for the public good, Sharp insisted that the franchise should be restricted to householders.[27] Nevertheless a few were willing to advance beyond this traditional position. Cartwright advocated universal suffrage, a policy that was also proposed by John Wilkes in the Commons and the Duke of Richmond in the Lords. With the sturdy common sense that generally characterized his arguments, he insisted that the poor had as great an interest in public freedom as the rich and were, indeed, more dependent on the probity of the legislature since the wealthy could employ lawyers to defend their property against the depredations of a corrupt legislature. His recommendation that the basis of representation should be changed from property to personalty marked a crucial stage in English political development, but should be treated with some caution. Cartwright did not anticipate the growth of a working-class movement; instead he seems to have been anticipating the deferential society of the following century when the work-

workmen might have the vote but generally expected to be represented by their social superiors.[28] Jebb and Brand Hollis gave the proposition greater clarity and invested it with a somewhat stronger moral imperative. They repudiated all suggestions that representation should be based on landed property and argued that "every man has an interest in his life, his liberty, his kindred and his country. The exercise of the poor man's elective right is . . . essential to his freedom."[29] But such arguments were pointers to the future rather than typical of current radical opinion.

Central to libertarian theory was the proposition that ultimate sovereignty in society was vested in the people and that the only justification for authority was their will. Radicals found it self-evident that a people could not be free if they were not governed by their own consent. Time and time again they reiterated their claim that the consent of the people was the true origin and "the happiness of all, the only worthy end of Civil Government."[30] Its lynchpin was the existence of a contractual relationship between citizens and their government. Sharp insisted that in all societies governed by law "some sort of *general covenant* must be understood to subsist between the several *Sovereigns* and their *Subjects* respectively."[31] Considering Cartwright's declaration that the king's title and authority rested in the common consent or will of the people as a fundamental constitutional maxim, it was hardly surprising that conservatives frequently threw the charge of republicanism against radicals.[32] But without this covenant the superstructure of legitimate government could not be erected.

Radical theory concerning the nature of society and the necessity for contractual government was matched by the belief that commonwealth principles were woven into the fabric of the English constitution. This conjunction was of vital importance for it provided the essential articulation between theory and actuality. Cartwright claimed that the British constitution was the best that had ever been framed by human wisdom. He believed that among the many obvious reasons, one was preeminent: "I mean that perfect harmony and correspondence which our constitution of government, in its genuine spirit and *purity*, holds with the great constitution of moral government, called the law of nature."[33] The constitution was the "means appointed by nature for the political salvation of us all"; common sense was all that was necessary to understand it.[34] Similarly, Sharp regarded the English constitution as the nearest possible to perfection, and Robinson contended that it was a declaration of the natural rights of mankind.[35] The theme permeated the minds of all radicals and is evident—sometimes explicitly, sometimes implicitly—in their correspondence and pamphlets and in the tracts they arranged to have reprinted either on their personal initiative or under the auspices of the Society for Constitutional Information. Their firm belief in the congruence between theoretical principles and the central postulates of the English constitution was of great importance in determining the nature of commonwealth radicalism; its natural consequence was that they were by preference reformers rather than root-and-branch revolutionaries, in spite of their disgust at the current state of politics.

A radical theory of the structure of government was well summarized by Viscount Molesworth, a Commonwealthman of the first half of the century, in his *Principles of a Real Whig*. According to Molesworth, the constitution consisted of the three estates of king, lords, and commons. The legislature was located in all three together, while the executive was entrusted to the first estate, but was accountable to the entire people in the event of maladministration. The executive had a right to the people's allegiance according to the rules of known laws enacted by the legislature; the subject had the right to protection, liberty, and property. He argued that monarchy was fully compatible with radical theory, but insisted that the monarch was not infallible. The constitution was a government of laws rather than of persons, and it was as much treason and rebellion against the constitution and laws for the king to break through them as for the people to rise up against their monarch.[36]

An alternative conclusion, that republicanism was the only legitimate form of government, was seldom drawn. Here, however, there is a question of definition. A loose application of the term "republican" to mean one who regards the object of government as being the good of all members of society and requires it to be grounded on the sovereignty of the people is sufficiently broad to encompass all moderate radicals, including such a stalwart supporter of the monarchy as Sharp.[37] If republicanism is equated with democracy, none were egalitarians. To be useful in an English context, it must include the vital ingredient of antimonarchism. This immediately excludes the large majority of old radicals and leaves only a small residue of men and women, most of whom were not in the first rank. Matthew Robinson-Morris described himself as a republican and a democrat, and Catharine Macaulay, it was said, "hates all the royal family—thinks them fools."[38] There were few others. Brand Hollis and Jebb may have been republicans in the strict sense, as perhaps were John Sawbridge and some other members of Mrs. Macaulay's family—Caleb Fleming, the dissenting divine and polemicist; Richard Baron, another minister; and an indeterminate number of men and women, such as Sylas Neville who lived in perpetual obscurity.[39] These were Commonwealthmen who were said to follow the strict canon by rejecting monarchy as incompatible with good government; they did little to convert their friends to their specifically republican views. Among the majority, Wyvill rejected Thomas Paine's claim to be considered a reformer because he wished to overturn the government, and Cartwright preferred at this stage to work through the existing structure though he took a different view much later in life. Men like Hollis, Burgh, Priestley, and Price denied accusations that they were republicans, accepted monarchy as a feature of contemporary English constitutionalism, and remained loyal subjects; they constantly reiterated their desire to work within the system, which they believed could be adjusted to meet the test of legitimacy in accordance with other criteria.[40]

A crucial qualification modifying the radicals' admiration for the British constitution lay in their insistence that they were referring to its "genuine spirit and purity." Setting the lines of discussion in his highly influential *Political Disquisitions*, Burgh declared that in principle it was unnecessary to change the constitution: "The present form of government by king, lords and commons, if it could be restored to its true spirit and efficiency, might be made to yield all the liberty, and all the happiness of which the great and good people are capable in this world."[41] Sharp expressed a common view that in spite of the inequality of the system as it currently operated, and of the efforts made to corrupt it, "yet it has been the principal instrument of preserving amongst us those remains of *natural liberty* which we still enjoy in a greater proportion than most other kingdoms."[42] The psychological consequences of this belief were substantial. By the standards of their time the radicals were advancing a highly innovative program. Yet they could bolster their courage (and reassure those to whom their arguments were addressed) with a misplaced confidence that their goal was no more than the restoration of a temporarily lost system.

Contemporary practice needed reformation in three respects if it was to be rendered consonant with the true spirit of the constitution. All were concerned with the purification of the House of Commons, since it was "the people's only *Palladium* against regal and ministerial tyranny." Perhaps surprisingly, the radicals were generally indifferent to the antilibertarian implications of a hereditary House of Lords.[43] One necessity was the formation of an equitable system of representation, through which citizens could delegate their consent to the operations of government. For some radicals nothing short of universal suffrage was acceptable; for others, compromise was both possible and desirable. All agreed that the existing structure of representation was defective. But this alone was insufficient for the House of Commons must be made more directly dependent on the will of the people by instituting more frequent elections. Wyvill was prepared to compromise on the matter by proposing triennial, instead of the prevailing septennial, parliaments, but he shared the view of Cartwright, Jebb, and the overwhelming number of radicals that annual parliaments were preferable. Sharp took the demand a stage further by insisting on elections for every session of Parliament, which sometimes would have required more than one election in a year.[44] In addition, radicals wished to reduce the number of placemen, pensioners, and other dependents of the crown in the lower house and so frustrate what they considered to be a dangerous increase in the dominance of the executive over the legislature. Lastly, the particular needs of Dissenters ought to be satisfied through the enactment of liberating legislation.

Not least among the problems facing radicals was an obligation to establish the legitimacy of their program, the specifics of which were far in advance of those currently acceptable to the orthodox majority of their fellow countrymen. To set out a body of normative values and demonstrate the moral legitimacy of their ideology were relatively easy at the highest level of abstraction; it became increasingly difficult the closer explication came to the point of actual proposals. Here it was necessary to satisfy the test of instrumental effectiveness as well as moral rectitude. In reply to any defense of the existing system based on prudential grounds, they could point not only to its refusal to permit adequate representation but also to its inability to resolve the gravest crisis for a generation, that is, the American dispute. Unfortunately, radicals could not readily prove the viability of their own proposals in positive instrumental terms; in particular, they needed to demonstrate the compatibility of political reform with social stability. Yet such a demonstration was highly desirable for its own sake, for argumentative purposes, and not least to fortify their own beliefs during a difficult period. The most attractive solution for such a problem would be to discover an exemplary model which could offer an analogue for the English situation. It was one thing, however, to postulate the desirability of a model and altogether another to find one that was suitable.

An immediately attractive source was the record of historical experience. According to Burgh, "History is the inexhaustible mine, out of which political knowledge is to be brought up," and, as Jebb told the leader of the Irish reform movement in 1783, none of the problems facing his country was unsolvable "when we reflect upon THE PAST."[45] Commonwealthmen had referred to the example of classical Rome for generations; unfortunately it was far distant in time, increasingly faint in the memory, and suffered the damaging defect of having collapsed through internal decay. More immediate in time, place, and remembrance was the putative Anglo-Saxon or ancient constitution that allegedly had been destroyed by the imposition of the Norman yoke in 1066.[46] Less sophisticated than its rival, the ancient constitution was more potent in certain respects. Since its historical justification went beyond the Civil War, it could be attractive to those such as Sharp to whom king-killing and the interregnum were anathema. And of crucial importance, it was a domestic model.

The doctrine had been formulated in the seventeenth century, but the most extensive and influential contemporary discussion of the constitution's provenance was to be found in an anonymous tract entitled *An Historical Essay on the English Constitution*, published in 1771.[47] Its tenets were a recurrent feature in radical writings. Williams, who like other radicals felt that the constitution was admired throughout the world, was on common ground in declaring that "the general outline of the English Constitution seems to have been brought by the Saxons from Germany; filled up and perfected by the astonishing genius of Alfred; almost totally defaced by the feudal alterations of William the Conqueror; and restored in some parts, by various attempts, from the Reformation to the Revolution [of 1688]."[48] When commenting on the *Historical Essay* for the *Monthly Review*, Andrew Kippis stated that the Saxon constitution would probably be found to be the most complete model of government ever put into practice. He agreed with the author on most points, especially with his emphasis on annual elections as its quintessence. Cartwright's political tracts were liberally studded with references to the ancient constitution, and its restoration was always a central element in his campaign for parliamentary reform, in spite of his skepticism as to the value of appeals to the past for verification of the rights of a free subject.[49]

Customarily radicals regarded the Glorious Revolution of 1688 as marking the grand renaissance of Anglo-Saxon principles after the vicissitudes of the intervening centuries and as a triumph for English liberty. They interpreted the offer of the throne to William of Orange as a vindication of the contractual principle in English constitutionalism; Catharine Macaulay's condemnation of the Revolution as a missed opportunity was exceptional.[50] Mrs. Macaulay's criticism was shrewd, for as the radicals believed, the Revolution had been followed by a disastrous decline in the morality and responsibility of English politics which seemed to have reached its nadir at the beginning of George III's reign. But in the face of a deteriorating situation, Commonwealthmen revered its memory ever more strongly as the epitome of English constitutionalism. References to 1688 were legion in radical tracts, and the membership of many moderate radicals in the Revolution Society, whose purpose was to commemorate it, symbolizes its potency.

Unhappily, the commonwealth tradition and its attendant model were dying by the second half of the eighteenth century. If consanguinity made the ancient constitution attractive, the passage of time weakened its hold on the radical imagination. A similar fate was overtaking the Real Whigs' seventeenth-century canon; the writings of John Milton, Algernon Sydney, and others were still read and occasionally reprinted, but there was little growth in the direct line.[51] Times and needs were changing, and the twin doctrines of radical tradition could no longer carry the full weight being thrust upon them: they needed refurbishing or possibly replacing.

The crisis in commonwealth ideology came at a crucial moment. When radicals compared their observations of the contemporary world with the historical experience of the past, the prospects for the future seemed at best ambivalent. Certainly there was much to encourage optimism. They regarded progress as an integral element in their cosmic system, possessed a fervent faith in the efficacy of what they conceived as "the truth" as an instrument of beneficial change, and believed that available evidence suggested that the human condition was improving and would continue to improve. But their optimism was modified by uncertainty and a profound sense of pessimism. Much experience in the recent as well as the distant past plainly indicated that improvement was far from an automatic feature of social change. Indeed, history suggested that the pattern of change was not a steady progression toward happiness and prosperity, but a cyclical rhythm of the rise and fall of many societies. There was, moreover, no certainty that their own community would be exempted from this process.[52] The dangers of disaster and a relapse into tyranny seemed both great and real. And when they considered the prospects for the world at large and their own country in particular, many radicals felt that the path facing mankind was anything but broad and easy; rather, it lay along the razor's edge between triumphant progress and total catastrophe.

An immediate consequence was to invest radical interpretation of the American Revolution with a complexity and importance that otherwise it might not have had. The normative values of commonwealth ideology alone were sufficient to mold radical attitudes toward the imperial conflict, but the crisis in radicalism itself superimposed fresh dimensions of understanding. It became necessary to set the survival of American liberty in an empirewide and even universal context. For as an experiment in government the Revolution provided fresh evidence of the viability of liberal principles. And such a demonstration had much potential relevance to the growth of English radicalism.

# 2

# A Transatlantic Community

Radical interpretations of the Revolution were refracted through a unique understanding of American society and its location in the imperial community. If their general principles logically directed Commonwealthmen to an interest in the colonial dispute, the warmth of their understanding gave it a distinctive coloring. Real Whigs were greatly exercised by libertarian causes wherever they arose—the fate of General Paoli and the Corsican nationalists, the black Caribs of St. Vincent, and Negro slaves everywhere—but on these issues their concern had a somewhat dry intellectuality. In contrast, the American crisis presented itself to them in immediate and concrete rather than abstract and distant terms. Their self-perception as members of a transatlantic community encouraged them in a far stronger determination to resolve the dispute in terms agreeable to their ideological system and made them more susceptible to the evangelical strain in the Revolution. The particular quality of their responses is apparent instantly when compared with their attitude toward another of Britain's most acute problems: their interest in Irish affairs manifested little of the intensity of their concern over America.

Commonwealthmen saw the Anglo-American community in

a particular form. Almost all Englishmen were warmly attached to the empire as an expression of British power and authority in the world. They accepted the reality of a transatlantic society all of whose members came largely from the same stock, and they were well aware of the commercial benefits of the empire.[1] Thus far the radicals were in accord with their fellow countrymen, for they were patriotic Englishmen and their American connections were in many respects a microcosm of the transatlantic community. Beyond this point the understanding of the orthodox majority and that of the radical minority diverged. Most Englishmen had only a vague knowledge and little comprehension of American society and accepted the validity of the political relationship as enunciated in the Declaratory Act; they considered the colonies to be inferior and subordinate members of the imperial community and applauded official insistence on the constitutional supremacy of Parliament. Such popular attitudes were repugnant to radicals since their experience of the connection with America was different in certain crucial respects that led them to see American society as a paradigm for the ideal society they desired and sensitized them to the force of Revolutionary rhetoric. Radicals easily believed that the colonists' situation was an analogue of their own. Like themselves the Americans were a discontented interest group who sought a remedy for legitimate grievances within the existing system—until the war. Later, in independent states, the revolutionaries were being called on to solve essentially the same political problems as those by which Real Whigs were exercised at home. If commonwealth ideology provided one-half of the conceptual framework within which radicals interpreted the Revolution, their understanding of American society and the transatlantic community provided the other.

One immediately manifest feature of the radicals' experience was its richness. They enjoyed far closer and stronger connections with America and its inhabitants than did most of their contemporaries. Many had close personal associations with individual colonists, sometimes through personal meetings in England, sometimes by correspondence, and they eagerly seized the opportunities to discuss a wide range of matters of common concern, including, of course, the growing tension between Britain and America.[2] In particular, the radicals were very well informed as to political developments since they counted many of the Revolutionary leaders as their friends. The understanding made possible by these personal ties was fortified by the ready availability in England of numerous commentaries on American life and society and many of the pamphlets and public papers through which the patriots elaborated their arguments.

Of all Americans who visited England before the Revolution, pride of place must be given to Benjamin Franklin. He first visited London as a young man to learn the printing business and, having made his fortune at home, returned to England in 1757 as agent for the Pennsylvania assembly. Save for the years 1762–64 he remained in London as agent for his own and other colonies until March 1775. A combination of a brilliant and supple mind, liberal politics, and genial sociability ensured for him many friends. While he lived in Philadelphia his English connections had been confined virtually to correspondence with William Strahan the printer, Peter Collinson the Quaker merchant and botanist, and John Fothergill the physician and scientist.[3] After arriving in Britain his circle of friendships expanded rapidly though it was strongest in the intellectual community. Among his friends in the provinces were Josiah Wedgwood in Staffordshire, Thomas Percival in Manchester, and members of the Lunar Society of Birmingham. The Lunar Society was especially concerned with natural science and its industrial applications; its members included several of his old friends and prominent industrialists such as Matthew Boulton and James Watt. Franklin, who visited the midlands on several occasions, met twelve of the "lunatics" at one time or another and was responsible for introducing William Small, Thomas Jefferson's tutor at the College of William and Mary, to the society.[4]

Franklin made his greatest mark in London. The capital was full of clubs and societies in the eighteenth century, and he was an enthusiastic joiner. He was a member of the Royal Society, on whose council he sat, and of many informal groups. One with which he was associated was the "Club of 13" whose members included Wedgwood and his partner Thomas Bentley, Thomas Day, and David Williams. Members of the club cooperated in editing a liturgy drafted by Williams on deistic principles. Franklin's friendship with Williams had matured rapidly; they only met in 1773 or possibly early in 1774, but when he felt he was in danger as a result of growing public hostility toward the colonies in general and himself in particular, he packed his papers in a trunk and spent several days in the privacy of Williams's house in Chelsea.[5] Probably the most celebrated of Franklin's informal societies in London was the "Club of Honest Whigs," which became his favorite meeting place. Among its twenty-five members were Price, Priestley, Kippis, and the schoolmaster James Burgh. Another dissenting minister who was probably a member was Theophilus Lindsey; certainly Priestley and Franklin attended Lindsey's first service at the Essex Street chapel and later dined with him. With a preponderance of ministers (about fifteen) among its members, the club might have been expected to concern itself principally with theology; in fact, its members were more concerned with philosophy, science, and politics.[6]

Many of his acquaintances were also political radicals. Richard Price was an early and affectionate friend. They were introduced during Franklin's first tour of duty as an agent; thereafter Franklin signed Price's nomination papers for the Royal Society and later attended his chapel in Hackney. Price considered Franklin the closest of his colonial friends and maintained a correspondence with him until the American's death in 1790.[7] Another of Franklin's especially close friendships was with Jonathan Shipley, the liberal bishop of St. Asaph. He stayed regularly with the Shipley family and began his autobiography at their Hampshire house. A possibly even closer friendship was with Priestley. They first met in 1766 while Priestley was on a visit to London from his post as tutor at the Warrington Academy. The initial source of their association was their scientific work—Franklin encouraged Priestley in the composition of his *History and Present State of Electricity*—but it rapidly became wider and deeper. Their friendship ripened especially during the years from 1773 to 1775 when Priestley was librarian to the earl of Shelburne and so was able to be in London during the winter. Not many days passed during this period when they did not meet; when the time came for Franklin to return to America he spent his last day in England with Priestley. As a devout Christian, Priestley greatly regretted that his friend did not share his religious beliefs; he willingly responded to Franklin's requests for theological works but ruefully acknowledged that the American probably had no time to read them during the war years. The intimacy of personal contact was not restored after the war, for Franklin returned to England only briefly in passage for the United States, but they continued to maintain an intermittent correspondence.[8]

Franklin never enjoyed in England the universal triumph that marked his years in France. The role he was required to play in London was very different, certainly humbler, and possibly more demanding. To the English public at large he was merely another colonist, and a schemer at that. Within the society in which he chose to move, his reputation was prodigious, and he gained much respect and influence among radicals. Thomas Hollis was distinctly unusual among them for his suspicion. The two men met occasionally at the Royal Society and the Society of Arts, but Hollis was shy of the American, and although he sent him as presents a number of Real Whig books, he considered Franklin a trimmer. The views of James Burgh were more in keeping with those of other radicals; he regarded his friendship with Franklin as "one of the most fortunate circumstances of his life."[9]

No one could match the peerless Franklin, but several other colonists were friendly with radicals in London before returning home to become prominent in the Revolution. One was Arthur Lee; his activities aptly illustrate one aspect of the Anglo-American connection. A member of the great Virginia family, he originally traveled to England for his education, spent some time at Eton, read medicine at Edinburgh, and returned to practice in Williamsburg. Life in the Virginia capital whetted Lee's appetite for politics, and about 1766 he went back to London to work for what he believed to be the cause of American liberty. He read law and then opened what soon became a lucrative legal practice. In December 1775 he was appointed a secret agent of the Continental Congress although it was not until the following year that he left London for the continent. During his years in England, Lee became an associate of John Wilkes and tried to invest the Wilkite movement with pro-American sympathies and objectives. He also published a considerable number of newspaper articles and pamphlets in support of the colonial position and was second only to Benjamin Franklin as a native-born American publicist in England. Lee had many friends, among them leading politicians such as Edmund Burke, Lord Shelburne, John Dunning, and Isaac Barré, and radicals such as

Price and Catharine Macaulay. His brother William was in London as a merchant and served as sheriff before entering the diplomatic service of the United States during the Revolution; Stephen Sayre of New York was also active in City politics and a minor pamphleteer. Yet another American who made many friends while in Britain was Benjamin Rush of Pennsylvania. Like Arthur Lee, he read medicine at Edinburgh before traveling south in 1768; many of those he met were fellow physicians, including Fothergill and his protégé John Coakley Lettsom, but he also met radicals such as the booksellers Edward and Charles Dilly, Mrs. Macaulay, and John Wilkes.[10] Nevertheless, it was not until his return to Philadelphia that his long friendship with Granville Sharp began.

Many Americans made only brief visits. Francis Dana and Josiah Quincy, Jr., of Massachusetts stayed for a short time but both met Price, who was greatly impressed by Quincy and commented that the American seemed to be "an able and zealous friend to his country."[11] Price was able to continue his friendship with Dana after the latter's departure in 1776, but unfortunately Quincy died on the voyage back to America. Henry Laurens, later president of the Continental Congress, lived in Westminster from 1771 to 1774 but associated mainly with merchants; Henry Marchant, who served as special agent for Rhode Island, established closer connections with radicals. A continual stream of colonial merchants visited London, and many were met by the radicals. Thomas Day, the poet, met a number of Americans during his period at the Middle Temple where there were more colonists than at any other Inn of Court; he became especially friendly with John Laurens, son of Henry.[12] Some of the men with whom the radicals associated were obscure; many merchants and sea captains had little pretension to political sophistication and only passed briefly through the London world before returning to a home in New England or Philadelphia. Others achieved distinction in their own colony and a few did likewise in England. Their presence in the metropolis was a reminder that London was the center of an empire; it also pointed up the nature of the transatlantic community.

Personal correspondence further strengthened radicals' understanding of the unity of English and American society. By the eighteenth century the North Atlantic had become less of a barrier than it had been previously. Ships carrying mail were frequent, if at times erratic, and sometimes the crossing was made in little more than three weeks. As a result radicals were able to enjoy extensive associations with many Americans prominent in colonial society. One of the longest exchanges of letters was that between Granville Sharp and Benjamin Rush, which continued for over thirty years. Rush, who had not met Sharp in England, heard of him through their mutual friend Anthony Benezet and wrote introducing himself in 1773; their friendship originated in their common interest in the antislavery campaign, but the subjects they discussed quickly broadened to include politics and other matters.[13] Many other exchanges also betokened a strong sense of community across the Atlantic. Thomas Hollis maintained a long correspondence with Jonathan Mayhew, the Boston minister; their association played an important part in the campaign by which the colonists sought to ensure that their views received expression in England. After Mayhew's death in 1766, Hollis corresponded with Andrew Eliot, another Boston minister, but did not find him an entirely satisfactory substitute. For his part, Mayhew wrote to several other English Dissenters including George Benson, Nathaniel Lardner, James Foster, and Micaiah Towgood, all ministers, and Benjamin Avery, a prominent layman. Price enjoyed perhaps the widest circle of correspondents in America, among them Charles Chauncy, Ezra Stiles, John Winthrop, Joseph Willard, and later Rush and other prominent Americans whom he had known in London. Much of the correspondence between the Americans and their English friends originated in a common interest in the theology of rational Christianity and the particular needs of the Presbyterian and Congregational churches in New England. Nevertheless, as with Rush and Sharp, its subject matter frequently extended to public affairs, especially during times of crisis. Letters received from America often treated political issues at great length, and their authors were at great pains to correct what they considered inaccuracies and distortions in official accounts.[14]

The coming of war in 1775 proved less of a barrier to the continuance of Anglo-American correspondence than might be expected. Some exchanges, such as that between Sharp and Rush, had to be suspended during the fighting, but others continued albeit somewhat irregularly. Price and Priestley maintained their friendship with Franklin by means of intermittent letters. News of American affairs and letters from American friends trickled through to the radicals by way of Paris, where Franklin and occasionally Arthur Lee were helpful intermediaries. Not that such communications were without risk; Benjamin Vaughan warned Franklin that all letters entering Britain were opened by the authorities and added that he assumed the same was being done to outward-going mail. Radicals accordingly felt it was wiser to consign their letters to friends for transmission, and as there was a small but fairly regular stream of travelers crossing the Channel who were willing to take them, the inconvenience was not too great. In this way some radicals enjoyed private sources of information on the progress of the war, and Franklin used the opportunity to impress on them the firmness of American determination and to encourage them not to abandon hope when the prospects seemed dark and unfavorable.[15]

Friendships such as these were important in arousing concern for America. They gave substance to what otherwise might have remained an essentially abstract relationship, informed radical understanding of the nature of colonial society, injected life and reality into the fabric of the Anglo-American connection, and directed the perceptions with which Commonwealthmen interpreted the imperial association. In this respect Franklin fulfilled an important symbolic role. For radicals he was no impertinent colonial to be put in his proper (and subordinate) place by Alexander Wedderburn during his examination before the Privy Council; he was a highly sophisticated politician, a brilliant scientist, and a man to be treated with complete equality. He could be seen as representative of the country from which he came, and the most profound inferences could be drawn from such an appreciation.

Another striking feature of the relationship between radicals and their American friends was the similarity of their social status when seen in English terms. Like the radicals (though for somewhat different reasons) the large and active American community in England was excluded from the highest levels of society and the inner circles of power. Its members traveled to Britain for a variety of reasons, but whether they came as students of law or medicine, or on commercial or political business, they mixed among the middle ranks of society, not among the aristocracy. Not even members of the most distinguished families of Virginia, Maryland, and the Carolinas could gain exemption from this rule of social standing; aristocratic though they may have been considered in America, they were indelibly middle class in England. In the empire as a whole, leadership and direction lay in the hands of the English aristocracy and their dependents. American colonists, however rich and influential in their local communities at home, and English radicals, drawn principally from the middle ranks of society, stood virtually side by side in relation to them.

In addition, personal connections and their associated correspondence gave radicals private access to colonial argumentation and an opportunity to debate the issues involved in the imperial dispute with men who were active and articulate proponents of the Revolutionary cause. They also suggested that the British empire transcended the formal links of administration, law, and the constitution and the economic ties of finance and trade; at heart it was a cultural community of a high order.

If they required further information about America the radicals could turn to the numerous books on the subject, and the contents of their personal libraries indicate that they did.[16] An argument in mitigation of the failures of British policy is that ministers suffered from a paucity of information concerning the colonies and colonial opinion. If this was the case, it was only because they did not read enough or read the wrong studies. In truth a great deal of information concerning America was readily available in the book shops and, as time passed, a great number of pamphlets through which the patriots expounded their arguments. Certainly the members of successive administrations need have been under no misapprehensions as to the colonists' frame of mind. Only a small fraction of the books and pamphlets printed in London related to America, but the proportion rose steadily in the 1760s as the worsening imperial problem encouraged greater interest in American affairs to reach about one-fifth during the crisis years of 1774 to 1779. In all, about one-tenth of the books, pamphlets, maps, and prints published in London between 1720 and 1784 were about America.[17] Government ministers might not have found them very useful; radicals found them illuminating.

Much of the literature relating to America was concerned with its natural history and exploration. In some cases discussion of the thirteen colonies was incorporated into a more general treatment of the continent as a whole, but there were also more specialized accounts such as William Roberts's *Account of the First Discovery and Natural History of Florida* and William Stork and John Bartram's *Account of East Florida*, both published during the decade before the Revolution. One of the earliest and most notable European travelers to describe the colonies of British North America was Petr Kalm, who recorded his impressions in his book *Travels in North America*, first published in Sweden between 1753 and 1761; the largest part comprised observations on flora and fauna, but he described the towns and communities he visited and commented on the various religious sects. As English interest in America increased the book was translated and published in Warrington by the press associated with the prominent Dissenters' academy in the town.[18] For many years John Oldmixon's *The British Empire in America*, first published in 1708 and reissued in revised form in 1741, was the standard description of the colonies. In 1755, William Douglass published the first account by a participant in colonial affairs; his *Summary View . . . of the British Settlements* was long, discursive, and somewhat conservative in tone, but supplied much information concerning the political and religious life of the colonies. By 1757 the rising tide of interest in America caused William Burke to publish *An Account of the European Settlements in America*. The book proved popular and by 1778 had gone through seven editions in London alone. As was common in such works, Burke included a long description of the Indians and discovery of all the Americas before proceeding to a discussion of the European colonies in North America and the West Indies. His treatment of the thirteen British colonies was largely geographical and to a lesser extent economic in approach, and his description of American society mainly confined to a somewhat critical analysis of the seventeenth century. Another very popular work was Andrew Burnaby's *Travels through the Middle Settlements in North America*, though it was not published until the year of Lexington.[19]

Supplementing the general studies of the American colonies, which necessarily suffered from the difficulties inherent in painting a broad canvas, were a number of regional studies. New England was especially well served. Daniel Neal, an English nonconformist minister, used Cotton Mather's *Magnalia Christi Americana* as the basis for his *History of New England*. First published in 1720 it was for long the standard work on its subject, certainly until the appearance of the Loyalist Thomas Hutchinson's *History of Massachusetts-Bay* in 1765 and 1770. Hutchinson was a member of an old New England family and initially addressed his work to his fellow Americans; there was much irony in its use by radicals to defend the patriots. William Smith, a leading New York lawyer and judge, felt it desirable to explain the importance of his colony to an English audience: his *History of the Province of New-York* was published in London rather than America in 1757. Pennsylvania was one of the most important colonies; it was analyzed in *An Historical Review of the Constitution and Government of Pennsylvania*, written by an Englishman, Richard Jackson, from materials supplied by Franklin, and published in 1759. Studies of the southern colonies were scanty, only Virginia receiving any attention of note. Oldmixon's *British Empire in America* infuriated a native Virginian, Robert Beverley, so much for its inaccuracies and misrepresentations that he decided to correct the record with a book entitled *The History and Present State of Virginia*.[20] These local studies had one notable feature in common. Whereas most general descriptions of America readily available in London were written by Englishmen and tended to be critical of colonial society, customs, and attitudes, the local studies were written by inhabitants of the colonies concerned or were based on native materials, and, not surprisingly, were far more sympathetic.

All these general and local studies, written by Englishmen, foreigners, and colonists, and on natural and human history together, made a wide range of material available in England from which to form an opinion as to the nature of American society. Moreover, as John Fothergill remarked, "With some little inquisitiveness, some little knowledge of the general history of the globe, some acquaintance with what passes commonly in the world, a very mean capacity must have unavoidably acquired not from system but by accident, perhaps, a general idea of the country, its inhabitants, its connections, its prospects. Such is the little stock upon which I presume to form any ideas of this most important subject."[21] The corpus of information was not, it is true, especially large, but it certainly offered adequate background to the political debates that opened after the Seven Years' War.

Last of the sources of radical understanding were the patriots' pamphlets, speeches, sermons, and public papers. In eighteenth-century England the pamphlet was an essential medium for public discussion of subjects great and trivial. The dispute with America encouraged a legion of writers to contribute to the debate, and the government's policy of subsidizing its own authors underlined its importance. Between 1764 and 1784 well over a thousand titles were published on the subject. Most were written by British authors, but many were reprints of tracts originally published in the colonies.[22] The *Monthly Review*, which as its title indicates was comprised of reviews of current literature, contained notices of large numbers of America pamphlets; over the years it served as a barometer of English interest in the colonial question.[23] At times when the American problem was a major concern the number of pamphlets selected for review burgeoned, but as the crisis temporarily receded so the output of tracts diminished. This pattern was especially apparent in the case of pamphlets of American origin: a number were reprinted in London during the Stamp Act crisis of 1765–66; there was a short lull followed by an increase during the rows over the Townshend duties, and a longer period before an explosion of reprinting during the years immediately preceding the war. In the earlier years most reviews of American pamphlets appeared in a section for short notices called the "monthly catalogue," but from May 1774 onward the volume of tracts on American affairs was so great that it required a separate section.

Most of the principal American pamphlets were on sale in the London bookshops within a few months or so of their initial appearance. Many of the leading patriots were represented. Daniel Dulany's *Considerations on the Propriety of Imposing Taxes in the British Colonies* was first published in Annapolis in response to the Stamp Act and reprinted in London the following year. Three works by James Otis were reproduced, including his *Rights of the British Colonies Asserted and Proved*. John Dickinson was the most widely read colonial writer in England; his classic tract, *Letters from a Farmer in Pennsylvania*, was one among five of his pieces to be reprinted. Other tracts that appeared at various times included pamphlets relating to the episcopacy affair by Jonathan Mayhew and Charles Chauncy and several provoked by the Boston

Massacre; in the year before the outbreak of war, American publications available in London included Thomas Jefferson's *Summary View of the Rights of British America*. There were also many sermons, addresses, and orations on various patriotic themes. Authors represented in London included Samuel and John Adams, Richard Bland, Stephen Hopkins, Thomas Paine, and Josiah Quincy, Jr.; perhaps the only notable advocate of the Revolutionary cause not to have any pamphlet reprinted was James Wilson of Pennsylvania.

Providing background material for didactic pamphleteering were numerous collections of documents relating to various aspects of colonial affairs and to relations with Britain in particular. Probably the most famous group of reprinted documents was the "Hutchinson Letters" published by Benjamin Franklin in 1774; there were many others. The great majority of the papers was published specifically in response to the issues of the day. They ranged in character from fundamental charters to diplomatic correspondence and included reports of debates, petitions, and protests according to the circumstances and political requirements of the moment. Thus when the debate over the Stamp Act led to a discussion of the extent of the authority enjoyed by colonial assemblies, the nature of representation, and implicitly the question of sovereignty, Jeremiah Dummer's old *Defence of the New England Charters* was reissued and the charters of Virginia, Maryland, Connecticut, Rhode Island, Pennsylvania, Massachusetts, and Georgia were reprinted first in the *Daily Gazeteer* and then as a pamphlet together with a narrative of the proceedings consequent on the act. Perhaps the largest single body of American material published during the prewar years was the bookseller George Kearsley's *American Gazette*, of which six numbers were printed between 1768 and 1770. As its subtitle indicated, the *Gazette* was intended to form a collection of all the authentic addresses, memorials, letters, and so on that related to the Anglo-American dispute; in his first volume Kearsley solicited contributions from any interested persons who wished to place information before the "tribunal of the public."[24] The peak came during the catastrophic years of the mid-1770s when the importance of pamphlets became increasingly evident. When the *Votes and Proceedings of the Freeholders and Other Inhabitants of the Town of Boston* was reprinted in London in 1773, John Noorthouck commented in the *Monthly*

*Review* that in it "we have a concise system of politics adapted to their situation as colonists, which is drawn up with great good sense and mature judgment."[25] Later the proceedings and declarations of Congress were published.

An important adjunct to the reprinting of colonial tracts and public papers was the work of American propagandists living in England. Each colony retained an official agent in London whose duty was to represent the interests of his client assembly. This was a limited if exacting task; some agents such as Edmund Burke were British and took a narrow view of their responsibilities, but others were American and often took a broader view. Two American agents in particular, Arthur Lee and Benjamin Franklin, took it upon themselves to represent the interests of the colonies in general and to act as political propagandists during the worsening storm. Vigorous, articulate, and combative, Lee agitated the American cause within the Wilkite movement and published extensively in several forms. For a time he composed letters to the newspapers in which he somewhat presumptuously signed himself "Junius Americanus"; later he reprinted them under the illuminating title *The Political Detection: Or the Treachery and Tyranny of Administration Both at Home and Abroad*. Having published *An Appeal to the Justice and Interests of the People of Great Britain* under the nom de plume "An Old Member of Parliament" in 1774, he followed it the next year with a *Second Appeal* and *A Speech Intended to Have Been Given in the House of Commons*.[26] The preeminent London agent for America was Franklin. He wrote extensively for the English newspapers, occasionally over his own name or initials, but more commonly over various pseudonyms. Usually he wrote in defense of all the colonies, not only his own province of Pennsylvania; only rarely did he write on any topic other than the immediate problems of the colonies.[27]

Not even the outbreak of war, the departure of the agents, and difficulties of communication could stop the publication of Revolutionary propaganda in England. Much of the news appearing in the newspapers was in effect censored by the government, to the great fury of opposition editors, but there were ways of circumventing this obstacle. Edward Dilly solicited pamphlets from John Dickinson and in anticipation of a demand for an alternative source of information the bookseller John Almon began one of the most notable publishing ventures of the war in 1776. His journal the *Remembrancer* set out to ensure that the American version of events would be publicized adequately in England and to provide a well-indexed selection of the principal accounts and documents relating to the Revolution in a permanent and convenient form. It covered the years 1775 to 1784, and reprinted news concerning the military campaigns, details of military supplies and disposition, American politics and state papers from both sides together with extracts from American newspapers, letters from Americans, and occasional letters from Englishmen. Almon always boasted that his information on public affairs, both foreign and domestic, was in general "early, interesting and authentic."[28] His success in reporting American affairs was due largely to his wide circle of informants in England and elsewhere: from Paris he received news and comment sent by his American friends Ralph Izard and Samuel Wharton, and the latter assured him that he would forward American newspapers as soon as he received them. Similarly the Philadelphia printer Thomas Bradford sent material and requested some of Almon's publications in exchange.[29]

With the transfer of the dispute to the battlefield the number of pamphlets published in America diminished sharply and this reduction was reflected in England. Among the tracts and public papers printed by Almon were an edited version of the journals and proceedings of the second Continental Congress which he published in 1776. The Dillys reprinted Smith's *Sermon on the Present Situation* and T. Evans published Jacob Duché's *Duty of Standing Fast* in 1775, E. Johnson printed Samuel Adams's *Oration at the State House* the following year, and Fielding and Walker printed John Witherspoon's *Dominion of Providence over the Passions of Men* two years later. By far the most famous American tract to be reprinted in England was Thomas Paine's *Common Sense*. Almon, its English publisher, took his impression from the third American edition, but since this contained vigorous criticism of both the king and the government which could not be printed without considerable risk, his version contained a number of gaps. Some omissions were short and the meaning remained obvious, but others were so long that it was impossible to guess the meaning of the missing passages.[30] Three years later a collection of Franklin's "Political, Miscellaneous and Philosophical Pieces" was assembled by his friend Benjamin Vaughan and printed by Joseph Johnson.[31] The greatest document of the war, the Declaration of Independence, arrived in England in August 1776 and immediately was reprinted in almost every newspaper, as a broadsheet, and in the various documentary collections.

Both before and during the war the English reading public had easy access to ample evidence to form an opinion on the American dispute. American pamphlets, state papers, sermons, addresses, and orations were available to supplement the information provided in the newspapers, and if the occasional need to subsidize publication suggests a limited audience, there was undoubtedly a profitable market for some tracts. Moreover, the success of Almon's *Remembrancer* confirms that a substantial public was eager to form an independent opinion on political issues. A comprehensive prospectus of American arguments, policies, and passions was presented as resistance to British policy stiffened and took shape during the difficult years that led to the breakup of the empire.[32]

Although the exact extent to which radicals read American publications is impossible to assess, the evidence suggests a considerable circulation among them. Thomas Hollis was not the only Commonwealthman to receive pamphlets direct from America. John Wilkes, who became a symbol of the English struggle for liberty in the eyes of many Americans, was sent several tracts by his colonial admirers, and both Catharine Macaulay and Richard Price received gifts of Revolutionary publications.[33] Hollis went a stage beyond merely reading the tracts. He devoted much effort, time, and money to reprinting American propaganda in England. Though reluctant to take a direct part in politics, whether English or American, he was passionately convinced that the individual had an important and influential role to play in public affairs and believed that he could most usefully contribute to the furtherance of the American cause and thus the broader interest of liberty by arranging for the insertion of colonial items in the newspapers and the reprinting and distribution of suitable American tracts. As he commented apropos his reprinting of the *Narrative of the Horrid Massacre in Boston*, "Service of this sort is the best it is apprehended, which I can render to the worthy, and now alas, distressed People of Boston—to cause their own Sentiments to be made known on this side of the water, on points of highest consequence to both of us."[34] The six volumes of his diary, covering the years from 1760 to 1770, contain frequent entries that testify to his diligence in carrying out his self-imposed task. He often subsidized newspaper and pamphlet publishers such as Noah Thomas, William Strahan, and Almon in order to get his material printed. When he gave Kearsley information for the *American Gazette*, Hollis gave him five guineas "to serve the cause of Liberty and the [Glorious] Revolution all he is able on every occasion."[35] An especially notable coup was his selection of articles from the *Boston Gazette*, which he considered one of the best pieces published in the colonies to that date. He gave the series the title "A Dissertation on the Canon and Feudal Law" and reprinted it first in the *London Chronicle* and then in book form; he was unaware at the time that it was John Adams's first notable contribution to the rhetoric of the Revolution.[36] After having arranged for them to be reprinted, Hollis distributed copies in large numbers to friends and in places where he thought they might do good. Many were concerned with the battle over the episcopacy in New England (he had already distributed some on behalf of his friend Mayhew), but he also circulated more obviously political pamphlets from time to time, as when he sent a copy of James Otis's *Considerations on Behalf of the Colonists* to Theophilus Lindsey in 1765. Franklin did much the same on occasion. Thus he distributed pamphlets concerning the dispute between the Massachusetts legislature and the governor which he had received from America and sent a copy of his article "Toleration in Old and New England" to Priestley and a bundle of tracts to his friend Thomas Percival for circulation in the Manchester area.[37] There well may have been many other such instances, for private distribution was common with political pamphlets. In the midlands Josiah Wedgwood was an avid reader and distributor of American tracts; writing in December 1775 he asked his partner Thomas Bentley in London to send additional copies of pamphlets he had already received, including six copies of Arthur Lee's *Appeal to the Justice and Interests of the People of Great Britain* (he was unaware of the author's American identity) and single copies of any other good pamphlets Bentley cared to send.[38] Many of the tracts were added to the libraries of radicals such as Lindsey who came to own a good collection of the leading English and colonial pamphlets on the American Revolution.[39]

The correspondence and publications of the radicals confirm that they read many American pamphlets. Dissenting ministers such as Caleb Fleming, Nathaniel Lardner, and Micaiah Towgood warmly approved of Mayhew's strictures on the Society for the Propagation of the Gospel as printed in his *Observations*; Catharine Macaulay read at least one of James Otis's tracts; James Burgh read John Adams's "Dissertation on the Canon and Feudal Law" and many of the tracts reprinted by Almon; Samuel Kenrick, a dissenting banker from Bewdley in Worcestershire, read among other things John Witherspoon's *Dominion of Providence*; and John Fothergill seems to have read American pamphlets regularly.[40] Citations of American sources in English writings provide additional indications that works such as William Smith's *Sermon on the Present Situation* and John Joachim Zubly's *Law of Liberty* were read, as well as Thomas Hutchinson's *History of Massachusetts-Bay* and *Collection of Original Documents*. Many tracts made a considerable impression, but above all John Dickinson was considered to be the prime authority on the colonial position. Arthur Lee claimed that his *Farmer's Letters* were much read and universally admired in England; certainly the radicals constantly referred to him and frequently cited one or another of his tracts in their own pamphlets. Thomas Paine's *Common Sense* was not widely admired when it appeared in England, but it was often read by radicals.[41] When pamphlets and books are added to the correspondence and personal friendships it becomes clear that radicals enjoyed an extended and detailed knowledge of America, a particular kind of knowledge since it was derived almost entirely from liberal sources. Its influence was profound.

Radical comment on the Revolution was based on an implicit view of the character of the American people and their society derived from reading and friendships. A warm admiration for the type of society they believed was exemplified by the colonies gave substance and direction to their political analysis. It justified their support for the Americans and raised it onto an altogether higher plane; without it their approval of the American position would have been abstract, largely legalistic, and empty.

American society was the fulfillment in actuality of an idealized version of what the radicals would have wished England to be. Their attitude was aptly summarized by an anonymous satirist. In the opinion of those who supported the colonists, he wrote, "America, . . . like Judea of old, is now the chosen land; that part of the world to which everything that is truly valuable is said to be returning; and in which, of consequence, there will be neither placemen nor pensioners, neither monarchy, nor nobility, nor church, nor clergy. In short, none of those things which at present shackle and enslave us, and hinder our progression towards that estate of popular and supreme liberty after which so many good souls seem to be panting."[42] Although he intended his words to be an ironic exposure of the radicals' dreams of past glory and their hopeful trust in the future, he described their feelings well. They were not indifferent to the horrors of slavery and other defects of American society, but they discounted them heavily in favor of its more attractive features. What they admired was a distinctive stereotype of colonial society whose formulation owed much to their own predispositions; no matter what its correspondence with any objective circumstances there can be little doubt that it represented the reciprocal of those conditions in England against which the radicals felt aggrieved. Moreover, the congruence between radicals' needs at home and the American stereotype abroad was strengthened by the particularity of their knowledge of the colonies. Their interests and connections gave them far more intimate knowledge of New England than of any other region (greater even than Pennsylvania), and it is scarcely an exaggeration to say that in their eyes America was New England writ large.

Joseph Priestley drove to the core of the matter for most radicals when he declared that the Americans, particularly in New England, were "chiefly *Dissenters* and *Whigs*."[43] Thus the colonists were believed to belong to the two most desirable elements in the English tradition. According to radicals, their ancestors had originated in the most enlightened part of the old world and had received by inheritance all the improvements and discoveries of the mother country.[44] There had been two types of emigrant; one had searched for material prosperity, but, more important, the other had fled from religious persecution in the search for liberty. Beyond this there was some disagreement, for the Puritan record of the seventeenth century was not untarnished. Thomas Hollis considered that "the fathers of New-England were persecutors with the stigmata of persecution fresh bleeding upon themselves," but this was an unusually harsh and uncompromising judgment.[45] Other radicals who were also Dissenters were embarrassed by what they knew of the intolerance of early Massachusetts but either argued that it had been only a temporary phase or ignored it in favor of the more charitable interpretation offered in Neal's *History of New England* and Hutchinson's later work on the same subject. In spite of the settlers' early blemishes (particularly their persecution of Quakers and Anabaptists) they were considered as friends to liberty and, as the founding of Harvard College demonstrated, of learning as well. Since those early days, American society had developed and matured. It had left behind the harshness of Puritan intolerance, its Christianity was well on the way to the benignity of Unitarianism and had already reached a high level of cultural sophistication.[46] It was no coincidence that radical connections were often with leading liberal clergy such as Mayhew and Chauncy and humanitarians like Benezet and Rush. And, of course, Franklin's presence in England was a living testament to American maturity.

The most spacious radical analysis of American society can be found in the writings of Richard Price. It was prefigured in the preface to the third edition of his *Treatise on Reversionary Payments* in 1773 and elaborated in the *Observations on the Nature of Civil Liberty, Additional Observations*, and *The Importance of the American Revolution*. There were, he argued, two general divisions of mankind, the wild and the civilized. Of the many different stages of civilization, from the most simple to the most refined and luxurious, the first or simple stages were those that most favored the increase and happiness of mankind. Society was agrarian, property was equally distributed, and the blessings of a simple life were easily supplied. In the refined state, property was engrossed and the natural equality of man subverted; great towns propagated contagion and licentiousness, luxury and vice; there was poverty, venality, and oppression. Ultimately all liberty, virtue, and happiness were lost.[47]

The colonies, Price believed, were for the most part in the first and preferable condition of civilization. Americans existed in the happiest conditions of society, "that state of civilization between the first rude and last refined and corrupt state."[48] When compared with other communities American good fortune was even more apparent. European society usually consisted of three classes of people: gentry, yeomanry, and peasantry. American society in contrast consisted only of yeomanry living off the land and nearly equal in status. At this point, Price had to acknowledge the presence of black slaves in the South—all radicals found slavery repugnant and embarrassing when they sought to defend American liberty—but he expected they would soon either become freemen or die out. In any case, he contended, it was not the fault of the colonists that there were so many slaves; they had enacted legislation against their importation, but it had always been disallowed by the British government in the interests of the African trade. The type of society Price admired was one such as existed in Connecticut. Its population consisted of an independent and hardy yeomanry, all roughly on the same social level. The citizens were trained in arms and well instructed in their civil and political rights. They had simple manners, dressed in homespun, and were strangers to luxury, made a good living from the soil without unduly arduous labor, married early, had large numbers of children, and lived long and fruitful lives. The virtues of a simple rural society had their corollary in political life. As members of a liberal community, the New Englanders were protected by laws that could not be oppressive since they had themselves made them and enjoyed the benefits of an equal government which, since it did not have lucrative places at its disposal, could not degenerate into corruption and intrigue.[49]

Price justified his preference for a homogeneous community on more than social grounds. He and other radicals were concerned that society should be virtuous and that its spiritual quality should be morally desirable. He believed that wisdom and goodness were not to be found among the upper classes or the great and mighty, but among the middle ranks of society and the "contemplative and philosophical who decline public employments and look down with pity on the scramble for power among mankind, and the restlessness and misery of ambition."[50] On similar social and moral grounds, Price preferred a society that was agrarian as well as homogeneous in terms of its class structure. He distrusted cities, with their opulent merchants, opportunities for vice, and changing and turbulent inhabitants. London and other European cities were at the front of his mind, and he was afraid lest the same conditions, with all their possibilities of decadence, should appear in America, and believed that American isolation had been an important factor in preventing contamination from outside. The least satisfactory aspects of American society were to be found in those areas that approximated most closely European conditions and were most susceptible to corruption of European influence, that is, on the coast. Its admirable features were to be found especially in inland communities. He asked rhetorically, "Where do the inhabitants live most on an equality, and most at their ease? Is it not in those inland parts where agriculture gives health and plenty, and trade is scarcely known? Where on the contrary, are the inhabitants most selfish luxurious loose and vicious; and at the same time most unhappy? Is it not along the sea-coasts, and in the great towns, where trade flourishes and merchants abound?"[51]

Such views were common among radicals even if they were not expressed at length. Granville Sharp's proposed system of compensated emancipation of slaves suggests that he had similar if more conservative views; he hoped that emancipation would lead to the creation in America of a "hardy Body of *Free Peasants*, serving either as trusty Tenants, or Farmers, to improve the Estates of Landed Gentlemen, or else as Laborious Cottagers, who might be employed with infinite advantage to the neighbourhood, wherever established."[52]

The size and wealth of the American continent made a profound impression on men like Price and his friends. Its resources were, they thought, more than enough to provide all the essentials of life, and its rivers and lakes provided a system of internal communications of a quality unknown elsewhere, so that the country had no need to develop overseas trade. As Price put it, "They possess within themselves the best means of the most profitable [internal] traffic, and the amplest scope for it. Why should they look much farther?"[53] This feeling that America should remain essentially an agrarian, self-sufficient society whose commerce would be limited to internal trade was common among the radicals. Priestley, for example, believed that the colonies would develop industry only if they were forced to do so; otherwise they would prefer to buy manufactured goods from England.[54] The radicals were, of course, correct in their assessment of the prodigious riches of the American continent, but the social conclusions they drew had strong overtones of utopianism. Belonging as they did to a society whose values were still essentially preindustrial, they used the fertility of the American soil to justify their belief that in the new world a social system actually existed which exemplified their own archaic socioeconomic values.

American progress and maturity were reassuring and exhilarating because they seemed to prove the validity of radicals' faith in the possibility of human improvement. Jonathan Shipley, in his sermon before the Society for the Propagation of the Gospel delivered on February 19, 1773, exclaimed: "Perhaps the annals of history have never afforded a more grateful spectacle to a benevolent and philosophic mind, than the growth and progress of the British colonies in North America."[55] They had taken root, acquired strength, and were rapidly becoming such a powerful state that they might promise an important change in human affairs. America had been fortunate because the colonies had reached their present flourishing condition at a time when the human intellect was able to use its powers freely and had learned to act with vigor and certainty. Thus the colonists were able to exploit not only the experience and industry of earlier times, but also the errors and mistakes. Under such circumstances the boundaries of science should be extended, and the vast resources of the American continent would provide ample opportunity for commerce and thought that might in turn lead to "considerable advances in the arts of civil government and the conduct of life."[56]

A certain piquancy ran through radical admiration for American society since the virtues they extolled in the colonies were those they felt had belonged to England in the golden past. Matthew Robinson-Morris, a strict believer in the Real Whig principles of the seventeenth century, believed that when they had emigrated to America the colonists had taken the spirit of liberty from England "at the time that it was in its greatest purity and perfection there, nor has it since degenerated by the climate."[57] American society came to represent in the eyes of radicals the antithesis of all that was being perverted in England. Britain was an old and great country, but also was irreligious, dissipated, and enervated by luxury and vice, encumbered by debts and heavy taxes, and poised for imminent decline. It was impossible to avoid the comparison with the vigor and virtuousness of America. In the words of Thomas Hollis, commenting on the qualities of the people of Massachusetts in the summer of 1770, they were a "virtuous, loyal, and magnanimous people."[58] Sterling, frugal, devout, and honorable, they had a strong attachment to liberty and a social system capable of supporting it. Price spoke with profound admiration of a country where there were "a number of rising states in the vigour of youth inspired by the noblest of all passions, the passion of being free; and animated by piety."[59] He found it painful to compare the condition of the two countries and was full of foreboding over the fate of his own country but hope for the future of the colonies. The contrast became all the more acute after the Anglo-American dispute had degenerated into war: "In this hour of tremendous danger, it becomes us to turn our thoughts to Heaven. This is what our brethren in the Colonies are doing. From one end of North America to the other, they are FASTING and PRAYING. But what are we doing? Shocking thought! We are ridiculing them as *Fanatics* and scoffing at religion.—We are running wild after pleasure, and forgetting everything serious and decent at *Masquerades*. We are gambling in gaming houses; trafficking for Boroughs; perjuring ourselves at Elections; and selling ourselves for places."[60] Men with a strong belief in the active role of the Almighty in human affairs could not doubt which side Providence would favor in the contest that was just beginning.

This contrast between a corrupt and a near-ideal society failed to shake the radicals' conviction that a transatlantic society did exist in which both America and Britain were integral and necessary components. They were aware, though not as fully as they might have been, that the dynamics of American society were distinctive and unique, and they were concerned for the well-being of its citizens for their own sake. But even if American society were different, it was not foreign and exotic; any assertion to the contrary would have conflicted with the historical record of colonial development and the manifest realities of the contemporary situation and been at variance with their own personal experience and observations.

And this experience told them above all that Englishmen and Americans held certain fundamental ideals and political principles in common. Men on both sides of the Atlantic claimed to belong to the most free society in the world. Unlike the French, the Germans, and other continental Europeans they were not subject to the harshness of arbitrary government or the terrors of *lettres de cachet* and military conscription, nor did they have to suffer under what many considered to be the tyranny of popery. Foreigners shared their view; Voltaire among others had long believed that English experience proved that tolerant, free, and human society could exist in actuality and was not merely a poet's ideal.[61] All were agreed that these blessings were the product of a free constitution and that constant vigilance was essential if they were not to be eroded, whether openly, by stealth, or by misfortune. Moreover, physical separation did not make the matter divisible. Liberty was a property to be shared equally and ought to flourish in both England and America; its fate in one part of the community was of direct relevance to the interests of the other. That relevance would manifest itself in many ways in the second half of the eighteenth century, for during the first decades of George III's reign many Englishmen and Americans came to feel that the liberty which had previously seemed so secure was endangered by the policies of the British government.

The temper of English politics changed sharply with the accession of the new king. His grandfather's reign had been quiet on the whole; reformers had slumbered and the colonies had been reasonably cooperative. Its climax had come with General Wolfe's triumphant capture of Quebec. Such a happy state of affairs was not to continue. An unseemly wrangle over the phrasing of George III's first address symbolically set the tone for the future of the reign.[62] Within twenty years the empire was in ruins, the government was widely accused of seeking to subvert the constitution, and there were noisy demands for reform. It is no longer necessary to accuse the king and his ministers of malevolent authoritarianism toward either his subjects at home or the colonists overseas; their intentions were well-meaning and honorable although their policies were often ill-judged. On the other hand, there was certainly greater sensitivity, in and out of Parliament, toward the continued use of such well-established practices as the issue of general warrants and the employment of ministerial majorities in the Commons to unseat obnoxious, recently elected members. For many of those within Parliament this was all part of the game of political tactics. Outside it was different, and the running series of conflicts between John Wilkes and the ministry encouraged men to believe there was system and purpose at work; to them it appeared that successive administrations were attempting to confine and subvert the hard-won liberty that was the pride of all Englishmen. Nor was this the only cause for alarm.

Simultaneously tension was growing between Britain and her American colonies. Its immediate origins lay in the attempt to organize and consolidate the new empire acquired during the Seven Years' War. Within a short time it gave rise to political and constitutional issues of the utmost gravity, for the effectual authority of colonial assemblies was being challenged by the legal authority of Parliament and the British government. At the heart of the matter lay the question of sovereignty, but the two sides saw it in different terms. British ministers saw the imperial crisis as essentially an organizational problem and regarded the preservation of the integrity of the empire as their prime obligation; many American colonists viewed it, in brief, as a threat to their liberty and sedulously propagated this view both at home and overseas. Such a divergence of interpretation was fertile ground for misunderstanding and ill-feeling, and each fresh development in the crisis aggravated the mutual distrust.

Radicals likewise became increasingly alarmed at the course of events. They were concerned over the government's policy toward the colonies, and the fears of Dissenters were heightened by the church's attempt to establish a bishopric in America. Taken together the two policies appeared to comprise a deliberate attack on the colonists' liberties. After the conflict had deteriorated into war, radicals realized that the very existence of the empire was at stake and struggled hard to avert its disintegration. The coincidence of the two crises, one at home, the other in America, both with profound libertarian implications, made them suspect that a conspiracy was afoot which transcended the physical barrier of the Atlantic Ocean. They began to ask whether there was in reality only one crisis and to conclude that there was indeed a vital connection between events in England and those in America.

# 3

## Liberty and Union

Over two long decades English radicals wrestled hard and desperately with the problem of empire. Attempting to balance several discrete considerations, they found that it was not easy to construct a workable formula. They were deeply concerned for the interests of their colonial friends and logically might have applauded whatever actions the revolutionaries chose to take and assisted in disseminating American argumentation in Britain; but this would have been far too simple. They increasingly suspected that English as well as American liberties were at risk in the maelstrom generated by the imperial dispute, and they needed to work out the implications of this fear. Third, whatever solution they proposed had to conform to the requirements of their ideological principles. Any solution had to operate within an imperial framework, for at all times the radicals believed that the connection between America and Britain brought substantial commercial, strategic, and cultural benefits to both countries, though they persistently argued that it could do so only if its political structure conformed to certain moral and constitutional principles. As Joseph Priestley put it, in terms that would have been fully acceptable to other radicals, the empire's welfare was dependent "on UNION and on LIBERTY."[1]

As the character of the imperial dispute changed considerably with the passage of time, the radicals modified their responses to keep pace with new developments. Initially they responded to particular issues such as the bishopric affair, the Stamp Act, and the Townshend duties. While the years passed and relations with the colonies deteriorated, the radicals' perception of the crisis sharpened; they saw the issues in a broader context, and they became increasingly alarmed at the prospect apparently confronting both countries. This deepening understanding encouraged them to offer their own distinctive contributions to the public debate, and by the time open warfare transformed the terms of the imperial dispute they had laid down the general principles of their theory of empire and begun to fill in the details. Simultaneously, the dispute stimulated a change of guard among the radicals themselves. The mid-century defenders of the commonwealth tradition were largely replaced by new men such as Richard Price, John Cartwright, and Granville Sharp, who would shortly play a prominent part in revitalizing the movement.

The conflict between Britain and America had two main components. First in time though subsidiary in importance was the struggle over the church's attempt to found a bishopric in the colonies; by its nature it was an issue of special concern to Dissenters. From an ecclesiastical point of view, the need for an American bishop was urgent and his consecration long overdue. In particular it would enable colonial clergy to be ordained in America instead of making the long, expensive, and hazardous journey to England. Such arguments were powerful and might have persuaded all moderate thinkers, but those many radicals who were also Dissenters saw a darker significance in the Anglican campaign. Drawing an analogy from the position of nonconformity in England, they feared that the establishment of an American bishop would seriously, and perhaps fatally, impinge on the status and freedom enjoyed by Dissenters in New England.[2] Worse still, the demise of religious liberty would probably lead to a drastic curtailment of civil and political liberty.

Intermittent attempts had been made to establish a bishopric since the beginning of the century, but the elevation of Thomas Secker to the archbishopric of Canterbury in 1758 signaled the onset of a far more vigorous and determined campaign. Much of its impetus was lost when Secker died ten years later, but it nevertheless continued almost until the onset of war. Its failure can be attributed in good measure to the systematic resistance of colonial Congregationalists and Presbyterians and the tactical deployment of the influence of their fellow Dissenters in England; there long had been close connections between Dissenters on each side of the Atlantic, and these were exploited to great effect. Responsibility for directing the English side was placed with a body of laymen known as the Protestant Dissenting Deputies. Comprised largely of businessmen, this committee took a cautious view of its responsibilities, but had operated for some time with considerable success as a political pressure group; its effectiveness was demonstrated once again over the bishopric. Several English radicals provided propaganda support to supplement their private pressure. Although he had declined to take any direct political part, Thomas Hollis was extremely active in ensuring that American pamphlets on the subject (notably those of Jonathan Mayhew) were distributed at times and in places where they might be expected to have most influence. He also arranged for the insertion of appropriate items in the newspapers and encouraged his friends the Reverend Caleb Fleming and Archdeacon Francis Blackburne to do likewise. The combination of private pressure and public argument was formidable and in this case, unlike that of so many radical causes during these years, successful as well. The church was deterred from pursuing its intentions.

Hostility toward the extension of episcopacy to America was based on ecclesiastical, not spiritual, objections. Andrew Kippis, the Westminster minister, rejected the charge that Dissenters were intolerant over the possibility of incorporating a bishopric in the colonies. He insisted that if American Episcopalians were to ask for a bishop "as a religious officer, to ORDAIN, CONFIRM and perform the other SPIRITUAL duties belonging to that character, they have a right to be indulged in their requests; and to deny that they have such a right, would be to contradict the fundamental principles of Toleration."[3] Instead, Dissenters believed that the issues at stake were the essentially different ones of liberty of conscience for all and freedom from secular intervention of ecclesiastical power such as that under which they suffered in England. The Englishmen wished to assist their American fellow Nonconformists to preserve the enjoyment of their civil and religious rights which they believed, with some justice, might be encroached upon by the arrival of a bishop. They had experienced the hardships produced by religious discrimination, understood that the hierarchy was determined to maintain this discrimination in England, and feared that bishops would attempt to introduce the whole panoply of ecclesiastical discipline, tithes, and authority once they got a firm foothold in the colonies. Kippis again expressed the general views of dissenting radicals when he remarked that English Dissenters would not oppose the dispatch of bishops to the colonies "who shall have no power or prerogative, OF ANY KIND, that may be detrimental to their fellow Christians, and who shall only put the Episcopalians upon a fair and equitable footing with other sects in matters of religion and conscience."[4]

Nor were the potential implications of an American bishopric confined to the enjoyment of freedom of conscience. As one of the great pillars of the constitution, the established church was powerful and firmly entrenched. Church and state marched together, and any issue such as that of episcopacy in the colonies was certain to have political implications. If one were successful in establishing a bridgehead, the other would not be far behind. Either way the outcome would be the suppression of liberty and the imposition of tyranny; a virulent hatred of popery, shared by Hollis and many other Dissenters, only served to exacerbate fears of high church policies. As the *St. James's Chronicle* argued in 1765, "The stamping and episcopizing our colonies were understood to be *only different branches of the same plan* of power."[5] Radicals clearly perceived the connection made by many Americans between secular and ecclesiastical affairs. Micaiah Towgood expressed their view with considerable vigor when he wrote Mayhew, "Perhaps the Reluctance you have shown to have the *Episcopal* Bit put in your Mouth may have hastened your being Saddled with that disagreeable [Stamp] Act. If that *order of Men* had been established [in the colonies] you would probably have found not only the Saddle fixed, but Riders also mounted on You. How Seldom has that order been favourable either to the religious or civil Rights of Mankind."[6] Although it is customary to discount colonial and radical fears of the possible consequences of an American bishopric, Anglican conduct toward Dissenters at home suggests that the fears may have had some validity. Any judgment necessarily must be speculative, but it seems unlikely that Episcopalians would have rested content with a bishop whose functions were confined to a spiritual nature. Returning to safer ground, the episcopacy affair, ostensibly and superficially apolitical in character, played an important part in setting the lines of division on both sides of the Atlantic in the years before the Revolution. It strengthened the links between English and American Nonconformists, sharpened their perception of a common interest, and heightened their understanding of the connection between political and religious affairs. Remembrance of it lingered for many years.

While the fight over a bishop for America rumbled in the background, center stage increasingly came to be dominated by more substantively political issues. By the end of the sixties the bishopric business, which earlier had been the radicals' principal colonial concern, was relegated to second place, and as Anglo-American relations continued to deteriorate in the seventies it faded into relative insignificance. In part this was a consequence of the Dissenters' successful resistance (though its permanence was far from assured), but mainly it was a product of changing political circumstances. Slowly at first, then with accelerating speed, the question of the ultimate survival of the empire came to overshadow all other issues.

The great imperial crisis began in 1763. Incorporation of vast new territories under the British crown imposed fresh imperatives on successive governments and forced them to reconsider the entire nature of the relationship between Britain and the American colonies. The task would have strained the most brilliant of minds. At the center of the great debate was the question of whether a genuinely representative system of government based on the consent of the people could survive. In America it focused on the British government's claim that Parliament enjoyed authority to levy taxes in, or on, the colonies without the consent of the local assemblies. The first phase of the story, which was precipitated by the need to rationalize the administration of the new territories by reorganizing defense and systematizing the development of western lands, came to a head over the Stamp Act of 1765. A second began with Charles Townshend's attempt to demonstrate the government's ability to impose its will on the colonies by seeking to raise revenue duties on American trade in 1767. After a lull in the early seventies it came to a climax with the Boston Tea Party of 1773 and the ensuing Coercive Acts. This legislation, which the colonists revealingly dubbed the "Intolerable Acts," precipitated a final crisis leading to armed resistance in 1775 and ultimately to separation.

Politics was initially a secondary concern for most radicals and, though they claimed the right and obligation to participate in public affairs, it took them some time to formulate a fully articulated response to the colonial dispute. At first they expressed their views largely in the privacy of personal correspondence; eventually the enormity of the crisis became so alarming as to require them to intervene actively in the national debate. The nature of their contribution closely matched the unfolding of the dispute. Most radicals chose to leave the Stamp Act affair to the parliamentary opposition, the colonial agents, and the merchants; few participated in the campaign to secure repeal of the offensive legislation. Three years later, however, the Townshend duties caused them greater concern and induced them to a more active response. By 1774 they were deeply alarmed by the crisis precipitated by the Boston Tea Party and entered a period of extended agitation. Over these years, several features of their rising concern stand out. First, perhaps, was their sensitivity to the cumulative effect of the unhappy sequences of events, and second was their increasingly manifest awareness of the thrust of colonial rhetoric. In America these influences led with seeming inevitability to independence; in England they were balanced in the radical mind by the conviction that the imperial association was worth maintaining and the perception of the colonists' position within the empire as somewhat analogous to their own position as an interest group pressing for parliamentary and religious reform at home. The practical effects of these forces on the articulation of radical policy were twofold. They led to a high correlation between American connections and radicals' contributions to discussion of imperial issues and to a determined conviction that the issues dividing the empire could be resolved by political negotiation. The lines of this policy were sketched out as early as 1765; radicals adhered to them throughout the prewar years.

Only three radicals were active in American affairs during the early and middle 1760s. One was Thomas Hollis, who was extremely active in the episcopacy business but confined himself to reprinting and circulating the tracts of others rather than publishing his own or acting as a direct intermediary with English politicians. John Almon, who was building a reputation for publishing American tracts, was the second, and the last was John Fothergill, the Quaker physician.[7] Surprisingly, perhaps, in the light of the raging fury it provoked in America, Fothergill was the only radical publicly to enunciate a thesis on Anglo-American relations during the Stamp Act crisis, although others expressed their views privately. His position, however, was somewhat different from that of most other radicals; he was already a close friend of Benjamin Franklin and, as a prominent Quaker, enjoyed an extensive correspondence with many Americans, including leading members of the Philadelphia mercantile community.

Fothergill set out his views anonymously in a pamphlet entitled *Considerations Relative to the North American Colonies.* Here he argued that the British Parliament had the capacity to do many things which it had no right to do; among them was the enactment of legislation affecting all British subjects. Fothergill found this unacceptable and asserted that Parliament should be governed by the supreme law of reason, any infringement of which was automatically void. Obviously the colonists could not be represented directly at Westminster because of the distance involved; consequently any attempt to subject them to legislation in the enactment of which they had not participated was to strike at the roots of the British constitution. Virtual representation, the other alternative, he ruled out (even if it had been feasible) largely because he feared the extension of political corruption to the colonies and the reduction of the Americans to the status of yet another army of government pensioners. He conceded that Parliament enjoyed the right to regulate imperial trade, but denied that it possessed authority to enact legislation such as the Stamp Act.[8]

As a member of the Society of Friends, Fothergill was specially anxious to promote a peaceful solution to the problem. In spite of his strong disapproval of the obnoxious act, which he saw as a threat to Britain as well as to America, he counseled his American correspondent James Pemberton to acquiescence and negotiation rather than resistance. He was unhappy over the turbulence of American reactions and feared that an immediate repeal of recent legislation might encourage the colonists to resist all future regulation even if it were genuinely in the interest of the empire. He suggested to Lord Dartmouth, president of the Board of Trade in the Marquess of Rockingham's administration, that commissioners be sent to negotiate American grievances, in the belief that mild treatment would encourage the colonists to see that their true interest lay in obedience to British regulation. This proposal, which set the tone for his later intervention in American affairs, perhaps was naive, but his advice that the Americans should ignore the Declaratory Act was shrewd and his insistence that they owed repeal of the Stamp Act to the Rockinghams rather than to William Pitt was politically correct.[9]

Though delighted at the repeal of the Stamp Act, radicals remained uneasy.[10] In the background the struggle over episcopacy rumbled on, and a return to the happier relations of earlier years seemed impossible. Nor did the formation of a ministry under the nominal leadership of the great William Pitt (now earl of Chatham) appear able to avert fresh conflict. On this occasion the damage was done by the chancellor of the exchequer, Charles Townshend. The chancellor's objective, to be attained by duties on tea, glass, paints, and lead, was to strengthen the colonial executives by providing them with sources of revenue independent of the assemblies. Here was a fundamental attack on the authority and functions of colonial legislatures, offensive in terms of both philosophical theory and the operative instruments of political power. Townshend's cunning but ill-conceived duties on American commerce incited anger in the colonies; they also provoked a much greater response among radicals in England than had the Stamp Act. From this point onward increasing numbers of Commonwealthmen took an active interest in Anglo-American relations and their implications for societies on both sides of the Atlantic. This process of involvement took some time to mature, but as it did, radical responses to the American crisis took on a distinctive and much richer quality than circumstances and natural rights theory alone might have dictated; they demonstrated a remarkable congruence with American arguments.

Several reasons can be adduced to explain the growing consonance between the radical and colonial positions. Knowledge of American rhetoric was more accessible than it had been a few years earlier, partly through personal connections and partly through pamphlet publications. Franklin's friendships among radicals were expanding and with them his already high reputation; his political work during the Stamp Act crisis had been largely among the merchant community. Arthur Lee was back in England with a self-assumed responsibility to promote the American cause, and Benjamin Rush and other more transitory visitors were also in London. Many were anxious to discuss politics, debate American issues, and promote the American cause.[11] Much of the pamphlet literature of earlier disputes was now available, and propagandists were working hard to ensure that the flow of information would continue unabated. Beginning with the Stamp Act crisis and resuming with the dispute over the Townshend duties, much of the relevant information was printed in the newspapers and a good deal reprinted as separate tracts; thus the activities of the Stamp Act Congress were widely reported in England, its proceedings reprinted, and in the late sixties George Kearsley was publishing his *American Gazette* with financial support and contributions from Thomas Hollis. A growing corpus of expository tracts was available to elaborate the colonists' arguments and to declare, as John Adams put it, that there seemed to be "a direct and formal design on foot, to enslave all America."[12]

Of all American tracts published in London during these years, one in particular stood out: John Dickinson's *Letters from a Farmer in Pennsylvania*, which appeared in the summer of 1768 with an introduction by Benjamin Franklin. Dickinson was already known to English readers, but this work established him as the most authoritative spokesman for the colonies before the war. His arguments were forceful yet moderate. He warned of the grave threats to colonial liberty posed first by the Stamp Act and suspension of the New York legislature and then by the Townshend duties, and he insisted that Parliament possessed no authority to tax America either internally or externally through the medium of duties on trade. But Dickinson also argued that Britain and her colonies comprised a single corporate entity, that the colonies were as dependent on Britain as was possible for a free society, and that their prosperity was founded on this dependency; in particular he insisted that they were loyal to the House of Hanover and had no wish to secede from the empire. The *Monthly Review* gave

Dickinson's pamphlet a long notice with extensive quotations in which John Noorthouck described it as a full inquiry into the government's right to tax the colonies and declared that if the dispute between Britain and America were to be resolved by reason, Dickinson would be hard to refute.[13] Certainly the radicals read him and were greatly impressed by the force of his logic. Towgood commented that the arguments advanced by Dickinson, Chatham, and Lord Camden had never been solidly answered except by resolutions in Parliament and the application of force; Wilkes received a copy from the Boston Sons of Liberty and told them that it showed a perfect understanding and able defense of the cause of freedom; and in later years the *Farmer's Letters* were cited frequently by Major Cartwright and other radical pamphleteers.[14]

Another very persuasive reason contributed to the sympathy radicals felt toward the Americans. Both groups were as concerned with the principles underlying the tension as with its immediate manifestations, as was demonstrated by the rhetoric of Dickinson's pamphlet. When the Englishmen read colonial argumentation they found that much of its ideological infrastructure was drawn from their own commonwealth tradition; one of the ironies of the Revolution was that Britain herself had supplied many of the arguments that were later deployed against her. Nor was this coincidence entirely accidental, for over the years the Real Whigs had sedulously fostered its growth in the colonies, and the fruits of their labor were now ripening.[15]

The ideological heritage of the colonies was a complex amalgam drawn from a variety of sources. It incorporated elements derived from the European Enlightenment, English common law, Scottish philosophy, New England puritanism, and the crucially unique ingredient of local domestic experience. Above all (as far as radicals were concerned) it was drawn from English political thought of the seventeenth and early eighteenth centuries. Thinkers such as John Milton, James Harrington, Henry Neville, and especially Algernon Sydney were a fertile source of inspiration for Americans of the Revolutionary generation as well as for the leading protagonists of contemporary English radicalism. Indeed, the consonance between colonial thought and contemporaneous English radical thought was so close that they can be legitimately described as two branches of a single tradition. Although there were differences of emphasis—the colonists felt closer to earlier eighteenth-century writers such as John Trenchard and Thomas Gordon, authors of *Cato's Letters*, and to Benjamin Hoadly than to the great authors of the previous century—the two lines of development ran close together, and their congruence was highly influential in determining the attitude of English radicals toward the Revolution. Theories of natural rights, contractual government, and representation ran through colonial pamphlets just as they did through radical tracts, and the conjunction was obvious and appealing to the radicals. Thomas Hollis was first attracted to Jonathan Mayhew by the spirit of liberty in his writings; the "general sameness of . . . views" added to the warmth of their friendship.[16] Franklin insisted that the Americans were "zealous whigs, friends of liberty, nurtured in revolution principles," and none could fail to be impressed by John Adams's reference to Hampden, Vane, Selden, Milton, Nedham, Harrington, Neville, Sidney, and Locke as the "greatest number of consummate statesmen ever."[17]

The kinship of radical and colonial thought was illustrated with special clarity and pertinence in the writings of Arthur Lee. A derivative rather than an original thinker, he carefully tailored the arguments of his "Junius Americanus" letters and later his *Appeal to the Justice and Interests of the People of Great Britain* to the predispositions of his English audience. The *Appeal* recapitulated the well-worn arguments of Commonwealthmen as expressing the political principles of its author as well as its readers. Taxation and representation were constitutionally inseparable, and the property of the people could be granted only by the consent of their representatives. This principle was founded on the law of nature, but it was also implemented in the British constitution. Moreover, Lee declared, "It is certain that originally, and before the Conquest, the right of being present in the great council of the nation, in which grants, if any were made, belonged to every freeman in the kingdom."[18] He insisted that the settlers had taken these rights to America and that they had been confirmed by the colonial charters. After laudatory references to the great men of the seventeenth century, he concluded the theoretical section of his pamphlet by affirming that "Upon these principles our own constitution stands; upon these principles the American claim is founded. If they are fallacious then were [English] claims usurpations upon the crown, and the glorious revolution itself was nothing more than a successful rebellion; Hampden, Pym, Sydney, Russell ... were sturdy traitors."[19]

When English radicals read arguments such as these in Revolutionary pamphlets they were able to recognize a great deal of familiar ideological content. Its similarity with their own principles did much to encourage and fortify their defense of the colonists during the years of dismay. For, as Noorthouck reminded readers of the *Monthly Review*, the Americans were "as well read in the nature and grounds of civil liberty as ourselves."[20]

A last but more alarming reason for the radicals' more vigorous response to the Townshend duties dispute was that the situation appeared to have deteriorated sharply since 1766. Official determination to suppress the colonists' liberties seemed to have hardened, the prospects for America seemed dark, and there was an unhappy conjunction with the Wilkes affair at home. Josiah Wedgwood believed that government policy was likely to accelerate American independence by a century; Hollis was much concerned over the general unease in the colonies and considered that equity lay with the Americans and that the Bostonians in particular had acted "as became an outraged, free & brave people."[21] Although he was out of town for most of the year (first at the Warrington Academy, then in Leeds), Priestley received reports from Franklin and anxiously watched the progress of American affairs. In a short pamphlet entitled *The Present State of Liberty in Great Britain and her Colonies*, he argued that British policy toward America was even more arbitrary and oppressive than that which it was pursuing at home; if Parliament were allowed to tax the colonists, they would be "reduced to a state of as complete servitude as any people of which there is an account in history."[22]

Priestley went on to develop a theory of imperial relations that had much in common with that currently being advanced by Americans, his purpose, like Dickinson's, being to reconcile local self-government with the need to retain central supervision. He argued that the colonists should be prepared to contribute to the cost of the recent war, but only through the agency of their own assemblies. Parliament had never previously levied taxes on unrepresented provinces, and the theory of virtual representation, which was made necessary by defects in the English electoral system, could not justifiably be used for the colonies. Although he was more perceptive than Dickinson in arguing that control of trade ultimately was tantamount to imposing taxation, Priestley hoped that moderation on both sides would enable regulation to continue. As far as internal affairs were concerned, the colonists' charters should be regarded as different in character from those of normal corporations and should not be withdrawn or revised. He went on, however, to place final responsibility for arbitrating on disagreement in the hands of the British and suggested no check on their exercise of that responsibility other than the duty to consider the interests of the empire as a whole and the recognition that Britain had more to gain from the profits of colonial trade that it would lose from the abandonment of American taxation. Two years later, another of Franklin's friends, James Burgh, published a series of articles under the title "The Colonist's Advocate," in which he demanded repeal of the Townshend duties on the central ground of the impropriety of taxation without representation.[23]

America also featured in the Wilkite agitation after 1768, although only to a limited extent. Accusations by John Horne Tooke that Wilkes hated the Americans and was an enemy to their liberties can be dismissed; they were made after the split between the two men in 1770, and earlier evidence suggests that Wilkes's public sentiments were genuine. His addresses during the Middlesex election affair contained no reference to America, but he was not entirely silent on the subject. His protestations of devotion to the cause of liberty in America as well as in England, made in his Boston correspondence, have a feeling of truth about them and went beyond simple expressions of political courtesy. Certainly Benjamin Rush, who visited Wilkes in jail, was entirely persuaded that he was "an enthusiast of AMERICAN Liberty"; Rush's comment that all Wilkes's friends were sympathetic to America also appears to have been true.[24] After the secession of Horne Tooke and his associates to form the Constitutional Society in 1771, the American Arthur Lee remained active in the Society of Supporters of the Bill of Rights and persistently attempted to inject the colonial issue into its propaganda. Working in careful consultation with Samuel Adams in Boston, he sought to establish a conjunction between the English and American causes, and in July when the Wilkite rump of the original Society of Supporters of the Bill of Rights prepared a program to which parliamentary candidates should be invited to subscribe, it incorporated an American plank at Lee's insistence. It urged that the House of Commons should restore the right of self-taxation, repeal obnoxious legislation enacted since 1763, and abolish the notorious excise which was incompatible with the principles of English liberty. Two years later the election of the American cousins John and Samuel Adams to membership was a further indication of its attitudes, and in March 1775, its members voted £500 for the relief of the townsmen of Boston and the fishermen of New England.[25]

During this same period the situation was worsening rather than improving. In 1770 radical fears were heightened by news of the Boston Massacre, which they saw as another instance of the tyrannous intentions of the British government on the one hand and the noble spirit of the American people on the other. During the years that followed they became increasingly pessimistic as to the future prospects for England and her American empire. As Richard Price remarked in November 1773, "America is the Country to which most of the friends of Liberty in this nation are now looking."[26] Six weeks later the Boston Tea Party precipitated the final crisis.

On 16 December 1773, a recently arrived cargo of Bohea tea was hurled into the harbor by a small group of colonists posing as Indians. Of itself the Boston Tea Party was little more than another instance of colonial sabotage, but it was immediately invested with a far greater significance than the facts alone would have sustained. Both sides construed the Tea Party as a fundamental challenge to British authority in America and drew the appropriate conclusions; Lord North on his part and the Americans on theirs were convinced that the time had arrived for a decisive test of strength. The first government move was the enactment of a corpus of legislation known collectively as the Coercive Acts. When news of these measures arrived in America the colonists recognized the seriousness of the situation and perceived that if they did not hang together they would surely hang separately—certainly metaphorically, and possibly literally. Their response was to summon a Continental Congress to meet in Philadelphia in September 1774.

The gravity of these new developments was equally clear to English radicals. Although Lord North's administration had remained carefully within the formal bounds of legality (by its own definition), they felt that the central tenets of liberty were at stake and probably the continued existence of the British empire as well. Thus the Tea Party encouraged a sharper polarization of attitudes in England, for while the generality of public opinion was becoming steadily more hostile toward the Americans, the radicals became increasingly aware that they must take a public stand on the issue. The consequences were far-reaching.

Having set the colonial dispute on an altogether more menacing plane, the Tea Party also stimulated the growth of English radicalism by encouraging fresh recruits. Before 1774 domestic political radicalism (as opposed to the movement for greater religious freedom) had been divided into two rough and sometimes overlapping divisions: Wilkite agitation in London and the propaganda of commonwealth ideologues. Now the London wing's strength in those ranks of society that previously had been outside the field of political activity was fading and would diminish still further with the elections of Wilkes to Parliament and the lord mayoralty. The City continued to pronounce on various public matters, including America and reform, but effective responsibility for the direction of the radical cause rested with the Commonwealthmen. And here the American crisis stimulated a new development. In the 1760s the ranks of active ideologues had been filled largely by Dissenters whose concern with America had been particularly directed toward the episcopacy question; other support for the colonists had been concerned principally with the commercial rather than the ideological aspects of the question and was essentially conservative in tone and character. This latest crisis in Anglo-American affairs encouraged men like the former Anglicans Lindsey and Jebb, who until recently had been involved in the subscription controversy, and Wedgwood and Kenrick, who normally were immersed in business affairs, to pay increasing attention to the American situation. It also stimulated Price, who previously had devoted himself to theology and financial matters, to speak out.[27] But all these men, and others besides, had links, however tenuous, with the liberal network that centered on Archdeacon Blackburne and rational Dissent. In 1774 there was a further and different accession to the numbers of radical publicists. Among them were two men in particular: John Cartwright and Granville Sharp. Cartwright had not been active in political affairs as he had been on naval duty in Newfoundland until 1770. Similarly, Sharp, who had connections with City politics through his brother James and had drafted an address relating to the Brass Crosby affair in 1771, had been particularly engaged in the campaign against slavery. Both published important pamphlets on the American crisis before going on to make valuable contributions to the radical cause in the years that followed. Their support for the colonists was much needed in the last months of peace.

Organization of resistance to official colonial policy was more difficult than it had been during the Stamp Act crisis. The government's command of domestic politics was in sharp contrast to its incapacity to master American affairs, and the struggle was always unequal. Worse still, the Americans could expect little effective assistance from their friends in Parliament; as Catharine Macaulay sadly conceded, her brother John Sawbridge had strenuously defended the Americans' rights, but his efforts had done no good. By the mid-seventies, opposition to North's administration had disintegrated into small groups too busy bickering among themselves to be able to mount any sort of concerted challenge; divided into squadrons led by Lord Chatham and Lord Rockingham, they were not united on the American issue. Although in accord in disliking North's policies, their fundamental disagreement over the Declaratory Act made them utterly incapable of agreeing on any alternative. In any case, they comprised only about one-tenth of the membership of the House of Commons in 1774 and could never hope to muster a majority from the ranks of sympathetic independents. The position "out-of-doors" was scarcely any better. As a group the colonial agents in London lacked vigor and were politically ineffectual; the merchants whose support had been decisive at the time of the Stamp Act had no longer any pressing commercial reason to support American resistance; and many City politicians who had supported the Americans earlier had used the issue primarily as a stick with which to beat the government, while the growing radicalism of others made any junction between the City and the parliamentary opposition impossible during the crucial months from the Boston Tea Party to the Battle of Lexington.[28]

In such a situation the role of radical publicists acquired a fresh and greater importance. Absence of effectual support in Parliament and the City meant that if colonial interests were to be fairly represented in England they would have to be promoted by men outside the formal perimeter of national politics; certainly the petitions presented by Americans resident in London were ineffectual. Thus the formulation of a liberal solution to what was rapidly becoming the question of the survival of the empire was left largely to men whose prime interests lay outside politics and who were essentially amateurs in the subtle arts of political life. For the first time in the eighteenth century radicals occupied a central, if unpopular, position in English politics; but although they tackled it with energy and devotion, the task facing them was forbidding, complex, and difficult. They exploited such connections as they had with leading government politicians, but their status as radicals meant that these were few, and their parliamentary connections were usually with men such as Shelburne who were in opposition and so unable to exercise substantive influence on the formulation of official policy. And since there was also no question of influencing government actions directly through the electoral process, radicals turned to the pamphlet as the best medium through which to arouse public opinion and thus to promote an alternative program.

Their support for the Americans was expressed in a major series of tracts which were published during the years 1774 to 1776 and thus spanned the outbreak of war. The tracts were an attempt to explore the elements of political society and to elaborate a liberal theory of empire. Many subjects discussed were far from new: sovereignty, the nature of liberty and the vital necessity for its defense, the need for authority and the proper means of circumscribing its powers, the character of representative government which alone could legitimate the exercise of power in the state; these had all been subjects for endless debate among Commonwealthmen for over a century. The imperial crisis gave them a fresh urgency and a further dimension after 1774.

Overarching the mechanics of the imperial problem was the question of the proper nature of the Anglo-American polity. Was it to be considered as a unitary structure or one that was articulated between Britain and her several overseas colonies? If it was intended to be an articulated society, what was the role of the colonies within it? Were they to be considered as underdeveloped and subordinate, or were they already sufficiently mature to be considered as equal components alongside Britain? If the latter, what rights should they enjoy and how should power and authority be distributed among the constituent parts; in particular, what powers should be assigned to Parliament at Westminster? Such problems had an essentially mechanical quality, but they were also suffused with difficulties of the greatest importance since radical thought was ultimately subject to certain political imperatives which effectively determined the nature of the solutions that it offered. Moreover, radical ethics required that the imperial structure of the Anglo-American community should not only be mechanically and politically satisfactory in its distribution of powers but also morally acceptable. The contrast pointed out by many writers between the increasing corruption and decadence of English society and the purity of colonial society should not be dismissed as rhetorical hyperbole.

Although it provoked little immediate public response, Major John Cartwright's *American Independence* must be considered as the first important English tract of these years. Originally published as an anonymous series of newspaper articles in the spring of 1774, then as a tract in the summer, it launched its author on a long and controversial career as a political publicist. Cartwright's decision to support the patriots demonstrates the value and influence of colonial propaganda since, though he had few if any American friends at this time, he was converted to the American cause by what he read in the pamphlet literature.[29] In his tract, he argued that a fully developed and articulated imperial system was required to avert the possibility of any recurrence of incidents such as the Boston Tea Party. In developing his theory Cartwright built on the fundamental premise that the colonies were already mature and possessed not only a theoretical right to self-government but the capacity to achieve it. This premise had profound implications for the superstructure of Cartwright's theory since it jettisoned almost all notions of colonial subordination that previously had been implicit even in radical thought in favor of the concept of Anglo-American equality. He argued that although the colonies had been dependent, they had always been free, and Britain's powers as a parent state had never extended to the right to act tyrannously. The people of the colonies had a right to choose their own governments, and it was self-evident that a people could not be free who were not governed by their own consent. Naturally, Cartwright repudiated the view that parliamentary authority extended to the colonies and rejected the British claim of the right to tax them.[30]

Thus far, Cartwright's thesis was concerned with the internal policy of the colonies; the crux of his pamphlet came with his proposals for resolving the problem of an imperial structure. His premise of colonial maturity made it possible for him to agree when Josiah Tucker argued that if Britain could neither govern the colonists nor be governed by them, and if she could neither unite with them nor subdue them, the only remaining course of action was to part on terms as friendly as possible. But the title of Cartwright's pamphlet was misleading. When he developed the theme of American independence he was not advocating total separation such as eventually occurred, but only legislative separation. His object was to "cement a lasting union with [America] as between the separate branches of one great family." He proposed that the colonies should be declared free and independent states, each subject only to its own legislature but still acknowledging the king as sovereign head in the same sense as he was head of the legislature of Great Britain. Parliament's authority in such a restructured empire would be curtailed, it would lose its universal legislative powers as specified in the entire system, guaranteeing the colonies against the depredations of foreign powers, and there would be a commercial and security league among Britain and the colonies. A corollary of the relocation of authority was that the crown would gain substantially; instead of many dependent colonies it would have fifteen independent kingdoms and three million free and contented subjects.[31]

Superficially, his system would substantially redistribute powers in favor of the colonies and to the detriment of British authority, but Cartwright intended it to operate to the mutual benefit of all participants. He conceded that if the colonies were granted their independence in this fashion they would act according to their own self-interest, but argued that this would be of advantage to Britain as well. As the common umpire charged with the responsibility of protecting the interests of the empire at large, Britain would become in effect the overall sovereign, providing she used her power and influence to maintain the common independence of all. This in any case would always be in her own interest. At home the government would be able to reduce the size of the standing army, which was both expensive and unconstitutional; and overseas a shortage of specie would compel the colonists to grant Great Britain exclusive trading rights. Reinvigoration of the empire would also, he hoped, greatly strengthen Britain's strategic position in relation to the outside world so that she would become "the dreaded, the dictatorial arbiter of Europe." Such proposals were unrealistic, but Cartwright's predictions as to the only alternative were more acute. At best, he believed, the colonies would submit reluctantly to British authority and there would be some temporary trade advantage. This would last for only a "very very short period"; discontent would soon fester into hostility and this in turn would develop into defiance and revenge, abetted, Cartwright shrewdly predicted, by the French. Time was short and it was too late for half measures, for "the multiplying millions of America must either be our deadly foe or our steadfast friends."[32]

Picking up a theme common among Dissenters, Cartwright added a further dimension which contributed an altogether more elevated tone and significance to his proposals. Many of his arguments were pragmatic and appealed to a sense of self-interest, but were sustained by a moral imperative beyond considerations of what was politic. To a patriotic Englishman such as Cartwright, Britain was "a kingdom, great and happy above all the kingdoms of the earth"; its Parliament was "nursed in the bosom of freedom and trained in the true principles of just government and pure religion, of which they are the guardians! If men, thus favoured of heaven, thus enlightened, thus elevated, shall not set examples of sterling virtue, where alas! shall we find it?" He was firmly persuaded that England and America had a providential responsibility toward the rest of the world: since the true principles of the English constitution were an expression of the laws of nature and the rights of mankind they, together with the principles of "pure religion," ought to be disseminated so as to enlighten all men. They would then become the chief instruments of God in bringing about the universality of Christianity and the harmony and happiness among all nations that were predicted in the prophetic passages of the Bible.[33] Such beliefs would have important implications when set in the conceptual framework of English reform.

The second recruit to the ranks of active radicalism, Granville Sharp, became involved in opposition to the government's American policy by a roundabout route. The theory of imperial relations he advanced in the summer of 1774 was derived from his analysis of the tactics of the Anglo-American campaign against slavery. His successful defense of the Negro James Somerset had aroused great interest in America and led to correspondence with Anthony Benezet, the Quaker abolitionist in Philadelphia. In one letter Benezet mentioned a proposed petition to the king and both houses of Parliament seeking abolition of the slave trade. Sharp was, of course, sympathetic to the objectives of the petition but detected important constitutional difficulties. In reply he made a point he had earlier made to Lord North: a colonial petition to Parliament concerning the slave trade was in order since the subject was a matter for imperial control, but the institution of slavery in America was outside the authority of Parliament. Slaveholding was a domestic matter which concerned the colonial legislatures alone, and it was essential that the Americans should protect the dignity and independence of their legislatures. Accordingly all petitions regarding slavery within the colonies should be directed to the king or the king-in-council, not Parliament.[34]

Embarrassed though he was by the incompatibility between the colonists' protestations on behalf of their own liberties and their continued tolerance of the enslavement of others, Sharp sturdily supported the American resistance to British policy. Throughout 1774, Benjamin Rush, whose friendship had followed from the correspondence with Benezet, regularly stressed the growing determination and increasing unity of the colonists and warned that if their grievances were not redressed a civil war was inevitable. At the same time Sharp was drafting his *Declaration of the People's Natural Right to a Share in the Legislature*, a tract intended to support the Americans while the government's coercive legislation was being enacted. When the tract was ready in July, he sent several copies to Rush and two hundred to Franklin for distribution in America in time for the meeting of the Continental Congress.[35]

Although Sharp, like Cartwright, realized that independence was possible, he firmly believed it was mutually undesirable. He rejected Dean Tucker's economic arguments in favor of separation and regarded such a course as disastrous and humiliating. It was also repugnant for another reason. A patriot as well as a radical, Sharp believed that it was treason against the crown to insinuate that the colonies could not be governed—and equally treason against the people to declare that union with America was impossible when there existed a constitutional method of maintaining it that would be acceptable to the colonists.[36] His pamphlet was intended to elaborate on this thesis.

As its title implied, Sharp's arguments were based on the doctrine of natural rights rather than on legal privileges originating in colonial charters, of which he confessed he knew nothing. Unlike most other radicals, Sharp rejected the great seventeenth-century writings for they were associated with the execution of Charles I which he found repugnant. Instead he looked back to Magna Carta, which he believed to be fundamental and unrepealable since it had been confirmed on previous occasions, and he denied the doctrine of parliamentary sovereignty. The heart of his imperial theory lay in the nature of its representative system. He felt it was iniquitous and contrary to natural law that freemen should not enjoy the right to free disposal of their property and argued, as he had in private correspondence, that there could be no legitimate taxation without full representation. Nor could defects in the prevailing system of British representation justify depriving the colonists of their rights. Sir William Blackstone's argument that since the colonies had been acquired by conquest, common law did not automatically extend to them, was also unacceptable; instead Sharp argued that the colonies were inhabited by British subjects who were entitled by right of birth to the benefits of common law and all other privileges enjoyed by Englishmen. He offered further support to his claim by declaring that common law was itself founded principally on reason, natural justice, and the eternal laws of God, and therefore all parts of the common law having these foundations must ipso facto have authority in the colonies.[37] Since natural rights and concomitant representation were the foundations of his political theory, Sharp's structure of empire was based on local legislative autonomy coupled with continued loyalty to the crown: he was fully persuaded that the empire would continue to develop provided that justice and the law of liberty were upheld by those who were responsible for the administration of government.

Sharp and Cartwright were joined in the debate by men who were already in the mainstream of commonwealth radicalism and enjoyed close associations with American friends. The immediate incentive was the prospect of a general election, for, as Archdeacon Blackburne's son Thomas remarked, the new Parliament "will have to do something to settle our American affairs."[38]

One leading writer who explicitly attempted to influence voters was Joseph Priestley. His contacts with his London friends, particularly Franklin, had greatly improved since he had taken the post of librarian to Lord Shelburne in 1773 and so could spend every winter in town. He later claimed that he had composed his *Address to Protestant Dissenters of All Denominations* at the suggestion of Franklin and Fothergill; this may not have been the case, but certainly he published it anonymously lest his readers might infer that he was speaking on behalf of Shelburne. In general, Priestley's comments on Anglo-American relations ran along the familiar lines: the colonists were entitled to enjoy a proper system of representation, and the Stamp Act had introduced a new principle that the Americans were subjects of Britain. He conceded that the East India Company had been injured by the Boston Tea Party but argued that the Coercive Acts were too harsh a punishment.[39]

James Burgh's *Political Disquisitions*, the most influential textbook of radical ideas to be published during this period, may have been intended to appear in time for the election.[40] It covered the wide range of domestic and imperial problems, but although the first volume appeared in plenty of time, the second, devoted exclusively to a discussion of the colonial issue, was published too late as the election was called earlier than anticipated. A notable feature of Burgh's colonial analysis was the degree to which it depended on Revolutionary argumentation: he used material from Franklin's "Letters to Shirley," his own "Colonist's Advocate" series, in the composition of which he had probably received Franklin's help, and two collections of American tracts reprinted by John Almon.[41]

Neither the pleas of Cartwright, Priestley, Burgh, and other pamphleteers such as Matthew Robinson-Morris nor the efforts of the Society of Supporters of the Bill of Rights were of any avail. During the election, North's American policy became an issue in ten constituencies at most. The Bill of Rights men had already incorporated an American plank in their platform, and in Middlesex the successful candidates, Wilkes and his friend John Glyn, bound themselves to seek repeal of the Coercive Acts in addition to pursuing various measures of reform, as did several other candidates in the London area. But their program met with little success outside the metropolis, and among their casualties was Stephen Sayre, who failed to outmaneuver the government forces at Seaford; eventually Wilkes returned to the House of Commons with only those followers whom he described as his "twelve apostles."[42] America also received some attention in Bristol, where Edmund Burke was a candidate, and in one or two other constituencies, but the effect on the ensuing Parliament was negligible. The opposition remained as small and divided as before.

By the time the autumn of 1774 was giving way to winter, a radical view of the relationship between Britain and the American colonies had been formulated. Many of its details remained to be added, but its outline was already clear. Once again it sought to satisfy the requirements of American liberty within the context of a continuing union. One of its central premises was a deep respect for American society, which in commonwealth eyes possessed many admirable qualities and appeared to have reached the level of maturity necessary for self-government. Within the transatlantic community it stood on far more equal terms with Britain than orthodox opinion would concede—a fact which radicals believed ought to be acknowledged on prudential as well as ethical grounds. They accepted full colonial independence at some future point, but believed that the proper moment for separation had not yet arrived in spite of the government's program. Meanwhile, the connection should be sustained for a variety of reasons, and they were convinced on the evidence of John Dickinson and others that the Americans shared their wishes. The radicals and their colonial friends were living testimony of the reality of the transatlantic cultural association, and though the parallel was not exact, there was some similarity between the colonial position and their own when viewed in the framework of an empire dominated by the great Whig oligarchs and controlled by a government displaying apparently tyrannous proclivities. The colonists were watching an attack on the authority of their legislatures, and the radicals saw the degradation of Parliament and felt the application of religious discrimination; in a still more speculative vein, it can be suggested that the radicals wished to retain the colonists as allies in their domestic struggle. But there were other, more specific reasons. Radicals saw the empire as being economically complementary; America contributed agricultural products, and Britain produced industrial goods, to their mutual advantage. Union with America also gave massive strategic advantages in the long struggle with France.

The radicals' various proposals, plans, and schemes were designed to satisfy considerations such as these. Organizationally they were intended to promote an empire based on local self-government, mutual respect, interdependence, and a minimum of central direction lodged in Westminster.[43] Arguably the radicals failed to appreciate the strength of the drift toward separation and so were being unrealistic. But one crucial point they had grasped with great firmness: the empire could survive only with the voluntary consent of its constituent members. Nor was this understanding based solely on the normative values of their ideological system, for it was powerfully reinforced by strictly pragmatic factors. Even assuming such a program could succeed, a policy of reducing the colonists to submission would in the process destroy all the benefits it was intended to produce. Coercion would be self-defeating.

The prospects were gloomy. Thomas Brand Hollis read aloud two letters from Massachusetts at a dinner party in November and, as Theophilus Lindsey reported to William Turner in Wakefield, "They were both very affecting. Full of deepest apprehensions for themselves and their own and for the parent country . . . the people in the country were hardly restrained from flying out with acts of desperation, on seeing a standing army sent again at them, and their port blocked up."[44] Yet radicals continued to hope for a political settlement.

Fortunately there could be no doubt about the steadfastness of the colonists. Benjamin Rush told Sharp in November that they were preparing for the worst; he added in tones that were both ominous and comforting, "We talk with less horror than formerly of a civil war."[45] In the same month a new emissary arrived from Boston in a desperate attempt to persuade the administration of the dangers inherent in its policies; he also mixed in radical circles, where he made a favorable impression. Throughout his stay in England, Josiah Quincy, Jr., regarded it as his duty to publicize the American position on all possible occasions. As he reported to his wife, "In *all* companies I have endeavoured to give a true state of the affairs of the Continent, & the genuine sentiments of its inhabitants."[46] Two days after his arrival in London he called on North at the minister's request and a few days later on Lord Dartmouth, who was still secretary for America.[47]

Quincy's advocacy on behalf of the colonies had little effect on the ministers, but it undoubtedly raised the morale of the many radicals whom he met. He had long conversations with several opposition politicians, notably Shelburne, Sir George Savile, Rose Fuller, and Isaac Barré, but his closest associations were with the "friends of liberty" such as Price, Priestley, Brand Hollis, Fothergill, Dilly, Micaiah Towgood's son Matthew, and other Dissenters in London. He also traveled outside the capital and had long conversations with Catharine Macaulay and probably Philip Furneaux, the dissenting publicist, in Bath.[48] A single theme dominated his discussions. As Lindsey reported of a dinner with Franklin, Quincy, Price, and Priestley, "We began and ended with the Americans"; on that occasion the friends also listened while Quincy read several recent letters from New England, which if nothing else offered the comfort "that our brethren on the other side [of] the Atlantic *will be free*."[49] Possibly her conversations with Quincy were what encouraged Catharine Macaulay to publish a short pamphlet on the American crisis at the beginning of 1775.[50] A vigorous woman whose opinions were sometimes more extreme than those of most radicals, Mrs. Macaulay's criticism of the government was trenchant. But in spite of the vehemence of her analysis, Mrs. Macaulay's recommendations were moderate to the point of being tame; she suggested that the Americans should send "unanimous and repeated" addresses to the throne and both houses of Parliament until the attention of every part of the government had been drawn to its own real interests and the dangerous condition of the empire.[51] Like other radicals she hoped for the resolution of the conflict within the confines of a continuing empire, though she feared the worst.

For all their pamphleteering, radicals were well aware that Westminster was the true cockpit of politics and the best place in which to defend their American friends. Several of them had close connections with the opposition, though unfortunately largely with the smaller of the two groups, that led by Shelburne with Chatham as its titular head. Price had been a close friend and adviser to Shelburne for several years and in late 1774 presented his views as part of a general program for the discharge of the public debt, the protection of liberty, and the preservation of the state. As an economist, he was able to demonstrate the prudential merits of repealing the Coercive Acts and restoring the situation that existed before the Stamp Act; such a policy would recover the affections of the Americans and would be financially sound since the revenue to be derived from exclusive trade with the colonies would be greater than that to be drawn from any other source. Later he was delighted, as was Lindsey, with Chatham's speech introducing his conciliatory motion of 20 January 1775, for "Your Lordship has Stepp'd forth to rescue us."[52] In contrast, he still believed that the government's policies were so wild (as well as unjust) that it would be overthrown within a couple of years and replaced by an administration that would establish colonial rights on a permanent and satisfactory basis.[53] David Hartley spoke in the House of Commons on several occasions, but his arguments met with no success.

Meanwhile another radical, John Fothergill, was exploiting his unique position as a prominent Quaker, friend of Benjamin Franklin, and fashionable physician to intercede in the worsening crisis. The key to his role lay in the fact that Lord Dartmouth was one of his patients. From November 1774 to January 1775, Fothergill and another prominent Quaker, David Barclay, worked as intermediaries between Franklin and Dartmouth in an attempt to construct a plan of reconciliation that would be acceptable to both parties. Its basis was twofold: repeal of legislation offensive to the Americans and acceptance of the principle that Parliament should have no control over the colonies' internal legislation. In particular, the colonies should not be taxed in peacetime but should be prepared to raise money at the request of the king (and the consent of Parliament) in wartime. The plan foundered because the government was unwilling to repeal the Coercive Acts, a concession regarded as essential by the Americans.[54]

Perhaps it had been too late anyway. Within a few weeks of the failure of Fothergill's efforts, the government imposed restrictions on colonial trade and fisheries and sent additional troops to America. Petitions were sent pointing out the commercial consequences of the American nonimportation agreement to the king and debates and motions in Parliament, but they did little good. On occasion the minority vote in the Commons was high—but the government's vote was always higher, and its majorities in favor of coercion were often extremely high by the normal standards of the eighteenth century. Though the prospect horrified them, radicals were coming to recognize that the dispute was likely to end in war. Priestley had forecast the possibility in his election address to Dissenters, and Jebb argued that "the English ministry must feel before they will repent."[55] The *Remembrancer* contained frequent warnings that the colonists were prepared to use force, and in the spring of 1775, Price was reported as believing that the sooner war came the better.[56]

# 4

## American Independence

The battle of Lexington inaugurated seven years of civil war during which the radicals were compelled to make a major shift in their position. They faced a problem that was complex and difficult, and in certain important respects the intellectual task confronting them was more formidable than that facing either the government in Westminster or the colonists in America. For them the questions raised by the conflict could not be refined to the single fundamental issue it became for most men on each side of the Atlantic. Lord North's administration was committed to preserving the empire by suppressing rebellion and could reserve to itself the right to employ any methods it deemed appropriate, including if necessary those that infringed the civil and political liberties of the colonists. For their part the American patriots were committed to the defense of what they regarded as their essential liberties, if necessary at the expense of severing their links with the British empire; as Arthur Lee told Samuel Adams, "The first wish of my heart is, that America may be free—the second is, that we may ever be united with this Country. But this union, however desirable, must not be upon dishonourable & slavish terms."[1] The radicals' objective was more subtle and far more difficult of attainment than either.

They desired as ardently as the government to preserve the Anglo-American connection and in particular to maintain the British empire as its formal expression, but they also wished as much as the colonists to protect and preserve American rights and liberties. Unfortunately their objectives proved to be in conflict, and their efforts to formulate a system of empire that would satisfy both criteria have often seemed like attempts to square the circle.

It took radicals several years to see the impracticality of their program. Initially isolated from the overwhelming majority of Englishmen, they had no doubt as to their obligations to stand fast in support of the Americans. Sometimes at the cost of personal sacrifice as well as unpopularity they argued privately and publicly that the fundamental issue of liberty was at stake and that the war ought to be halted in the interests of both America and Great Britain. They promoted the cause of reconciliation long after it had ceased to be feasible, but as the war continued they were forced to choose between loyalty to the empire and devotion to the principle of liberty. In the ultimate test they held true to their prime concern for the preservation of liberty and welcomed the success of American resistance even though it meant an end to the imperial connection. Nor was radical policy determined only by a limited desire to support the colonists in their refusal to submit to what they regarded as the intolerable pretensions of the British government; they were firmly persuaded that the outcome of the struggle in America would have profound implications for the fate of liberty in England and the rest of the world.

The colonists' actions could not be condemned when news of the outbreak of fighting reached England. The right to resist a tyrant was an integral component of radical ideology and had been sanctified by the events of 1688. It was not, however, an unqualified right: the use of force had to be morally legitimate in the particular circumstances, and it had to be pragmatically necessary in order to achieve an acceptable objective. In earlier years, when hope remained of settling the dispute entirely by negotiation, the radicals had been equivocal over the use of violence. If Edward Dilly described the Boston Tea Party as "a noble exertion of the just rights of the people against Ministerial encroachments," James Burgh regarded it as inexcusable.[2] Similarly, Cartwright thought the Tea Party warranted by the law of nature, but did not approve every act of tarring and feathering and disorderly conduct.[3] But now the Americans had no choice; as David Hartley insisted, "I shall never call these men rebels, nor their cause rebellion, but a justifiable resistance."[4] Nor were the Quaker radicals any exception. In March, John Fothergill had advised an American Friend to submit to the "prevailing power," by which he meant the "general voice of America," and although he constantly urged negotiation as a means of settling the dispute, he never condemned the use of force; certainly his protégé John Coakley Lettsom welcomed "the noble action of Concord."[5] Indeed, the radicals felt much anxiety and uncertainty about whether the colonists could hold out against the onslaught of the British army. John Jebb, shortly to play an important role in the metropolitan reform movement, had doubted the firmness of the American union before the news of Lexington arrived, and Price was known to be dubious and at times despondent over the American ability to stand firm. After arriving in Paris as a representative of Congress, Franklin tried to raise the morale of his English friends by sending news of the course of events in America. He asked Priestley in October 1775 to tell Price that with the exception of a few Tories and placemen, America was unanimous and utterly determined to resist. He continued dryly, "Britain, at the expense of three millions, has killed one hundred and fifty Yankees this campaign, which is twenty thousand pounds a head. . . . During the same time sixty thousand children have been born in America. From this *data* his mathematical head will easily calculate the time and expense necessary to kill us all, and conquer our territory."[6] In reply, Priestley assured Franklin that the members of the Club of Honest Whigs often thought of him and that their zeal for the American cause was unabated.[7]

On the other hand, the radicals had no intention of organizing any complementary action in England. The tone of their writings was far removed from the rantings of *The Crisis*. This scurrilous newspaper, published in 1775–76 and devoted to the American conflict, expressed many of the radicals' views but in a most extreme form and frequently in the most hysterical fashion; in particular, several issues contained savage personal attacks on George III and scarcely veiled threats of a domestic revolution. The authors probably included the pamphleteer William Moore and the historian Philip Thicknesse and did not represent any significant movement. Certainly they did not represent the radicals.[8]

Their support for the American cause emphasized the separation of Commonwealthmen from the rest of the country. A few wishfully believed that their views were acceptable outside their own ranks: David Williams commented in retrospect that it was to the honor of the great body of the people of England that they abhorred the government's attempt to reduce the Americans "beneath the ranks of British subjects," and Samuel Kenrick, the Bewdley banker, believed that not only Nonconformists but also many Anglicans were sympathetic toward the Americans.[9] Most of the evidence is against them; radicals were probably never more isolated than at the outbreak of the War of Independence.

Reports from many parts of the country clearly indicate that the ministry's efforts to suppress rebellion in "our" colonies received general approval. Cartwright had conceded in *American Independence* that the people of England unanimously favored the use of force. This was an exaggeration, but the feeling was widespread, and had been noticed by Franklin before the war that the subjects of the king in England were superior to those in America. As Price remarked, "The meanest person among us is disposed to look upon himself as having a body of subjects in America; and to be offended at the denial of his right to make laws for them, though perhaps he does not know what colour they are of, or what language they talk."[10] The argument, according to Cartwright, was that if the House of Commons had legislative authority over the colonies the English people ultimately had the same right since the House derived its constitutional authority from them.[11]

Public opinion had moved sharply against the colonists before the outbreak of fighting. Commenting on popular attitudes in the midlands and the north in January 1775, Josiah Wedgwood told his partner Thomas Bentley that "all the world are with the Minister and against the poor Americans."[12] A month later he made a short visit to Manchester and reported that Dr. John Roebuck, a leading government supporter, had denounced the colonists with great violence and encouraged people to petition for enforcement of the coercive legislation. Roebuck had done the same in Leeds and Halifax and although moderates believed him to be a hired agent he had been very effective, even among Dissenters. Wedgwood was forced to conclude that there was a general infatuation in the north; most people regarded the Americans as rebels and considered that they should pay the required taxes for Britain's recent defense of them.[13] William Turner of Wakefield confirmed this evaluation of Yorkshire opinion, to the considerable dismay of Lindsey in London.[14] Alarming inferences could be drawn from the petitions to the House of Commons of January and February. True, the majority demanded restoration of trade with America (cut off by the Association of 1774), but they did so on commercial grounds, not out of sympathy with the Americans; and some, notably one from Birmingham and another from the West Riding of Yorkshire, insisted that the government should continue to assert its authority in America.[15]

News of Lexington and Concord strengthened the government's popular support. The orthodox press insisted that the correct order of priorities in dealing with the Americans was for the rebellion to be crushed first and only then for Britain to deal justly with her refractory colonies.[16] A flood of addresses to the king during the second half of 1775 offered further support for official policy. Many came from communities where a significant number of Dissenters lived, which might have been expected to be sympathetic toward the colonies; thus loyal addresses were received from London and Bristol, Nottingham and Taunton (both of which had large dissenting populations) and Kenrick's home town of Bewdley. When Richard Champion went round Bristol in October 1775 to solicit signatures for an antigovernment petition, he obtained more than a thousand signatures but admitted that a Tory address had probably secured still more.[17] Provincial opinion continued to give general support to the government during the early years of the war. Liverpool was divided but the majority supported the government in spite of economic difficulties caused by the war. The rapidly expanding and increasingly sophisticated town of Birmingham was also divided: it had two debating societies, the pro-American Robin Hood Free Debating Society and the progovernment Amicable Debating Society, but if anything it came down on the side of the ministry.[18] The general sentiments of Manchester were staunch loyalty to the government, and it raised a regiment for service in America. Of the two principal interest groups in the nation at large, the landed interest was strongly in favor of coercion, and the merchants, who had been so active in defending the colonists in earlier years, were far more divided than previously.[19]

Ministerial popularity at the beginning of the war was reluctantly acknowledged by leading members of the parliamentary opposition. Edmund Burke told his leader, the Marquess of Rockingham, in August 1775, "If any indication is to be taken from external appearances, the king is entirely satisfied with the present State of his Government. ... His Ministers too are perfectly at their Ease"; in a long letter composed over two days, he went on to declare, "As to the good people of England, they seem to partake every day more and more of the Character of that administration which they had been induced to tolerate."[20] Even the merchants had largely abandoned the American cause, and the majority were beginning "to sniff the cadaverous Haut Gout of a Lucrative War."[21] Rockingham could only agree; all the information available confirmed that most people had been deceived by the misrepresentations and guile of the ministry, the court, and their supporters so that violent actions directed against America were accepted and approved by the majority of people in all classes, professions, and occupations.[22]

If Americans expected to receive unanimous support from the ranks of Dissent, they were disappointed. Several well-known dissenting clergy, including Edward Pickard, John Martin, John Clayton, and David Rivers, approved government actions. Caleb Evans of Bristol declared that many Baptist laymen, including some members of his own congregation and some ministers whom he knew personally, supported the administration. A London minister, John Rogers, was reported as being a Whig on the American issue but opposed to independence. One of the most prominent of dissenting laymen, Sir Henry Hoghton, who made several attempts to secure parliamentary relief for Dissenters, supported the war to the bitter end.[23] Methodists generally disapproved of rebellion in the colonies. Their leader, John Wesley, whose influence over his followers was very persuasive, was a staunch Tory who believed the British constitution was as near perfect as any reasonable man could expect. He rejected the notion that the colonists had been treated cruelly and believed that they were demanding an illegal privilege in claiming exemption from parliamentary taxation. As a "mite toward putting out the flame which rages all over the land" he published *A Calm Address to Our American Colonies* in the summer of 1775. It was largely plagiarized from Samuel Johnson's earlier pamphlet *Taxation no Tyranny* and did more to fan the flames than to extinguish them.[24] The outbreak of war posed a difficult problem of conscience for Quakers; they enjoyed close ties with colonial members of the Society of Friends, but their religious principles prohibited encouragement of military action. They were thus faced with the unenviable choice of repudiating their religious convictions or in effect condoning British policy by remaining passive. Some made the first choice, most (including their leaders) made the second. Official policy, accordingly, was to urge the American Friends to remain faithful to their principles of nonviolence. This attitude toward the war was held especially strongly by the richer, conservative merchants who believed that the rebellion endangered their capital and trade and saw its suppression as their only relief.[25]

A further feature of the radical isolation was official hostility. It has long been known that the government financed replies to radical pamphlets, notably to Price's *Civil Liberty*; further evidence shows that radical critics of the ministry's American policies were the target of extensive political and legal harassment. Much was no more than the spite of rumormongers, such as the allegations that John Fothergill was an American agent who did intelligence work in London and that some of Franklin's friends had trained the most active of the Gordon Rioters. On occasion the government refused to act on information provided by informers, as Viscount Weymouth declined to proceed on information concerning the activities of American supporters in Bristol, much to the chagrin of his informant.[26] Other threats, such as the rumor that radical correspondence was being intercepted, were more serious, and prosecution was always possible.

One of the most useful weapons in a government's armory against what it considered as intolerable criticism was prosecution for seditious libel. It had been employed against Wilkes during the 1760s and was brought out again at the beginning of the American war. Within a few days of the arrival of news of Lexington, the government was informed when the Constitutional Society placed notices in several London newspapers soliciting subscriptions for the relief of widows and other dependents of those who had been "inhumanely murdered by the King's troops" and immediately instituted proceedings against the publishers of those papers in which the first and subsequent notices had appeared.[27] But the centerpiece of the government's actions was the prosecution of the former Wilkite and active radical John Horne Tooke. When he eventually came to trial in 1777, Horne Tooke, who admitted authorship of the offending notice, was sentenced to a year's imprisonment, fined £200, and ordered to provide sureties for his good behavior for three years. Possibly it was the prospect and consequences of this prosecution that kept him unusually silent during these years; certainly Horne Tooke believed the attorney general deliberately had been dilatory in bringing him to trial.[28] Nor was the Lexington notice the only instance of prosecution for pro-American sympathies during the war. In 1781, Joseph Cooper, printer of the *London Courant*, was prosecuted for seditious libel after publishing a poem in the 23 January issue which argued that the king had invaded the rights of the people, ignored their prayers, infested the seas and land with lawless rapine, and caused the Americans to rebel, thus bringing about the loss of the empire. Earlier, in 1775, a prosecution of Stephen Sayre for an alleged plot to send the king back to Hanover had collapsed and Sayre had been awarded £1,000 damages for false imprisonment in the Tower.[29]

Radical fears that their unpopular views would lay them open to prosecution received added substance by the decision to suspend habeas corpus in 1777. Since its formalization in 1679, the right to apply for a writ of habeas corpus had come to be considered an essential bulwark of English liberty, and its suspension was regarded as highly alarming. Sharp pointed out the dangers inherent in this action in a strongly critical pamphlet, and Catharine Macaulay feared that if she were to hold conversations with Franklin or any other Americans during a visit to Paris in December of that year she might be subject to immediate imprisonment on her return to England. Richard Price also became increasingly afraid of the possible consequences of his American sympathies during the course of the war.[30]

There can be no doubt that the position of radical supporters of the Americans was difficult and often lonely. Fothergill's esti-

mate that America's friends in England had been reduced to insignificant numbers by the beginning of 1775 cannot be accepted, for
he was being unduly pessimistic, but Sir George Savile's comment
two years later that "we are not only patriots *out of place*, but
patriots *out of the opinion of the public*" was all too true.[31]
Certainly the government's majorities in the House of Commons
reflected its general popularity—until things began to go wrong.
Lord North made a legitimate point when he protested against
criticism of his American policy in a Commons debate in 1785
that "the war was a war of the people, begun at their instance, and
at the instance of that House."[32]

Conscious that they were members of a small and unpopular
minority, many Commonwealthmen made considerable sacrifices
in order to remain true to their principles. For several the outbreak
of war created substantial personal difficulties. Jebb's political
views during the war caused tension between himself and his
cousin Sir Richard Jebb, who was surgeon to the king, and ham-
pered his new career as a physician. Priestley refused to quarrel
with his Tory friend the engineer Matthew Boulton, but also
refused to pass on information which he feared Boulton would
exploit to the detriment of the Americans. Had he wished to,
Cartwright could have resumed his naval career on the outbreak
of war, but he declined to serve against the colonists. Later he felt
he might have been appointed to a command "of some importance" in the American service, but he told his niece that although
he refused to bear arms against American liberties he had an
obligation to his country from which nothing could absolve him;
he accordingly spent several years on active service in the county
militia, during which he was appointed to his majority.[33]

The difficulty posed by war was especially acute for Granville
Sharp. A man without private means, his employment as a clerk in
the Ordnance Department at the Tower of London gave him
sufficient income and free time to indulge in his many philanthropic
activities. But as a strong friend to the colonists he refused to assist
in the shipment of supplies to British troops in America after
Lexington. At first he obtained leave of absence in order to avoid
embarrassment, and finally he resigned; thereafter Sharp had no
paid employment and lived with members of his family.[34] Thomas
Day, who always took a cooler view of America than most radicals,

suffered embarrassment of a different kind. As a vigorous critic of the institution, he found the continued existence of slavery a serious impediment to his support for colonial resistance. He previously had condemned the colonists for cruelty to their slaves in a poem entitled *The Dying Negro*; in 1776 he drafted a strongly worded attack on the inconsistency between southerners' noble principles of individual liberty and their actual practices toward American blacks: "How dare the inhabitants of the Southern colonies speak of privileges and justice? . . . If there be an object truly ridiculous in nature, it is an American patriot, signing resolutions of independence with one hand and with the other brandishing a whip over his affrighted slaves."[35] Such scathing criticism could only damage the American cause so he withheld it from publication until after the war had ended. In the meantime he publicized his support for the Americans.

For several months after the outbreak of war radicals were uncertain what course to follow. Pamphlets such as the widely admired *Sermon on the Present Situation of American Affairs* by William Smith of Philadelphia confirmed their automatic assumption that the colonists still wished to settle the dispute within the framework of empire. At first they hoped the government would respond to the Americans' proposals for reconciliation—thus Sharp was hopeful of the outcome of the Olive Branch petition though Fothergill was not—but this hope was soon frustrated. They naturally urged the Americans to guard against deceptive offers from the government, but some were almost as skeptical of the policies of the parliamentary opposition as of those of the ministry. Cartwright had a poor opinion of its members and in retrospect believed that the crucial distinction between radicals and the leaders of the parliamentary opposition was that the parliamentarians had, almost without exception, accompanied their vigorous defense of the colonies with an assertion of parliamentary sovereignty whereas he, Price, and the anonymous pamphleteers had insisted that Parliament did not enjoy sovereignty in America.[36] Certainly radicals were more in sympathy with the views of the Chatham-Shelburne group than with the Rockinghams, though Sharp did not accept Chatham's supposed distinction between taxation and legislation. At one point, in October 1775, Joseph Priestley told Savile, who had close connections with the

Rockinghams, that if ever there was an opportunity for negotiation the Americans would prefer to deal with his patron Lord Shelburne rather than with Lord Rockingham, whose Declaratory Act was anathema to them.[37]

As 1775 gave way to 1776 many radicals were almost in despair. Although men such as Fothergill continued to frame schemes of reconciliation and others were thinking implicitly along similar lines, some were becoming more realistic. In November, John Wilkes warned the House of Commons that the country was on the brink of separation unless reconciliation was achieved immediately. Capel Lofft wrote a perceptive analysis of the nature and future prospects of the war, concluding that taken in any light it seemed "full of discouragement."[38] They were not alone. Turner was deeply pessimistic about the prospects for the new year; it would be blackened with "deprivation, slaughter and public misery."[39] He thought there was little hope to be derived from a peace mission being sent to America since it was only a disguise for not doing what ought to have been done immediately and hoped it would not divide the colonists. Turner's London correspondent, Lindsey, who had been impressed by Arthur Lee's *Second Appeal*, agreed that the administration's American policy was disastrous and that only ruin could follow from the attempt to subdue the colonists. Although as time passed radicals became increasingly depressed at the government's bellicosity, they remained certain that the American cause was honorable and hopeful that it would be successful. As Kenrick put it, with the assistance of Providence, truth and liberty would ultimately flourish "in those extensive fertile regions, to destroy which British arms are at present hastening."[40]

During these difficult months the most important and influential English defense of the American colonists was published. Richard Price had been concerned with American affairs for several years and had made private recommendations to Lord Shelburne. He had also approved the principles of Cartwright's pamphlet *American Independence* (though he considered it would be difficult to obtain sufficient support for its recommendations), but as yet had published nothing substantial on the subject. Only after waiting several months since hearing of Lexington did he decide to make his first venture into political pamphleteering. He began his tract, *Observations on the Nature of Civil Liberty, the Principles of Government and the Justice and Policy of the War with America*, in October 1775, though it was not ready for publication until the beginning of the following February. Since he already enjoyed a notable reputation as a writer, Price's views commanded considerable attention, and edition followed edition in quick succession.[41]

Radicals received it with enthusiasm. Priestley commended it as "a most excellent pamphlet," Lindsey thought it "noble indeed," and Cartwright considered that it reiterated every substantial principle laid down in his own pamphlet *American Independence*.[42] News of *Civil Liberty* spread rapidly. Wedgwood had already seen extracts by 21 February and asked Bentley to send him a copy, commenting, "The Nation, like the Old Man at Gataker [*sic*], wants something to frighten it." Bentley had anticipated Wedgwood's request and sent a copy before being asked. Three days later Wedgwood wrote to thank him for "Dr. Price's most excellent pamphlet" and asked for some copies of the next edition; in his view, "those who are neither converted, nor frightened into a better way of thinking by reading this excellent and alarming Book may be given up for hardened sinners, beyond the reach of conviction."[43] Kenrick would have agreed; he sent a copy of *Civil Liberty*, the principles of which he approved, to his friend James Wodrow in Scotland in an unsuccessful attempt to persuade him of the justice of the colonists' cause. Somewhat surprisingly, Ralph Griffiths, the liberal editor of the *Monthly Review*, was only lukewarm toward the pamphlet, believing that Britain should only negotiate with the colonies from a position of strength. *Civil Liberty* served to win friends for the Americans as well as to confirm the views of those who were already sympathetic. Thomas Hardy, later to become a prominent figure in the radical artisan movement of the 1790s, arrived in London shortly after the onset of the war. He immediately became involved in discussions and debates over the issue. He was unable to believe that the administration was quite as bad as its critics made out and often found himself defending it. But as soon as *Civil Liberty* appeared, Hardy was utterly persuaded by its arguments and came to believe that an American victory was necessary not only for the well-being of the colonists but also in the interest of the future happiness of the entire globe. The greatest formal accolade came when the Common

Council of the City of London, led by the lord mayor, John Sawbridge (who remained a zealous advocate of the American cause), offered Price the freedom of the City and voted to thank him for laying down "those sure principles upon which alone the supreme legislative Authority of Great Britain over her Colonies can be justly or beneficially maintained."[44] Such wide popularity among other radicals makes it appropriate to examine Price's arguments at some length, for they can stand as broadly representing the radical view of the nature and prospects of the imperial dispute after the outbreak of war.

Like other radicals, Price was firmly persuaded that the American question should be examined in relation to the general principles of civil liberty as well as the narrower grounds of particular problems and circumstances. He insisted that the basic issues were reason, equity, and the rights of mankind, not simply precedents, charters, and statutes.[45] From this premise he considered the Americans in three interrelated contexts: as men entitled to be different from Englishmen because they inhabited a different continent, as fellow countrymen who were members of the same political and social system as himself and so entitled to the same rights and privileges that were the property of all men and other benefits as members of the British empire, and lastly as citizens of particular local communities. Nor was this the only consequence of Price's preliminary analysis. Since the empire was in many important respects a single community, the operation of government policy in its various parts interacted; and since the fate of mankind was indivisible, the ramifications of affairs in America were potentially capable of reverberating throughout the world. It followed that Englishmen should be concerned for the fate of liberty in America partly in the particularist interests of the colonists, but also for their own sake and that of mankind.

Price also perceived that if the American problem was to be assigned such potential importance, the central issues required more extensive exploration than was customary among political pamphleteers. Accordingly, he opened his discussion with an analysis of the nature of liberty, which, although necessarily somewhat brief and dependent on his earlier philosophical work, gave his tract greater depth and substance than its contemporaries had.[46] Moving forward in his argument, Price insisted that if a government was to be free, it had to be a creature of the people. Its legitimate authority originated from them, it ought to be conducted under their supervision, and it had no purpose or justification other than the furtherance of their happiness. By itself, though, this was insufficient. As a Dissenter, Price suffered infringement of his liberty through legal discrimination and knew that legislation could be enacted by one man or group in their own particular interest rather than by common consent in the interest of the community as a whole; observance of the maxim "government of law not of men" was inadequate as a means of protecting the liberty of the citizen. Unfortunately, the consequent requirement to devise a coherent system whereby the consent of the citizenry was given to the operations of government in an advanced and complex society posed a difficult problem. Price's preferred solution was a small state in which every man could indicate his assent in person: such a system provided an ideal environment in which liberty could flourish, but failing that he was prepared to accept representation in a larger state. To balance this concession he insisted that "government . . . is, in the very nature of it, a TRUST: and all its powers a DELEGATION for gaining particular ends."[47] Further difficulties arose, however, when the principle had to be applied to a complex empire such as that of eighteenth-century Britain.

The laws of civil liberty (which to Price was almost synonymous with political liberty) and the intermediate principles of government decreed that no one country could possess any power or authority over the property or legislation of another unless the other was incorporated into the first by just and adequate representation. Only then could a state be free, and since only through representation could it be governed by its own will, any country subject to the legislation of another without representation or control was in a condition of slavery. Such a form of slavery was worse than that of one person over another for although an individual might die, a body of men was self-perpetuating. Worse still, there was no fellow feeling among states as there was among men, especially between those separated by the expanse of an ocean. The governing country could not observe the consequences of its oppression or be a competent judge of the circumstances and abilities of the people whom it was administering; also inherent in the relationship was that the two societies must have separate interests to a large degree. Last, although the enslavement of a people by internal despots might be limited, there was little to circumscribe the authority of one state over another. Such authority could only be sustained by force, and Price cited the fate of Massachusetts to illustrate his point.[48]

In the light of these principles, Price felt inescapably bound to condemn British policy toward America. The Declaratory Act of 1766 purported to enunciate an absolute power enjoyed by Parliament over the colonies; this was an infringement of the Americans' right to the benefits of civil liberty; maintenance of the unity of the empire was undesirable if the cost was the enslavement of one half. Like other radicals, Price reiterated the proposition of "no taxation with representation" and denied that the Americans had given their consent to taxation through the medium of "virtual representation" in Parliament. Far from establishing her own constitution in America (which was undesirable since the colonies had their own chartered governments), Britain was violating it by her actions there. He saw the object of the war as being to extend British power by destroying the American constitutions and substituting military force.[49] A society, Price believed, should always possess the right to determine the nature and extent of its own liberty and happiness. He rejected the argument often advanced in defense of ministerial policy that the Americans would be happier under British rule than their own and that their liberties would be safer under the British government than in their own hands. This theory was inherently fallacious; although different classes within a single kingdom shared the same concerns and interests, there was not necessarily reciprocity of interest among different communities forming an empire. They inhabited different areas and were governed by different legislatures, and these factors had considerable influence on their interests and outlook. The potential clash of interests among different communities could lead to a situation in which the constitution of government might be consistent with liberty in one part but entirely inconsistent with it in another.[50] The implication of this proposition was plain: even if the present structure of government was consistent with liberty in England (and Price was severely critical of its current mode of operation) it was not consistent with liberty in America.

What was appropriate in England was not necessarily suitable in the colonies for local circumstances were different. Britain should not consider herself superior to the colonies for wealth tended to corrupt rather than to give dignity, and the Americans were probably as knowledgeable and virtuous as the British. The colonists were a mature people and well able to determine what was desirable in their own communities. No attempt should be made to extend the machinery of British government, as distinct from its constitutional principles, to America. As a parent state, Britain should have been relaxing control, not increasing it, as the colonies developed. She should be pleased to observe free states developing within the empire, each enjoying an independent legislature similar to her own; she should have aimed at binding the colonies to her only by ties of affection and interest and might have acted as a friendly umpire and defender. Price's views were strengthened by the belief that in fifty or sixty years the American population would be double the size of Britain's. The colonies would then form a powerful empire which would comprise a number of states, all equal or superior to Britain in the arts and accomplishments that gave dignity and happiness to human life. And the idea of a small group of men on one side of the Atlantic controlling a vast continent on the other was risible.[51]

Much of Price's argument very properly was concerned with principles and political ethics, but he also criticized official policy on prudential grounds. The government still could draw back, he believed, and if it did not do so voluntarily it might be compelled to later with greater disgrace. Raising troops was becoming difficult, and naval power would be of little use against the Americans since they did not depend on trade. The war was already having a harmful effect on Britain. She was throwing away the advantages of a very profitable trade, which had been one of the mainsprings of her opulence and splendor, the empire was being dismembered, and the blood of thousands was being shed in an unjust quarrel. At home her strength was exhausted, her industry was suffering, and there were dangerous consequences for her financial stability and revenue. At such a time the country's natural enemies who were eager to see her downfall would seize the opportunity to take advantage of it.[52]

Price refused to take his argument to the logical conclusion which, it might be thought, was demanded by much of his analysis. In one further step he could have advocated independence, but this was the antithesis of his purpose as a pamphleteer. His central purpose was to promote reconciliation between Britain and the American colonies, for he was a warm, if not unqualified, supporter of the British empire. He therefore felt it essential to devise some machinery to protect the Americans' liberties and preserve the imperial connection at one and the same time.

To achieve this Price moved considerably beyond Cartwright's earlier proposals by recommending the establishment of a formally constructed federal community. Each state would be internally self-governing, and a general confederacy comprising a senate of representatives from each state would provide the necessary articulation between the particularist interests of its individual members and the general needs of the empire at large. The senate would possess authority to manage all common concerns, adjudicate in disputes between members of the confederacy, and have the common force of the states at its disposal to enforce its decisions. He defined the purpose of the scheme as being to give each state security from oppression and interference from its neighbors; disputes would be arbitrated as they arose and thus universal peace would be maintained.[53]

Such proposals were impractical in the circumstances prevailing in the early months of 1776. Price's schema, which called for British and American representatives to sit together in the same assembly, was far more advanced than that proposed by Joseph Galloway at the first Continental Congress, yet its generosity toward American aspirations and interests and its understanding of the imperative need to secure colonial consent to the operations of empire concealed several grave weaknesses. For the Americans it raised the old problem of representation in a Westminster legislature (though in a different form), and, more crucially, Price's proposals probably were not relevant to rapidly changing circumstances in which independence was gathering both speed and strength. His plan implicitly called for drastic changes in the British constitution, particularly in the authority and powers of Parliament, and could hardly have formed the basis for discussion at a time when the British government, with the support of a large majority of the population, was determined to suppress the rebellion and convinced of success. Price conceded the improbability of securing the requisite support in England. Thus he recommended proposals made by Lord Shelburne in the House of Lords as the basis for reconciliation—proposals that were clearly related to his own sketch of a year or so earlier. What Shelburne had suggested was altogether more modest: hostilities should be suspended, the recent Restraining Act, the Coercive Acts, and the Quebec Act should be repealed and other legislation set aside for later revision. But he insisted that certain regulatory legislation should never be abandoned because one of the central principles of the imperial structure was that Parliament possessed the right to regulate trade in the common interest of all its members. Shelburne also argued that the British national debt should be made the responsibility of the entire empire; other legislation was open for negotiation, but in any case the colonies should be exempted from parliamentary taxation and their charters should be acknowledged as sacred.[54]

Unfortunately Price's efforts were being overtaken by the course of events. On the western shores of the Atlantic a movement of the most profound importance was gathering strength: the Revolutionary leaders were coming to the firm conclusion that the connection with Britain should no longer be sustained. Several colonies were organizing governments whose authority purported to be no longer dependent on the crown, and the argument was gaining that diplomatic, military, and domestic considerations made independence imperative. On 7 June 1776, Richard Henry Lee introduced into Congress a formal motion that the united colonies were, and of right ought to be, free and independent states, that they were absolved from all allegiance to the British crown, and that all political connection with Britain was dissolved. Within a month Congress had accepted the decision to secede from the empire, and on 4 July it issued a Declaration of Independence.[55]

News of the American decision was not unexpected when it reached England. From May onward London newspapers had been full of rumors that the colonists were about to secede, and their correspondence columns included animated discussions of the likelihood, consequences, and propriety of such action. Confirmation of the rumors arrived in mid-August, and within a few days the text of the Declaration was printed in several papers and as a broadsheet.[56] It had little effect. Ralph Izard of South Carolina, who was in London at the time, commented that it was laughed at in St. James's, and although William Lee believed that it had made some impact in September, a month later he had to concede that it seemed to have been forgotten; neither in conversation nor in the newspapers was it being mentioned as a matter of the least importance.[57] Such an anticlimactic response was, of course, to be expected from the public at large as they still expected the rebellion to be crushed.

The response of the radicals is at first sight more surprising. As an affirmation of the most cherished articles of their political faith and an expression of the Americans' determination to resist the allegedly tyrannous intentions of the British government, one might have expected the Declaration of Independence to have been received with enthusiasm by America's friends in England. Such was not the case. Wilkes applauded it in the House of Commons but made it clear that he hoped for reunion; very few other radicals seem to have made any comment. The authors of *The Crisis* printed the Declaration but later implied that union was still feasible. Lindsey, whose correspondence with Turner before the war had been full of comment on American affairs, did not mention it when their correspondence resumed in September 1776; Cartwright is said to have hung a copy of the Declaration of Independence in a place of honor in his dining room, but he probably did not accept it at the time in terms that would have been acceptable to its author. Commenting in the *Monthly Review*, Griffiths criticized its long recapitulation of grievances against the king as appearing frivolous and peevish and thought them likely to detract from its more important arguments.[58] Price, who already had been the object of much abuse for his public sympathy for the Americans, certainly remarked, "The Congress has declared war and independency, and there is now an end of all hope of reconciliation. The next news we may hear is that they have formed an alliance with France"; yet these words were misleading for he did not anticipate a permanent separation at this stage.[59] Responses such as these make it clear that radicals missed (perhaps deliberately) the central thrust of the Declaration of Independence in spite of its clarity of argument and distinction of style.

In reality, this lukewarm response to the Declaration is readily explicable since it was entirely consistent with well-established radical attitudes toward the American crisis. Englishmen who supported the American cause had anticipated that the two countries would separate at an unspecified point in the distant future, but they neither wished nor expected independence to come immediately.[60] In a sense they anticipated an American 1688. That Glorious Revolution had been an almost bloodless affair; it had put an end to the tyranny of James II and had produced an eminently satisfactory basis for the government of a free nation. Looking at the Anglo-American dispute, radicals acknowledged that it had been right and necessary for the patriots to take up arms, but denied that the differences between the two countries were irreconcilable. Instead they believed that a reunited empire would enter a new era of prosperity, harmony, and freedom. Richard Watson had had the temerity to make the explicit analogy with the Glorious Revolution in a sermon preached before the chancellor and other members of the University of Cambridge in May 1776. He declared that the colonists' resistance on the issue of taxation without representation was reasonable and warned of the dangers emanating from the tyranny of a legislature and the terrible possibility that the crisis might get out of hand. Instead of a second 1688 the situation might develop into a catastrophe similar to that of the Civil War, which from small beginnings had ended in devastation, carnage, the oppression of the people, and the ruin of the king, nobility, and constitution. Kenrick in Bewdley and many others insisted throughout the war that the Americans had never deliberately sought independence.[61] Men like Major Cartwright, who had advocated friendly separation before the first shots had been fired at Lexington, were extremely rare, and even Cartwright argued only for legislative independence.

Price, Cartwright, Sharp, and other radicals had always been ready to defend the colonists on "American principles" because they believed those principles were synonymous with their own, but in the summer of 1776 they failed to recognize that the Americans had extended their principles to incorporate the new axioms of total independence and republicanism into those of the radical creed. This change in the terms of the conflict was of considerable importance to the development of an American nation but was unacceptable and largely irrelevant to the immediate concerns of English radicals. For them loyalty to the crown (with few exceptions) and the integrity of the empire were central components in the structure of their political ideology; had they realized the true purpose and significance of the Declaration, their dilemma at a time when reconciliation appeared superficially possible would have been intolerable. Accordingly, they ignored its true meaning and continued for some time to respond to the crisis in the context of an Anglo-American empire which would retain constitutional as well as cultural associations. Their duty remained, in their eyes, the same as it had been before the war: to preserve the union as well as to maintain liberty.

Despondency was common among radicals during the dark and uncertain middle years of the war, though they never gave up hope of a satisfactory outcome. Taking the opportunity of a fast-day sermon to try to influence a congregation that was probably not as sympathetic to the Americans as he was, Newcome Cappe of York suggested that God's patience with Britain was running out and that there were clear symptoms of a national decline. He went on to point out that even if their adversaries were wrong, there was little consolation in that; furthermore, a war between parent and child was especially horrible.[62] After news of General Burgoyne's surrender at Saratoga had arrived in Staffordshire, Wedgwood commented sarcastically that those who had opposed the Americans now seemed to think that the war could best be ended by granting them everything they had previously demanded; he commented on the tragic incongruity of their change of heart, "what fools we must have been to expend so much blood and treasure for something worse than nothing at all."[63] When Fothergill heard of the Franco-American alliance, he lamented that although Britain had long enjoyed the privilege of being as good, as virtuous, and as happy a nation as any, it had neglected those things that could have made it both great and happy in the future. Instead, the country was immersed in pleasures and corruption and the public good had been ignored. Even those members of the parliamentary opposition who might have been expected to give assistance were divided among themselves and concerned to pursue their own individual interests. There was, he believed, little to be hoped for in such circumstances, and he felt that the justice of Providence was displayed by the reduction of a "powerful, enlight-

ened and yet haughty nation to the threshold of destruction"
because of its refusal to acknowledge its dependence on Providence
and for plunging into an unjust war.[64] Lindsey despaired when he
discovered in October 1778 that the government was still determined to continue the war. Worse still, soldiers returning from
America were reported to believe that if twelve thousand troops
had been sent instead of the Carlisle peace mission, the Americans
would have been defeated. When he heard a rumor that the
government had rejected an offer of peace from Franklin early in
1779, Lindsey concluded that the only future course was to wait
for the long-anticipated consequences of the government's wicked
measures.[65]

Pessimistic though they often were, the radicals' prime objective remained reconciliation. Even Wilkes, who had explicitly
defended the Declaration of Independence in the House of Commons as a "wise and political measure" in October 1776, was still
arguing a year later that although America could not be recon-
quered, it might be regained "by the mild arts of lenity and justice,
by temper and moderation."[66] For some time many of them worked
hard to restore the traditional union between Britain and America
until slowly, one by one, they were forced to recognize that a
resolution of the conflict between the two countries could only be
achieved on a basis of total separation.

While many Commonwealthmen lacked access to the circles
of power, Granville Sharp was sufficiently well connected on both
sides of the Atlantic to feel that he had the right and the duty to act
as an intermediary. To be the son of an archdeacon and the
grandson of an archbishop carried prestige and influence in the
eighteenth century, and although Sharp did not move continuously
in high society, his acquaintances included the earl of Dartmouth,
who had been American secretary from 1772 to 1775 when he
became lord privy seal, Lord North, and several bishops. Once he
had resigned his clerkship at the Board of Ordnance, Sharp was
able to devote much of his time to promoting reconciliation;
initially he sought to achieve a restoration of the Anglo-American
union, but later he worked for peace on a basis of separation. His
first major effort came in March 1777, when he had a long
interview with Lord Dartmouth, whom he begged to acknowledge
the expediency of making peace with the Americans. On the basis

of an earlier conversation with some Americans in London, he insisted that an attempt to bring Americans back to an allegiance to the crown would be successful, provided a proof of British sincerity was offered, and he recommended the reformation of Parliament, to be implemented within six months.[67] The government made no such move, but Sharp refused to give up hope. On hearing the news of Saratoga, he sent the duke of Richmond (a leading member of the Rockingham group in the House of Lords who was also radical in his politics) a copy of the proposals he had made previously to Dartmouth. Sharp insisted that America still would be willing to return to the empire and declared that his tract *A Declaration of the People's Natural Right to a Share in the Legislature* had demonstrated the necessity and advantage of preserving the "ancient Constitutional Connection" with Britain by means of a direct relationship between the colonies and the crown. The pamphlet, he said, had been well received in America, and this demonstrated that the majority of the people there were not really committed to republicanism.[68]

Having pleaded earnestly for reconciliation before the outbreak of war, Major John Cartwright continued his efforts to secure a negotiated settlement after 1776. Working perhaps in concert with Sharp, in April 1777 he attended a royal levee and presented the king with an address recommending peace with America and proposing a plan for maintaining the union; the nature of his proposals emerged in the second edition of *The Legislative Rights of the Commonalty Vindicated*. As a preliminary the government should nominate a day of national fasting and humiliation, British troops should be withdrawn from America, a declaration of peace made, and commissioners who were not already compromised by involvement in the war should be dispatched to America. The next stage would be to call a general election in England in which all members of Parliament would be elected on a countywide basis by those who already enjoyed the franchise. A proclamation should be issued to the effect that the people should instruct their members to enact legislation to restore the independence of the House of Commons to the true theory and standard of the constitution. A second act of the new Parliament would be legislation to bring about reconciliation with America along the lines proposed in *American Independence* three years earlier. It was, however, essential to allow the colonists sufficient time to realize that opinion in Britain had changed and to appreciate the benefits they would enjoy as members of the "grand British league and confederation."[69]

At the beginning of 1777, Price made a last despairing effort to influence public opinion on the American question. He originally intended his *Additional Observations on the Nature of Civil Liberty* to be a brief elaboration of his earlier tract, but it grew beyond those limits. Sensibly adapting his arguments to the need to influence public opinion, he laid far more stress on strategic factors than he had done previously and argued that Britain could be neither safe nor prosperous without America. Sooner or later the loss of the colonies would be felt in Britain's commerce and finance; it would be even greater in military terms since they had given additional strength to the navy and assisted Britain in her wars, and the country's position in relation to France and Spain must be maintained. In his view the Americans were "worth any price—our existence depends on keeping them."[70] This was going to extremes (the tenor of much of the tract suggests that he was overwrought), but there was good sense in much of what Price had to say. He insisted that the Americans had not deliberately sought independence and argued that the only possible method of retaining them was by reconciliation, for coercion would destroy their value and render them useless. Also, if America were to be recovered by force, it would have to be retained by force, and, he predicted, the failure of the coercive policy would unleash a general war and destroy the empire; he was afraid as he wrote that America might have already concluded an alliance with France, in which case the die would have been cast. But, he commented, "let events turn out as they will, I shall always reflect with satisfaction, that I have, though a private person of little consequence, bore [sic] my testimony, from deep conviction, against a war which must shock the feelings and reason of every considerate person."[71] A few months later Price informed his friends Lee in France and Winthrop in Massachusetts that having done what he could, he was now in the position of a silent spectator "waiting, with inexpressable anxiety, the issue of a most important struggle"; the following year he declined a formal offer of citizenship and an invitation to assist in organizing American finances coupled with a warm personal invitation from Lee to emigrate to the United States.[72]

Of all America's radical friends, David Hartley was in the best position to intercede on their behalf and to promote the cause of reconciliation. As a member of Parliament he spoke frequently on American affairs in the House of Commons and made eight motions in favor of reconciliation between 1775 and 1779. Unfortunately his mannerisms, reputation for eccentricity, and the inordinate length of his speeches seriously diminished the effectiveness of his arguments. He shared the radical belief that the colonists had carried the seeds of the British constitution to America and argued that the justification for their resistance could be found in the English Bill of Rights. When on 7 December 1775 he offered proposals for reconciliation with America, Hartley suggested that a veil should be thrown over all theoretical disputes concerning the rights of subjects, either as colonists or as men in general, and restrictive legislation should be repealed so that the Americans would be restored to the position they had enjoyed in 1763. Then, as an "auspicious beginning to lay the first step of universal liberty to mankind," an act of Parliament should be passed entitling all slaves to trial by jury in criminal cases; this would be the first step toward complete abolition of slavery, which each colony should undertake according to its own circumstances.[73] By 1777, Hartley had come to believe that the best way of dealing with the colonies would be to grant them national rights as free and independent states, and he hoped that this would provide a basis for a perpetual bond of affection and alliance with Britain as beneficial to both countries as the previous connection had been. A year later, in April 1778, he traveled to Paris, with North's knowledge but without any official authority, to sound out Franklin and Adams about the prospects for peace. He virtually ignored the Franco-American alliance, much to the Americans' annoyance, and returned to England convinced that he had discovered a basis for ending the war. As heads of negotiation, Hartley proposed that America should be declared independent (according to his own restricted definition of the term), that the two countries should agree not to enter into any treaty offensive to the other, and that there should be free trade and mutual naturalization between Britain and America. A final hint of unreality about Hartley's proposals was that, although he knew that the Americans were adamant on the issue of independence (that is, they intended to fight for total separation), he proposed that Franklin should be invited to go to America with a British representative to negotiate a federal alliance between their two countries.[74]

Hartley continued to hammer away at this theme during the remainder of the Parliament. He also took advantage of his friendship with Sir George Savile to press his views on the Yorkshire Association for parliamentary reform in 1780 by writing a long letter to Wyvill, its chairman. He defended the Americans for making an alliance with France and urged that even if France were using America for her own purposes, Britain should still be conciliatory. She should make a sincere offer of peace to America, beginning perhaps with a truce, and then offer a federal alliance. He argued that it would be particularly appropriate for the Yorkshire Association to take the lead since the continuation of the American war was the most pressing of all evils. Hartley was seldom precisely clear as to what he meant by "American independence" and a "federal alliance," but when speaking in a debate in the House of Commons on 22 June 1779 he expressed the explicit hope that the proposals he was then recommending would lead not only to peace but to reunion as well.[75]

Nor were these hopes confined to a tiny group of particular individuals. Others such as William Pulteney and James Hutton, the Moravian pastor, tried to promote reconciliation, and still others vainly wished to see a restoration of the union some time after the war was to all intents and purposes over. Like Cartwright and Sharp, John Jebb believed that the introduction of parliamentary reform probably would lead to a federal union with the American states and commended Price's 1776 proposals in an *Address to the Freeholders of Middlesex*, delivered on 20 December 1779. Capel Lofft, who earlier had defended the Americans against the attacks of John Wesley, believed that if a thorough parliamentary reform were initiated, the crown would preside over a united, happy, and invincible people; then Britain might expect to renew the interrupted connection with America "on free, permanent, truly beneficial terms, as with brethren and equal friends by a FEDERAL UNION."[76] The City of London Common Council was arguing the same point in April 1780, no doubt under the influence of its radical members, and even the more conservative reformers of Yorkshire were expressing similar sentiments. A motion offered at a meeting of the Yorkshire Committee of Association held on 3 May 1780 thanked those members of both houses of Parliament who had opposed the attempt to reduce America to unconditional surrender and urged that they should not give up hope of effecting a "speedy reunion with that Country on beneficial, just and honourable terms."[77] As late as 1782 the London Livery drank a toast to the fond hope, "May the acknowledgment of the Independence of America be no baulk to a reunion with that people."[78]

The course of events could not be ignored, and by 1782 the possibility of reunion between England and America was long dead. Like the rest of their fellow countrymen, although for different reasons, radicals had hoped that the British empire could be preserved; they had also been convinced that it could be done without violating the fundamental liberties of their American friends. Gradually they came to realize that their aspirations were at variance with the realities of the war and to face the fact that the dual goals of liberty and union were unattainable. And since maintenance of the union was no longer feasible, they abandoned their objective in favor of continuing their support for the defense of American liberty; instead of working to preserve the empire they advocated recognition of American independence.

General Burgoyne's surrender in October 1777 was the turning point for most radicals. Alone among them Priestley had anticipated separation (apparently in the fullest sense) as "a certain and speedy event" in the spring of 1776 and regarded Shelburne's proposals as having little hope of acceptance; when news arrived from Saratoga he hoped even the most confident advocates would be convinced that the war was certain to end in disgrace and ruin. As librarian to Lord Shelburne until his resignation in 1780, Priestley was nearer than most other radicals to the cockpit of political life and became involved in political negotiation. Shortly after the Franco-American alliance had been reported in London, in March 1778, the prime minister attempted to persuade Shelburne to join his administration. North's emissary, William Eden, called on Priestley, who introduced him to his patron and then left. Priestley was greatly alarmed at the prospect of his patron entering the government and wrote him a long letter claiming to represent not only his own views but those of Price and Shipley as well. He urged that Britain should disconcert the French by joining them in recognizing American independence. Such a policy would detach the Americans from their alliance with France, and if the French persisted in war, the country would be united against them in defense.[79] North's attempt to bring Shelburne into his administration failed—but so did Priestley's attempt to persuade him to recognize American independence.

Others were slower than Priestley. John Fothergill seems to have abandoned the possibility of reunion late in 1776 or, more likely, sometime in 1777, but he continued to advocate the appointment of negotiators to treat for a commercial union. Early in 1777, Cartwright was urging the City to petition the crown for a new ministry which would (by implication) pursue more conciliatory policies; a year later he conceded that Chatham's proposals and his own for a grand confederacy were outdated and publicly declared, "It is our duty to cease hostilities, to acknowledge the independence of America, and so obtain the best terms we can."[80] At much the same time Wilkes was declaring in the House of Commons that America was irrecoverably lost, and by the spring of 1779, Price was confident that American independence was already secure and that there was no longer any prospect of subjugating the former colonies.[81] Sharp's recommendation that a measure of parliamentary reform should be implemented as an indication of conciliatory intentions toward America had been ignored. By January 1778, only a few weeks after he had expressed the view that reunion was possible, he realized that peace was attainable only if Britain acknowledged the independence of the United States. He supported Richmond's motion of 7 April calling for withdrawal of the army from America as the most reasonable proposal currently being offered and urged the government to seek conciliation with the Americans on terms that would preserve their goodwill.[82] Later he drafted a memorandum for consideration by the citizens of London which advocated that they should petition the king in favor of peace on the basis of American independence as the only way to end the war with France and Spain. In the summer and autumn of 1781, Sharp resumed his efforts for, as he told the bishop of Peterborough, the United States "have been independent in fact for several years and why should the truth be any longer denied?" The earl of Dartmouth and Lord George Germain were unresponsive, and the war was left to follow its natural course.[83]

To all intents the war ended with the surrender of General Cornwallis at Yorktown. As the London Livery bluntly told the king, "'Your armies are captured; the wonted superiority of your navies is annihilated; your dominions are lost.'"[84] Jebb had long abandoned his hopes for a reformed empire when news of Yorktown arrived. He urged the Westminster Committee for parliamentary reform to demand an immediate recognition of American independence, but its other members were unwilling to go so far and contented themselves with demanding an end to the war. Price was delighted at the course of events in America but horrified by the apparent determination of North's government to continue the war; events, however, were moving rapidly and the prime minister was forced to resign in March 1782.[85] By this time the American problem had been reduced largely to a question of tactics. Not that there were no points of substance remaining for debate. Much public opinion would have imposed punitive restrictions on American trade as a corollary of the American withdrawal from the empire. This was unacceptable to radicals for although they were now eager to recognize American independence they worked to preserve commercial relations and were firmly convinced that there was an essential unity of interest between the two countries. Their desire to run two horses together raised the question of priorities, and each one had to decide for himself whether the formal acknowledgment of independence should be delayed in an attempt to negotiate a commercial agreement.

Different men took different positions, of course. Thomas Day welcomed the advent of the Rockingham administration, with its commitment to independence, but it proved a disappointment to Price, largely because of the policies pursued by his patron. Lord Shelburne had been appointed to the secretaryship of state in charge of negotiations with America and in July became prime minister, but still seems to have been hankering after some form of reunion. Possibly he was under the influence of Thomas Pownall—certainly the former governor of Massachusetts had been touting a plan of reunion to Franklin in the summer of

1781—but his policies were also in general accord with the grandiose schemes for the exploitation of the American west which he had drafted over a decade earlier.[86] Price, on the other hand, would have recognized American independence immediately following the appointment of the new administration; evidently he tried to persuade Shelburne of the desirability of such a course, but without success.[87] Jebb was concerned with tactical problems for different reasons; he was afraid that the question of American independence was becoming entangled in negotiations for a general peace settlement and feared that difficulties with other belligerents would be used as an excuse to protract negotiations with America. For him the acknowledgment of independence was not only morally correct, it was prudentially essential. A complete restoration of friendship with America was, he believed, essential to the future welfare of Great Britain, and he argued to the Westminster Committee that such a policy would be expedient as well as honorable, "for in politics as well as in the private concerns of life, justice and expedience are inseparably united."[88] A similar theme was taken up by Andrew Kippis when he defended the preliminary articles of the peace treaty on behalf of his friend Lord Shelburne. On the other hand, David Hartley, who had agitated so hard for reconciliation, voted against the preliminary articles on the grounds that they conceded too much to the Bourbon powers. He later accepted appointment by Charles James Fox as negotiator in April 1783, with instructions to conclude a definitive treaty and a commercial convention. In this he was unsuccessful, and in September the preliminary articles were accepted as the definitive treaty.[89]

Yet another tactical problem flowed from the interaction between the termination of the war and the progress of the parliamentary reform movement at home. For the more advanced radicals there was little difficulty: the war had to be ended. But Christopher Wyvill, the shrewdest tactician as well as most moderate among the radicals, saw very clearly that the climax of the American crisis could easily distract attention from the cause of parliamentary reform. He believed that the addresses from London and the surrounding counties that followed news of the disaster at Yorktown were misconceived in that they concentrated on demanding an end to the war, and when it was suggested that Yorkshire should follow the metropolitan lead he promptly scotched the idea. In January 1782 he told F. F. Foljambe that for Yorkshire to have adopted a remonstrance would have been a dereliction of duty toward parliamentary reform in order to obtain a peace treaty on slightly better terms and somewhat sooner through a change of ministry than was likely under the present one. As the negotiations slowly got under way, Wyvill declared that he favored an immediate grant of independence to America but felt it was not so indispensable that all other parliamentary considerations should give precedence to it. If anything, priority should be assigned to reform. After all, honest men could disagree over the timing of independence for America, but all real friends to the constitution would agree that a substantial improvement in Parliament was in the general public interest.[90]

Whatever the tactical problems of negotiating political reform and independence for America, the fact remained that the radicals had failed in one of their principal objectives. They had attempted to formulate a system to preserve the empire and protect American liberties. Their overriding motives were ideological, but much empirical good sense underlay their recommendations. They were as anxious as anyone to protect and promote Britain's strategic and commercial interests, particularly in relation to France. But they also saw more clearly than did their critics that America could form an element in the grand design only with the voluntary consent of the colonists themselves. In other words, attempts at coercion were likely to be self-defeating, and in this sense the radicals were shrewder realists than their more orthodox opponents. Thus their ardent desire to preserve both liberty and union at one and the same time was logical and prudential as well as ideologically sound; unfortunately their constitutional proposals, while perhaps not totally impracticable, faced formidable barriers. Fundamentally they were concerned with principles of political morality, and they discovered during the war years that no matter how deep their devotion to the Anglo-American political community, its importance was secondary to that of the cardinal principle of liberty. They had started from the promise that their political ideology, which they shared with the colonists, was fully congruent with the constitutional fabric of the empire. And although the proposition was never disproved, they came to see that in the immediate circumstances of the time the political connection could not be sustained. In such a situation, and for reasons that will be examined later, they were able to give warm support to the Americans in the defense of their independence; they were also able, with little difficulty, to reformulate the Anglo-American community in terms rather different from those prevailing before the war.

Several factors contributed to the radicals' failure. Some were inherent in their political status. Initially they were pleading for an unpopular cause: the majority of the public and its parliamentary representatives firmly believed that the proper order of ministerial priorities was to suppress the rebellion and only then to discuss the colonists' grievances, about which they were gravely skeptical. Later, when the war expanded and turned sour, popular opinion wished to terminate it, not because of any new found sympathy for the Americans and their aspirations, but solely because its consequences were proving disastrous. And although a good number of people formed a temporary alliance with the radicals during the reform campaigns that began in 1779, the motives behind their attitudes toward the American war remained at variance with those of men like Price and Cartwright. Worse still, the radicals lacked a firm political base from which to advance. Some were undoubtedly close to the circles in which political decision making took place, but their connections were with the wrong people. Priestley could urge the earl of Shelburne not to join North's administration, but Shelburne was not a powerful politician, as was demonstrated by his fate in 1783. Hartley was only an outrider of the Rockingham faction and his unfortunate mannerisms limited his effectiveness; Sharp was very well connected, but mainly with Lord Dartmouth, who was North's stepbrother, a member of his ministry, and mildly sympathetic toward the Americans, but had been relegated from the American secretaryship in 1775 for that very reason and carried little weight in the government.

These were crippling weaknesses, but primacy must be assigned to another factor. The radicals' conciliatory proposals were all predicated on the assumption that an Anglo-American union ought to continue, for they thought of America and Britain not simply as two associated nations but as two branches of a single nation. When the question of separation was raised they found it extremely difficult at first to grasp the point that their American friends were making. They could not understand that when the Americans declared their independence in July 1776 they meant what they said: that they wished to sever the link with Britain utterly and irrevocably in order to become in the fullest sense independent. And although many Englishmen—Chatham, Shelburne, and Burke as well as the radicals—continued to search for an acceptable formula by which to bring about reconciliation, the American revolutionaries ceased to do so once the Declaration of Independence had been issued.[91] For them the alternatives were simple and stark, the choice was between complete independence and total surrender. There was no middle course.

In spite of this disappointment the radicals' mood was one of optimism and triumph as the American war came to an end. They had always placed the American crisis in a broad context and never conceived it solely in the narrow terms of an imperial problem. Now the Revolution as a colonial conflict had ended. As the "opening of a grand scene and Design in Providence," to use John Adams's words, it remained.[92]

# 5

# Liberty and Reform

While the British empire was disintegrating overseas, a vigorous revival of radicalism occurred at home. Beginning in the 1760s with the Wilkite movement in the metropolis, climaxing with the associated counties and metropolitan campaigns of 1779 onward and effectively ending with William Pitt the Younger's second Commons motion for parliamentary reform of 1785, radical agitation was a major feature of domestic politics for almost two decades. The largely extraparliamentary character of radicalism was one of its most notable qualities, for it marked a significant extension of public participation in national politics. Much of the urgency and force behind radical protest during these years necessarily was derived from purely English circumstances, needs, and pressures, but the contemporaneity of the American Revolution raised the inescapable question for radicals of whether there was any reciprocity between the two crises, and if so what form it took. In an immediate sense the disasters of the war substantially if temporarily extended the radical constituency, but radicals themselves also inquired whether the Revolution had a deeper pertinence to the English predicament. Being moralists, they viewed the issues primarily in the light of ethical rather than prudential considerations (though these remained important). Thus they perceived a sharp contrast between the moral standing of English and American society and drew important inferences from the new governments to supplement their understanding of the Revolution's importance to their ideology; their conclusions were to have a long-range significance far beyond the immediate occasion of the war years.

In virtually all its aspects the first phase of the domestic crisis, from 1763 to 1775, revolved around the enigmatic person of John Wilkes. It began with the grotesque comedy following his attacks on the peace treaties that concluded the Seven Years' War and on Lord Bute, the minister held responsible for them in Wilkes's journal, *The North Briton*. Number forty-five, which enraged the ministry, was undoubtedly scurrilous, but the government's consequent prosecution was mismanaged and its decision to employ a general warrant against Wilkes and his printer in a politically sensitive situation was unfortunate, no matter how venerable the precedents.[1] The business dragged on for over a year in all its complexity and enabled Wilkes to pose as a champion of individual liberty against the power of an authoritarian government, though how far his protestations were an expression of genuine principle rather than mere opportunist tactics is open to question. What is certain is that opposition politicians in Parliament and critics out-of-doors vigorously condemned the administration for unconstitutional conduct, arguing that the use of a general warrant was illegal and protesting against purported infringements of the freedom of the press. And whatever its intrinsic merits, by the time the affair was over it left a strong residual suspicion that those in power lacked a proper regard for the liberty of the citizen and the spirit of the constitution.

A second high tide in the Wilkite affair, which ebbed and flowed throughout the remainder of the decade and into the following one, came with the general election of 1768. Under pressure at home, Wilkes had fled to Paris where his financial recklessness once more placed him in imminent peril of prosecution. Faced with the unappetizing prospect of imprisonment and a fine if he returned, the only promising course still open was to obtain immunity from prosecution by becoming a member of Parliament once more. Accordingly, he returned to England and seized the opportunity presented by the general election to stand as a candidate first for the City of London, where he came bottom of the poll, and then for the county of Middlesex, which gave him a majority of 465 over his nearer rival. From this point the Middlesex election took on a heightened significance, for Wilkes goaded the government into fresh folly and in February 1769 he was expelled from the House of Commons. A discreditable series of by-elections followed, and finally the House resolved the dispute on a straight vote between the government and its critics by declaring that Wilkes's defeated opponent had been duly elected.

Narrowly construed, the Middlesex election was of minor importance. Until the passage of Grenville's Act in 1770 such disputes provided a commonplace opportunity to test a government's strength in the House, but Wilkes managed to transform a standard device of parliamentary tactics into an altogether more substantial issue by pointing firmly and vociferously to its constitutional implications. Seen in this light, the core of the question was whether the Commons, in the course of regulating its membership, could nullify the express will of the electorate, and whether, by creating an incapacity not known to the law of England, it was doing what it could not constitutionally do—assuming the power to legislate by itself and without the concurrence of lords and crown. Wilkes successfully persuaded substantial segments of the public that it could do neither. Although in the short run he was unsuccessful and was forced unexpectedly to serve a term of imprisonment, he was able to build considerable strength in the City. A recapitulation of the conflict probably was averted only by the government's acquiescence when Middlesex elected him once more in 1774. Superficially, therefore, the dispute was concluded, but in a more general sense it created a widespread sense of unease, which did not dissipate as rapidly as did the ostensible issues.

Once was enough, twice was too much. Whatever the particular merits of the two affairs, it was beginning to look as if system and purpose were behind them. In Parliament various opposition members seized the Wilkite issue as a stick with which to beat the government and insisted that a secret cabal of advisers was working behind the skirts of the ostensible cabinet with the purported object of extending executive power. Out-of-doors this thesis was sedulously propagated by John Almon and others, and, more importantly, Wilkes was able to attract the support of the small freeholders and tradesmen of the metropolis (in itself a phenomenon pregnant with great significance for the development of English politics in general and radicalism in particular) and a quarter or more of the voting population in the country at large.[2] Furthermore, if such special interest groups as the Dissenters' and Quakers' organizations and obscure and usually ephemeral debating societies like the Robin Hood Society are excluded, the Wilkite affair produced the first modern political organization in the shape of the Society of Supporters of the Bill of Rights. And parliamentary reform was already in the air.[3]

By the standards of participation that prevailed later, the Commonwealthmen and their associates responded somewhat mildly to the Wilkite affair. Intellectually, Wilkes operated within their own ideological tradition, but his personal reputation caused the morally upright Real Whigs considerable embarrassment, and he received less public support from them than the logic of the argument might seem to have required. Even though he supplied Wilkes with confidential information concerning the court, Caleb Fleming believed that no such irreligious and immoral man could possibly be a true friend of liberty; Richard Price was cautious over Wilkes's personal character but shared in substance Hollis's view that in spite of Wilkes's irregularities his personal cause was invested with public interest. Alone among the Commonwealthmen Priestley expressed his views in a public pamphlet, albeit anonymously. He knew Wilkes well and did not doubt the authenticity of his political principles; he also insisted that Dissenters should be friends to the Wilkite cause "because it was the cause of liberty and the constitution" and particularly because they were especially dependent on the maintenance of a broad public liberty.[4]

Subsequent events were to demonstrate that the public moderation of this reaction was misleading, for the Wilkite affair marked marked the unfolding of a new phase in the development of commonwealth radicalism. Before the business over Wilkes, the small band of Commonwealthmen had confined themselves in practice largely to the defense of the particular interests of Dissenters, including the preservation and extension of religious liberty in England and resistance to episcopacy in America; as far as the wider public was concerned their secular program had remained private and virtually dormant. Now, in the late sixties and seventies, a new guard took over from the old. Publicists such as Hollis, Fleming, Philip Doddridge, and the elder Towgood were superseded by a new generation who had a broader vision and were able to carry the old tradition into more active participation in public affairs. Under the spur of immediate events they were also, more importantly, able to attract more substantial public attention for their arguments than had been achieved in earlier years. As public demands for parliamentary reform continued and grew more strident in the early seventies, the Real Whigs and their associates in effect formed a junction with City radicalism and also became much more active as pamphleteers. And while Sawbridge was moving the first of his annual Commons motions for shorter parliaments and the Supporters of the Bill of Rights were demanding that candidates at parliamentary elections should be required to work for the shortening of parliaments, reduction in the number of placemen in the House, and a more equitable system of representation in 1771, Commonwealthmen were pulling together the threads of two crises (one at home, the other overseas), concluding that reform was vital if the much-admired liberties of Englishmen were to be preserved, and attracting fresh recruits to their ranks. Much of the Real Whigs' success, at least in the mid-seventies, was attributable to the American crisis and the implications they perceived in it for English circumstances.

Right or wrong, Commonwealthmen believed that at bottom there was only a single crisis, the ramifications of which spread throughout the empire. The argument was attractive and the conjunction easy to establish. At home the traditional fear of placemen in the House (a Tory as well as a radical complaint) was supplemented by alarm provoked by the use of general warrants, infringement of the liberty of the press, the St. George's Fields massacre of 1768, nullification of the will of the Middlesex electorate, and a little later the unsuccessful attempt to suppress reporting of Parliament; in America there was episcopacy, the financial policies beginning with the Stamp Act, the Boston Massacre of 1770, and the coercive legislation of 1774. These are only the bare bones of the growing tension. Radicals increasingly believed that the whole fabric of British political society was at risk and that this included the American component of the transatlantic community. The noble principles of the ancient constitution and the Glorious Revolution were in jeopardy, and tyranny, not liberty, was the likely prospect for Britain unless current practices of the administration were speedily terminated. According to radicals, colonial policy was a vital link in the ministry's program; it was systematically establishing despotic control in America as a preliminary stage in its long-range plan for imposing an authoritarian regime in Britain. Once this initial object had been achieved, it would exploit America as a source of patronage and as a base from which further attacks could be made on the constitution at home.

The worsening colonial crisis fortified radicals' horrified belief that policies ostensibly directed toward America could, and probably would, be turned against England as well. The conspiratorial hypothesis was adumbrated during the Wilkes affair. America remained unnoticed in speeches on the Middlesex election, nor was there any pressing reason for it to appear in a debate focused on a fairly specific issue, but it did emerge in Wilkes's correspondence. Men from New England and elsewhere insisted that "*the fate of Wilkes & America must stand or fall together*," and Wilkes reciprocated their sentiments, at the same time turning his comments to English as well as colonial circumstances; union between Britain and America was, he insisted, essential if an invasion of liberty by despotic ministers was to be resisted.[5] No wonder Americans like Rush and Arthur Lee paid court to him while he served his sentence in the King's Bench prison. At this stage, however, the connection was not fully established. Writing on both the colonial and domestic issues in 1769–70, James Burgh pointed out the parallels but otherwise treated the two questions separately. Similarly, Priestley discussed the defense of liberty in America and at home in his first political tract, *The Present State of Liberty in Great Britain and Her Colonies*, but was prepared only to make the brief point that Britain and the colonies shared a common interest, leaving his readers to infer for themselves the connection between the fate of liberty in America and their own position in England.[6]

The conspiratorial thesis was vigorously hammered home by Americans resident in London. Like his brother William, Arthur Lee was totally persuaded of the malign intentions of the British government and immediately joined the Wilkite Society of Supporters of the Bill of Rights in an attempt to promote the defense of the colonies. Lee drew a parallel between the course of events in America and the Middlesex election; the grievances of the colonists and of the British electorate were very similar, he argued, and the differences merely ones of degree. He went on to declare, "The Ministry have adopted, and already executed, in one county here, Mr. G[renville]'s, or rather my Lord Bute's plan for enslaving America. It were, indeed, the last degree of folly to suppose, that if arbitrary rule was once suffered to establish itself in *America*, it would not speedily traverse the ocean, and finally fix itself in England"; it followed, he argued, that Americans and Englishmen should fight together to resist the torrent of arbitrary power: "The Cause is common, let us be united in its support."[7] Similarly, Sayre, who possibly assisted Lee with his Junius Americanus letters, insisted that the countries shared a community of interest "in order to engage the body of the people on our side."[8]

Their advocacy fell on welcoming ears. Many radicals were thinking along similar lines as the Boston Tea Party set the fuse for war. In his address to Dissenters, published anonymously in preparation for the general election of 1774, Priestley directed his argument far more closely than he had done previously to the implications of the American crisis for England. He argued that the measures being taken against the colonies were indicative of the court's attitude toward Dissenters in England. The time, he urged, was critical, and he called for all the efforts of the friends of liberty: as the particular privileges of Dissenters and the general liberties of the country at large were inextricably interconnected, and those in power were as much the enemies of civil liberties as of Dissenters, it was necessary to stand in defense of both. Insistence that English Dissenters should realize that their own as well as American liberty was in the balance was a central theme of his pamphlet. He warned them,

Do you imagine, my fellow citizens, that we can sit still, and be the idle spectators of the chains which are forging for our brethren in America, *with safety to ourselves*? Let us suppose *America* to be completely enslaved, in consequence of which the English court can command all the money, and all the force of that *country*; will they like to be so arbitrary *abroad*, and have their power confined at *home*; especially as troops in abundance can be transported in a few weeks from America to England; where, with the present standing army, they may instantly reduce us to what they please. And can it be supposed that the Americans, being slaves themselves, and having been enslaved by us, will not, in return, willingly contribute their aid to bring us into the same condition?[9]

These were words of bitter fear and perhaps hysteria, but they were written during a period of great concern for Priestley and his friends. Not only had the Coercive Acts (and, for some, the possibly worse Quebec Act) been imposed on the Americans, but at home recent attempts to relieve Anglican ministers from the obligation to subscribe to the articles of religion had failed, as had the related motions to secure relief for dissenting clergy and schoolmasters. A growing suspicion that the shadows of tyranny were lengthening was heightened further by the observation that their progress was even more advanced on the continent of Europe.

Nor was Priestley alone in his fears, for it was a recurrent theme in private correspondence as well as public rhetoric. James Burgh argued that ministers were imposing taxes on the colonies in order to augment the number of places and pensions available for their dependents and thus to extend the power of the court. Bad ministers, he believed, were always inclined to increase taxation since they needed revenue to retain power; if they were successful, the colonists' spirit would be broken by oppression, and corruption would spread throughout the empire. England was in acute danger, and Price feared the systems of government proposed for North America would serve as models for emulation in England; "and as far as they can succeed in America, their way will be paved for success here."[10] Thomas Brand Hollis expressed similar feelings to an American friend: "We have no hopes but in your zeal & perseverence, the same measures pursued against you will return upon us with greater force if they succeed in America"; in Catharine Macaulay's opinion, there was "a formed design to enslave the whole empire"; and in attempting to rouse his English fellow countrymen to the need for reform Major Cartwright argued that ministers had struck a deadly blow at the English constitution "through the sides of America." One of the few radicals in the House of Lords, the earl of Abingdon, declared that if the liberties of fellow citizens in America were to be taken from them, only an idiot could suppose that Englishmen could preserve their own:

"The dagger uplifted against the breast of America is meant for the heart of old England."[11]

Such views had wide currency among a host of minor, often obscure, and sometimes anonymous writers, and as the war progressed the tone of criticism became increasingly strident. Richard Goodenough argued that the Americans actually were defending the true principles of the constitution; he insisted on the essential unity of that constitution and believed that even if there was no deliberate plot by the executive to establish despotism in England, a denial of the principles of the constitution in one part of the empire comprised a repudiation of them in all other parts. Another pamphleteer declared that the war was being prosecuted by a small number of ambitious and perhaps sinister men for their own temporary advantage; similar arguments were expressed in 1777 by the author of *The Case Stated on Philosophical Grounds*, leaving "Constitutionalis" to develop the charge of malevolence at greater length. This anonymous writer argued that at the beginning of George III's reign the king's ministers had formulated a plan to make themselves absolute. The first stage was to subjugate America in order to provide the patronage necessary to maintain a majority in the House of Commons; when the colonies "asserted their just rights, exactly on the plan of the Bill of Rights in England" and petitioned the crown, Parliament, and people "in most dutiful and affectionate terms," Lord North arrogantly rejected their petitions, the government attacked them with troops, and they were compelled to take up arms in their own defense.[12]

Radicals lost no time in discovering the locus of responsibility for the war. In the first instance they placed it firmly and inescapably on the shoulders of the British government and argued that the corruption of Parliament enabled it to execute its antilibertarian policies. They did not, however, regard the political hypothesis, horrifying though it was, as a fully adequate explanation: devout men that they were, they searched for a more profound diagnosis and found it readily enough in the context of their ethical system.

A desolating sense of the moral corruption of their country pervaded the minds of all radicals. As early as 1765, Hollis had noticed a decline since the great days of William Pitt; Price commented to Shelburne in 1774 that Britain had sunk far into distress and that luxury had undermined the foundations of public liberty;

Cartwright remarked on the low state of public spirit and casti-gated those who supported the current system as "subverting their own moral principles, and sapping the very foundations of all integrity in society, both public and private"; and Mrs. Macaulay urged Englishmen to rouse themselves from the state of guilty dissipation in which they had rested for too long.[13] Such national immorality was indeed "the sure harbinger of *public misfortune* and *approaching slavery*" in the eyes of Sharp, and Price declared in 1779: "Never, perhaps, was there a time when men shewed so little regard to *decency* in their vices, or were so *shameless* in their venality and debaucheries."[14]

The same theme recurred constantly in the sermons of dissent-ing ministers who gave supporting strength to the activists. Their titles often gave a clear indication of the tone of the argument. Rees David gave one in Norwich entitled *The Hypocritical Fast with Its Design and Consequences*, Joshua Toulmin another called *The American War Lamented* in Taunton, and Samuel Stennett a third under a still more explicit title: *National Calamities the Effect of Divine Displeasure*. Newcome Cappe's sermon given in York on 13 December 1776 (a national Fast Day) illustrates the general line of exposition. In it he offered his congregation a sustained jeremiad directed against the present state of English morality, which, he declared, represented a severely distorted sys-tem of values. Society, he argued, was grossly corrupted and vices had been elevated into virtues: intemperance had been exalted into sociality, lewdness into gaiety, hypocrisy into politeness, and so on. Conversely, the highest virtues were described by the most ignominious appellations; devotion had become enthusiasm and integrity transformed into obstinacy. No wonder Ebenezer Radcliff told his congregation that the most striking features of national life were contempt for religion and an insatiable appetite for pleasure, from which sources a multitude of evils had sprung and deluged the land.[15]

Inescapably the radicals, especially those who were ministers of religion, were driven to the view that England deserved punish-ment and that the American war was truly a manifestation of the working of Divine Providence in the affairs of mankind. They believed it was a mistake to assign only secondary causes for political evils; such things could not be ascribed entirely to "the clashing of human interests and passions, the imprudence of governors and the misconduct of statesmen"; those who took a broader view would search for the hand of an overseeing deity who, though he worked through human means, never failed to accomplish his own objectives.[16] Sharp, who devoted much attention to the explication of biblical prophecy, came to believe that the war was divine retribution on both sides for their oppression and wickedness in continuing to tolerate slavery and the slave trade; he was convinced that Britain and America were both preparing themselves for mutual destruction and considered it all too evidently merited on both sides. Other radicals admired the steadfast virtues of the Americans (which Sharp himself admired), but generally agreed that England, like Sodom and Gomorrah, had been guilty of grievous sins and was being punished for her waywardness. All countries required a leaven of virtuous men, but England had too few and was being called upon to accept the chastisement of Providence; as Toulmin declared, "War is a *Judgment* of *God*; ... by public calamities nations are disciplined, and bear the punishment of their iniquities."[17]

For Real Whigs the implications for their view of American society and its role in world affairs were profound. To men whose political system was directly regulated by the ethical imperatives of a theological cosmology, the corrosive effects of moral decay were horrifying and the apparent manifestations of divine retribution fully justified; when coupled with political decline and the temporary eclipse of the reform movement because of popular association of its advocates with disloyal support for rebellion, they stimulated an apocalyptic vision of the future. Human progress, for which radicals had entertained such great hope, seemed to have ended in jarring failure for Britain; no longer could she claim to be the model of liberty. In its place Commonwealthmen substituted a millennarian vision of America. Such a view long had been latent in the English mind, but during the Revolution the contrast between the health of American society and the decadence of English was especially sharp and bitter; in America, Price declared, "every inhabitant has in his house (as a part of his furniture) a book on law and government, to enable him to understand his civil rights; a musket to enable him to defend these rights; and a Bible to enable him to understand and practice his religion."[18]

England had failed in its duty as the guardian of freedom; America would have to assume her responsibility and become the asylum of liberty.

A feeling of sadness, failure, and regret underlay radical belief that America was ready and able to fulfill this new role. Eighteenth-century Englishmen had prided themselves on living in a free society, and although the claim was somewhat tarnished there was much to give it substance. Radicals had shared this popular belief while always careful to distinguish between the theoretical virtues of the constitution and the frequent imperfections of its implementation. As they came to believe that America, which long had shared this vital role, would have to assume sole responsibility for providing the refuge necessary for the future happiness of mankind, their sense of desolation was mitigated by a conviction that England and America remained parts of a single community.

America's function as an asylum of liberty took two forms. At its simplest, the country was a haven for individuals who felt themselves oppressed in their own country. Such a refuge was becoming important for Englishmen as well as for others. Sylas Neville, the republican, noted in 1768 that ten thousand people a year emigrated from northern Ireland and commented, "May they flourish and set up in due time a glorious free government in the country which may serve as a retreat to those free men who may survive the final ruin of liberty in this country: an event which I am afraid is at no great distance."[19] The Supporters of the Bill of Rights expressed similar views to the South Carolina Assembly, encouraged no doubt by Arthur Lee, and a few years later Lindsey remarked that if Providence were permitting the ruin of England and the independence of America, it would turn out for the best since there would be one place in the world where Englishmen could be free. Price told his New England friend Charles Chauncy in February 1775, "I consider America as a future asylum for the friends of liberty here, which it would be a dreadful calamity to lose!"[20] War intervened to frustrate this hope for several years, but the concept of America as a haven remained potent in radical thought for many years, and the emigration of numerous refugees to the United States during the repression of the 1790s was an especially eloquent tribute.

The second form of asylum was bound up with the notion of

an experiment in the government of a free yet powerful and orderly society. In many respects the second form was potentially more important than the first since the haven for emigrants was essentially nihilistic in its implications for British society and those who remained there. The opportunity to escape oppression was of great benefit to individual victims but did nothing to advance the cause of reform at home; if anything, it weakened the radical movement by enticing away some of its natural leaders. At a time when liberty was decaying in England and, as Priestley noted, in Europe as well, the experiment comprised a renewed attempt to prove that liberal principles could flourish in one part of the world when apparently they had died in others.[21] If the experiment were successful, it could be cited as proof that the principles of liberal government were as valid in practice as they seemed to be in theory. The radicals' assessment of the experiment was strongly colored by their belief that American principles of government had flowed from English sources. Matthew Robinson-Morris, who though personally retiring proved to be an influential pamphleteer, believed that the spirit of patriotism that was dying at home had been taken to America at the time of its greatest purity in the seventeenth century. There it was flourishing and, he asked, who could say whether the "sacred flame may not at this time burn brightly and strongly in America, which once showed forth such wonders in Greece and in Rome and from whose ashes it still enlightens a great part of mankind."[22] Such sentiments became increasingly general among radicals as the crisis worsened. Shortly after news of Lexington reached England, Jebb came to feel that the American crisis would be decisive for the security of liberty in both countries. Fearing that Britain would slide back into barbarism, he found consolation in the belief that America would emerge as a free country for, as he told his friend William Chambers, "Liberty has an asylum on that continent."[23] By the middle of the war, Price was in despair for Britain was going backward in its sentiments on government and liberty, but he was much consoled by the new vision opening across the Atlantic. He hoped the United States would preserve its liberty, set an example of moderation and magnanimity, and establish such forms of government as would render it an asylum for the virtuous and oppressed; for him a new era was opening.[24]

Indeed, Congress's decision to make a bid for total separation had transformed the central terms of the dispute. After 2 July 1776 a negotiated settlement was impossible. The imperial connection could be maintained only by coercion, and the asylum of liberty could survive only if the United States achieved its goal. Liberty was dependent on disunion. Radicals were slow to appreciate this, but once they had accepted the necessity of separation they were elated by the vindication of independence. Thomas Day believed that the success of the United States would teach those who possessed power to use it with moderation and, more important, declared that the establishment of so many free states on the purest principles of civil and religious liberty afforded most encouraging prospects for the friends of humanity; Jebb told Wyvill even before Yorktown that he thought American independence would be a notable event in the history of mankind and that its probable effects on the happiness of mankind had not yet been fully considered. Kippis believed that any parallel to the Revolution would be difficult to find and expected its effects to extend to both hemispheres.[25] Speaking perhaps for many of his friends, Price told Franklin in November 1782, "After many doubts and fears during the course of this war I now see with unspeakable satisfaction the object [of independence] secured, new constitutions of government favourable to liberty civil and religious established in America, and a refuge there provided for the friends of truth and humanity. This is the consummation of the present contest which has been all along the object of my anxious wishes."[26]

As an imperial crisis the effects of the American Revolution were profound. In prudential terms, whatever the ethical qualities of the political system, the policies pursued by the government had led to disaster and the most effective way to avoid any repetition would be a reformation in the manner of parliamentary representation. But more important, radicals were directed by essentially theoretical considerations of how a just and proper system ought to operate. In moral terms, British decadence had led to divine retribution, whereas the virtue of the Americans had been rewarded with triumph; by the standards of political ethics a defective constitution had enabled the executive to get out of hand with the consequence of a concerted policy of suppressing liberty in both England and America. Here the lesson of the Revolution stood out in stark clarity. One particular outcome was confirmation of America rather than England as the asylum of liberty. This could possibly have led to a radical migration to the United States, or improbably to armed revolt on the American model; in actuality it led back once more to an insistent demand for parliamentary reform in England. And this in turn led to consideration of the exemplary function of the Revolution and the value of the new system of government as a possible model.

In retrospect the year 1779 can be seen as the turning point in orthodox English attitudes toward the American Revolution. Overseas, the conclusion of the Franco-American Alliance of February 1778 had translated a colonial rebellion into world war. At a time when the whole fabric of the British empire was disintegrating, the country was compelled to face the revengeful hostility of its worst enemy and shortly, with the accession of France and Spain to the ranks of her opponents, found herself diplomatically and strategically isolated at a moment of great peril. Repercussions were felt in the West Indies and off the coasts of Africa and India; worst of all, for several weeks during the summer of 1779 a French fleet controlled the English Channel and an invasion of Britain herself was averted more by good luck than military skill. British armies in America were still to enjoy their most notable successes, but the dismay that was setting in proved to be irreversible. The country's will to sustain the fight slowly but steadily sapped away until there came a point in the spring of 1782 when it evaporated entirely; radical pamphleteers, Liverpool businessmen, City merchants, and Yorkshire gentlemen could agree that government policies were bringing unfortunate consequences in their train. At home many of those who had applauded ministerial efforts to reduce America to obedience were unwilling to accept the consequential expense entailed. They objected that the war was leading to higher taxes, a sharp rise in the national debt, and disruption of the economy; lamented that trade, manufacturing, and rents were declining and all classes of society were being ruined; and pointed out that not far away the Irish were attempting to apply the lessons of the American experience to their own situation. Their discontent and frustration were exacerbated by the general air of incompetence exuded by Lord North and other members of the administration. Men disillusioned by the course of the war sought an explanation, attempted to locate responsibility, and searched for a way out of the intolerable situation in which the country found itself ensnared. The only way to attack the government without appearing unpatriotic in time of war was to attack the sources of executive power, condemn the corruption of Parliament, and demand a restoration of the constitution to its original and proper purity.

Thus a policy of peace and reform became very attractive, and radicals enjoyed for a short term the support of a broader element of English society than they had been able to attract in the past except briefly over the Middlesex election. In the mid-1770s the dominance of the American question in public affairs and the patriotic backlash against the known sympathies of many reformers for the American cause contributed to the decline of the first, Wilkite, phase of the reform movement. True, an apparently extremist London Association was founded early in the war, but its political principles affirmed the commonwealth program, it protested loyalty to the House of Hanover, and it was of little importance.[27] A few years later, demands for political change struck a more responsive chord in the public mind when heard against a background of military danger and severe domestic difficulties.

Unhappily for the radicals, its echo soon faded. Conservatives still could deter potential supporters by arguing that agitation for reform would impair national unity at a time of crisis and equating sympathy for the Americans and advocacy of reform with republicanism and disloyalty. Fresh recruits to the ranks of parliamentary reformers frequently offered only qualified backing and proved to be only temporary adherents; radicals had negligible success attracting support for the ideological components of their program. Most Englishmen who came to condemn the war and demand reform did so very largely because of the degree to which it impinged on internal affairs. They were not for the most part concerned with the political and moral justice of the war and seldom came to accept the legitimacy of the American cause; they would have been just as appalled by a war against the king of Ruritania if its domestic consequences had been similar. Such men could be comforted by news of British successes and were willing to rally to the government during the Gordon Riots; when they demanded peace and the recognition of American independence they did so on prudential grounds, not as a matter of principle.

Support of this kind could be crucial in bringing an unhappy war to a close, even if it was not based on "American principles," but was far less trustworthy in promoting reform. For many, probably most, of these new adherents, parliamentary reform was little more than a means by which to end a misbegotten conflict; like the radicals they would insist that the war was a product of parliamentary corruption and argue that reform would terminate it. But their analysis was doubly incorrect. In reality the question of corruption had been irrelevant to the attempt to suppress rebellion, and an unreformed Parliament eventually torpedoed North after Yorktown. The implications of this latter event were unfortunate for the radicals; once the war was ended and the American dispute settled, reform became redundant in the eyes of their new supporters. At least one of the Commonwealthmen foresaw this. Writing in March 1780, when the associated counties movement was getting under way, Richard Price warned Sharp, "I do not much expect that the present efforts of the people will terminate in any thorough reformation. We must, I am afraid, suffer more before we are brought to this."[28] Events shortly justified his prediction.

This temporary alienation among discontented government supporters turned out to be only peripheral to the central concerns of radicals. It was tactically necessary to make allowances for the interests and attitudes of those who were normally acquiescent toward the manner in which the political system operated, for their assistance could be useful and perhaps vital. But to men like Price, Cartwright, and Sharp, matters of principle were at stake that transcended the effects, however unpleasant, of an unsuccessful war. To Commonwealthmen, the loss of America was only one malign product of a perverted constitution; corruption ought to be extirpated for long-term as well as immediate reasons. Demands for reform went hand in hand with pleas for peace but retained a life of their own.

The campaign for domestic reform contained several main elements. One, the demand for economical reform (as the program for reducing the expense of government and the influence of the crown in the House of Commons was called) associated particularly with Edmund Burke and the Rockingham group, was moderately successful but was also largely parliamentary in character and less radical than the others. Economical reform was no doubt desirable, and the reformers out-of-doors supported it; it did not necessarily require reform in the system of representation. In the sense that demands for financial reform were stimulated by the expense of the war, they were directly connected with the American Revolution, but in relation to the growth of English radicalism financial reform was limited and it can be left on one side. Two other elements were of greater importance: the county, petitioning, or association movement and the metropolitan movement exemplified especially by the activities of the Westminster Committee. Another group, the Society for Constitutional Information, disseminated radical propaganda, and its membership overlapped that of the other two groups to a considerable degree.

Agitation for reform received its most substantial eighteenth-century expression in the association movement of 1779 to 1785. The movement originated in two widely separated localities, Middlesex and Yorkshire, and its strength was variable; even at its peak it included only a minority of counties—four around London and several in the Midlands and southwest in addition to those in which it originated—and a number of boroughs. In Middlesex it developed from an unsuccessful attempt by the Wilkites to turn a by-election in 1779 into a cause célèbre similar to the affair over Wilkes's attempts to enter the House of Commons as a member for the county a decade earlier. The activities of the Middlesex group were soon overshadowed in the metropolis by those of the Westminster Committee (to which many of the Middlesex men migrated), and Yorkshire provided the petitioning campaign with the greater part of its strength. Within a short time Yorkshire had produced in the person of Christopher Wyvill a national strategist, but apart from a few major politicians who muscled in, the leaders were predominantly local. Outside London the members of the association movement were drawn largely from the upper gentry who felt oppressed by the high taxation made necessary by the war. They were men who were already within the limits of the political nation but felt neglected, rather than members of an unenfranchised group; the six hundred people estimated to have attended the first great Yorkshire county meeting of 30 December 1779 were said to have represented property worth £800,000 per annum.[29] There was no suggestion of any frustration of the lower orders: the days of artisan, let alone working-class, radicalism were still in the future.[30]

Wyvill's initial ostensible intention was to petition Parliament for economical reform in order to reduce government influence in the House of Commons. He was not sanguine about the prospects of success but regarded it as a first step toward more extensive parliamentary reform. Ultimately he intended to restore what he regarded as the ancient right of full and free representation; this, he hoped, would create a constitutional system purged of its corruption and responsive to the wishes of the people, by whom he implicitly meant the gentry. Theoretically reform implied annual parliaments and universal manhood suffrage, but Wyvill recognized the tactical necessity to moderate both demands, and his attachment to such propositions was at best lukewarm. The response outside Yorkshire was disappointing. Of the many counties and towns prepared to petition for economical reform and a reduction in the influence of the crown, only twelve counties and four cities and boroughs sent delegates to a general meeting summoned by Wyvill in March 1780. The meeting recommended that a general association should be established to press for economical reform, annual parliaments (a traditional demand of Commonwealthmen), and an additional hundred county members in the House of Commons. Wyvill was able to persuade Yorkshire to establish an association, but he modified the program to demand triennial rather than annual parliaments in order, he hoped, to secure the approval of Lord Rockingham and thus the support of a group within Parliament. Even so, only five other counties approved the entire Yorkshire program and expressed their willingness to associate.[31]

London was a different kettle of fish. Both the City and Westminster were more radical than the rural counties, and their program came more directly under the influence of radical theoreticians.[32] Wilkites were still influential in the City, and the Common Council's stance on reform was modified by the views of Granville Sharp. Sharp thought Sir Joseph Mawbey's Commons motion demanding the publication of lists of placemen and Burke's program of economical reform were no more than palliatives tinkering with superficial problems. During the critical years 1780 and 1781 he corresponded extensively with the various county committees, but received no support for his pet scheme of frank-pledge.³³ Since the keystone of his constitutional edifice was frequent elections, he was bitterly disappointed when he heard that Wyvill and the Yorkshire committee had declared themselves in favor of triennial parliaments; such a reform was better than septennial parliaments but was no substitute for the "ancient constitutional right" of choosing representatives at least once a year. At Sharp's prompting his brother James persuaded the City of London Common Council Reform Committee to support a demand for elections to be held annually "or more often if need be"; in other respects the City kept step with Yorkshire.³⁴

Various other metropolitan committees were the chief expression of urban discontent. Two, those of Surrey and Southwark, were of minor importance; the others, from Middlesex and Westminster, were more influential in the reform movements. The Middlesex committee was a meeting of freeholders who originally had intended to wait for Yorkshire to give a lead, but by January 1780 had been pushed to a position that allowed more radical action. The Westminster committee, established in February 1780, became more influential; both were markedly unlike the Yorkshire group. Differences between them were more than those of urban and rural memberships and interests. Where Wyvill had successfully excluded undue parliamentary influence from his organization, others were unable or unwilling to keep the parliamentarians out of their ranks. Parliamentary influence was especially marked in the composition of the Westminster Committee. Charles James Fox came in from the wilderness to act as its chairman, and other members included Burke, Shelburne, Richmond (who was rapidly moving to an extreme radical position), Isaac Barré, and Wilkes; partly in consequence it was less representative of its constituency than was the Yorkshire association. In one final important respect the Westminster Committee differed sharply from the Yorkshire movement: it included a powerful radical and speculative element.³⁵ One consequence was considerable competition between the Yorkshire and metropolitan groups for leadership of the reform movement as a whole.

The activities of a subcommittee set up on 27 May to combat expense and influence at the next election gave Westminster a reputation for extreme radicalism. Two radicals in particular,

Jebb and Brand Hollis, were appointed to it; they obtained permission for the subcommittee to consider general matters concerning the election of members of Parliament, took the bit between their teeth, and galloped away with it. Brand Hollis was possibly the more extreme of the two men, but Jebb was the more influential. Formerly a fellow of Peterhouse and now a physician, he had been active in reform politics for several years before placing his most radical views in front of the Middlesex freeholders in 1779. His scheme called for the establishment of an association, or body of delegates, to supervise the activities of the House of Commons. It would be elected by the counties and towns in proportion to their numbers and would have the ultimate right to dissolve Parliament and supervise the election of a new House of Commons. This scheme, based on one advanced by Burgh in his *Political Disquisitions*, represented the most advanced position reached by radicals of the Real Whig tradition.[36] The Westminster subcommittee's report anticipated the proposals of the People's Charter by more than half a century. Rejecting the requirement for property qualifications for voting on the grounds that even a poor man needed the suffrage in order to protect his freedom, it advocated universal suffrage and demanded annual elections, single member constituencies of equal size with paid members elected by secret ballot, and total exclusion of placemen from the House of Commons. Jebb looked on the proposals as attainable goals, although not in the immediate future, but they bore little relation to the practical politics of his own time. He and Brand Hollis were adept at maneuvering their proposals through a small and unbalanced group, but were only just able to persuade the main Westminster Committee to circulate the recommendations to other committees. Their near failure here was partly due to the greater conservatism of the parent body, but also to the presence of parliamentarians such as Fox.[37]

Although at their extremes the rural and metropolitan reform movements were far apart, there was considerable overlapping among the more active members. Cartwright worked with the Westminster Committee and as a Nottingham representative, Jebb served on the Huntingdonshire committee; both, together with Brand Hollis, were members of Wyvill's crucial St. Albans Tavern conference in March 1780 which promulgated the associated counties' platform.[38] But by 1785, after a number of ups and downs, the movement was dead. The Westminster Committee had become a machine whose purpose was to secure the election of Fox to Parliament in the election of 1784, the Yorkshire association had disintegrated in the same year, Wyvill's final attempt to repair the broken unity of the reformers initiated at the Thatched House Tavern on 7 May speedily collapsed, and William Pitt, the object of so many of Wyvill's hopes, was on the road to apostasy. Disunity in the ranks no doubt contributed to the movement's failure; so did the extremism of Jebb's proposals, though Wyvill's more cautious tactics were scarcely any more fruitful. More crucially, the reformers' lack of success can be attributed to their inability to attract a substantial body of support either inside Parliament or in the nation at large.[39] And resolution of the American crisis probably contributed substantially to the reform movement's loss of impetus.[40]

The Society for Constitutional Information soldiered on. Founded on Cartwright's initiative in April 1780, its original members included Jebb, Brand Hollis, Day, and Capel Lofft; these names clearly demonstrated that the society was to be the mouthpiece of advanced opinion in the 1780s. Other members were Charles Dilly, the bookseller, Kippis, and Horne Tooke; in December 1787, Thomas Paine (recently returned from America) was elected as honorary member.[41] As its name implied, the society's object was the dissemination of propaganda in favor of parliamentary reform: an understanding of the need for reform was to be inculcated into the people of all classes by restoring to them a knowledge of their rights under the ancient constitution. This purpose was to be fulfilled by distributing contemporary tracts written by society members and others, but perhaps more important by reprinting and circulating extracts from earlier commonwealth canon. The size of the society was never very great because of the relatively high subscription of one to five guineas a year; such a rule also ensured that although membership nominally was open to anyone, it remained the preserve of the comfortably off and the rich. By the late 1780s the SCI was almost moribund, but it enjoyed an Indian summer revival during the first years of the French Revolution, when its membership became markedly more radical in tone. It was finally killed off by the government prosecutions of 1794.[42]

Much propaganda of the Society for Constitutional Information and the rash extremism of Jebb and Brand Hollis were in a different world from the tactical caution and even conservatism of Christopher Wyvill. To cite only one instance, there was a vast chasm between the theory of representation based on personalty advocated by Jebb and Cartwright and the Yorkshireman's more traditional attitudes toward reform which were implicitly based on the principle of property and the representation of an agrarian society. These differences were reflected to a considerable degree in the differing responses of various elements in the reform movements to the American Revolution. All could agree that the social and economic consequences of the war were calamitous, but they differed as to the political and constitutional inferences to be derived from it.

The first problem requiring examination was the old one of the relationship between British policy toward America and the preservation of liberty (in which the issue of parliamentary reform was incorporated) at home. Necessarily, this involved tramping over old pastures when the question of the origin of the war was raised, but other issues were to be considered. What would be the consequences for reform if the war were to continue? What effect would a successful reformation have on the relationship between Britain and America? The answer to both questions would be conditioned to some extent by the assessment of the British government's purpose in waging the war.

When the gentlemen, clergy, and freeholders of the county of York petitioned for reform at the first county meeting of 30 December 1779, they made the unexceptionable declaration that the American war had been most expensive and unfortunate. Many colonies had declared themselves independent and allied themselves with Britain's inveterate enemies; taxes and the national debt had risen and trade, manufactures, and rents had declined; at a time when frugality in government was necessary, much money had been squandered on sinecures, exorbitant emoluments, and pensions. Three months later the Yorkshiremen agreed that much of the country's unhappiness arose from the war, "which was unjust in itself, impolitic in its tendencies, and had been, in many instances, prosecuted with a degree of cruelty which was disgraceful to the character of this nation, and even to mankind."[43] Such misfortunes demonstrated an urgent need for a "free and uncorrupted parliament," which could only be effected by the united action of independent men throughout the country.[44] In January of the following year the Yorkshire committee of association expressed itself more forcibly. The system of corruption, they claimed, had reached maturity, and the crisis point had arrived. They went on to declare, "The Amputation of that poisonous Tumour, the Excrescence of our vitiated Constitution, must therefore be resolved on, or political Disolution must soon be the unavoidable Consequence."[45] Plainly the war was a source of corruption and its consequences were malignant, but neither the gentlemen nor Wyvill felt it necessary to inquire more deeply into its origins. For them the purpose of the association movement was the limited one of making technical adjustments in the existing modus operandi of parliamentary politics. They could be, and were, unhappy about the war and concerned about its effects on the empire; they saw no need to set the Revolution in a broader context.

Another, albeit subsidiary, object of the petitioning movement was the consolidation of national unity in the face of the French threat. If nothing else, it ought to have been sufficient to rebut the charge of disloyalty. Richard Watson argued in a petition he drafted for the county of Cambridge, which was almost unanimously approved on 25 March 1780, that economic reform would unite the country against the Bourbons.[46] Three days later the Yorkshire county meeting unanimously resolved that "the prosecution of an offensive war in America is most evidently a measure which, by employing our great and enormously expensive military operations against that country, prevents this from exerting its united, vigorous, and firm efforts against the powers of France and Spain."[47] A sidelight on the degree to which the reform campaign was coordinated is revealed by the passage of almost identical resolutions at the Hertfordshire meeting of 17 April and the Dorset meeting of 25 April.[48] At this stage, however, there were dangers in associating the reform movement too closely with the war issue. When the electors of Middlesex met on 7 January 1780 to discuss their petition for reform, it was suggested that it should include a charge that the government had driven the Americans into the arms of the French. The suggestion was popular, but was dropped for fear that it would alienate those who had supported the American war in the past but were now prepared to sign the petition.[49]

Radicals in the metropolis shared these inherently patriotic sentiments, but were unwilling to stop at such a restricted analysis. They saw a much closer connection between peace and reform, which members of the Society for Constitutional Information expressed at its simplest when they drank a toast to "America in our arms and Despotism at our feet."[50] Cartwright insisted that the war had been a war of the government, not of the people, and that if there had been a pure House of Commons the colonies would not have been lost.[51] In the City, the Common Council had regularly passed resolutions and presented petitions against the war. Its arguments, like those of the Westminster Committee, were to a considerable degree prudential. In 1782, however, the Livery declared that the corruption of Parliament had been one of the principal causes of the disaster.[52] Taking the analysis a stage further, Watson argued that the war showed that the crown could do anything through the instrumentality of influenced parliaments; why, he asked, should a minister take responsibility for unpopular measures when he could obtain the consent of Parliament to almost any measure he might propose?[53] Wyvill's conference of deputies at the St. Albans Tavern was markedly more forthright on the origins of the war than any meeting held in Yorkshire or the provincial centers; when offering their reasons for proposing a plan of association, the deputies argued that Britain was bowed down under intolerable oppression, by which they meant "the enormous, the compactly-accumulated, the all devouring, influence of the Crown." They went on to assert that it was "by the unhappy war with America, begotten in the first insolence of this despotic system, and nursed with a view of giving completion to it, this fatal influence had been armed with a more ample means, than it ever enjoyed before, for enslaving Parliament in the private application of no small part of those moneys which have far exceeded the supplies of former wars, and have been obtained under the pretext of necessary public service."[54] Significantly, no doubt, the members of the conference included the old Wilkites James Townsend and Brass Crosby, Cartwright, Jebb, Brand Hollis, and occasionally Day.

A measure of the extent to which those who were more extreme in their views on domestic issues were also more advanced in their perception of the American crisis can be obtained from a tract published by the Society for Constitutional Information. In it Day examined at some length the relationship between reform and the American war. He began by developing the argument that the ministry was conspiring to subvert liberty throughout the empire; the government, he claimed, had found that "one nation was too small a theatre for rapine, and therefore it was decided to scatter death and havoc over the whole Western Continent, and to disperse enmity, division, rage and mutual desolation through all the parts of the noblest Empire in the Universe."[55] There was an acute difference between the moral standing of the two combatants: on the one side stood the right of nature, the interests of mankind, and a rising empire founded on the principles of equity and reason and destined to be a refuge from European tyranny; on the other side only "selfishness, avarice and cruelty."[56]

Vigorous condemnation of the government for its policies toward America was by itself insufficient in a Society for Constitutional Information address, for the society was centrally concerned with political reform in England and always held very close to this principle. Day, therefore, had to demonstrate the nature of the connection between the war and the situation at home, and he went on to discuss the effect of administration policy on internal affairs. His words are worth quoting at length because they express with considerable vigor the essence of the radical thesis on the importance for England of the attempt to coerce America into submission. In Day's opinion,

the weakness of their measures was equal to the iniquity of their councils. That noble country, which had so long been the bulwark of European liberty, was doomed at length to submit to the common yoke, a just reward for having deviated from its former principles, and become the instrument of oppression. Instead of the triumphs it expected, instead of seeing the spoils of the persecuted Colonies poured into its territories, instead of seeing the commerce of all the subject West enrich its merchants, baits which the vile incendiaries of the war had made much use of with too much success, it was doomed to experience the very ill it had endeavoured to inflict; its wealth was destined to circulate through the very country it had devoted to destruction; its commerce was gradually diminished by the depredations of its enemies and by the intolerable impositions which were levied upon the people. Universal poverty and despair seemed to pervade the land; all ranks and orders of Men began to share in the general distress . . . excepting the few who received the spoils of their sinking Country, infected with its curses and polluted with its blood. They now began to perceive . . . that they had been deluded by the grossest articles, to throw away the noblest prize that was ever possessed by mortals: —America was irreparably lost; yet there was no term proposed to their distress, no hope of peace, no attention to spare the last resources of an exhausted nation. In this extremity of public and private distress some remains of the ancient English spirit seemed to burst forth from the embers under which it had been so long concealed. All the real and disinterested friends of Public Freedom, all who had viewed with silent sorrow and indignation the progress of venality and the diminution of the People's influence, thought it necessary to unite in one last effort; and to prevent, if possible, their Country's ruin.[57]

The reform movement was that "one last effort"; radicals were determined to exploit their opportunity.

All radicals were agreed that there was a direct relationship between the American war and their own campaign for parliamentary reform; evidence also suggests that they were interested in the political procedures and constitutional practices that were developing in the United States. The question is, what effect did these practices have on the radical mind at this time? John Adams of Massachusetts had no doubt that the American states were providing a model for emulation on the other shore of the Atlantic. In a series of articles intended for publication in England he remarked that in the new states the laws resembled those of the democratic Swiss cantons and differed from the monarchical and aristocratic components of the British constitution. He went on to claim that in no country were the principles that power lay with the people and that authority was derived from them more widely believed than in America and asserted that it was in the interest of all Europe to enjoy these forms of government since they were best adapted to preserve peace, and the people always desired peace. The articles ultimately were published in England in 1782; but it is probable they had circulated privately two years earlier and had been seen by the members of the Society for Constitutional Information.[58]

One obstacle which might have prevented a favorable radical response had been eliminated already. By placing responsibility for the war firmly on the shoulders of a corrupt government and Parliament, the Commonwealthmen had removed all blame from the colonists. According to this interpretation, resistance had been legitimate and the Americans could not be regarded as rebels in the same sense as, for example, the Jacobites. Thus the radicals could use the American example as a political model yet remain loyal members of their own community. Other difficulties remained, since it was by no means self-evident how the experience of the United States could be applied to English needs and circumstances.

Some promising sources of inspiration for English reformers were to be found in American techniques of political agitation. One was the highly successful system of establishing committees of correspondence in the various towns and colonies. In the latter months of 1779 several newspapers contained suggestions that Britain should follow the American example of forming associations in order to combat oppression and to achieve parliamentary reform.[59] A letter in the *Public Advertiser* of 4 December pointed to the example of American unanimity in defense of liberty and cited the associations which, though despised at first, "have set an Example before Freemen how to act when oppressed." The Irish had already followed suit, and the moral for Englishmen was clear: "When James II was driven into exile, it was by a national Association; and when similar attempts were designed . . . then Association becomes the Duty of all."[60] Such sentiments had their echo in the pamphlets. Perhaps the clearest illustration of American influence among the pamphleteers can be found in a tract published in 1783 under the title *A Solemn Appeal to the Good Sense of the Nation*. Its author, who signed himself "An Ancient Constitutionman," believed that vigorous action was needed; accordingly, he urged the people to associate "in the defence of their Constitutional Rights, by establishing Committees of Correspondence, by appointing Delegates to confer in Congress" in order to achieve reform.[61] Price also used the term "national congress" (though his meaning is uncertain), and there were similar reflections in the terminology of other reformers. The Yorkshiremen established a "committee of correspondence" in January 1780 and used the well-known term "Plan of Association"; and both the Westminster committee and the very cautious gentlemen of Gloucestershire also used the phrase "committee of correspondence."[62] How far the use of such phraseology was based, whether consciously or unconsciously, on American practice is impossible to say, but certainly Charles James Fox felt it necessary to warn the chairman of the Essex committee to avoid using terms such as "delegate" which had acquired unfortunate connotations during the American crisis.[63] At one point Cartwright suggested that the British should emulate the American nonimportation agreements as a method of applying economic pressure in order to obtain the franchise. Those who were excluded from representation should refuse to pay their taxes; if their goods were distrained he thought it probable that a people "associated to oppose the tyranny of tax without representation" would enter agreements not to buy, similar to the successful American agreements not to import goods from Britain.[64] Events in America (and also in Ireland) demonstrated the need for cooperative effort in attempting to achieve reform, but it would be unwise to claim that the American associations and committees of correspondence were the sole or even prime precedent followed by the English reformers in establishing their organization. There was no positive link between American practices and the creation of county committees and associations, but since they had been widely reported for several years and had not been a customary political form in England, there may have been a degree of unconscious emulation, both of organizational techniques and terminology.

Far more important than such essentially tactical devices was the nature of reform itself. Here the American model soon had an important part to play, for it provided empirical evidence of the validity of radical arguments. In the first instance the radicals looked to their own national experience. As Wyvill told the Volunteers of Ireland when they sought his advice in 1783, when a free people attempted to improve their legislature, they should retain the ancient foundations and every part of the fabric that could be repaired.[65] The more conservative reformers were scarcely willing to go beyond this position and construed it in a way sufficiently narrow to avoid the crucial matter of the franchise. Men like Cartwright also looked to their own tradition for primary inspiration—his declaration of rights owed nothing to the declarations of rights incorporated into the American state constitutions—but were prepared to take a broader view of the extent of relevant experience. This flexibility was fortified by their belief that the Americans were implementing the best principles of England's own constitution, a view well expressed by Day when he referred to "the majestic form of the English constitution, with all its admirable proportions and noble simplicity, imitated and improved by a multitude of rising states, which glorified in their common origin, and limited dependence upon this country," which was to be found in America.[66]

As they looked across the Atlantic, radicals probably did not fully grasp one important point. In spite of the many evangelical claims made on its behalf, the new system of government being formed in the United States was intended for particular American purposes; the needs of others were only secondary in its construction. Moreover, each of the thirteen states implemented common political principles in its own fashion in order to conform to its own requirements, and superimposed on the states was a national dimension. The whole system underwent substantial change between the Declaration of Independence and the acceptance of the federal Constitution. The citizens of other countries were invited to examine the new (and changing) model for its potential relevance to their own situations, but the criteria by which suitability was to be determined were implicitly exterior to the model and not inherent in the objectives of its construction. Thus the question to be asked is not whether the Commonwealthmen were successful in perceiving and emulating the essentials of the transatlantic model (as defined by Americans), but whether the model had any value in assisting Englishmen to meet the requirements of their own ideology. One immediate benefit accrued from this change of perspective: certain components highly prized by Americans could be discarded without impairing the model's value to Englishmen. In particular, the doctrines of republicanism, strictly defined, and federalism, as it was emerging, could be set aside. More important was the pertinence of other elements to radical needs.

These requirements were substantial. Radicals found themselves in a changing and increasingly disagreeable world. In ethical terms their country was declining into moral degradation; in politics there was an accelerating divergence between general acceptance of common goals and the manner in which the political system actually operated; and in social and economic terms, if one may judge by the admiration radicals felt for American society as a paradigm, the processes of industrialization and urbanization were repugnant. There was one exception to this growing distaste: they were deeply grateful for the stability of English society and the security of which they were among the beneficiaries. In short, the radicals were caught between their wish to maintain stability and their desire to direct the processes of change along a channel that it seemed reluctant to take.

In such a situation radicals urgently needed a model that would conform to the normative values of their ideological system and give it instrumental legitimacy by providing a path through their dilemma.[67] It would have to possess the virtues of social stability (preferably in a somewhat more egalitarian form than in contemporary England), an agrarian-rural economy, an acceptable political system, and, as a vital ingredient, a morally upright people. One model, classical Greece and Rome, having disintegrated, and a second, the ancient constitution, being in decay, there was an obvious attraction across the Atlantic in the newly founded United States. As a model it enjoyed several particular advantages. Unlike the others it was contemporary in time; it was also external in the sense of existing outside Britain, yet internal in the sense of having grown from the commonwealth tradition. Its social structure was, with the exception of slavery, admirable, and the fortitude of the American people had proved their moral integrity. There was, however, an important caveat. The mechanics of the model could be modified in the light of changing circumstances; but its high moral and social standards must be rigorously maintained; hence the radicals' constant concern for the continued stability and morality of the new republic. Any decline would have devastating effects in England as well as the United States. During the war years there seemed little danger of such a relapse, and radicals could safely look to the United States for political encouragement. They were most attracted to the Americans' evident success in uniting respect for equal political rights to the obligations of effective authority and the requirements of social stability.

Since commonwealth ideology focused on representation as the fulcrum through which consent could be channeled in order that power could be harmonized with liberty, it was principally to this aspect of American constitutionalism that the radicals addressed themselves. This understanding of the central processes of political organization was strengthened by the terms of the imperial dispute; wishing to preserve both the imperial connection and American liberty, radicals had concluded that only a satisfactorily articulated system of representation could achieve their objective. Thus everything directed them to look to the new legislatures in order to find instrumental legitimacy for liberal and effective government; a corollary was that they paid little attention to the declarations of rights that accompanied the new constitutions.

Beyond this point, radicals faced a technical problem of analysis. During the early years of the republic they were most familiar with the constitutions of the state governments, but had small knowledge of their operation. They knew little of the Articles of Confederation and the administrative structure of Congress but much about its operative success. The solution was to conflate the two: they tended to draw theoretical conclusions largely from the experience of the states and empirical observations as to actual practice from the Continental Congress.

Just as each state adapted uniform principles to its own circumstances, so radical opinion varied in response. Indeed there was sufficient variety for all radicals, whether cautious or bold, to draw encouragement. One of Franklin's friends, Benjamin Vaughan, preferred the more conservative politicians, while another, the Quaker John Fothergill, admired the Massachusetts decision to permit affirmation in place of oath-taking. A third radical also took encouragement from Massachusetts. The earl of Abingdon saw the process by which it formulated its new government as demonstrating the essential distinction between a constitution and enacted legislation and vindicating the role of the people as the constituent power.[68] But though his perception was acute (he anticipated Thomas Paine by more than a decade as far as England was concerned), he was a peripheral figure in the Real Whig movement, and his views had little influence on other radicals. What is at first sight more surprising is the lack of interest shown by Commonwealthmen in the notable American innovation of the constitutional convention. Jebb's proposal for a body of delegates to superintend the conduct of Parliament, which was in its way extremely revolutionary, had points of consonance with the American conventions, but its ancestry went back to Burgh's prewar

*Political Disquisitions.*[69] The crux of the matter was that such bodies were superfluous in England since the operation of the constitution in its pure form was expected to be entirely satisfactory.

A far more important component of any representative system was the franchise, and several states provided useful evidence. Cartwright was dismayed to discover that many of the state constitutions included property qualifications for the franchise. Though he respected "the wisdom so conspicuous in those constitutions," he declared that he could not admire any rules in practice that violated the clearest American reasoning and "the eternal principles of truth and justice."[70] But conversations with Henry Laurens after his release from the Tower of London about the success of the ballot in South Carolina persuaded Cartwright to persist in recommending it for introduction in England.[71] For his part, Christopher Wyvill rejected the secret ballot as a cowardly way of resisting pressure at the polls and thought universal suffrage inappropriate in his own time. In this opinion he was encouraged by the recent example of America as well as those of modern Europe and of antiquity. He pointed out that in America property was much more equally divided and the behavior of the people simpler, more orderly, and uncorrupt than in Britain and Ireland, but even so property qualifications had been thought desirable in some states. Indeed, he declared, in Massachusetts and some other states the landed qualification exceeded that of any English freeholders. Price was on close terms with many of the extreme radicals such as Sharp, Jebb, and Cartwright, but his views on the suffrage were somewhat more conservative. He conceded that the principles of civil liberty required that everyone in a state who could be presumed to have a will and capacity to judge of his own should be entitled to vote, but as yet, he believed, it had seldom been practicable to extend the franchise that far. He argued that it was best to aim for what was practical rather than for what was ideal, hence his view that it was wise to confine the proposed reforms to a limited extension of the franchise and the substitution of a hundred additional county members for a hundred borough seats. Even in America, Price pointed out, where the new forms of government were more liberal than any the world had yet seen, the right to vote was restricted to those who paid taxes and owned property.[72]

Of all the radicals John Cartwright was the one who made most use of a state constitution. Both his choice and the purpose to which he put it were significant. His admiration (which he retained to the end of a long life) was directed toward the first Pennsylvania constitution of 1776, and he used what is generally accepted as the most advanced of all the early frames of government to support the most advanced radical program of its day. Moreover, he used it to give instrumental legitimacy to a previously constructed theoretical system. In his pamphlet *Take Your Choice!*, written early in 1776 but not printed until October, Cartwright had discussed the origins and objectives of the war but otherwise had made little reference to America; his argumentation was solely English in tone. Shortly before he published a second edition in 1777 under the title *The Legislative Rights of the Commonalty Vindicated*, Cartwright saw a copy of the Pennsylvania constitution which had been drafted the year before. What he read deeply excited him, for he believed that it contained all the essentials of his own proposals.

As a model, its terms were ideally suited to Cartwright's needs. It provided that all freemen should be eligible to vote for representatives to the assembly, all elections should be by ballot, county elections should be by district, and elections to the assembly should be held annually on the same day each year. A requirement that members should be incapable of sitting for more than four years in every seven would ensure rotation of power, and he was pleased to note that elected representatives were prohibited from holding any other public office except in the militia. Thus the Pennsylvania constitution incorporated all those principal elements that Cartwright had urged as necessary for an honest and responsible legislature: universal suffrage, equitable distribution of seats, frequent elections, and, especially, freedom from the corrupting influence of placemen. He regarded it as the best commentary that could be made on his own work and a practical demonstration of the validity of the principles he had been advocating. "Where, now," he asked, "is the impracticability of making our representation *equal*; where the difficulty, the expense, or trouble of annual elections?"[73] Three years later Cartwright believed that his judgment was fully vindicated. The contrast between the corruption and servility of the English Parliament and America was sharp. America told Britain what Parliament ought to be by her own example: legislative bodies were elected annually by the people at large, the elections were held at specified times, not at the whim of the executive, and were not dissolvable at government discretion.[74]

Yet most radicals' knowledge of the operation (as distinct from the structure) of American government was drawn from observation of the Continental Congress rather than from the states. In particular, Commonwealthmen found the conduct of Congress strikingly superior when compared with the prevailing corruption of Parliament. Especially impressive to critics of the unreformed House of Commons was the representative character and integrity of Congress—though they do not seem to have understood the exact mode of election to membership. Shortly after the outbreak of war, Sharp told Benjamin Rush that he was

most sincerely interested in every point which may affect the *honour* of the most extraordinary popular Council or Parliament that was ever assembled. I mean that Parliament which is *respectable* by being convened without even the suspicion of undue influence or corruptions; and is *important* because it is a *representation* not merely nominal, but *really* deputed in *equal proportions* from the free Inhabitants of several great and flourishing Regions, widely extending through a variety of Climates, and including altogether a larger proportion of the Habitable World perhaps than was ever before *freely* and mutually united in *one common interest*, since the general *Pheligah* or Division of the Earth.[75]

Similarly, Lord Abingdon argued that if ever the sense of any people was taken, it was done in America, and Price considered Congress to be the most respectable and important assembly in the world.[76] Within a few years, therefore, the United States had successfully met both radical criteria. The new governments had conformed to libertarian principles and at the same time provided effective administration and direction—matters on which the course of the war provided conclusive evidence.

The development of English radicalism had taken giant strides during the decades before the acknowledgment of American independence. Partly under the influence of American propagandists, the Wilkite affair had been reinterpreted as one element in a single crisis affecting both wings of the empire. The imperial crisis had encouraged new men to participate in active radical politics and so to inject fresh life into a tradition that was dying rapidly in the hands of Hollis and his associates. At the height of the war, the Revolution stimulated a substantial if temporary accession of support, but more important were the ideological implications of the new American governments. In their campaigns for political reform the radicals urgently needed to be able to demonstrate the legitimacy of their program. American constitutionalism made a substantial contribution to meeting this need, for it conformed to the normative values of radical ideology and demonstrated its instrumental effectiveness; it showed that certain specific principles and institutions that previously had existed only in theory or in a far distant (and grossly distorted) historical memory were feasible in practice.

Nor did the American contribution to radical development end with the conclusion of the war. As they had searched for an acceptable formula for reconciliation during the imperial conflict and struggled to persuade their fellow countrymen of the necessity of parliamentary reform, the radicals had become increasingly aware of the potential significance of the Revolution in a broader context. But just as the processes of American constitutionalism were incomplete in 1783, so the radicals had insufficient time to analyze their full implications before the conclusion of the peace treaties and the collapse of the associated counties reform movement. Unlike other Englishmen, the Commonwealthmen maintained their interest in the United States long after the formal act of separation had been consummated and continued to ponder the significance of the Revolution for many years.

# 6

# The New Republic

For the radicals to have abandoned their interest in America
after 1783 would have been strange. Like Benjamin Rush (and
partly under his tutelage) they were always careful to distinguish
between the War of Independence and the Revolution. The war
had concluded formally with the Treaty of Paris, and with it had
disappeared the major part of Britain's American empire; thereafter the two countries would pursue separate and sometimes
conflicting courses. No such final curtain could be drawn across
the Revolution, and the process of founding the republic continued
long after the war had ended. The Englishmen's interest in America
necessarily changed somewhat after the war since there was no
longer any constitutional connection between the two nations, but
the extent of the change should not be exaggerated. In the past
radicals had admired the moral and social qualities of American
society in contrast to those of England, and in the dark days of the
seventies they had assigned to America the vital duty of becoming
the asylum of liberty. This was not a role for only one season, and
although the radicals had tried desperately to prevent separation,
the terms in which they ultimately welcomed American independence made it plain that their expectations for and of the United

States would continue to be high. Once the fighting was over they restored the lines of communication that had been cut, opened fresh ones, and resumed their active concern for the progress of the new republic. In part they wished to offer advice in the interests of the United States, but they also firmly believed that liberty was a universal virtue, and its fate in one country was of concern to all others. The successful defense of American liberty during the war was a beginning, not an end. If the new political order was to be of value as a model it would have to demonstrate continuing pragmatic effectiveness as well as acceptance of high ideological goals. And potentially the working out of libertarian issues in America had particular relevance to England.

Friendly relations between Americans and English radicals continued long after the war was over. Many friendships were kept up by correspondence, and when British acknowledgment of United States independence brought an influx of Americans to London, a good number of them made the acquaintance of radicals. Although the flow of American pamphlets had almost dried up, a trickle of American books appeared in the press to supplement (and often correct) the information available in the newspapers.

Several Commonwealthmen maintained an extensive correspondence with American friends. Richard Price wrote to several New Englanders including Joseph Willard, Ezra Stiles, John Lathrop, a number of politicians, and several others; his prewar friend Charles Chauncy was unfortunately too old and sick to write. Another of his correspondents was Benjamin Rush of Philadelphia, with whom a prime topic of discussion was the progress of the United States. Rush was profoundly optimistic and constantly anxious to dispel any misconceptions; he was aware of the perils facing the new nation, but enthusiastically reported the growing strength of Congress and the prospects for drafting an improved system of government at the Philadelphia Convention. Granville Sharp also resumed his interrupted correspondence with Rush, but in his case the topics were confined to the foundation of an American bishopric and various philanthropic campaigns, including particularly the crusade against slavery; he also corresponded with James Manning, president of Rhode Island College (later Brown University), on the same subjects. Several Baptists, including Caleb Evans, wrote to Manning but confined themselves largely to religious matters. Thomas Brand Hollis corresponded with Willard and others. The Society for Constitutional Information had some communication with America in its corporate capacity, but made no efforts beyond the courtesy of replying to letters received.

Of all Americans with whom radicals corresponded, pride of place was taken yet again by Benjamin Franklin. Although he had been the greatest of Americans in London before the war, he returned to England only for a brief call at Southampton on the voyage home in 1785. Nevertheless he missed the companionship of his old friends and had resumed his friendships by correspondence at the earliest possible moment; only his death terminated the exchange of letters with men such as Price, Priestley, Shipley, and Wedgwood and newer acquaintances like Brand Hollis and Wyvill. Inevitably one of the principal topics discussed was the progress of the new nation. Shipley indicated that he preferred to learn from Franklin rather than from others "with what prudence and success your countrymen proceed in reviving and establishing that civil liberty, which is extinguished everywhere else."[1] Franklin was anxious to counter what he regarded as misleading accounts of American affairs being printed in English newspapers and replied from Philadelphia that a number of experiments were being made, not all of which he approved, but assured Shipley that "we are daily more and more enlightened, so that I have no doubt of our obtaining in a few years as much public felicity, as good government is capable of affording."[2] Another subject was the campaign against slavery, with which Sharp, Price, and Wedgwood were particularly concerned; Wedgwood sent Franklin a number of cameos depicting a chained Negro with the comment, "This will be an epoch before unknown to the world and while relief is given to so many of our fellow creatures immediately the object of it, the subject of freedom itself will be more canvassed and better understood in the enlightened nations."[3] Sharp also enlisted Franklin's assistance in his campaign to found an Episcopal bishopric in America; on this occasion there was no public resistance comparable to that which had frustrated the previous attempt.[4]

Many Americans visited London during the years immediately following the war. Among them John Jay, Jr., William Bingham, Joseph Reed, John Witherspoon, Solomon Drowne, John Wheelock (president of Dartmouth College), Elhanan Winchester (the Universalist minister), and many others made the acquaintance of radicals. The benefit gained from these connections could be considerable, for as Rush remarked when introducing Richard Peters to Price, "The friends of liberty & mankind however distinguished by country are all members of one great family"; Peters's knowledge of American affairs would enable him to satisfy all Price's inquiries.[5] Even so, the situation was not quite the same as it had been before the war. The new visitors normally stayed only briefly in London before returning home or going elsewhere; no one could replace Franklin as America's most brilliant representative in England; nor was there any replacement for that determined and combative publicist Arthur Lee. John Adams spent three years in London as the United States's first minister to the Court of St. James's, but although he made many strong friends among the radical fraternity his role was far more circumscribed than that of either Franklin or Lee before the war. The other outstanding American living in Europe during these years, Thomas Jefferson, played a much smaller part in reviving Anglo-American friendships. He necessarily spent most of his time in Paris performing his duties as minister to France and was seldom able to visit England. When he was in London, Jefferson met several of Adams's friends, including Price and Jebb, and also Lord Shelburne; he struck up a warm friendship with Price which the two maintained after his return to Paris.

The last important line of communication between America and the radicals was the press, but again the situation was not the same as before 1775. With the conclusion of the peace treaty American affairs became intrinsically less interesting to Englishmen than they had been a decade earlier, and the quantity of material on American subjects available in London diminished accordingly. English newspapers continued to treat Anglo-American relations at some length, but their main themes were hostility toward America stemming from the war, fear of the strategic implications of independence, apprehension over the future of American trade, and annoyance at the plight of loyalists and holders of prewar debts.[6] Pamphleteers, concerned with affairs of the immediate moment, turned for the most part to other issues of pressing public importance such as the Regency crisis. The attention given to American affairs by periodicals like the *Gentleman's Magazine* also declined, though they continued to print the principal American state papers.

American books and tracts often appeared in England only after some difficulty. Charles Dilly, the bookseller, was anxious to reprint works of American origin if they were likely to be commercially viable, but he had to be cautious. He had enjoyed considerable success with Paine's *Letter to the Abbé Raynal* in 1782 and solicited Rush for anything similar; unfortunately, he was forced to inform Rush later that he did not believe a memoir on the Revolution in Pennsylvania could be printed successfully in England and added that he was doubtful of the prospects for David Ramsay's *History of the Revolution in South Carolina*.[7] There was no counterpart to the sustained propaganda disseminated by Hollis, Franklin, and Lee; William Bingham of New York published a *Letter from an American Now Resident in London* to defend American trading interests in 1784, Adams printed his mammoth *Defence of the Constitutions of Government of the United States* in 1787 and 1788, and the young Marylander William Vans Murray produced a small tract under the title *Political Sketches*. Bingham's pamphlet went through a second edition, but only Adams's work stimulated any significant response.

Like Franklin before him, Adams believed that one of his duties as official representative of the United States was to get American news, tracts, and books reprinted in London. This was a much more difficult task than before the Revolution, even allowing for the need to subsidize many of the colonial pamphlets. Adams complained that booksellers were reluctant to publish pamphlets unless the authors were well established; a new author had difficulty breaking into the market without the government's assistance. In the past the parliamentary opposition comprising many peers and gentlemen, whose status gave them great influence, had been able to stimulate interest in many American publications, but now the politicians had lost interest in America.[8] If anything, he believed, the situation with the newspapers was worse. Almost all were abusive and would not print even the acts of Congress and the states and other public documents without payment of advertisement rates. Adams could not afford to pay large sums of money, nor could he offer publishers promotion as if he were an opposition politician; indeed, American paragraphs only seemed to provoke hostility. The worst slanders might be contradicted in private conversation but this involved expensive hospitality. And, as he informed John Jay, "To talk of Republican Symplicity [sic] is to make it worse. Every Republican Idea is detested and they think themselves bound in Duty to ridicule it and beat it out of Countenance in Self defence."[9]

Although some London booksellers were sympathetic toward him, Adams found it difficult to secure publication for American books. John Stockdale, with whom he had stayed on a previous visit to England, had already printed a number of American pieces, but Abigail Adams reported in 1785 that he had accepted a government pension of £400 a year and become a different man in consequence.[10] On this occasion Mrs. Adams was unduly harsh in her judgment, for Stockdale continued to print material from the United States. Sometimes Adams toured the bookshops of Stockdale, Cadell, Dilly, and Almon in order to promote the sale of American books, but it was a long and delicate task. The works with which he was particularly concerned were Ramsay's *American Revolution*, William Gordon's *History of the American Revolution*, and Timothy Dwight's *Conquest of Canaan*. Ramsay had sent sixteen hundred copies of his *History* to Dilly for distribution, and there were suggestions that an expurgated edition should be printed in England but nothing came of it; ultimately the American edition filtered out and received praise from Shipley, Price, and Priestley.[11] Similarly, Gordon had considerable difficulty getting his book published in England, where he felt it would have a better chance of success than in America. Finally Charles Dilly took the risk; when it was printed the initial subscribers included Mrs. Macaulay, Brand Hollis, Kippis, and Price, and by 1790 two hundred copies had been sold.[12] Joel Barlow, one of a group of nationalist poets and shortly to be active in English and European radical politics, asked Adams and Price to get his epic poem *The Vision of Columbus* published, and Dwight sought assistance for his poem *The Conquest of Canaan*. Price sent both poems, together with one by David Humphrey entitled *The Happiness of America*, to Thomas Day for his opinion. Day was unimpressed and advised against reprinting any of them, and Price was compelled to warn Barlow that no bookseller was likely to publish his work at his own expense or give him nearly as much as he was asking for the copy. He suggested that Barlow try to get it printed in America or France, but finally Dilly and Stockdale agreed to publish it in England.[13]

There remained a small market for American books, works about America, and tracts of various kinds. A buyer did not find newly printed works as easily as before, but he could find something. Leman Thomas Rede claimed in his *Bibliotheca Americana* that all publications of any importance in size and expense were reprinted in Europe and generally in London, Dublin, or Edinburgh; and although this was probably something of an exaggeration, certainly quite a number were to be found in the libraries of radicals.[14] One of the most notable foreign commentaries on American society, Crèvecoeur's *Letters from an American Farmer*, was originally published in London in 1782 and received a long eulogy in the *Monthly Review* from Edmund Cartwright, brother and close friend of the major.[15] Other European reports included a few years later *Travels* by the Marquis de Chastellux and Brissot de Warville besides the Abbé Mably's commentary on American government. Early postwar publications of American origin included *A Circular Letter from General Washington* and the Congress's *Address and Recommendations to the States*, both printed by John Stockdale in 1783; two tracts by Franklin, one on the savages of North America and the other his famous warning to intending immigrants concerning the realities of American life, published in 1784; and an edition of Adams's Novanglus Letters under the title *A History of the Disputes with America from Their Origin in 1754*. Later came works such as Jefferson's *Notes on the State of Virginia*, Jeremy Belknap's *History of New Hampshire*, and David Humphrey's *Poem Addressed to the Armies of the United States of America*; in addition, works such as Timothy Dwight's *Conquest of Canaan* often were circulated privately, and occasionally authors such as Noah Webster would send copies of their work to one of the radicals.[16]

Correspondence, personal acquaintances, and books all contributed to keeping America in the radicals' minds. In general they offered a comforting corrective to the unflattering image more usually presented in the newspapers and set the United States in a different perspective from the narrow self-interest customarily portrayed in England. Still less did the exultant Americans attempt to disguise their absolute conviction that the relevance of their actions was not confined to the United States; as Stiles proclaimed in a eulogy, a copy of which was sent to Price, "Great and extensive will be the happy effects of this warfare, in which we have been called in Providence to fight out not only the liberties of America only, but the liberties of the world itself."[17] Without disguising the problems of the early years of independence, the picture presented was one of vigorous, prideful, and self-aware nationhood. This image was drawn from very particular sources in American society; with few exceptions, the radicals' friends came from the more conservative and nationalist wing of Revolutionary politics, which had considerable effect on their assessment of the importance of the Revolution.

At the end of the war, radicals hastened to congratulate their American friends and to express their hopes for the future of the United States. Samuel Stennett, the Baptist minister who had castigated Britain for her moral decadence, congratulated his American correspondent Manning on the outcome of the "extraordinary Revolution" and declared that "God is no doubt bringing about his great purposes."[18] David Williams congratulated Franklin on his part in "an Event of such astonishing magnitude, as the Emancipation of your Country."[19] Delighted at having been elected to the recently founded American Academy of Arts and Sciences, Thomas Brand Hollis pointed out the contrast between European societies, which were much too contracted, and the liberal minds of Americans, which saw things in a more extended perspective. American societies, like their governments, would be generous commonwealths for true science to flourish. For Price, a man who firmly believed in the fundamental integrity of the physical and human world and the importance of human reason, the indications of progress were clear and universal: Herschel's discovery of the planet Uranus, the development of balloon flying in France, and the American Revolution were complementary. Together they made the present time "a new *epoch* in the affairs of mankind"; a little later he added, "Perhaps I do not go too far when I say that, next to the introduction of Christianity among mankind, the American Revolution may prove the most important step in the progressive course of human improvement"; the American example had already done much good, he believed.[20] Another of America's sturdiest and most enthusiastic friends, Cartwright, was preoccupied with family affairs for most of the 1780s and took little active part in politics, but to the end of his life he retained a warm admiration for "that happy land, where real freedom gives a reasonable assurance, that whatever measure shall be proposed by a known wisdom and tried virtue for the people's welfare will be adopted."[21]

The abiding interest in the progress of the new nation was the product of several closely interwoven elements. In part it was the benevolent solicitude of men of goodwill for the prosperity and future welfare of a recently emancipated nation, an attitude neatly expressed by the Society for Constitutional Information in its corporate capacity. When thanking the Reverend John Lathrop of Boston for some sermons on civil government in 1784 the society affirmed that they

have ever felt themselves interested in the preservation of the liberties of America as well as of Great Britain. They beheld with equal grief and indignation the unjustifiable attempts to invade the rights of the former, and they rejoiced that those attempts were defeated. As peace is now happily established, it will afford them the utmost satisfaction to see the ancient friendship restored between the two countries, and such inter-courses opened as may be equally advantageous to both. It is their wish that the commercial intercourse between Great Britain and America and whatever regulations may be entered into concerning it may be on the most just and equal and liberal terms. They also sincerely wish for the lasting continuance of American freedom; and as they formerly sympa-thised in its distresses, shall now view, with the utmost satisfaction its increasing prosperity. Nor have they any doubt but that their friends in America, having improved their own plan of representation, and thereby secured their liberties, will view with similar pleasure the efforts of the inhabitants of Great Britain and Ireland to obtain a more just and equal representation of the people in the great council of the Nation.[22]

Such a view was restricted in scope but readily explicable. The purpose of the society was not so much to formulate policy as to disseminate propaganda; only limited significance could be as-signed to such expressions of benevolence. At the other extreme the annunciation of concern for the fate of liberty in general, such as the society's toast to "the United States of America and may the cause of Freedom flourish in every region of the Globe," was un-avoidably diffuse in character.[23]

Linking the two extremes, and so articulating a coherent intellectual response, was the radicals' belief in the relevance of the fate of liberty in America to its situation in western Europe in general and Britain in particular. Thus a sustained interest in the United States was not only an end in itself but had an exterior purpose, and as radicals wrote about America, whether publicly or privately, they not only dispensed advice but pondered its significance for themselves. They implicitly sought through their advice to direct America toward developing a stereotype model community that would exemplify the requirements of their own ideological system. Their task was made easier by the familial intimacy of American public doctrine and the English common-wealth tradition; and their belief in the continuing reality of an Anglo-American community provided a highly convenient, and perhaps essential, vehicle for the achievement of their objectives.

To these radicals, England and America remained essentially two parts of a single community even after the Revolutionary War. The point was neatly expressed by an American. Writing to Price, Governor Jonathan Trumbull of Connecticut argued that although the link with Britain as fellow subjects had been broken, "other bonds will unite us—similarity of manners, character and dispo-sition, national consanguinity, national interests and wants, sup-ported & interchanged by commerce must yet connect us."[24] For Commonwealthmen the division of the English-speaking world into two distinct states did not imply a total divorce, and one or two still vainly hoped for reunion. The normally levelheaded Christopher Wyvill, while discussing parliamentary reform with Franklin in 1785, expressed the hope that success in the attempt to reform the English constitution might in due course bring the two countries to "that modified reunion which recent events will admit, & which you seem to agree with me in thinking would be equally honourable & advantageous to Both"; very untypically among radicals, Matthew Robinson-Morris believed that the United States was immature and that independence had come a century too soon; Price and others were agreed on the desirability of close commercial connections.[25] Radicals' reluctance to abandon the connection with the former colonies was expressed with especial clarity when discussing America: Sharp used the term "British Americans" in a letter to Franklin, Lindsey referred to "American Englishmen" in one to Adams, Robinson-Morris hoped that "Americans should nevertheless be considered and continue as Englishmen" (including the right to elect two or three members to Parliament), and in 1790 Priestley commented that it was just as possible for people in England to manage without a national church as for "Englishmen" on the other side of the Atlantic.[26] It was natural for radicals to take this view. Many contemporary Americans were conscious of those features of their society that distinguished it from Britain (and their judgment has been confirmed by the retrospective opinion of later generations), but radicals had been firmly convinced of the existence of a transatlantic community. And when they employed the term "British American," they used it not in a possessive or patronizing sense but in a familial sense and to imply equality between the two branches of the community.

Working within this conceptual framework, radicals saw the possibility of a continuing relevance for the Revolution. As the Southwark minister John Rippon insisted, "To this hour we believe that ye Independence of America will for a while secure ye liberty of this country, but that if ye Continent had been reduced Britain would not long have been free."[27] Jebb hoped that America's example would be a model for many years and that it would inspire Englishmen with the same spirit should they be injured in the same way. America's fate hung on Brand Hollis's mind "as a grievous weight" for he believed that the United States could provide an example of the successful application of his own theoretical principles. As he put it in a letter to Franklin in 1785, "The divine rights of human nature are declared [in America] and established against the arts of priests and Tyrants and there is now an Asylum for the injured and oppressed"; the Americans were becoming "the preceptors of mankind, as once the English were."[28] The concept of the asylum of liberty permeated a pamphlet of advice to the United States written by Thomas Pownall. In sending copies to America for members of the Continental Congress, he told its secretary, Charles Thompson, "An anxious Concern, which hangs, as it were suspended in my mind, looking to this great Event and which engaged me in these works, arises from a decided Conviction & belief that America will, in some future day, be the only Residence on Earth wherein the Rights, Liberty and political happiness of Mankind will be found established."[29] He also argued that knowledge of America was essential to the rulers of Europe, though he did not believe British statesmen were capable of benefiting from it, and he insisted that the United States should set an example for the rest of the world.[30] The Revolution gave Price hope of universal progress, with specific as well as general relevance for Britain: "a revolution by which Britons themselves will be the greatest gainers, if wise enough to improve properly the check that has been given to the despotism of their ministers, and to catch the flames of virtuous liberty which has saved their American brethren."[31]

In another sense the American Revolution appealed to the radicals' secular and theological millenarianism. They viewed it not only in political terms and as the historical experience of human society, but in the context of grand cosmology. They adhered to a theory of cyclical historiography with its unavoidable implication that growth and maturity were ineluctably succeeded by decline and decay, but they also accepted as an article of faith the principle of human progress. They resolved this paradox by assigning a crucial role to the will of Divine Providence and sought evidence of his intentions in the political behavior of their society. And as George Walker, dissenting minister and radical activist, declared when discussing the humiliating terms of the peace of 1783, "Who can forbear to acknowledge the hand of Providence in the fate of this country?"[32] Somehow the radicals hoped that Providence would step in to break the normal cycle of rise and fall in human history at a point at which man could make the much-hoped-for exponential progress toward universal happiness. A good deal in eighteenth-century experience suggested this was possible, but there were also many warnings of the difficulties that would have to be overcome.

The Revolution was vital at least as much in this context as in the narrower field of technical improvements to the British constitution. One recent bid to break the cycle had already failed: previously Britain herself had been regarded as a model of liberal society suitable for emulation by other nations; unfortunately her political system had since decayed and become corrupt. Her moral standing had suffered accordingly, and the struggle over America and the failure to restore the constitution to its ancient purity were manifestations of this decline; as a result Britain had to suffer the political consequences of a decadent constitution and the moral chastisement of Providence. In contrast, the Americans had escaped the disaster. Their political system, based on principles shared with the radicals, was still undefiled and represented the most advanced position yet achieved in the science of political organization. Thus the Revolution was seen as the manifestation of the Providential will, and more precisely as the fulfillment of biblical prophecy. As Sharp informed Franklin, many of the most important psalms were prophetic in that they revealed the purposes of Providence and in particular offered assurances of "a glorious interference at length in behalf of *popular Rights*, Justice & Peace"; he concluded that these happy times might not be too distant, and there would be truth, justice, and peace on earth, a general vindication of the poor, the entire destruction of all wicked and arbitrary governments with their standing armies, and vengeance on wicked individuals.[33] Largely because of this ethical role they had assigned to the United States, men like Sharp and Price were greatly concerned over the continued existence of slavery in America.

Their conviction of the importance of the American Revolution was intensified by revulsion at the course of English politics in the 1780s. Price and others found the political union of Lord North, the erstwhile oppressor of their American friends, and Charles James Fox, who had claimed to be one of the patriots' principal defenders in Parliament, utterly repugnant. The failure of the reform campaign made matters worse. Christopher Wyvill was prepared to negotiate with William Pitt once he had become prime minister, but the associated counties movement had split and collapsed over the issue, and radical disillusionment with parliamentary politicians deepened still further. By 1788, Brand Hollis utterly despaired of the British government, which seemed to be operating on purely mercenary principles without regard for the consequences. Some radicals concluded that reform would be achieved only after a major upheaval which would destroy all government.[34]

By imposing such momentous responsibilities on the United Staues the radicals also made a profound commitment to the prosperity of the new republic. They were very well aware that the progress for which they had such great hopes would not be attained automatically, but demanded conscious will and determination. Accordingly, if the American people were to fulfill the role assigned to them they must maintain the high standards of public morality that had been so admirable during the war and adhere to the highest normative criteria of political ideology. They also must demonstrate the instrumental legitimacy of the principles they shared with the radicals by displaying a capacity for vigorous and effective administration coupled with social stability and respect for individual liberty. Such an achievement would not only benefit the Americans, but would give massive new strength to radical ideology. Similarly, failure would not only be a catastrophe for the United States but would inflict severe damage on the radical cause in England and vindicate the prudential arguments against reform.

In practice radicals expected the United States to conform to a particular code of behavior—to avoid lapsing into luxury, dissipation, and impiety in favor of simple and virtuous manners. In socioeconomic terms it should continue to adhere to an agrarian economy, pursue an orthodox financial policy, and maintain or even extend its relatively equal distribution of property. This last requirement gave added importance to the need to abolish slavery, for radicals feared that its continuation could endanger the liberty of white men and form the basis of a new aristocracy.[35] Politically, Commonwealthmen increasingly believed that the central government must be strengthened, though not to the extent of establishing that most obnoxious of institutions, a standing army. In short, for radical as well as American interests, the United States must conform to the requirements of both virtuous conduct and effective administration.

As the initial euphoria of independence subsided, radicals had doubts on both counts. Thomas Day, who was often cooler toward the United States than most radicals in spite of his vigorous insistence that the reality of American independence should be acknowledged, was somewhat disappointed by its progress in the mid-eighties. He claimed that he had never considered the virtue of the Americans to be superior to that of the rest of the world, nor the duration of their liberty and happiness to be absolutely certain; reports he received were of governments without power and the people divided into hostile factions; as he commented early in 1786, "I hear but little of that country which I can depend upon, and that little gives me no pleasure."[36] A similar concern is apparent in the correspondence of other radicals. Always worried over the potential dangers inherent in standing armies, Sharp was alarmed at reports of conflicts between the American army and the government. He warned Rush of the conflict of interest between a standing army and the people at large and urged that even if the American army's intentions were honorable at present, there was no guarantee that they would remain so. He was horrified to learn of the establishment of the Society of the Cincinnati and feared the emergence of an American Cromwell; he trusted Washington, but warned that a successor would not likely be so disinterested and honest. He was also shocked to receive reports that Tory settlers had been attacked in South Carolina, that there had been violence in Pennsylvania (where some settlers from Connecticut had been dispossessed), and that there had been serious disputes between New Yorkers and Vermonters. Not even Rush's mollifying words could entirely assuage Sharp's fears, for in his view, "These circumstances are manifest indications of public danger, and of the want of an effectual government."[37]

Even Price found much to disappoint him during the immediate postwar years. On receiving unhappy news of a deterioration in American manners he wrote in some distress to Joseph Willard, "There is, I am informed, among them an avarice, a rage for foreign fineries, an excess of jealousy etc., etc., which are likely to do them the greatest injury, and to disappoint the friends of Liberty."[38] If this account were true, it was evident that his friends had pitched their hopes too high, and the Revolution, "which had revived the hopes of good men and promised an opening to better times, [would] become a discouragement to all future efforts in favour of liberty and prove only an opening to a new scene of human delinquency and misery."[39] Much of the news coming from America in the mid-eighties was pessimistic, and he was very relieved to receive some grains of comfort from Franklin: "I rejoice to find that the u.s. [sic] are not yet in that confusion and distress which we are led to believe here. For the sake of the world I wish them all possible prosperity."[40] He was disappointed that the British government refused to concede commercial reciprocity with America, but consoled himself with the thought that the British restrictions would check American enthusiasm for trade and so make the United States more self-supporting and thus more independent.[41]

Against this background of hope coupled with uncertainty, several radicals wished to offer advice and guidance. They did so in a series of pamphlets echoing those of 1774–76 with one important difference: now they were predicated on independence and directed toward its success. Though each writer had his own way of analyzing the problems facing the United States, all were concerned to a greater or lesser degree with the same issues.

Among those who were especially anxious over the success of the American experiment was Thomas Pownall. In many ways Pownall stood apart from the other radicals, although he shared their seventeenth-century intellectual heritage; not least of the qualities that distinguished him from the others was his actual experience of American life. Though his relative lack of emphasis on the necessity of guarding individual rights and his sympathy for the interests of administration separated him from the orthodoxy of contemporary radicalism, in the course of time his views on America moved closer to those of other radicals. As a member of Parliament in May 1780 he requested permission to bring in a bill that would empower the king to make peace with America, and in July of the following year he told his old friend Benjamin Franklin that he was confident that between them they could devise some means of preventing or averting the ruin which he believed faced both countries. His proposal was for a federal union to be negotiated on a basis of perfect reciprocity after the British government had declared the colonies to be free states.[42] His hopes for a federal union disappointed, Pownall accepted the reality of separation but considered that the time at which independence was recognized was also the moment of greatest danger to the new nation. Accordingly, he prepared a pamphlet of advice in which he urged the classical mixture of popular, aristocratic, and monarchic elements and suggested in particular improvement in the system of representation and a much stronger central government that would be able to enforce the uniform execution of its policies by the states.[43]

But once again it was Price who published the most notable pamphlet on American politics. In it he combined and interwove advice for the future development of America society and, as its title *Observations on the Importance of the American Revolution* indicated, an exposition of the relevance of American affairs to the progress of liberty at large. Price initially printed and published the tract at his own expense in 1784 and distributed it principally among Americans; later it was reprinted in several American cities as well as in London.[44]

Like Pownall, Price believed that the years immediately following independence would be crucial for the United States. America was a secluded continent with many natural advantages, and already its governments were liberal to an unprecedented degree; there were no laws against heresy and religious nonconformity and no social hierarchies. Another advantage was that the United States did not suffer from the ingrained conservatism that frustrated attempts at reform in England. In Britain, suggestion of reform brought an immediate outcry that any attempt to repair the constitution would terminate in destruction. In America there were no such prejudices. "*There*, abuses have not yet gained sacredness by time. *There* the way is open to social dignity and happiness; and reason may utter her voice with confidence and success."[45] Price accordingly hoped that the newly independent nation would be able to develop free from the corruption of the outside world; he believed that other nations were plotting to trap America by luring her into dangerous intercourse, and he advised the United States to avoid involvement in European affairs. "Is there," he asked, "anything very important to them which they can draw from thence—except INFECTION?"[46]

America's natural position gave her substantial advantages, but Price was fully aware that internal dangers posed a far greater challenge than any external threat. One was that the relatively equal division of property would diminish: Price believed it was vital for the continued good health of American society and the maintenance of liberty that this equality should continue. In his view, the United States existed in the happiest condition of man: a comfortable agrarian society poised halfway between the savage and the refined in which the rights of the individual were fully protected and the powers of government restricted only to essential functions; he dreaded the possibility that the evils bedeviling Europe might reappear in the new world. Perhaps the two greatest dangers facing America, in Price's opinion, were disintegration leading to civil war on the one hand and the emergence of a powerful unitary state on the other. A strong political union, which gave all necessary weight to its central institutions but no more, was essential if the new country was to enjoy credit strength and respectablility abroad combined with liberty at home. The somewhat uncertain and hesitant unity that emerged from the Revolutionary War led him to suggest that the powers of Congress should be substantially strengthened, but at the same time he opposed the establishment of a unitary parliament superseding the individual legislatures by which the states governed themselves; such a body would encroach far more on the freedom of the states than would enlargement of the powers of Congress.[47]

A financial writer of note, Price appreciated that a viable society was dependent on a sound economic base as well as a stable social structure. As befitted the author of schemes for a sinking fund in England, he was especially eager to offer advice on financial matters. The United States, he considered, should strengthen its financial position by redeeming its debts and giving the members of the Continental army adequate pay before demobilizing them. Such an orthodox policy should not be too difficult to implement for, if Price failed to appreciate the possibility of exploiting the national debt to create fresh capital, he saw very clearly the inestimable potential of the country's vast natural resources as a source of wealth. The land would augment in value as the country was settled and could be sold to immigrants and former soldiers to extinguish the national debt; though even without the riches of the land the United States was capable of bearing sufficient taxation to abolish it. Complementarily to this program of retiring the debt, Price insisted that Congress should be granted authority to procure the necessary funds to defray the expenses of the Confederation and authority to contract debts and obtain funds to discharge them; it was especially important that Congress's financial powers should not be thwarted by the opposition of a minority among the states.[48]

Although Price himself attached considerable importance to the social and economic bases of society, his analysis of the problems of interstate relations and the powers of Congress attracted greater attention in America.[49] His suggestions were concerned more with the functions of government than with its structure and were so remarkable for their inherently nationalistic implications that it is doubtful whether he fully comprehended the direction they were leading. As he saw, one of the greatest difficulties facing the union was conflict among the several states. Price argued that peace should be maintained by courts of law; the Articles of Confederation had made some advance toward this position in that disputes between states were to be determined by Congress, but no provision had been made for enforcing its decisions and they were ineffective. He concluded from his analysis that the powers of Congress should be enlarged to include the necessary means to coerce the states, which would, he thought, submit if they knew that such a force existed. One possibly essential instrument under such circumstances was a regular army, but Price shared the traditional mistrust of such a body. He insisted that the United States should not have a standing army, for everywhere they were to be found as the "grand supports of arbitrary power, and the chief causes of the depressions of mankind."[50] Instead there should be bodies of armed citizens, well regulated and ready to turn out to execute the law, quell riots, and keep the peace. If necessary Congress should be empowered to call out quotas of militia from the states; Price conceded that it would be difficult to guard such a power from abuse, but felt that a militia would be the lesser of two evils.[51]

A third radical, Granville Sharp, who also gave considerable thought to the problems facing the United States, offered as a highly distinctive remedy the Anglo-Saxon system of frankpledge. The tract in which he elaborated on his theory, *An Account of the Constitutional Polity of Congregational Courts*, was, he claimed, nominally drawn up as if for the reform of Great Britain but actually intended for the United States; again, like Price, he had it privately printed and distributed the majority of the first impression among his friends and other leading Americans before having it published in England.[52] In reality, however, his ostensible motive for composing the tract was also the true one. He informed Franklin that frankpledge was the basis of the common law and constitution of England, but when he added that since he no longer hoped to do any good with it in England his only object was to promote its adoption in the American states, and that the system was as suitable for a republican or popular government as for a limited monarchy such as that of England, his words were misleading. Beneath his genuine concern for American prosperity and well-being, Sharp was encouraging the United States to construct a model system that would serve as a stereotype for later emulation in England.

Frankpledge was a broadly articulated political system that encompassed all levels of the political structure from local affairs to Parliament. It comprised a pyramid with the householders of the nation divided into groups of ten (called tithings), fifties, hundreds, and thousands. Householders were defined as owners or renters-by-the-year of their houses; they were required to pledge each others' good conduct and be responsible for every individual under their roof. Sharp argued that such a system would meet the basic desiderata of a liberal society by ensuring that all persons would be both amenable to the law and free. Regular courts, called tithing courts, would keep the peace and adjust differences between neighbors without expense. There would also be an "annual view of frankpledge," and all free men would have their own weapons so that they could serve on "watch and ward" to obviate the need for a standing army. Magistrates (by which he meant legislators) and other officeholders would be elected annually "or more often if need be." At all stages from the tithing court to Parliament the suffrage was to be vested in householders.[53]

Such a scheme had merits as well as many disadvantages, but one feature was of particular relevance to the analysis of the relationship between the American experience and English radicalism. Frankpledge was a tightly interlocked system whose object was to promote an integral community of interest among all its members and especially between the citizen and his government. It was, above all, designed to ensure that the legislature would be directly and absolutely subordinate to the will of the people through the medium of an extensive (though not universal) franchise and the device of frequent parliaments. Divested of its archaisms it contained much that was congruent with the most advanced of the early American state constitutions, that of Pennsylvania. Like Cartwright, who in some respects was more advanced, Sharp was much impressed by the Pennsylvania constitution, for it appeared to exemplify his own principles, and he defended it against attacks made by the Abbé Mably in his *Observations on the*

*Government and Laws of the United States of America*. Sharp found it fully consistent with and indeed borrowed from the ancient constitution. The desiderata which Mably claimed to be unable to find in it—those features that united the interests of the citizens and created the harmony which kept the departments of state in equilibrium and gave them a common spirit—could be supplied by frankpledge. Sharp was especially impressed by Article XVI of the Pennsylvania Declaration of Rights, which asserted that "the People have a right to assemble together to consult for their common good, to instruct their Representatives and to apply to the Legislature for redress of grievances, by address, petition or remonstrance." Here was the heart of what Sharp believed to be the traditional English constitutional system, for "the right of holding frequent *Folkmotes* on all occasions is the very basis of King Edward's laws, and their *popular assemblies* (whilst due order was maintained in them by the Regularity of the *Tithing Divisions* in Frankpledge) never had, nor ever can have, any bad effects."[54]

If the frankpledge system was to be implemented there was one essential prerequisite: equality of landholding. Although other English commentators remarked on the relative equality of property distribution in America, Sharp believed that progress was not sufficient. He told Franklin he would like to see the adoption of a general agrarian law in America to restrict the amount of landed property held by any one person since a monopoly of land in the possession of a few families was one of the most baneful evils in the contemporary world. His perception of the social consequences of inequality was acute: "It increases pride and aristocratical arrogance and introduces a dangerous inequality among the members of every state wherein it is permitted, so that the bulk of the people who cultivate the land is thereby rendered dependent and servile; and an internal National weakness is the necessary consequence!" The "fatal effects" of the concentration of landholding in England should be a warning to America.[55] Sharp proposed to introduce a system of equal distribution of property among the sons of landholders based on his understanding of the Anglo-Saxon law of gavelkind. The existence of moderate amounts of land in the hands of freeholders and the provision of ample quantities of cottage land for the laboring poor and common land for all other householders would benefit every community. It would have the added advantage of encouraging men to find other uses for their capital, preferably in trade, commerce would be stimulated, and the whole community would profit. Sharp also urged the need for immediate action. Land would be very difficult to obtain in future years if care was not taken while it was plentiful to reserve some cottage and common land round every town, new settlement for the accommodation of poor but industrious families, and also small parcels for the maintenance of schools and other public establishments.[56]

Within only a few years, however, two new developments did much to allay radical fears and give the men fresh hope. The first was the appointment of John Adams as American minister to the Court of St. James's; the second was the Philadelphia Convention. Adams's arrival in London in the spring of 1785 gave the radicals an opportunity to discuss the implications of the Revolution with an active and articulate participant. Two years later the federal Constitution suggested that it was possible to construct a more effective government without disturbing the proper respect due to individual rights. At the same time a model was created that was sharply different from the most widely known American state constitution, that of Pennsylvania.

As far as his official duties were concerned, Adams's stay in England was unhappy. He had been well aware of anti-American feeling in England before he left Holland, and his fears were soon confirmed. Shortly after arriving in London, he wrote William Gordon that "the same Pride and Vanity and the same Contempt of America which produced the late War and their inhumane Conduct in the Course of it is still industriously kept up in the Nation"; he attributed part of the hostility to the work of the loyalists and was astonished at their "incorrigible Wickedness and obstinacy."[57] Such feelings were a constant refrain in the Adams family's letters to their American friends, and before the end of the year Adams told John Jay, the secretary for foreign affairs, "I am like to be as insignificant here, as you can imagine"; he had reached the end of his tether.[58] He was particularly incensed that the British government was spreading lies about America in order to discourage emigration. In 1787 his wife Abigail reported that public hostility toward America was no less than it had been during North's administration; the sort of pinprick insult the Adamses had to endure was the Royal Academy's decision to confine invitations to its annual dinner to the ambassadors of crowned heads only, thus pointedly excluding the American minister.[59]

Moreover, the leaders of the parliamentary opposition were no warmer toward America than was the government. Fox and Burke had as little goodwill toward the United States as North; Shelburne would be more liberal but had no chance of recovering office, and even if he had, he would not have been able to implement his proposals as the opposition set against him was so virulent. Adams's insight into the forces that drove the parliamentarians forward was sharp and perceptive, if perhaps a little cynical; he accused some of them of foreseeing the American success in the Revolution and using it "as a scaffold on which to mount into power; but having arrived at the Summit, they neglect the ladder."[60] The British government behaved correctly but without warmth; Adams's instructions required him to negotiate a commercial treaty with Britain, but the government procrastinated, and the objective was never achieved. On the eve of his departure for America, Adams commented that the government and opposition had treated him with "the same uniform Tenor of dry decency & cold Civility" which both seemed to have intended from the beginning.[61]

Circumstances were very different in the Adams family's private life. Although official coldness and public hostility made Adams feel uncomfortable in London, he had to admit that in many respects his situation was most pleasant as he was able "to enjoy the Society of Persons of great worth—and if I please of high Rank."[62] Adams's boast that he was able to associate with men of high rank was somewhat exaggerated. He certainly met men such as Lord Shelburne and the earl of Abingdon on occasion, but was not very impressed by their attitudes toward America. His closest friends were the radicals, and it was with them that he spent many of his private hours. He met some of them, notably Theophilus Lindsey, on his first brief visit to England at the end of 1783. At that time he was invited to attend a meeting of the Revolution Society to commemorate the anniversary of the Glorious Revolution, though probably he did not attend.[63] When he returned to London in 1785 his circle of friends expanded considerably. Among those whom he met were John Horne Tooke, David Hartley and his brother Winchcombe, Abraham Rees, William Smith the dissenting member of Parliament, Thomas Belsham, Micaiah Towgood, Joseph Towers, Matthew Robinson-Morris, Andrew Kippis, John Disney, the bishop of St. Asaph, several members of the Vaughan family, Joseph Priestley, Granville Sharp, Theophilus Lindsey, John Jebb, and Richard Price.[64] Some he knew only moderately well. Priestley was out of town for most of the year, and although Shipley married Adams's daughter Abigail to Colonel William Smith their relationship was never as close as that between Shipley and Franklin before the war. Adams knew Sharp quite well and discussed slavery and the creation of an American bishopric with him, but they were not on terms of intimate friendship.

Of all Adams's English friends, three stand out: Brand Hollis, Jebb, and especially Price. Brand Hollis and Adams met frequently in London, and the Adams family visited at his Essex home, The Hyde, in the summers of 1786 and 1787. Adams met Jebb on his first visit to England and told Stockdale he had the highest esteem for Jebb as "one of the best Citizens of the little Commonwealth of the just upon Earth."[65] Jebb visited Adams on many occasions to discuss politics, and sometimes brought his wife Ann, who was also actively interested in public affairs, much to the delight of Mrs. Adams. He talked of visiting America, but his health was poor and he died in March 1786. Richard Price had corresponded with Adams before his arrival, and the family met him shortly after they reached London and thereafter went regularly to hear him preach in Hackney; at one point Adams offered to endow a pew in Price's chapel, but his offer was declined. The friendship between Price and the Adams family was very close—Price christened John and Abigail Adams's first grandson William Smith—but Adams thought Price overoptimistic on the degree to which mankind could be expected to improve as a result of the American Revolution. A fourth friend with whom Adams conducted an extensive political correspondence though they seldom appear to have met in person was Matthew Robinson-Morris. Much of their discussion concerned reciprocity of trade which Robinson-Morris was anxious to promote and believed would be acceptable to the majority of the British people; when they discussed wider issues, he was proud to observe that Adams frequently concurred with his political views.[66]

The central intellectual feature of Adams's friendships was the discussion of politics and of American government in particular. During the years in which he probably had in mind the composition of his *Defence of the Constitutions of Government of the United States of America*, Adams told Jebb, "I have long wanted to communicate with some of the Enlightened Friends of liberty here upon some Parts of our Constitutions."[67] Whatever benefits Adams obtained from discussions with the radicals (and it is reasonable to suppose that they were substantial) the opportunity he presented to them was both unique and invaluable. One of the central deficiencies suffered by radical publicists of the Revolutionary era was that in spite of themselves they were far too dependent on theory to the detriment of practical experience. Almost none had any significant direct experience of politics, and only one—Governor Pownall—had experience of administration as distinct from legislation. But although radicals were particularly strong in the theoretical aspects of politics, they were far from being only speculative and abstract thinkers. Their political principles were intended to be implemented in the real world, and one of the central and most fundamental features of their intellectual system was the intention to marry theory and a priori principles to the empirical evidence of actual experience; this conjunction was, after all, one of the most important features to them of the American Revolution. Thus, the opportunity to discuss politics with Adams took on a profound significance for those radicals fortunate enough to be able to seize it. In him they saw a man who stood squarely within their own political tradition and at the same time possessed the actual experience of politics that they lacked. Moreover, his experience had been wide-ranging, covering agitation, diplomacy, legislation, and the ultimate opportunity of constitution making. Furthermore, when they knew him, Adams was standing at the high peak of success in his career and was eager to discuss the fundamentals of the human experience in politics and to draw conclusions that encompassed both theory and practice. Adams could no more replace Franklin in London than Jefferson could in Paris, but in this respect his potential contribution to the world of English radicalism was greater than that of his predecessor. Whereas Franklin had been admitted to the radical circle initially as a scientist, Adams was welcomed as an American. And, as Brand Hollis put it, "Americans have excelled in the art of government."[68]

Although almost all record of Adams's political discussions with radicals has vanished, the hints and scraps that remain are sufficient to suggest that they were extensive. The most substantial fragment surviving is in a series of letters between Adams and Jebb written in the summer of 1785. Jebb had been delighted to receive Adams's invitation to discuss the American constitutions, for as he told Adams he considered that nothing could be more pleasing than an inquiry into the acts of free men. Many of their conversations centered on the Pennsylvania constitution, which was distinctive not only for its radicalism but also for its popularity among Englishmen; in particular the thirty-sixth article, relating to the payment of officials, was the subject of extended debate between them. Adams argued in favor of the payment of the holders of public office. He pointed out that if there were no salary, only men of private means could afford to take office; he also cited the bribery and corruption of English elections as evidence of the consequence of not paying members of Parliament. Jebb accepted Adams's point that remuneration of officials should be a matter of justice rather than gratitude and acknowledged that professionals such as civil servants and judges should be paid. He also believed that a provision that the only men eligible for office were those who had sufficient income to maintain themselves and their families would lead to "aristocratic despotism & every evil you describe"; his great fear was that as soon as offices became essentially professions, they would also be "incentives to ambition & inordinate affection that can influence the human heart."[69] Essentially Jebb was arguing that a man should be prepared to make some sacrifice in the performance of his public duty, but that he should be recompensed if the sacrifice was substantial. Adams recognized that Jebb had moved some way toward his position, but insisted that officials should be paid not only as of right but because payment would make them more responsible and add to their prestige among the people, and he cited the Massachusetts constitution as evidence. The difference between the men was small though significant, grounded on the different experiences of their respective countries, but Adams was glad to find that he and Jebb agreed on the same principles of morals, religion, and politics. Accordingly, he told Jebb that he wished to continue their discussions on the American constitutions, for he believed they needed amendment and hoped for guidance from him.[70]

Adams gave as his reason for writing the *Defence* his desire to refute the opinions on American government expressed by the French statesman Turgot and given general currency when Price printed them as an appendix to his *American Revolution*. Price had been hesitant about publishing Turgot's views and regretted not adding a note expressing his disagreement with them but ultimately he was not entirely sorry as he found the *Defence* a very convincing treatise. He believed that the nature of civil government was currently better understood than at any other time and that Adams's work would assist further improvement. Jebb was dead by the time the first volume came out in January 1787, but the Society for Constitutional Information, of which he had been one of the principals, printed an extract from the preface in the newspapers. Others of Adams's radical friends, such as Robinson-Morris, were also impressed. The reviewer in the *Monthly Review* found the *Defence* deeply disappointing, but Theophilus Lindsey expressed the laudatory tone of the radicals when he described it as "a work which is the result of deep thought and of the largest experience and observation of what is now passing or has ever passed on this globe of ours, and full of such easy practical lessons of the truest wisdom with respect to civil governments that it is to be hoped they will in time be followed not only by American englishmen [*sic*], but by all nations."[71]

The *Defence* was intended to warn the United States against the perils of continuing the course it appeared to be taking in the mid-1780s. Adams, like many of the radicals, had received numerous reports of a purported decline in the standards of American political and social behavior. Thus a sense of pessimism underlay his work. But the radicals were more impressed with the superficial optimism that pervaded the preface, with its references to progressive improvement, the growth of a single European community, and improvements in the theory and practice of government. Above all, they responded to Adams's claim that America exhibited perhaps the first example of governments based on the simple principles of nature.[72] But Adams's work went further than this; it had the substantive effect of redirecting the response of several radicals to the crucial process of constitution making.

Radicals were most conversant with the Pennsylvania constitution, which, with its single-chamber legislature and its institutional insistence on subordinating the operation of government to the will of the electorate, was most untypical of the general pattern of American state constitutions. Adams's *Defence* set out, inter alia, to challenge this model and to offer instead a system of checks and balances. Thus the radicals faced two alternate interpretations of the American experience, one of which appeared to be fully congruent with theory and the other substantially modified by practice.

Sharp immediately recognized the importance of Adams's book as an analysis not only of the American constitutions but of government as a whole. His comments on it serve, however, to highlight the degree to which he was permanently committed to his archaic conceptual framework of frankpledge and its associated concomitants. He perceived that even the most sophisticated political system probably could operate effectively only if there was a reasonable degree of economic equality. Thinking as he did in agrarian rather than urban terms (and responding to the existing structure of the American economy), Sharp argued that Adams's political structure still required an agrarian law to limit the greed of monopolists and to invest unoccupied lands in the community at large. In other respects, Sharp's comments were derived from his overall insistence that liberty was best preserved by subordinating the functions of government to the will of the people without the intervention of any regulatory mechanism to frustrate abuses. Adams's statement that in New England the offices of justice of the peace and elected representatives were dominated by three or four families drew Sharp's condemnation that such a situation was a strong argument in favor of free elections. On the other hand, Sharp approved of the refusal of the Americans to give the executive a veto over the actions of the legislature and of the preservation of the traditional right to elect officers of militia; this was an ancient and fundamental right of the English constitution, it was the only true way of preserving popular liberty, it made the

Commons respectable, and provided an antidote to the evil of standing armies. Above all, however, Sharp was disappointed by Adams's proposal to form a triple balance of power by establishing an upper house in the legislature. He acknowledged that Adams was arguing from the best and most patriotic intentions, but insisted that frankpledge was the best balance of power and would provide the most effective means of maintaining the various American constitutions within proper limits without harming any of Adams's well-intentioned plans.[73]

Other radicals took a different view of Adams's tripartite balance. Priestley, who in some respects was more advanced than Sharp, was also more sophisticated, in certain respects more orthodox, and thus more sympathetic. He had discussed the structure of government with both Franklin and Adams and declared in 1790 that he had always favored Adams's arguments in support of a tripartite system in preference to Franklin's defense of a pure republican government incorporating a unicameral legislature. Later, however, he modified his views somewhat. In reply to a gift of the three volumes of the *Defence*, Priestley told Adams that he now thought rather more favorably of the pure republican form than previously and added that a comparison between the American and French governments some years hence would make possible a better judgment. Price, who never analyzed the nature and functions of government with the same thoroughness as Priestley, was fully persuaded of the force of Adams's arguments in favor of the separation of powers among a legislature, an executive, and a judiciary and also the distribution of the legislative power among "three independent states"; they completely refuted the arguments of patriarchs of the commonwealth tradition such as Marchamont Nedham.[74]

Brand Hollis, who probably had provided the text from which Adams took his extracts from Nedham, was also won over to the more conservative position by Adams's arguments. He read the work several times, and his comments were scarcely short of eulogistic: the Americans, he believed, had profited from the experience of former ages and had outstripped Europeans in their knowledge of whatever concerned the dearest interests of mankind; they had put into practice principles that previously had been considered visionary by establishing free states on the only possible basis of rotation of power and equal laws. At the beginning of the decade Brand Hollis had attached great importance to the need to introduce universal suffrage. Adams made him see that other factors were of great account and took him back to the Montesquieu model of the constitution in preference to the soidisant purer republicanism of the commonwealth and Anglo-Saxon tradition. Brand Hollis told Adams that hitherto he had considered that a balance of powers was unnecessary in a society where there was no distinction of rank, but that the *Defence* demonstrated the necessity of it and the impracticability of a single-chamber assembly. He lamented that the English constitution, so admirable in theory, was in practice lost, but in spite of his insistence on his republican principles and his references to the commonwealth tradition, Adams apparently had effectively brought him back to a position much closer to the current system, although not, of course, to the methods by which it was presently manipulated.[75]

Although fragmentary, the surviving testimony is sufficient to suggest that the discussions held between Adams and his English friends were of substantial significance in the development of political analysis on both sides of the Atlantic. For one thing, those such as Price who knew him especially well responded far more favorably to his arguments than those such as Sharp, who did not. But more importantly, as far as all Commonwealthmen were concerned, Adams stood firmly within the broad avenues of their own intellectual heritage.[76] His arguments, expressed as they were through a massive accumulation of evidence from the historical past and the more immediate experience of the United States, were powerful and directed firmly away from the extremity of the Pennsylvania model toward a system that was empirically more feasible and (of considerable importance) closer to the realities of the English constitution. Above all, it reminded radicals that where there was divergence between theory and practice, theory would have to be adjusted to practice, and not practice to theory.

The last American contribution to eighteenth-century radicalism was the federal Constitution of 1787. Although radicals were more aware of the problems within the states, and when they considered the problems of constitutionalism were concerned with the state constitutions, they were also concerned over the fate of the nation of large and aware of the difficulties of unity. Their conception of the nature of the federal relationship was at best somewhat hazy (some appear to have conceived of the Continental Congress as a popularly elected body rather than a group of appointed delegates), but their awareness of the problems of federalism intensified as the decade progressed, and they expressed great interest in the new Constitution drafted at Philadelphia in 1787.

Price was especially anxious about the evident weakness of the Continental government. Jefferson told him in February 1785 that Congress's lack of power had soon been realized as a potentially destructive flaw in the Articles of Confederation. Public opinion on the eve of his departure from the United States the previous summer had been swinging in favor of increasing the powers of the central government. He was not convinced that this would occur until two states actually attacked each other; only then would the public demand that Congress should be given sufficient powers to prevent a recurrence of such an event. Jefferson's predictions were unduly pessimistic but they were sufficiently alarming to prevent Rush's assurance that "Republics are slow in discovering their interest, but when once they find it out, they pursue it with vigor and perseverance" from dispelling all of Price's misgivings.[77] Price had been pleased to learn that a conference was to be held at Annapolis to discuss the enlargement of the powers of Congress, but his fears were once more accentuated by the news of Shays's Rebellion. He commented to Joseph Willard that suffering was a severe teacher and it seemed to be destined to be America's teacher: what fatality was it, he asked, that prevented the Americans from recognizing that their true interest consisted in frugality and simplicity, in avoiding luxury, in finding all they wanted within themselves, and in obeying their own laws and strengthening their federal government? Nevertheless, within a fortnight Price told another correspondent that the United States enjoyed a situation such as had been scarcely before known to mankind and that he was delighted to see that in several instances its advantages had been improved upon.[78]

Price believed that the outcome of the Philadelphia Convention would be critical, not only for the United States, but in some measure for the happiness of the world at large. If a vigorous and wise federal government were to flourish in America, a haven would exist should calamities come, and what happened in Europe would be of less importance. A year later he told Franklin how pleased he was that the Constitution had been ratified by the states, for this justified his hopes that the new American government was more favorable to human rights than any that had been known previously. He remained optimistic about the progress of the new federal regime until his death.[79]

Brand Hollis was even more delighted when he read the Constitution and told Adams that the more he considered it the more he rejoiced and congratulated him: "It is the wisdom of ages reduced to practice."[80] He believed that Adams's *Defence* had influenced the convention in favor of a balance and separation of powers; although a more perfect form of government might be imagined, it was also necessary to consider what the times and people would tolerate and so, bearing these factors in mind, the Constitution was admirable and suitable to be put into execution. Brand Hollis approved the appointment of a president, senate, and assembly (house of representatives). The president had been given considerable, though not perhaps quite enough, power, but could not become absolute as he was required to seek the advice of the senate. Nevertheless, perhaps his reelection should have been forbidden. The danger of an increase in his power was great and almost inevitable and although the danger of an aristocratic tyranny had been frustrated, there remained the danger of a single tyranny. Brand Hollis approved the provisions for electing part of the legislature every two years as being in accordance with the doctrines of Harrington and Milton, but the requirement that the votes of members should be publicly recorded was too democratic for him. He was afraid that it would affect their freedom of voting by subjecting members to the influence of party pressure; he suggested that instead citizens should be able to instruct their representatives. Brand Hollis also criticized a number of other points. He argued that books should be exempt from tax and was especially disappointed that the freedom of the press was not explicitly mentioned in the new federal Constitution. It was protected by all or most of the states but should have been included in the federal Constitution as it was of fundamental importance as the guardian of liberty and a right which despots most feared. He also insisted that the suspension of habeas corpus could not be too much guarded against. Other provisions Brand Hollis disliked were the right to issue letters of marque, which he contended were unchristian and a disgrace to human nature, and the tax on the importation of slaves which he mistakenly took to refer to all immigrants. He urged that admission should be granted freely to all and expressed his concern lest an emancipated people should be unwilling to share its blessings with the rest of the world. Brand Hollis's correspondence with Adams continued after the latter had returned to America; in 1790 he told Adams that he had read the *Federalist* and found it valuable and was pleased to learn that Rhode Island had joined the union.[81]

Of the other radicals, Sharp was somewhat disappointed in the Constitution. He argued that the method of establishing a stable, united, and free government was not as difficult as members of the convention seemed to have thought. In particular he was disappointed that they seemed to have been obsessed with the question of a balance of power between three estates. This attempt to follow European patterns was full of danger for, in spite of a zeal for liberty among the people, statesmen and timeservers usually succeeded in tipping the balance to one side—that of monarchy. In the American system the senate was extremely dangerous since it was apt to produce obnoxious aristocratical distinctions among the people. He objected on the same grounds to the indirect system of electing the president. The system that Sharp thought preferable was, of course, frankpledge. He consoled himself by reflecting that the convention had left scope for the introduction of the system by proposing a census to determine the distribution of representatives among the states; the best method of doing this, he suggested, was by the numerical division of the people in frankpledge. He was greatly disappointed that his attempt to popularize frankpledge in America had failed and concluded that it was Adams's sedulous propagation of the doctrine of a triple balance of power that had frustrated his efforts.[82]

Catharine Macaulay, the only English radical to have visited the United States since its independence, had waited anxiously for the news of the convention. She had been afraid lest the Constitution should be based on monarchic and aristocratic principles, but unlike Sharp she felt that it was grounded on simple democracy. Its principles were so well guarded that in the present circumstances of the United States they might well last for many years without being corrupted. She considered that if it were to be put into effect the Americans would rapidly become the happiest people in the world, but urged that they should pay less attention to commerce and European luxuries and more to the cultivation of the land and the domestic manufacture of essentials. Although she saw the urgency of establishing a government that could control the conflicting interests of the states, she was fearful of the centralization that this might involve. She had originally been fearful of the dangers inherent in the possibility of a perpetual president. After reading some Antifederalist pamphlets sent by Mercy Warren her reservations grew stronger. To Europeans the new system had the appearance of perfect freedom, but to Americans, accustomed to liberty "in its most pleasing garb" it must look different; she was not surprised that there were apprehensions concerning a system that appeared to give undue trust to "that faithless ambitious animal, man."[83] Later she was confident that George Washington as first president would counter the progress of every opinion inimical to the rights for which Americans had fought and would set an example to his successors.[84]

Priestley's only reference to the Constitution in the English edition of his *Lectures on History and General Policy*, which he published in 1788, was to the division of powers. Although he had been sympathetic to Adams's system of balanced powers, he felt that it was absurd to incorporate more than one will in a state as it gave one part a veto over the actions of the remainder; this could be useful as a device for preventing precipitate action but otherwise the American, like the English, Constitution was defective. Three years later he pointed out that the United States had confounded the critics of its government. There had been general predictions that as soon as they achieved their independence the Americans would degenerate into universal confusion and start cutting each other's throats. But even though the break from England had been violent and had drained the country of valuable resources, the Americans had never suffered from a lack of government. In the years following the war they had tolerated an imperfect system, but after much careful thought had adopted a more comprehensive one. Priestley, however, was cautious in his praise. He believed the Americans had only intended to make a trial of the new Constitution; if it were not suitable they would no doubt attempt to improve on it.[85]

Men such as Lindsey praised the "new and wise" Constitution, and the dissenting historian William Belsham declared that it was "one of the happiest and most extraordinary efforts of human virtue, wisdom and ability."[86] Comments such as this and criticisms were made in good measure in an American context—because of concern with the fate of the new republic. But the processes of constitution making in America could also be seen in an English context, and this the radicals were more than willing to do. They did not feel that the distinctively American devices of government appropriate to the circumstances of the United States would be suitable in England any more than they believed that the detailed provisions of the English constitution should be implemented in America. Their task was to translate the American experience into terms that would be comprehensible in English politics.

The first stage in the process was to point to the elements of similarity. Priestley thought that the Americans were imitating the English civil constitution and adopting a form of government similar to the British. Sharp believed there was sufficient congruence between the United States Constitution and the Anglo-Saxon model for his pet system of frankpledge to be implemented there as well as in England. Cartwright took this line of analysis still further. One of the features of the American Constitution that particularly appealed to him was what he believed to be its origin in the same Anglo-Saxon system as the English constitution. He rejected the concept of balanced powers and remained faithful to the unitary system and direct democracy exemplified in the Pennsylvania constitution of 1776, but the merits of the practice of formulating written constitutions remained in his mind. Later Cartwright formulated a written constitution for his own country which illustrated well the uses that could be made of an American model. Cartwright's proposed constitution was comprised essentially of a codification of English principles and practices purged of contemporary corruptions, rather than a frame of government in the American style, but probably it was a product of his observation of American affairs.[87]

More representative of the uses made of American constitutionalism were the views of Wyvill at one end of the radical spectrum and Price toward the other. For Wyvill the crucial and determining factor was the difference between the social and economic circumstances of the two countries; to him the American environment was what made the American system distinctive. He believed that the American society was healthier and the condition of her citizens better than that of the British. He attributed this to the generosity of British treatment of the colonies before the Revolution which had permitted their inhabitants to put themselves in a more favorable position than that of any other nation in the world. Americans enjoyed the benefits of equal distribution of property without the disorder normally associated with democratic states and enough territory to meet the needs of a rapidly increasing population; they paid very few taxes and supported a very modest governmental machine, and yet they had acquired the influence of a substantial state and would soon stand on an equal footing with the world's leading countries. But in spite of these enormous advantages, Wyvill considered that America had been unable to form a government that was both perfectly consonant with the principles of liberty and friendly to the rights of property. Even the Americans had thought it necessary to impose property qualifications for voting. Wyvill conceded that they probably had good reasons for stopping short of theoretical perfection, but in his view this merely demonstrated the folly of attempting to transplant American institutions into the very different circumstances prevailing in England. The American system of government obviously gave great benefits to the Americans themselves, but it would not be suitable to Britain unless the circumstances were the same; without this similarity it would create more problems than it would solve.[88]

Price's theoretical position was considerably more radical than that of Wyvill, but he held similar views on the suitability of American institutions in England. He approved the general structure of American government, especially after it had been reorganized at Philadelphia, but he was seldom concerned over the precise mechanics of political systems and did not wish to transfer the American system to England. At times he fulminated against priests, bishops, and kings, but he explicitly rejected the ideas of republicanism (as it was understood in America) and pure democracy. He believed that the will of the community undoubtedly should govern, but that there were different methods of determining what that will was and then of executing it. Moreover, in America, republican government was appropriate because of the simple manners and relative equality of property there, but like Wyvill he recognized that the situation was very different in England. In any case, Price admired the English constitution. Even during the American war he had been willing to acknowledge the excellence of its general principles and structure, in spite of the need for reform. The government of the country was, he felt, so well balanced, and the institution of the common law so admirable, and they had taken such deep root that the country could bear much decay before its liberties fell. Ten years later he declared that "so far am I from preferring a government purely republican, that I look upon our own constitution of government as better adapted than any other to this country, and in THEORY excellent."[89]

English radicals as well as Americans believed that ratification of the federal Constitution marked the climax of a momentous period in human history. They welcomed the Constitution as setting a fresh course for the continued development of the new nation (and had devoted much thought to the problems facing it), but were also firmly persuaded that the Revolution had an importance that transcended the local concerns of the United States. Joseph Priestley set the Revolution in its broader context when he remarked in the first edition of his *Lectures on History and General Policy*, "As all other sciences have made very rapid advances in the present age, the science of government bids fair to keep pace with them. Many ingenious men have of late turned their thoughts to this subject, and valuable treatises upon it have been published both in this country and abroad. But what is of much more value, we have now a vast stock of important facts before us for contemplation. The old governments of Europe are arrived to a considerable degree of maturity. We may rather say they are growing to decay; so that their several advantages and defects are becoming sufficiently conspicuous, and the new governments in North America are so many new experiments, of which political philosophers cannot fail to make the greatest use."[90] The radicals had no intention of missing the opportunity.

On the eve of the French Revolution, Commonwealthmen believed that certain conclusions could be drawn safely. There could no longer be any doubt that America had fulfilled its obligations to the outside world as well as to its own citizens. The United States had successfully constructed a system of government within the framework of radical ideology and demonstrated that it could be effective. Moreover, Adams's arguments brought the American model closer to the structural forms of English constitutionalism, and the work of the Philadelphia Convention showed that adjustments could be made should they prove necessary. Thus a modern liberal order had been created without need for devastating social upheaval. Radicals recognized that circumstances were uniquely favorable for the achievement of libertarian goals in conditions of social stability and that many of the devices employed for use across the Atlantic were unsuitable, or unnecessary, in England. But they also believed that general principles were applicable and that the American example demonstrated the feasibility of political reform in their own country.

# 7

# Religious Liberty

The American Revolution had particular relevance to another of the most pressing concerns of English radicals, the defense and promotion of religious liberty. To men such as Joseph Priestley religion was "the great business of life" and theological inquiry was superior to the study of all other subjects.[1] But their religion was far from eremitical and did not require them to abstain from intercourse with the secular world. Rather the reverse; one vital corollary was that religious principles bore a substantial relationship to the affairs of political society, though to define the exact nature of the connection was a problem of profound complexity. In one form it was expressed in the ethical basis of political morality and behavior, and much of the radicals' response to issues raised by the Revolution was grounded ultimately on what can be conveniently described as political theology. In another respect it was manifested through the differential political status accorded to various religious denominations, and particularly through the alliance between the state and an established church. This union of secular and spiritual authority was a central component of the eighteenth-century constitution. The state assessed loyalty to itself partly in terms of religious affiliation (assuming that Catholic Dissenters were inherently untrustworthy and Protestant Dissenters uncertain) and imposed confessional qualifications on officeholders. Refusal to conform to the established church was deemed to be evidence of seditious intent. The state acted on the premise that a gift of entrenched privileges to the dominant sect would conduce to greater social and political stability and made such a grant to the Anglican church while denying it to the dissenting sects. In return the state received substantial moral and political support from all levels of the Anglican church. This association invaded most areas of public life and was deeply insulting to many loyal citizens; its power was formidable.

These ecclesiastical arrangements were a source of bitter grievance to lay and clerical Dissenters and to many liberal Anglicans as well. They potentially infringed the individual's right to freedom of conscience and worship and certainly reduced those who refused to conform to the condition of second-class citizens; the fact that their declared purpose was secular rather than spiritual made them all the more obnoxious. One inevitable consequence was a series of campaigns to obtain relief from the operation of offensive ecclesiastical legislation and so to restore to Nonconformists their right to full enjoyment of religious liberty. Many of the arguments deployed by Dissenters and liberal Anglicans during the successive battles were essentially theoretical in character. Partly because the grounds of establishment were prudential pragmatic evidence was offered in support of dissenting insistence that some at least of the apparatus of establishment could be safely dismantled. Here the experience derived from the reordering of church-state relations in America was of great value. A substantial extension of religious liberty had produced harmony, not disaster, as was cited frequently during the successive attempts to secure repeal of discriminatory legislation in the late 1780s. Although these campaigns were unsuccessful, the model of religious liberty in the United States continued to fortify an important component in dissenting ideology.

Radicals had no doubt that a close connection existed between religion and politics. Among Anglicans, John Jebb, who resigned his preferments because of the refusal of the church to incorporate Unitarian heterodoxy, was convinced that the evils of government, lack of felicity among the governed, and absence of patriotism arose from the want of a moral and religious principle that only the Gospel could provide. Christopher Wyvill, who remained formally within the church, told the dissenting member of Parliament William Smith that universal religious toleration was "a cause on which the advancement of Rational Religion and the preservation of Civil Liberty appear chiefly to depend," and Granville Sharp, a devout Trinitarian, always insisted that his political views were based on religious principles.[2] For Dissenters the connection between religious belief and political principle took on even greater significance since, unlike Anglican radicals, their very status as Nonconformists brought inherent political disabilities and offensive obligations. Robert Robinson, the Baptist propagandist, declared in his *Plan of Lectures on Nonconformity* that modern Dissent naturally led to the study of government. Priestley, in his pamphlet addressed to Dissenters during the general election of 1774, emphasized the indissoluble link between civil and religious liberty, pointed out that although Dissenters were immediately concerned with religious liberty, civil liberty was a necessary basis, and claimed that Dissenters had always been noted for their vigorous exertions in favor of both and that whatever civil liberty was enjoyed in England could be ascribed to them.[3] Priestley's remarks were fulsome in some respects, but in others they were apt, for they serve as a reminder that if Dissenters' principles invited a devotion to religious liberty, their legal status made it an urgent imperative.

Religion and the ecclesiastical polity in eighteenth-century England were dominated by the ubiquitous presence of the national church. Its position, functions, and privileges had been broadly set out during the reign of Charles II and confirmed with various modifications by the Revolution Settlement of 1688; at the same time, the status of Dissenters was defined and restrictions on them were imposed. Statutory arrangements for an established church complemented by limited toleration for Protestant Nonconformists and minimal toleration for Catholic Dissenters were immensely satisfying to Anglicans but far from agreeable to others. The few remaining Catholics observed the virtually absolute requirement of discretion, and Quakers obtained limited concessions on matters such as oath-taking and largely withdrew from the political life of the nation. Members of the three principal denominations of Protestant Dissenters, on the other hand, struggled hard and long, though somewhat intermittently, to modify the system in their favor, but with little success until the nineteenth century.

As a group the Dissenters inherited the extreme Protestant elements of the seventeenth-century church. Many of their predecessors had been ejected from their parochial livings in the purge of St. Bartholomew's Day 1662 and had chosen to remain outside the church rather than conform. In the early days the theology of Dissent was largely Calvinist, but during the eighteenth century its character changed substantially with the advance of what was frequently described as "rational Christianity." Calvinist theology did not disappear entirely, but liberalism was much more common among prominent clergy such as Price and Priestley among the Presbyterians and Robinson and Toulmin among the Baptists. In institutional terms an unhappy feature of eighteenth-century Dissent was its decline in numbers. Of the three principal groups, the Presbyterians were moribund and the Congregationalists or Independents remained about level in numbers; only the Baptists showed any increase in membership. Socially the Dissenters were drawn largely from the middle ranks of society; they included few from the highest and lowest strata. As a political group they neither formed a party nor identified themselves with any particular faction; instead they existed as an "interest" in the same sense as the "landed interest" and the "commercial interest." Their political views tended to be liberal, but distinctive dissenting political principles also were held by at least some members of the established church.[4] They placed unusually high significance on the protection of religious liberty, which became increasingly important after the middle of the century when Anglican hostility toward Dissenters revived during the reign of George III following a period of relative acquiescence.

By religious liberty, Dissenters meant freedom of private conscience and the enjoyment of both civil and political rights without any impediment of religious discrimination. A representative committee, the General Body of Protestant Dissenting Ministers, expressed their fundamental principles succinctly and with clarity when they declared, "The Principles upon which we have acted are Liberty of Conscience, the Right of Private Judgment, the sufficiency of scripture and the authority of our Divine Master and Saviour. It is to human authority and human articles in matters of

Faith that we object."[5] These propositions had critical implications when lay Dissenters attempted to apply them in public affairs.

Dissenters enjoyed restricted freedom of conscience and worship under the Act of Toleration of 1689. But their ministers and academy teachers were required to subscribe to all but the organizational Articles of Religion (Baptists were also excused from subscribing to the article relating to infant baptism) and to register with the local diocesan or ordinary. These requirements caused considerable friction over the years. Calvinist and doctrinally orthodox ministers, particularly some Presbyterians, were not greatly troubled since their heterodoxy was largely organizational, but as many ministers moved toward "rational Christianity" and even beyond toward Unitarianism, the statutory obligations caused increasing difficulty. Misled by the terms in which the Anglican "Feathers" Petition for clerical relief from the requirement to subscribe to the articles had been rejected in 1772, the ministers petitioned twice (in 1772 and 1773) for an end to the need to subscribe, but without success. A few years later, in 1779, they and the teachers were allowed relief sequence of concessions made to Catholics the previous year. This was the only concession made to Dissenters until the next century.

Dissenters argued that religious liberty incorporated not only the right of private judgment but also a right to enjoy the free exercise of religion and freedom from secular discrimination on confessional grounds. The last proposition implied that civil magistrates exceeded their authority by demanding a religious test before men were allowed their full political rights. They resented the encroachment of the church on their everyday affairs, its interference with them from birth and until after death. Following the passage of Hardwicke's Marriage Act of 1753 even Price and Priestley were compelled to have their marriages solemnized in Anglican churches. Interference with Dissenters' civil rights was irritating and humiliating. Political disabilities were more damaging in the long term. The legal basis on which the political position of Protestant Nonconformists rested derived from legislation enacted during the reign of Charles II. The most important statutes were the Corporation Act of 1661 and the Test Act of 1673 that required officeholders of profit under corporations and the crown respectively to fulfill certain requirements. The most repugnant was the taking of the Sacraments according to the rites of the Church of England. In theory this excluded Dissenters from office, and although many employed subterfuges such as occasional conformity, others rejected the practice as a matter of principle.[6] By a curious quirk they were not disbarred from sitting in Parliament, though few did so.

Discriminatory legislation remained in force until the nineteenth century, but if the letter of the law was harsh, its implementation was less so.[7] From the Glorious Revolution onward various devices were employed to ameliorate the position of Protestant Dissenters. The cornerstone of Nonconformist liberties (such as they were) was the Toleration Act. It formed part of the religious settlement of the Revolution and listed criminal acts of which the penalties were not to apply to Protestants. Significantly, its preamble stated that the act was passed in the interest of the state, not for the benefit of the subjects. Nevertheless, the act substantially eased the lot of Dissenters in civil matters and after some ups and downs was followed in the eighteenth century by legislation intended to alleviate some of the consequences of their second-class political status. From 1727 onward indemnity acts were passed in most years to suspend the penalties of the Test and Corporation Acts in the case of those officeholders who had failed to comply with their provisions. But these acts promised more than they fulfilled. They may have relieved the minds of some Dissenters, but they were a mere palliative since they were not reliable and the original laws remained in force. As their title implied, they offered retrospective relief after illegal acts had been committed, not future immunity, and there were many gaps and loopholes. The most notorious exploitation of a loophole was the device by which the City of London elected to the shrievalty men who would not take the Sacrament to qualify for office and then fined them for refusing to serve when elected. Only after protracted litigation was the practice outlawed in the Sheriffs' Case in 1767, and even on this occasion the Dissenters' victory was not unalloyed. Lord Mansfield declared in his opinion that Dissent could not be considered a crime, but two years later Sir William Blackstone asserted in his *Commentaries on the Laws of England*, which were explicitly intended to be descriptive and expository, that it could. Dissenters believed they had considerable cause for complaint, and the evidence of this and other cases goes far to support them.[8]

Dissenters did not wish this unsatisfactory situation to continue without protest, especially as they felt with some justice that the security of the Glorious Revolution and the successor House of Hanover rested in part on their own sense of loyalty. Their activities in defense of their interests were directed by two complementary organizations, the Body of Protestant Ministers of the Three Denominations in and about the Cities of London and Westminster, founded in 1727, and the Protestant Dissenting Deputies, a representative body of laymen founded five years later. Of the two groups, the Body of Protestant Ministers had the narrower range, but nevertheless directed the ultimately successful campaign to secure relief for ministers and teachers. The Deputies were more vigorous and had wider responsibilities: to supervise the civil affairs of dissent and to give advice and assistance to Dissenters who felt that their grievances derived from their religious beliefs. The Deputies organized the campaigns for repeal of the Test and Corporation Acts in the 1730s and again in 1787, 1789, and 1790. Such organizations were essential to transform generalized grievances into consolidated pressure on public opinion and on the government, but they did not pretend to be more than a vehicle for the mobilization of argument. They had few counters with which to bargain for relief, and necessarily their chances of success depended on their powers of rational persuasion.[9] When they constructed their arguments (both for private instruction and public debate) the Dissenters, being men of wide intellectual horizons, were prepared to look outside the narrow limits of domestic circumstances. In the 1730s this willingness brought little reward, but half a century later it encouraged them to consider the practices of the United States.

Although the Dissenters' campaigns for relief began long before Anglo-American relations became a critical issue in English politics and continued long after the matter was resolved, the Revolution played an important if subsidiary role in the formulation of Dissenting attitudes and policies on the question of discrimination. The affair of the colonial bishopric was the first substantive problem to direct Dissenters' attention to America. Because ecclesiastical-political policies and imperial relations were intertwined, fundamental questions affecting the religious liberty of their fellow Nonconformists were raised, and Dissenters worked enthusiastically and successfully to thwart the church's intentions. The nature of the victory was significant, for although the preservation of liberty in America and its fate in England were connected, on this occasion the Americans depended on English assistance, and their potential capacity for constructing a model relevant to the needs of domestic argument remained undeveloped. More important was the breaking down of discrimination on religious grounds in America during the Revolution and the consequent extension of religious liberty. Even though such liberty was far from complete by the end of the century and church-state relations remained an active issue in American politics for many decades, the Dissenters detected within American practice many features that were much in advance of contemporary English practice and of great relevance to their own circumstances. Thus in this respect the American Revolution operated in England as a model and an example.

Argumentation on both sides of the dispute over the status of Dissenters was extended and complex.[10] Nevertheless the debate can, for the purposes of this discussion, be reduced to two issues, one substantive and the other procedural. The first was a conflict between individual rights and the interests of the state.[11] The second was the need for Dissenters to persuade an overwhelmingly Anglican Parliament not only of the propriety of their demands but of the safety of making concessions. The arguments adduced by Nonconformists in support of their claims form a classic example of an attempt to establish legitimacy by reference to normative values and instrumental efficacy.

Dissenters insisted on the right of the individual to enjoy full freedom of conscience and full civil rights based on the theory of natural rights and its concomitant, the Lockean postulate of social contract. The counterargument .was the assertion that the state possessed authority to intervene in the interest of the community at large in matters of religion that were of communal concern. Such powers were not wholly inconsistent with the theory of contract; certainly most men deemed them essential in the political circumstances of late seventeenth-century England. Opponents of toleration could argue that in the years between the Restoration and the acceptance of the House of Hanover (perhaps until the succession of George II was secure) the establishment of a single dominant and almost entirely comprehensive church, whose position was bolstered by discriminatory legislation directed against both Protestant and Catholic Dissenters, was essential for national stability. Indeed, many Protestant Dissenters implicitly conceded the point when they argued in favor of the continued maintenance of discrimination against Catholics on political grounds. By the 1730s, however, the sociopolitical structure of the country had settled so that no danger could be rationally anticipated from Protestant dissent, although Sir Robert Walpole insisted on diverting the Deputies' first attempts to secure repeal. Fifty years later, when they inaugurated the second series of campaigns, the danger would seem even more remote. Yet on both occasions the Dissenters' applications aroused sufficient feelings of horror and fear that the orthodox could frustrate them.

In part the Dissenters' argument was derived from an affirmation of supremacy of natural rights of the individual, upon which was constructed a complex superstructure of logic. Once this doctrine was destroyed, the remainder fell. The argument of the state's interest had to be neutralized if the Dissenters were to have any chance of success. Thus they were compelled to demonstrate that state interest could be congruent with individual rights.

Two reciprocal lines of argument were possible, both based on empirical evidence rather than abstract logic. One was to demonstrate that an increase in the number of Protestant sects and sectarians was so great that public safety would be better secured by the extension of rights than by the maintenance of special privileges for a single favored group. The other alternative was to demonstrate that the number of sectarians had declined so as to render them innocuous. Both arguments could be advanced only by reference to experience, and in practice the latter circumstance had occurred in the eighteenth century (although the former was to mature in the nineteenth). The argument from empirical evidence contained a possible deficiency. Dissenters could argue from the experience of the recent past that they no longer posed any conceivable threat to the body politic (persuasively in the eyes of the external observer) and that they could therefore be trusted with the same rights and privileges enjoyed by members of the established church. They could not demonstrate from the experience of their own country what the consequence of emancipation would be. Thus they would remain vulnerable to the argument of safety and the desirability of avoiding risks. But this argument could be blunted if the grounds of experience could be extended to incorporate other, similar, societies. If reference could be made to other nations that had safely emancipated their Dissenters, the analogy could indicate that the twin pillars of church and state were not irrevocably doomed to collapse if England followed the same course.

At this point the American Revolution acquired a distinctive relevance to the English situation. The analogy between English circumstances and American experience was not perfect, but the considerable congruence between the two had much merit. In America the process of liberalization and secularization had taken substantial and significant steps during the Revolution. Subsequent experience suggested that the confessional state was no longer an essential requisite of social and political stability and that Dissenters could be safely let off the leash. Should such a program be thought too dangerous for emulation by England, the case of New England suggested a means by which the maintenance of an established church could be rendered less obnoxious and devices by which Nonconformist churches could participate to some degree in the benefits of state protection. The United States still had a long way to go along the path to a total separation of church and state, but it had already amassed a corpus of experiential evidence that was available for use in English battles.

A helpful, and possibly essential, preliminary to the interpretation of the American model of religious liberty was a favorable picture of colonial Nonconformity and the secular treatment accorded to religious belief. By and large, English Dissenters (especially their ministers) possessed a good knowledge of the state of American religion. As was shown in chapter 2, there were many close connections between English Dissenters and those colonists who were not members of the Church of England; coordination of resistance to the episcopacy proposals is only one instance. Moreover, the image purveyed of colonial religion and its political circumstances was both attractive and congruent to the interests and desires of English observers. Following a parallel path to the growth of English Dissent, American religion had bifurcated in the eighteenth century into a rational, essentially Arminian, and almost Unitarian wing and a Calvinist, evangelical, and revivalist wing associated especially with Jonathan Edwards. English Dissenters directed themselves to the liberal wing; by a sad irony the greatest figure of eighteenth-century American theology was held in low regard and was little mentioned. The great figures with whom Englishmen corresponded were, of course, Jonathan Mayhew, the pope of Bostonian Arianism, and Charles Chauncy, scourge of the Revival. These men accepted the doctrine of the congruence of civil government with moral and religious considerations, and their social values were similar; as Alan Heimert has remarked, "They did not speak to incite the multitude but wrote to convince the respectably intelligent."[12]

The generally congenial image of colonial society presented by English books further encouraged Dissenters to take a favorable view of American ecclesiastical practices. Most important of the descriptions of the religious condition of the colonies was Daniel Neal's *History of New England*. This work, first published in 1720 and based largely on Cotton Mather's *Magnalia Christi Americana*, was deeply informed by the ideology of Puritan religion. In his dedication, Neal claimed that "oppression and Persecution here, the greatest Vices Men can be guilty of, gave Birth to *New-England* at first; and Liberty among you the most publick Blessing, had yielded Nourishment to it ever since and will always keep it vigourous and healthy"; he told New Englanders, "You have the Character of a Religious People," and though conceding that the early Puritans had persecuted the Quakers, he argued that the Friends' activities struck at the very foundations of the colony.[13] Later, Mayhew, when attacking the Society for the Propagation of the Gospel, declared as a preliminary to his argument that the first settlers had migrated chiefly on account of their sufferings as Nonconformists in England: "They fled hither as to an asylum from episcopal persecution, seconded by royal power"; the settlers were, he declared, "a sober, virtuous and religious set of people in general."[14] Neal claimed that although there were two sides in New England politics, religion was not involved because there were no sacramental tests for office and all groups were satisfied: "Happy People! as long as Religion and the State continue on a separate Basis. . . . May they long continue on this

Foot a Sanctuary to oppressed Protestants in all Parts of the World!"[15] Not all Dissenters accepted this benign view of the state of religion in New England—Ebenezer Radcliff declared that the Americans had "stained the merit of their integrity with persecution"—but there is little doubt that it fitted their needs very well and its defects were generally overlooked. New England was presented as a tolerant rather than persecuted society in which even Anglicans were accorded the same rights as members of other more orthodox sects.[16]

For the most part Dissenters said little about the state of religion in the colonies south of Mason and Dixon's line, but they were greatly impressed by the situation in Pennsylvania. Robert Robinson, one of the most articulate and vigorous critics of the English ecclesiastical establishment, greatly admired the declaration of religious rights contained in William Penn's fundamental constitutions, and this view was echoed to a greater or lesser extent by many other Dissenters. Such adulation led to the comments that religious diversity in Pennsylvania produced harmony and stability rather than discord; here was "an example worthy the imitation of all Europe, beaútiful in itself, but placed to infinite advantage when contrasted with the unnatural persecutions of many other lawgivers."[17]

Although the view of American society was favorable (perhaps unduly so) its potential remained dormant during the two campaigns to extend religious freedom in the 1770s. The plea of liberal Anglican clergy to be relieved from the obligation to subscribe to the Articles of Religion and the request for relief for dissenting ministers were argued out in terms of abstract rights, theoretical principles, and the operation of logic. At this stage little need was felt to refer to experience; major works such as Israel Mauduit's *Case of the Dissenting Ministers* and Philip Furneaux's *Essay on Toleration* made no reference to American practice, and it was seldom referred to in other pamphlets.[18] There was, however, one important exception. Shortly after the Dissenters' relief bill had been rejected for the second time, Benjamin Franklin wrote a piece in the *London Packet* defending New England against the charge of religious persecution. He recapitulated the accepted version of the origins and early history of the northern colonies, conceded that there had been persecution in the early days, but argued that they should be judged by their present rather than past conduct. He pointed out that although Anglicans in Massachusetts were required to pay taxes, these were assigned to the maintenance of the church to which the payer belonged; he also attempted to deflect the charge that New England Dissenters sought to prevent the appointment of a bishop. The climax of Franklin's argument was the definition of a "persecution account" arranged in accordance with his well-known felicific calculus. In New England, he declared, where almost all men were Dissenters, there was no test to prevent churchmen from holding office, the sons of churchmen had the full benefit of the universities, and taxes for support of public worship, when paid by churchmen, were given to an episcopal minister. He scarcely needed to specify the circumstances prevailing in old England.[19] Franklin's arguments impressed many Dissenters; Price advanced the same arguments when soliciting Lord Chatham's support during the second reading of the bill in the House of Lords; Priestley, who had read the article while unaware of the identity of its author, was much impressed; and Radcliff attached it as an appendix to his *Two Letters*. Later Benjamin Vaughan included the article in his collection of Franklin's works, but it seems to have had a greater effect after the Revolution than before.[20]

Only Priestley took up the American example to any considerable extent during these years. He was already a rigorous and vocal critic of the very existence of an established church in England, thus placing himself at the most advanced position in ecclesiastical politics along with a few others such as Caleb Fleming and Robert Robinson. He pointed to America as an example of harmony among the sects in those colonies that had no establishment and as an example of the least offensive form of establishment in those provinces that did consider one sect superior. He argued that Pennsylvania should be investigated together with other appropriate colonies and foreign countries, to inquire of the consequences of the liberal regulation of religion.[21]

During the war years the intellectual arguments over religious liberty were temporarily subordinated to the more pressing imperatives of immediate circumstances. Nevertheless, the subject was not forgotten on either side of the Atlantic. In August of 1776, Samuel Adams declared in his *Oration Delivered at the*

*State-House in Philadelphia* (which was quickly reprinted in London) that the United States should remain an asylum of religious freedom. The connection between civil and religious liberty was emphasized by John Witherspoon in his Princeton sermon of May of the same year.[22] In England earlier arguments were recapitulated and somewhat expanded. Richard Watson told Jebb (who had earlier been skeptical about the liberality of American arrangements concerning religion) that Connecticut and Massachusetts had set an example worth imitation by all Christian states in their disposal of revenue for the support of religious ministers. Franklin's friend Jonathan Shipley, bishop of St. Asaph, referred to the American practice during the debate on the bill for the relief of dissenting ministers in 1779. He pointed out that there was a multiplicity of sects, including some from Germany, and that they were all tolerated and enjoyed the same privileges; in consequence all had been peaceful and harmonious and religion had not been a disturbance to government for the last century.[23] Although American examples were most commonly used to support the Protestant Dissenters' case for relief, they could also be used to bolster arguments in favor of relieving Catholics from their much more severe disabilities. During an age when Dissenters and liberal Anglicans like Thomas Hollis and Archdeacon Francis Blackburne were rabid in their hatred of popery, Priestley compounded his sins in the eyes of the orthodox by publishing a pamphlet in support of the Catholics in 1780. By referring (somewhat misleadingly) to the role of Catholics in Maryland, he demonstrated that even Catholicism need not necessarily be hostile to civil liberty, and he closed his pamphlet by reprinting Benjamin Franklin's celebrated parable against persecution. Franklin's piece was specifically recommended to the attention of the reactionary Protestant Association by a contributor to the *Monthly Review*.[24] The popular response to these pleas was the Gordon Riots.

As the war continued and it became increasingly evident that America would be independent and so free to pursue her own course in matters relating to religious as well as civil liberty, the tone of radical response underwent a subtle change. The United States was now seen as offering new and complete experimental evidence of the operation of religious freedom on a scale not apparent during the colonial era; Price visualized the emergence of a rising empire that was not only without nobles and kings but without bishops as well. The contrast between Massachusetts and England was sharp: a great people was likely to be formed "into free communities under governments which have no religious tests and establishments! A new aera in future annals, and a new opening in human affairs beginning, among the descendents of Englishmen, in a new world."[25] Similarly, Jebb had overcome his skepticism toward the end of the war. Looking forward in September 1781 to the establishment of American independence (which he anticipated in the fairly near future) he thought it would be a great day in the religious as well as the civil history of mankind: "Its probable effect on both the religious and civil Happiness of Mankind has not yet been fully considered. The gospel will triumph in consequence on the true Spirit of Toleration being established in the transatlantic world."[26]

In the early days of independence Price offered moral advice to the new nation. He believed that religion was necessary for the future greatness and happiness of the United States, and he hoped it would be a better religion than had been taught elsewhere. It should enforce moral obligations but should also be tolerant and catholic and stress peace and charity rather than persecution and damnation. Judging the Revolutionary settlement by these criteria, he considered the new Massachusetts constitution to be very liberal, but not far enough; similarly, he disapproved of residual discrimination in Pennsylvania, Delaware, and Maryland. He advised the new nation that not only all Christians but also men of all religions ought to be eligible for state protection insofar as they behaved themselves honestly and peacefully.[27] Price's advice was well meant and well received, but it was already being overtaken by events in America.

The days when colonial Dissenters had required the assistance of their London colleagues were now past.[28] With the firm consolidation of the American republic and the rapid, though incomplete, extension of religious freedom, the status of America as a model rather than as a dependent became more apparent. Already, as Franklin had pointed out to Price in 1780, Massachusetts had made substantial advances in eliminating religious tests, and a still more liberal policy was anticipated when its constitution was revised.[29] From this time onward the position of religion in

America and its relationship to the state would be a matter for great envy among those who resented the power of an established church in England.

More important, the understanding of the usefulness of the American model in an English context was also changing. Before the Revolution the American model had been essentially one of moderation. Dissenters' references to complete religious freedom in Pennsylvania were characterized by a general tone of wishfulness; they knew in the depths of their hearts that such a system was unlikely to be implemented in England in the forseeable future. They looked instead to the alternative example proffered by the congregational colony of Massachusetts Bay. Their enthusiasm for this model was no doubt stimulated at least in part by Franklin's shrewd pragmatism and conciliatory ministrations; if there had to be a confessional state the Massachusetts pattern was the least repugnant for it gave sanctity of conscience to all Christians and offered the services of the state to assist in the maintenance of nonconformist sects as well as of the officially established church. This arrangement would be advanced for several years as a compromise system that might be tolerable to Anglicans, though it did not go far enough to satisfy many Dissenters.

After the Revolutionary War the newly independent states provided an even more stimulating alternative model when the auguries for the future liberality and prosperity of mankind appeared to be especially favorable on a variety of grounds. This second model took the implications of the earlier one to their logical extension. It retained the function of government as having a general oversight of the moral conduct of its citizens and conceded that morality was an essential prop to the secular state, but went no further. The method of implementing these principles was to dismantle the apparatus granting privileges to particular sects and to arrange for the total disestablishment of all religion. In the 1780s there were considerable variations in practice, but sooner or later all the states moved in this direction, though some delayed for several decades, and a minor residue of discrimination remained still longer. The United States Constitution of 1787 imposed an absolute prohibition on any federal establishment or restriction on religious liberty.

Virginia's actions, and in particular Thomas Jefferson's Statute for Establishing Religious Freedom, aroused most admiration in England. The statute was enacted in 1786; copies arrived in England in the summer of that year and quickly appeared in the press. It made an instantaneous, deep, and lasting impression on Dissenters; they had expected much of the United States and believed that the statute vindicated their faith in the new nation. Thomas Brand Hollis had it printed in his local Essex paper, the *Chelmsford Gazette*, and remarked that it "surpasses for spirit and good sense anything of its kind in Europe and gives us an example of what we may expect from men emancipated from subjection, perfectly free with the powers of the human mind, at full liberty to range through the civil and intellectual world and peruse truth and knowledge and follow their dictates." John Disney printed it as a note to his memoirs of Jebb to confirm the liberality of American religious legislation.[30] Price was especially delighted; the statute was the first of its kind and a "noble example of legislative wisdom and liberality."[31] In order to give the statute wider currency in England he printed a broadsheet edition with a brief introduction in which he argued that if the principles that informed it always had been acted upon by governments, there would never have been any persecution, honest inquiry would not have been discouraged, truth and reason would have enjoyed fair play, and many of the evils that disturbed the peace of mankind and obstructed its development would have been avoided.[32]

Jefferson's masterpiece was in many ways an appropriate model for English Dissenters. Its argument was powerful and its literary style distinguished, but these considerations were insufficient by themselves, as the reception of the Declaration of Independence had demonstrated ten years earlier. More important was its precise suitability to the Dissenters' situation and needs. The Virginia statute went to the limit of their demands for intellectual freedom and formalized the final disestablishment of an Anglican church. It also demonstrated the lack of utility in an establishment, though Dissenters were careful not to make too much of this in their propaganda, and the safety possible in denominational equality. While its political basis was drawn from the particular circumstances of the Old Dominion with a growing multiplicity of sects, its intellectual underpinnings owed much to theories of natural rights, government, society, and religion common among English

Dissenters. In composing the statute Jefferson had used tracts by Locke, Shaftesbury, and Furneaux, and his friend and collaborator James Madison had read Priestley's *Essay on Government* in addition to Furneaux's *Essay on Toleration*, the latter being regarded on both sides of the Atlantic as the leading statement of the principles of religious liberty.[33] Perhaps more important than the statute's formal rejection of the concept of the confessional state was its declaration of the individual citizen's rights to a general freedom of the mind and implication that intellectual liberty was essential if human progress was to be achieved. Eighteenth-century Dissenters saw intellectual liberty largely in terms of religious freedom for good reasons, but they were also much concerned with secular speculation and considered it just as much entitled to protection from government interference. It is hardly surprising that radicals regarded Jefferson's statute as the most important document to emanate from the American Revolution.

Writing to Arthur Lee in February 1787, Price declared that the widespread circulation of the Virginia statute had not been without effect.[34] He may well have been right, for within a few months of its publication in England the Dissenters began their second great campaign of the century to obtain repeal of the Test and Corporation Acts.

The winter of 1786–87 seemed propitious for the renewal of the campaign for relief. William Pitt the Younger was secure in office, and although he had given up the cause of parliamentary reform there was still reason to suppose that he would be sympathetic toward the Dissenters. He was the son of a good friend of earlier days and had received considerable support from Dissenters in the general election of 1784 (largely because of their revulsion against the Fox-North coalition). When a delegation of Deputies visited him in February 1785 to protest about the unfortunate implications of the newly enacted Registry Act, they left with the impression that he was very sympathetic toward their wishes.[35] Their optimism was followed by a long hiatus before a meeting of two hundred laymen and ministers discussed the situation in December 1786. The American example may have contributed significantly to the decision to go ahead; certainly the Virginia statute was read to the Society for Constitutional Information in November, Price had it printed in the *Gentleman's Magazine* for January

1787, and it circulated widely during the campaign.[36]

The Deputies' application abjured the extreme theoretical arguments of Price, Priestley, and Robinson in favor of the more limited and moderate arguments of men such as Philip Furneaux and stressed the disabilities suffered by Dissenters rather than the general and radical criticisms of establishment associated so unfortunately with the others.[37] They also sought to demonstrate the safety to the constitution-at-large of the course that they were advocating. One immediate consequence of this tactical decision was to assign an increased importance to the evidence of experience. Here the American example was apposite. Unfortunately, it was also potentially hazardous since the archbishop of Canterbury and many others argued that the Dissenters not only had been king-killers a century earlier but were republicans and had been disloyal during the recent American war. The charges against the recent behavior of Dissenters were both easy to make and unjust in their premises; they were also inevitable and would have been leveled even had the Dissenters not made any reference to America.[38] If they were charged with sympathy for rebels, they might just as well secure any advantages that could be derived from the American model.

The active campaign began with the meeting of dissenting ministers and laymen in December 1786. This led to the nomination of an ad hoc committee under the chairmanship of Edward Jeffries, which was charged with the responsibility of conducting the application. The committee met the prime minister, who expressed polite interest and then fobbed them off with the comment that he needed time to think about it (Pitt shortly turned against the Dissenters). The committee then prepared a printed *Case*, which they rapidly distributed in appropriate circles in London and throughout the country.[39] The argument was carefully constructed to avoid the charge of narrow self-interest on the one hand and of extremism on the other. In particular the *Case* steered well clear of the attacks on the fabric of the establishment made by Priestley and others that had imposed self-inflicted and severe harm on the general dissenting cause. Instead it briefly referred to the philosophical basis of the Dissenters' demands, then delineated the handicaps imposed on Protestant Dissenters by discriminatory legislation and insisted that Parliament could accede to the Dissenters' requests with total safety to the fabric of both church and state. But of themselves, these arguments were insufficient. What was necessary was not only a statement of principle and a protestation of loyalty but also empirical evidence to exemplify them.[40]

Here American experience was particularly germane for, as Capel Lofft commented when he sent the resolutions to the *Gentleman's Magazine*, they appealed to principles of beneficent and just policy similar to those of the recently printed Virginia statute. Article XI of the *Case* made the point forcefully:

The situation of foreign countries with regard to Britain offers strong arguments for repeal of these oppressive laws. . . . The United States of America in addition to the ease with which they permit foreigners to become naturalised, make no distinctions as to religious sects in relation to public offices . . . and in [many] other countries many persons dissenting from their respective establishments have been employed in the highest offices, who by the most signal services have manifested this important truth: THAT A DISSENTER FROM THE ESTABLISHED RELIGION OF A COUNTRY MAY BE A TRUE FRIEND TO ITS GENERAL INTERESTS AND PROSPERITY.[41]

There is also evidence that John Adams, who was still in London during the first phase of the campaign, was consulted about the preparation of the Dissenters' propaganda. Vaughan, who was among those added to the committee on 30 January, sent the sheets of a pamphlet to Adams with an invitation to correct any errors. The tone of Vaughan's letter and the thoughts implicit in it suggest that this was not the first occasion on which Adams had discussed the position of the Dissenters and the discriminatory legislation that impinged so severely upon them. Certainly Adams knew several members of the committee and had discussed religious liberty with Price, and after he returned home, Brand Hollis wrote to him about a later phase of the campaign.[42]

The pamphlet that Adams was invited to comment on was almost certainly Samuel Heywood's tract, *The Right of Protestant Dissenters to a Compleat Toleration Asserted*. Heywood was a shrewd tactician. He realized that the Dissenters' only hope of success lay in dividing the church so that the low churchmen would support them rather than indulge in a frontal assault. He accordingly conceded the arguments of Bishop William Warburton and Archdeacon William Paley as to the need to sustain an establishment but sought to turn their flank to the advantage of his cause. Part of the pamphlet comprised an extended history of the two offensive acts from their origins onward followed by a discussion of the current position and a declamation against the injustice of religious tests. Then Heywood urged that relief for Protestant Dissenters would not endanger the church, that it was expedient, and that the present period was especially favorable for such a concession. His most astute argument was to cite William Paley himself on establishment. Paley attached great importance to the expediency and efficacy of institutions, and, as Heywood pointed out, had suggested that if a number of sects were competing for position and more harm than good might be done to advance one over the others, it might be desirable to introduce a system similar to that obtaining in certain parts of the United States.[43]

Some of the strongest argumentation of empirical evidence came in an appendix to the main body of the tract. Before Vaughan could get Heywood's pamphlet published, the opponents of repeal had wheeled out some heavy artillery from the earlier struggles in the form of Bishop Sherlock's defense of the Test Act in which he argued that a Presbyterian establishment would be a persecuting one.[44] Such an attack at a crucial time required an immediate response. Heywood, or probably Vaughan, added a somewhat hastily composed appendix in an attempt to rebut his opponent's arguments. As he pointed out, "There is another style of argument on this subject, even yet more convincing than the foregoing"; it was drawn from the conduct of Protestant Dissenters in America.[45] He pointed out that most Dissenters lived in states that had the most liberal test laws and declared that the statute of the state of Virginia respecting religious liberty "is a masterpiece, deserving record in letters of gold."[46] He further defended the New Englanders against the charge of intolerance by quoting Franklin's letter of 1772 at great length, including the felicific account in which he demonstrated that New England was more benevolent than the old country.[47] Moreover, he added, the Declaration of Rights, which was the basis of the new Massachusetts constitution, laid down the principle that all peaceable denominations were entitled to the equal protection of the law and prohibited the subordination of one sect to another. He argued, "Certain it is, that no countries under the sun, shew more indulgences to variety in religious opinions than the United States of North America; and since so large a majority of their citizens are Dissenters, nothing can be more clear than the proof it affords, that the modern disposition of the Dissenters, as Dissenters, is not intolerant."[48] The clergy, Heywood insisted, would run no risk by acceding to the Dissenters' request.

Motions for the repeal of the Test and Corporation Acts were introduced in the House of Commons on three occasions during the ensuing three years. On 28 March 1787, the first was defeated by 176 votes to 98; on 8 May 1789, the margin came down to 124 to 104; and on 2 March 1790, the last motion of the century was defeated by a crushing 294 votes to 105.[49] The first two motions were proposed by Henry Beaufoy, Andrew Kippis's former pupil and a Quaker who had conformed, and seconded by Sir Henry Hoghton, a prominent Lancashire Presbyterian. Both men were careful to avoid giving the smallest unnecessary offense while pressing their case as firmly as possible.[50] Neither referred to the United States. For the third motion a different approach was used in view of the failure of Beaufoy's motions. In place of the two backbenchers the brilliant opposition spokesman Charles James Fox was invited to lead. Fox had spoken on behalf of the Dissenters in 1789, but Pitt had effectively trumped his highest card. In answer to his attempt to distinguish between opinions and actions and his insistence that the test laws should be repudiated because men should be judged by their actions rather than their opinions, Pitt had replied crushingly, "The government has a right to guard against the probability of civil inconvenience being produced; nor ought they to wait till, by their being carried into action, the inconvenience has actually arisen."[51]

The prime minister had explicitly based his opposition to relief on the grounds of expediency, not principle, and in the 1790 debate Fox attempted to meet the argument by reference to experience. He denied that Dissenters were strenuous advocates of toleration when out of power, but were intolerant when in authority, and he argued in favor of toleration by reference to the United States. In America, "the different religious sects, unembarrassed by any *religious* monopoly, enjoyed their rights in common! Nearly all the provinces of the Thirteen States varied in the nature of their religious opinions; but, as the most enlightened and general principles of Toleration were adopted, all acted with that liberal cordiality, the imitation of which, at the present juncture, would reflect the highest credit upon ourselves."[52] Pitt's reply that circumstances in America were different from those in England since the American Constitution resembled the English neither in state nor in church and that the United States possessed no establishment in need of protective test laws was only half true, but it was tactically effective in the context of a parliamentary debate.[53]

Although references to the extension of religious liberty in America were perhaps unwise in the House of Commons, the transatlantic model continued to provide an encouraging example for the Dissenters outside the house and played an important role in the exposition of their propaganda. As the Baptist minister Caleb Evans reported to James Manning, "We are clogged here with Test Laws, and are struggling to get rid of them. You know no such shackles."[54] The official *Case* of the Dissenters, containing the reference to the United States, was reprinted several times. The Birmingham Dissenters printed a collection of *Extracts from Books* in connection with the renewal of the application for relief in 1790; most of the selections it contained were English in origin, but it concluded by printing the American Quakers' Address to the President of 3 October 1789 and George Washington's reply in which he recapitulated the principle, "While men perform their social duties faithfully, they do all that Society or the State can with propriety demand or expect, and remain responsible only to their Maker for the religion or modes of faith which they may prefer or profess."[55] Vaughan collected a similar though briefer *Collection of Testimonies in Favour of Religious Liberty,* which he published in London in 1790. There were twenty-one items in all, mainly from the eighteenth century; they included the Quaker address and Washington's reply, the Virginia Statute for Religious Liberty, his friend Franklin's parable against persecution, and extracts from Heywood's tract, including Franklin's discussion of toleration.[56] But the best evidence of the continuing attraction of the American model can be found in the resolutions of a meeting of Dissenters held shortly before the beginning of the last attempt to obtain relief. The resolutions repeated many of the old propositions and went on to announce that the Dissenters would not cease their efforts. Finally, though they saw their campaign in good measure in terms of an internal debate within England, they also derived much sustenance from the successes of others, for they declared "that we are encouraged to perseverance by the establishment of religious liberty in America."[57]

In spite of the failure of Dissenters to obtain relief from the Test and Corporation Acts, the years around the beginning of the last decade of the century were ones of optimism. As Priestley said, "We every day see signs of the nearer approach of those glorious times, in which truth, virtue and liberty, will diffuse themselves over the whole earth, and when error, vice and tyranny, will in every country fall before them."[58] There was now one country, the United States, in which the separation of church and state appeared to have been completed; the results thus far seemed entirely beneficial, and France seemed about to follow suit, even if England lagged behind.[59] The American model was not simple, of course, even though English reformers tended to treat it as if it were. Rather, it offered a complex example and could be used for somewhat different purposes. For many its most attractive feature was the cohabitation of an establishment and a body of Dissenters who were not only free from discrimination but were themselves given assistance by the state. This was to some extent a misapprehension (some of the admirers do not seem to have appreciated the full significance of the Virginia Statute for Religious Freedom), but they were tactically wise in emphasizing the model of Massachusetts when trying to persuade members of the established church to make an important concession. Perhaps the full significance of the most advanced aspect of the American model took some time to sink in; a good deal of evidence to this effect can be found in the publications of Joseph Priestley.

Priestley never disguised his desire to go beyond the elimination of discriminatory legislation. He consistently and intemperately made it plain that he wished to bring about the destruction of the whole fabric of establishment. During his last years in England he returned frequently to the example of the American model, but initially his references were, for him, moderate. Immediately after the first failure in March 1787 he composed a harsh and ill-judged attack on Pitt for his opposition to repeal. The pamphlet, written independently of the official Dissenters' organizations, comprised to a considerable extent an attack on the concept of establishment, but the only reference to America was a restricted one. This moderation was repeated when he came to discuss establishments in his *Lectures on History and General Policy*, which were published for the first time the following year. In them he pointed to the example of Pennsylvania and its multiplicity of sects coupled with an absence of any establishment, but went on to cite the Massachusetts practice of requiring every citizen to pay a certain sum toward the maintenance of religion but allowing him to determine to which sect it should be allocated.[60]

During a bitter clash with Spencer Madan, vicar of St. Philip's, Birmingham, Priestley developed his view of the more radical importance of American religious arrangements. Madan had delivered a sermon shortly before the third repeal debate in which he made numerous hostile remarks about the Dissenters. Priestley was bound to reply and did so in a series of "Familiar Letters" to the citizens of Birmingham. One of Madan's premises was that no country could exist without some system of religious tenets. Priestley commented that this could apply to heathenism and cited an instance of a nation that prospered without need for an officially supported church. His words are worth quoting at length as an illustration of his line of argument:

Mr. Madan certainly never thought of America, when he wrote his sermon. For that country had been *permanent* and *flourishing* for near two centuries, without any such system, as he imagines to be *absolutely necessary*. In many of those provinces no man was ever compelled to pay to the support of any particular species of religion approved by the state: for the state left every man to chuse his own. And in Pennsylvania, which unfortunately for Mr Madan's hypothesis, was from the first, and was continued to be, the most flourishing of them all, no man was compellable to support *any* religion, yet there never was any want of religion, or of good morals, in that province.

All the states of America are now in the same situation. They have no national religion at all. In that respect every man does *what is right in his own eyes*, and all persons without distinction are admissible to every civil office; and yet they see no cause to apprehend that ruin and destruction which Mr. Madan forebodes will be the consequence of the dissolution of *our* national establishment. Since their emancipation from the power of this country, the North Americans . . . wisely avoid everything like the *ecclesiastical part* of [our constitution], as the clergy always affect to speak.

If these establishments of Christianity were so *necessary* as Mr. Madan represents, the American States could not have subsisted a single year without one; and in the late unsettled state of their civil government, when the ecclesiastical constitution was certainly as Mr. Madan himself would say, most wanted, they found no want of it at all. They have now done without one, in a state independent of England, fourteen years, and for anything that appears, they may do as well four score, or four hundred years.

He concluded by asking why Englishmen could not manage without a state church if similar men in America could.[61]

A year later Priestley's view of the establishment had become even more severe and his tones more strident. In his *Letters to Burke*, written to refute his former friend's *Reflections on the Revolution in France*, the alliance between church and state had degenerated into nothing more than "a league between two parties in the state against the common liberties of the country."[62] There were compensations, for an alliance of the state with such a weak partner as the Church of England would either collapse or be dissolved, and Priestley claimed that the Dissenters' only goal was to achieve a peaceful separation. America provided once more an appropriate model: "Happy is such a country as America, where no such alliance as that of church and state was ever formed, where no such unnatural mixture of ecclesiastical and civil polity was ever made. They see our errors and wisely avoid them. We may also see them, but when it will be too late."[63] Nevertheless, he had little doubt that following the American example, all the governments of the world would in due course confine themselves to matters of civil concern. In turn, truth of all kinds would be triumphant, the true principles of civil government and universal peace would prevail.[64] Declarations such as this made Priestley an object of popular hatred and one of the most vilified men of his day. He closed his attack on Burke's defense of religious establishments by quoting from David Ramsay's *History of the American Revolution*. Ramsay had pointed out that one of the features of the new American governments was their abolition of religious establishments and severing of the alliance between church and state; the world, he had declared, would soon see the consequences of such an experiment and would be able to decide whether the happiness of society was increased or diminished by the absence of establishments. Priestley added that the experiment was sufficiently large to be valid and that the result might be expected in a reasonable length of time.[65]

After the failure of the third motion in the House of Commons the Dissenters virtually gave up any active attempt to secure repeal for a generation. This did not mean that they had come to terms with the apparatus of discriminatory legislation or that they had abandoned hope of introducing a system of religious liberty that went beyond the limited right to freedom of conscience and the free exercise of religion. The French Revolution encouraged them onward in this direction—especially the intellectuals among them —but the example of America remained a potent supplement to abstract rights and theoretical justifications. In part it became increasingly attractive as a refuge for the victims of religious persecution, but this was only one element. The American system was attractive even to moderates such as the liberal Anglican Wyvill who felt that however strong was their commitment to religious toleration, its lessons were not necessarily applicable to England. It demonstrated that religion could perform its necessary meliorative functions through the agency of the community at large without the need for privileged establishments, that equality among the sects reduced the conflict among them, and that leaving the human mind free and unfettered enabled the Christian religion to demonstrate its truth without the assistance of a civil magistrate.[66]

The Dissenters' perception of the extent of religious liberty in America, which they so enthusiastically regarded as a notable success, may not always have accorded fully with the realities of the situation, but this was not the point. They did not observe the American scene in a spirit of academic disinterestedness nor were they concerned solely with the welfare of the Americans themselves though they certainly wished them well. They were asking, implicitly or explicitly, what relevance the American experience had for England and for them and were selecting those elements that seemed appropriate. Faced with a powerful and seemingly intractable opponent in the Church of England, they needed encouragement from the successes of others, and, more important, they needed empirical evidence that their theoretical principles of religious liberty and the separation of church from state were operable. Such evidence could be invaluable both for their own self-justification and in their vain attempts to persuade their opponents, when they applied for relief, that they need not fear its consequences, or, after the event, of the folly of resistance. All this evidence, if not absolutely essential to the argument in favor of religious liberty, came very close to being so, and could be provided by the American Revolution. As the early historians of Dissent put it, the Revolution was important because of the "connection which dissenters had with ministers and people of that country, and the interest they felt in the unhappy contest; its influence on the cause of religious liberty throughout the civilised world; and the many important lessons which by placing the citizens of America in a state respecting religion unknown before, it has taught and is still teaching mankind."[67]

# 8

## A Middle Way

After 1789 nothing could be the same. Revolution in France convulsed all Europe for a generation. Social upheaval, political turmoil, bloodshed, and war spread in greater or lesser degree throughout the western world from the gates of Moscow to the American frontier. England was fortunate in avoiding revolution within its own shores, but did not escape entirely unscarred. Fear of contagion from foreign revolution moved Pitt's government to a policy of harsh repression; spies, informers, trumped-up charges, and savage sentences gave expression to a deep-seated alarm among the orthodox. This reaction was totally opposite from the excitement the French Revolution generated in the minds of radicals. Whether they had been agitating for reform for years or were artisans engaging in politics for the first time, it seemed like a triumphant vindication of their most cherished principles. Joseph Priestley spoke for all commonwealth radicals when he declared in 1791, "How glorious, then, is the prospect, the reverse of all the past, which is now opening upon us, and upon the world. Government we may now expect to see, not only in theory, and in books, but in actual practice, calculated for the general good, and taking no more upon it than the general good requires; leaving all men the enjoyment of as many of their *natural rights* as possible, and no more interfering with matters of religion, with men's notions concerning God, and a future state than with philosophy or medicine."[1] A year later the Sheffield Constitutional Society brought out five or six thousand workingmen to celebrate the victory of the sans-culotte army at Valmy.[2] In some respects, though, this unity of response among old and new radicals was misleading. While the two groups were united in many ways, in others they were fundamentally different, and these differences were apparent in their response to revolutions overseas.

In spite of the more immediate attraction of events across the Channel, America was not forgotten. Although new men were joining the ranks of English radicalism and the number of Commonwealthmen was being depleted by death, in some ways the model of the American Revolution became more important, not less, during the 1790s. Many of the new recruits were artisans and tradesmen whose social status dictated fresh political conceptualizations and objectives—in brief, they were lighting the torch of working-class radicalism—but their ideology remained partly dependent on elements derived from the older tradition. Like the Commonwealthmen, they were encouraged by the existence of the American republic. Both groups placed it firmly in the sequence of international revolution which had come to a grand climax in France, saw it as a haven from oppression, and had direct connections with America, especially through Thomas Paine. From this point their understandings diverged. The new men were particularly impressed with the egalitarianism they believed to be inherent in American society, though they did not overlook other aspects of its political life. In contrast, the older radicals continued to attach greater importance to its libertarianism; to them America represented a middle path between conservatism and the democratic extremism represented by the later excesses of the French Revolution.[3]

The new generation of radicals was born in December 1791. In that month a group of artisans formed a Constitutional Society in the new industrial town of Sheffield, marking the distinction between "old" and "new" radicalism. Shortly afterward, and probably partly in emulation of the Yorkshiremen, the London Corresponding Society (LCS), "composed chiefly of tradesmen and shopkeepers," was founded, followed by other societies similar to a greater or lesser degree, in Manchester, Birmingham, Stockport, Norwich, and elsewhere.[4] During the same period the SCI, founded by Commonwealthmen a decade earlier, was captured by men clearly more advanced in their views. This new form of radicalism appeared to have been born fully grown. In reality it was formed by the conjunction of many small streams whose origins can be traced back far beyond 1789: to some of the supporters of John Wilkes and, in a different form, to the Gordon rioters of 1780, for example. Some of the new societies included rich men, such as Thomas Walker of Manchester, but they sought to advance the interests of the lower orders, and they introduced a new element by demanding social change as well as political reformation. When the Birmingham Society for Constitutional Information told readers of a broadsheet, "*You have rights equal to all*," they were saying nothing that was in itself new; what was remarkable was that they were addressing workmen.[5] A chasm had opened in English political life, extending to the structure of radicalism.

Preservation of liberty was the central object of the old radicals; promotion of equality was the aim of the new. The two concepts had been linked for generations, but the new radicals moved the emphasis so much more onto equality that their view of politics can be considered as a new conceptualization. Led by manufacturers, the Manchester men went least far along the path; they insisted on an equality of rights, which meant that all men were equally entitled to benefits that would enable them to start fairly in the race of life, but denied that they sought to institute equality of property and urged that there should be no more talk of leveling. The London Corresponding Society took the intentions of the new radicals a stage further. They repudiated "so wild and detestable a sentiment" as the equalization of property, but argued that they were "friends of *Civil Liberty* and therefore to *natural Equality*, both of which we consider as the Rights of Mankind."[6] And they understood that social equality required acknowledgment of equal rights, equal laws for the security of those rights (including particularly equal representation), and above all, administration of the law in such a way that the poor would be protected from the rich and vice versa.

If the reports of a government informer are to be believed, the views of the new members of the SCI were yet more advanced. At a dinner attended by about one hundred and fifty persons in April 1793 (long after the majority of commonwealth radicals had left the society), many of those present were certain that a revolution would soon take place in England and a toast was proposed: "May government soon cease to be a conspiracy of the few for the rights of the many."[7] John Thelwall, son of a silk mercer but also one of the ablest theorists of the LCS, declared himself bluntly to be "a Republican, a Downright *Sans Culotte*"; his lectures had strong overtones of class antagonism, and he attacked the aristocracy for its wealth and power and its corrupt manipulation of government. For him the time for action had come.[8] These, however, were the rumblings of extremists. Few among the new artisan radicals, not even Thelwall, were prepared to go as far as Thomas Evans, who reformulated Thomas Spence's scheme of communal property into a program of land nationalization. Nor did the subterranean ramblings about arming and drilling, referred to at the treason trials of 1794, represent anything more than the actions of a miniscule minority; far more typical was the declaration of the LCS that "peaceful reform, and not tumultory revolts" was their intention.[9]

The importance of the developments that took place during the 1790s cannot be underestimated. An entirely new class of actors had marched onto the stage of English politics, expressing views that were often very different from those of the old radicals and frequently repugnant to them. As yet this new radicalism was undeveloped. It made less use of the circumstances of an urban and industrial society than it was to do in the nineteenth century though it did consciously attempt to set out the distinctive interests of the lower orders and place them in juxtaposition to those of their social superiors. Whether the improvements and changes the new men envisioned were to be accomplished by armed revolution or by steady amelioration, they were all predicated on fundamental changes in the social order. Here was an ideology that could offer far more nourishment to an embryonic working-class movement in the nineteenth century than could the more circumscribed arguments of the Commonwealthmen.

The social origins and advanced nature of the new radicalism should not be permitted to obscure its connections with more traditional forms. Much of its ideology was a logical extension of the Commonwealthmen's insistence on liberty rephrased to meet the needs of a new class, and it stood firmly in the line of the ancient constitution and commonwealth heritage. Thomas Hardy, shoemaker, secretary, and organizer of the LCS, had read extensively in the earlier tracts of the SCI (given him by Brand Hollis) and pamphlets by Sharp, Cartwright, Jebb, and Price. His society was organized on the basis of the Anglo-Saxon system of tithings (derived perhaps from Sharp); it talked about the restoration of annual elections and equal representation and regarded Magna Carta as declaratory of the English constitution. Joseph Gerrald, a propagandist who was transported to Botany Bay after the Edinburgh Convention of 1793, looked back nostalgically to the golden days of Alfred and recapitulated the mythology of the imposition of the Norman yoke. Henry Yorke invoked the spirit of Hampden, Russell, Pym, Vane, and especially Sydney, and lauded the merits of the ancient constitution. Similarly, Thomas Spence's periodical *Pig's Meat* was stuffed with numerous extracts from the commonwealth canon, as was a collection published under the title *Manual of Liberty*.[10]

Radical connections with America continued throughout the 1790s, albeit on a somewhat diminished scale. With a few notable exceptions, they were sustained almost entirely by members of the older radical group. Some continued to correspond with American friends—Brand Hollis exchanged letters with Adams, and Sharp wrote to Rush and others—but this line of communication was seriously attenuated with the deaths in 1791 of Price and of Catharine Macaulay. Later in the decade the reports of recent emigrants became an increasingly important source of information on the condition of American society. Fewer Americans were in England than in the previous decade, though Sharp held long conversations with John Jay and Charles Pinckney, and Brand Hollis talked to Benjamin Trumbull as well as to Jay; in neither case did any significant political consequences follow.[11] Elhanan Winchester, the Universalist preacher, had been in London for several years and established contacts with several Dissenters; in 1792 he felt it his duty to give an oration commemorating the tercentenary of the discovery of the Americas. In his address, which he later reprinted at his own expense, he reinforced the argument that America was the birthplace of civil and religious liberty and could teach the world several valuable lessons. American experience, he argued, demonstrated that a large country could be ruled by a republican government without need for monarchy or aristocracy, that equality among religious sects was the wisest policy, and that the milder the government the more happy the people and so the stronger it was.[12] The new radicals had fewer personal connections. Thomas Hardy had supplied Adams's son-in-law William Smith with boots and shoes during the eighties. One American visitor to travel in the provinces was John Francis; he met several members of the radical groups in Sheffield and Manchester, but refused to discuss politics (English or American) on the grounds that he was a foreigner. Untypically, Gerrald had spent several years in Pennsylvania, an experience reflected in his writings.[13]

If radical connections with America were thin in numbers, they were not in qualitative terms. Two Americans actively contributed to the reform movement and sought to impress on it the lessons of American experience; one was Joel Barlow of Connecticut, the other was the most brilliant and provocative radical of his generation, Thomas Paine. Barlow had arrived in England on business in 1788, having already dispatched a copy of his poem *The Vision of Columbus* in the hope that it would be reprinted in London. Paine had preceded him by a year, having become to all intents an American during the War of Independence. Both were well acquainted with radicals old and new, and both later played an active part in the French Revolution before returning to the United States.

Few American publications appeared in London after 1789. Some official publications of Congress and other branches of the federal government were reprinted, and American papers seem to have circulated fairly widely among the better-off, supplemented by the occasional political tract and addresses such as Adams's Fourth of July oration of 1793 and David Ramsay's of the following year. A sign of the times was that when John Quincy Adams's *Letters to Paine* were printed in London they had been given to Stockdale by a government official.[14] Ironically, one of the difficulties facing Americans who wished to reprint their work in London was the practice of pirating; one victim was Jeremy Belknap, who discovered that William Winterbotham, the Plymouth Baptist minister, had incorporated much of his work in his *Historical View of the United States*.[15] Toward the middle of the decade a new source of information concerning the United States became available in England: formal reports on America as an area suitable for emigration written by men such as Harry Toulmin, son of the Taunton minister, who later became Kentucky secretary of state. Not all the reports and comments were favorable, and to some extent radicals' knowledge and understanding depended on memories of the past, but in general the image remained attractive, at least until news of the crisis over the Alien and Sedition Acts reached England.

One consequence of retaining the American Revolution in the radicals' memory at a time when domestic issues were imposing severe imperatives on the growth of radicalism was confirmation of its international status. Radicals had consistently repudiated the judgment that the Revolution was little more than a local crisis and were convinced that what they believed to be the triumph of liberty in America had a relevance beyond the shores of the United States. The outbreak of revolution in France appeared to vindicate this article of faith, besides many others, for it seemed to demonstrate the validity of the idea of human progress. At times the French Revolution seemed to have a magnitude infinitely greater than any other, but at least the American Revolution had the honor of being its precursor. Price was delighted that the principles adumbrated in his pamphlet of advice to America appeared to be in the process of implementation in France. He asked, "What gratitude is due to the American states for the resistance and that diffusion of just sentiments in the subject of government which have led the way to this Revolution?"[16] Such opinions were held by many radicals. As Priestley insisted, American liberty was the parent of French liberty, and the experience of actual events was worth more than a thousand treatises; America's example was its vital contribution to the new era. Brand Hollis wrote, "The glorious revolutions in America & France have propagated truths which will never be extinguished for Truth is like a spark of Fire which flyeth up in the face of those who attempt to tread it out."[17] The Revolution Society delineated most clearly the bloodstock line that had come to such noble maturity in France: "What Plato finely imagined, Harrington nobly planned; Rousseau improved and added character; and you generous Frenchmen! agreeing with Locke, that where law ends Tyranny begins and being stimulated by the resistance the English Nation made to Tyrants, and seizing the sacred flame of Liberty from America, have magnanimously brought it into execution."[18]

This memory played a far smaller part in the ideology of the new radicals than the old, yet it was by no means dead. The LCS—with the approval of the SCI—spoke of a triple alliance of the people of America, France, and Britain, and many individuals saw a causal relationship between the two revolutions. William Godwin, the radical theorist, put the American Revolution in the context of a transatlantic movement, William Winterbotham insisted at his trial that France had attempted in Europe what had been so successfully achieved in America, and Charles Pigott, a vigorously class-conscious and frequently libelous pamphleteer, declared that the American Revolution operated as an example to France and the French Revolution would operate with equal effect on England.[19] From a man like Pigott the potential implications of such an opinion were far more extreme than they would have been from one of the older radicals, and they give a hint of the different uses to which the two groups would put the American experience. It was hardly surprising that he was prosecuted for seditious libel.

One of America's most central responsibilities during the 1790s was its function as a haven for the oppressed. Several Revolutionary leaders had enunciated the obligation a decade earlier, but relatively few Englishmen had taken it up before 1790. The steady trickle of emigrants during the 1780s (among whom Burke's friend Richard Champion of Bristol was perhaps the most notable) had seldom been motivated by political considerations.[20] But the stream gathered strength and changed character after 1791 when the bitter pamphlet war over Priestley's ecclesiastical views and the Birmingham riots made many Dissenters feel they were the object of official persecution as well as popular hostility. By 1793 the desire to emigrate was widespread, and as government attacks on individual liberty intensified, so did the importance of America as "an asylum to the virtuous & distrest where the long hands of Tyrants cannot reach." Liverpool boats sailing for Pennsylvania carried many refugees, and in March 1795 Lindsey reported that he knew of five American ships filled with parties of Englishmen.[21] Both new and old radicals were affected; Priestley, Thomas Cooper of Bolton, Joseph Gales of Sheffield, and John Binns were only a few who fled to America. Many others such as Hardy, Gilbert Wakefield, who was later prosecuted for blasphemy, and the unfortunate Thomas Fysshe Palmer who was transported to Australia, thought about emigration but did not leave.[22]

At this point, the task of the American Revolution might be thought complete as far as English radicalism was concerned, but it was not. As a preliminary to the French Revolution its function was necessarily confined, and it could operate only at a remove in England. It was a much-needed haven for particular victims of oppression, but did nothing to advance the cause of radicalism; indeed Charles Marsh, a Norwich radical, argued that "departure to America was a gross violation of the duty to stay and check the precipitate degeneracy of the age."[23] But as a model of political behavior its importance was far from spent, and it continued to make a positive contribution to the development of the increasingly divergent ideologies of old and new radicalism.

The new radicals had less concern with America than did the Commonwealthmen. Evidence of their interest is scattered, often rather thinly, across dozens of pamphlets and journals and in the mass of documents seized by government agents. References to America were fewer than in the writings of the old radicals; there were none, for example, in the correspondence of the various societies and in the minute books and addresses of the London Corresponding Society. But the relative paucity of references must be judged in a wider context and is perhaps misleading. Allusions to the French Revolution were also remarkably few considering its proximity in distance and time.

Reasons for such insularity are not hard to find. The intellectual range of the new men was more limited than that of the old. Necessarily their attention was directed largely to the English circumstances and affairs that created the new societies and impinged on them with the force of immediacy. Nor was there any prohibiting reason why their battles could not have been fought exclusively with English weapons. Radical artisans shared with their fellow countrymen a confidence in the superiority of Englishmen over all foreigners and, in spite of the universality of their principles and their dedication to a common cause, their attitudes held a latent strain of xenophobia. Only a faint element of doubt appears in the LCS remark, "If it be true that the People of Britain are superior to other nations. . . ."[24] Although they felt a community of interest and brotherhood with the revolutionaries in France, their emotion was not as intense as that of the Commonwealthmen toward their American friends. And in this respect America's standing was more limited. Its revolution had already entered radical mythology as a peculiarly abhorrent civil war and a demonstration of the consequences of rule by an unrepresentative and corrupt regime, but the actual events had taken place a decade earlier, their impact was somewhat diminished, and the friendships and connections to keep it fresh were fewer.[25]

Joel Barlow and Thomas Paine brought to the new radical movement direct experience of the American Revolution and a powerful enthusiasm for its wider importance. Barlow had moved in radical circles for some time, but only in 1792 with the publication of his tract, *Advice to the Privileged Orders in the Several States of Europe*, did he reach prominence. In his tract he insisted on the general relevance of American experience to the European situation and lamented that the example of American republicanism was too little known to carry great weight. He argued that the obviously different circumstances of America had encouraged Europeans to imagine additional differences and so prevented their application of principles founded in nature and not dependent on variations between countries. Besides, he insisted, European poverty and ignorance were the effects, not the cause, of slavery. Offering his advice to the old world in general, he stressed the importance of an equality of rights as existed in America. Bringing the argument of the American model directly to bear on the politics of English radicalism, he declared that it demonstrated the operation of the very principles enunciated by Price in his notorious *Discourse on the Love of Our Country*: the people of America "are in the habit of *'choosing their own governors'*, of *'cashiering them for misconduct'*, of *'framing a government for themselves.'* "[26]

For a short time, Barlow was an active participant in radical agitation. John Horne Tooke, who was picking up the threads of an erratic political career, was impressed by his pamphlet and secured his election to the Society for Constitutional Information.

Never backward in disseminating his opinions, Barlow presented copies of his various political tracts to the LCS and the Association of Friends of the People as well as the SCI.[27] In November 1792 he was appointed to the committee that prepared the SCI's address to the French National Convention and was responsible for the drafting of its text. It was the only SCI address to France that incorporated any reference to America, and the marks of Barlow's pretentious rhetoric were clearly evident. He was also appointed to join John Frost, one of the most active of the new members of the SCI, in forming a delegation to present the address to the convention, but thereafter faded from the world of London radicalism.[28] At best his contribution to English radicalism was minor, though he did help to keep America as an active ingredient in its argumentation.

Thomas Paine was altogether more influential. In many ways an American, he had remained an Englishman, and it was largely through his writings that the lessons of the American Revolution were refracted to the new radicals. He had arrived in England with a ready-made reputation based on *Common Sense* and had quickly made contacts with a wide range of politicians from Edmund Burke and the old Shelburne set to more advanced Commonwealthmen such as Brand Hollis. With the appearance of his *Rights of Man*, the first part of which came out in 1791 and the second in 1792, his English reputation as a vigorous proponent of American independence was extended to fame as a brilliant and iconoclastic advocate of extreme political and social reform.

The first part of *Rights of Man* was a success, the second a triumph. In sparkling prose and dazzling argument Paine transformed the terms of English radicalism. Much of his analysis was as concerned with constitutionalism and political rights as the arguments of the Commonwealthmen had been, so many of them welcomed his book. His argumentation was distinguished from theirs by the ruthlessness with which he stripped away the inessential paraphernalia from their rhetoric, exposed the bare essentials of their natural rights philosophy, and reconstructed a fresh and vastly different superstructure on their foundations. In particular he developed the concept of equality to an extent that they had been unwilling to do. This emphasis on equality led him to hypothecate the existence of two distinct classes in society (those who paid taxes and those who received and lived on them) whose political interests were in conflict, and in the final chapter of Part II he expounded a system of taxation and social policy that presaged an almost total restructuring of society. Thus, although his various pamphlets were not specifically addressed to the lowest orders to the exclusion of those of higher standing, his *Rights of Man* provided an ideological basis for a working-class movement. In E. P. Thompson's words, "Few of Paine's ideas were original. . . . What he gave to English people was a new rhetoric of radical egalitarianism, which touched the deepest responses of the 'free-born Englishman' and which penetrated the subpolitical attitudes of the urban working people."[29]

In Part I, which he began before the publication of Burke's *Reflections* and adapted to rebut his erstwhile friend's charges, Paine defended the actions of the revolutionaries in France and laid the philosophical groundwork of his argument. His first theoretical postulate was a declaration of faith that men enjoyed natural rights that originated a priori at the moment of their creation. At one stroke he had assaulted Burke's theory of an organic society integrally connected with generations past and future, thus rendering his doctrine of precedent nugatory, and made the old radicals' model of an ancient constitution redundant. Paine added as a corollary to his system the proposition that each individual and generation philosophically participated in an independent accession of rights. He insisted on the unity of mankind, a concept to which he gave a distinctly more egalitarian tone than his predecessors had been willing to do. By it he meant that men were "of *one degree*" and so born equal and the possessors of equal natural rights. By natural rights he meant those which appertained to man's very existence, as distinct from the civil rights he enjoyed as a member of society. In return men had two obligations, one to God and the other to do unto his neighbor as he would be done by. His version of the contractual basis of legitimate government differed from that of John Locke in emphasizing that the compact was formed between groups of individuals, not between individuals and government. Following partly from this, Paine also emphasized the distinction between constitutions and governments and legislation; the operative function of a constitution was superior to that of a government for it enshrined the basic matrix of society's rights and principles. And being brutally unfair to Burke's argument (not for the first time), he declared that since no one could produce a formal English constitution, none existed.[30]

Up to this point America had played little part in Paine's exposition, though the brief recapitulation of its principal elements is sufficient to demonstrate that they had been nourished by the experience of his years in the United States. Almost all his supporting evidence was drawn from recent French experience, and the only use he made of the American model was brief references to its religious liberty, republicanism, and equality of rights. Otherwise its principal function lay in its relationship to the revolution in France; he declared, "What we now see in the world, from the Revolutions of America and France, are a renovation of the natural order of things, a system of principles as universal as truth and the existence of man, and combining moral with political happiness and national prosperity."[31]

Paine's book was well received among radicals. Members of the Society for Constitutional Information who had already elected him an honorary member and most of whom were still moderates, approved it and published a broadsheet commending it.[32] The tract sold well, at three shillings, and was not so outrageous or incendiary that the government thought it necessary to take any action. A year later the second part appeared. It delighted the new radicals (though it distressed many of the Commonwealthmen) and provoked a massive outburst of government anger. It also offered the most systematic analysis of the relevance of the American Revolution since Price's pamphlet on the subject almost a decade earlier.

From the opening paragraphs of its introduction to the close of the analytical chapters, Part II of *Rights of Man* was dominated by the example of America. Moreover, the use to which Paine put it was distinctive and even startling. He was passionately devoted to the success of the French Revolution as well as that of his "beloved America," but in constructing an argument that would have universal application at one level and relevance to England at another, the use he made of the two revolutions was quite different. His treatment of events in France in Part I was essentially defensive in face of Burke's assault (they were hardly mentioned in Part II) and reflected the emotion of the moment. When, after further consideration, he drew out the implications of his theoretical premises and sought to demonstrate their empirical validity he turned to America, not France. Moving directly to the core of the matter, he declared with his customary vividness of imagery, "What Archimedes said of the mechanical powers, may be applied to Reason and Liberty: '*Had we*,' said he, '*a place to stand upon*, we might raise the world.' The revolution of America presented in politics what was only theory in mechanics."[33] Such mechanistic metaphors were common among radicals rather than original, but Paine paved the way for an unusually advanced deployment of the American Revolution in the context of what he had referred to as the "revolution of the world."

Paine saw by instinct and logic that if any attempt was to be made to relate the American experience to European (and particularly English) circumstances reference only to its physical and social situation would be insufficient. America was indeed fortunate in its position and was the only place in the world where the principles of universal reform could develop, but the liberality of its society stemmed only partly from its environmental advantages. Similarly, as he so sharply perceived, "the independence of America, considered merely as a separation from England, would have been a matter but of little importance, had it not been accompanied by a revolution in the principles and practices of governments."[34] What the Revolution did, Paine argued, was to create a government founded on moral theory, universal peace, and the indefeasible hereditary rights of man. In spite of its heterogeneous population, American society was harmonious because the construction of its government on proper principles of society and the rights of man brought all elements into harmonious unity. Condemning hereditary government as an imposition on mankind and insisting on the sole legitimacy of republicanism, he pointed to the United States, whose government was based wholly on representation, as the only true republic in existence. Its principles were moving from west to east, and he advanced the conjunction of a superstructure of representation built on a foundation of democracy in explicit terms as a model for the modern world.[35]

Having enunciated his basic principles, Paine developed his analysis of legitimate government a stage further and incorporated a substantial body of supporting evidence. Taking up points he had made in Part I, he argued that although no single form of republic was acceptable, still republican principles could be defined more exactly; above all, he insisted, it was essential to distinguish between a society's constitution and the functions of its government. He indicated the necessary processes by which the principles should be implemented by citing at length the examples of his own former state of Pennsylvania, the drafting of the Articles of Confederation, and the work of the Philadelphia Convention of 1787. Drawing on this experience, Paine suggested that several elements were necessary: a special convention summoned for the sole purpose of drafting a constitution, the drafting of the constitution itself that should incorporate a declaration of rights and define the structure of government, and a procedure for amending the constitution to meet the changing requirements of successive generations. In the case of the Pennsylvania constitution of 1776, he declared, "We see a regular process—a government issuing out of a constitution, formed by the people in their original character; and that constitution serving not only as an authority, but as a law of control to the government."[36] He believed that England had no constitution, that its derivation of authority from precedent was vile and nonsensical, its system of representation a farce, and many of its laws tyrannical and their administration problematical. Thus the creation of a just society consistent with the rights of man required the execution of a far-reaching program of radical social reform, which he expounded in a final chapter of "ways and means." The opportunities facing England in 1792 were great, and since America was so far away, France was the principal standard-bearer of freedom in Europe.[37] But in matters of reformation, America, not France, was the most appropriate model.

The second part of *Rights of Man* was an even greater success than its predecessor. It circulated with extreme rapidity among the new radical groups in Manchester, Sheffield, Norwich, and elsewhere and was warmly welcomed as a work of the highest importance. In London the SCI, which one report said it revitalized, resolved to contribute its utmost assistance to Paine (largely in the interests of freedom of the press), but discreetly declined an offer of £1,000 from his profits. A proclamation against seditious writings was intended to suppress the pamphlet, but had the opposite effect, and when Paine learned that a prosecution was imminent he arranged for the publication of a cheap edition. By Christmas, Paine had retreated to France and Messrs. Chamberlayne and White, the Treasury Solicitors, were frantically chasing copies all over the country and seeking assistance in the prosecution of those concerned in circulating Paine's alleged libels on the constitution. Hundreds of thousands of copies were sold within a few years. To supplement them, five editions and ten variants of *Common Sense* were published between 1791 and 1793, and the SCI distributed twelve thousand copies of his *Letter to Secretary Dundas*.[38] Many others than conservatives found his more extreme views repugnant; but the artisans and new men entering the political scene considered Paine's works not only a new version of society, but an ideological system that could sustain their efforts to achieve it.

Other ideologues of artisan radicalism attached a somewhat different emphasis to the various components of American experience. As a group they had a more diffuse and attenuated understanding of its nature than Paine or the older Commonwealthmen, as shown by the uses to which they put it in the development of their rhetoric. In general their remarks were less sharp and perceptive and display the marks of mythologizing much more clearly than did those of the other radicals. Where Paine, as a participant, had drawn sustenance directly from American political action and argued its primacy over the more obvious advantages derived by the United States from its environment, their interpretation was a conflux of the two and placed greater emphasis on the environment. Also, in crucial distinction from the old radicals, they called upon America to fulfill and validate the criteria of an advanced egalitarian model.

At its simplest, America revived the memory of a pastoral utopia for new radicals as well as old. It was a land of opportunity in which infant industry promised the intending immigrant abundant riches, and the fertile soil, the agreeable climate, and pleasing prospect were irresistibly attractive.[39] Thelwall, who claimed to speak for the desperately poor and condemned the generation of property as corrupting, introduced a note that was both sharp and sour when he remarked that the American people had too much veneration for property, religion, and law. His acerbity was unusual, but even he conceded that the condition of laborers was better than in England, for in America "every hired cultivator is enabled, by tolerable diligence and sobriety, to become, in time, a master and proprietor himself; and servitude is not, of moral necessity the life estate of any man."[40] More common were the views of Joseph Gerrald, who had spent several years in Pennsylvania before returning to England and becoming one of the leading theoreticians of the LCS. To him America was not only a garden of Eden, but a society whose structure and values were the antithesis of those current in England. More important, he drew from his own observations certain conclusions that incorporated a harsh note of class awareness. "In America," he declared, "that country which God and man have concurred to render the blissful habitation of abundance and of peace, the poor are not broken down by taxes to support the expensive trappings of royalty, or to pamper the luxury of an insolent nobility. No lordly peer tramples down the corn of husbandmen, no proud prelate wrings from him the tythe of his industry. They have neither chicanery in ermine, nor hypocracy in lawn. The community is not there divided into an oppressed peasantry and an overgrown aristocracy, the one of whom lives by the plunder of the state, while the others are compelled to be the object of it. Plenty is the lot of all, superfluity of none."[41] In essence, Gerrald was describing the same social phenomena as Price a decade earlier, but he was placing the accent in a different place and using American experience to support a class-oriented ideology alien to the social mores of the Commonwealthmen.

Social egalitarianism merged into a political radicalism more explicitly advanced than that of the Commonwealthmen. Price's notorious remarks about America as a country with no bishops and no kings were misleading and untypical of himself and his friends; Henry Yorke's citation of the United States as a society of equal rank and privilege which had discovered "that the sun will shine & the grass grow without Kings or lords" was far more central to the ideology of new radicalism.[42] Moreover, it had also become an explicit model of formal republicanism. In 1794, Thomas Spence printed a new song titled "The Americans Happy without the Assistance of Royal Proclamations." One verse went:

America, behold! O happy, happy, clime;
Her triumphs will be told, until the end of time!
There liberty is law,
And joy o'erspreads each cheek,
No more 'tis "vive le roi!"
But "vive la REPUBLIQUE!"[43]

Similarly, for Thomas Cooper the American success demonstrated the uselessness of hereditary privileges, and for Charles Pigott the number thirteen stood as a symbol for the United States, which "like all good Republics, renounced the bug-bear of royalty."[44]

In short, America was an eyesore to the despots of Europe for it was "the sole monument of equal freedom on earth."[45] To a man like John Oswald, who openly advocated revolution in England, the emancipation of America, together with other independence movements, and the fall of the Bastille indicated that the human soul was awakening from a long lethargy. William Vaughan, author of *The Catechism of Man*, insisted that the best form of government was that which promoted the people's prosperity and happiness in the "highest degree and at the least expense"; it required that laws should be made by those whose conduct was to be regulated, taxes imposed by those who were to pay them, and any person of the necessary talent should be able to rise to the highest office regardless of his occupation or religion. These privileges could only be found in the United States, where the best form of government had flourished since the break with England and the Constitution arose from the will of the people. On occasion American experience could be drawn upon to bolster specific radical policies—as Felix Vaughan cited the beneficent effects of conventions in America when defending Daniel Eaton against a charge of seditious libel—but this was unusual.[46] Most commonly it was deployed in general terms to rebut the constantly reiterated claim that innovation was dangerous. Henry Yorke, who was much impressed with the quality of American society and life, made the most explicit assertion of the point. He declared, "We are charged with broaching doctrines that are injurious, speculative and impracticable. But our enemies have in no instance pointed out what injury would accrue from these doctrines, where a good theory ought not to be practised, where theory & practice do not in any physical instance agree, nor have they asserted the truth, when they declare the doctrines impracticable. For America exists to give the lie direct to their assertions. She presents to us a pleasing & lively image of national felicity."[47]

Although Yorke and others incorporated into their arguments much that was familiar from the rhetoric of the old radicals, there were important differences in their application of American experience to English circumstances. In part the passage of time, the pressing needs of English society, and the eruption of the French Revolution had muted the folk memory of America, but the differences were more fundamental than this, for they went to the core of eighteenth-century radicalism. As the self-styled sans-culotte, Thelwall acutely noticed a distinct and notable difference in the social status of those who were impressed by the American and the French Revolutions: "In the former instance, it was the gentry, the optimacy [sic], the aristocratic interest that moved—that agitated, and conducted everything; in the latter, the great body of the people—the *common mass*, had the audacity to judge for themselves, and inquired into the nature of their rights."[48] Even after allowing for hyperbole, there remained more than a grain of truth in Thelwall's remarks and as reflected in the demands imposed by the two groups on the American Revolution. The new men called upon it to strengthen their advocacy of social leveling and (to the annoyance of the government) an abrasive republicanism; it implied a fundamental reconstruction of society. These objectives were anathema to the old radicals for they went far beyond their own intentions. Instead, for Commonwealthmen the American Revolution took on a new and rather different significance.

During the 1790s the Commonwealthmen used American experience to redress these extremist tendencies. By the middle of the decade many old radicals were appalled by the "horrible excesses" of the French Revolution; they remained convinced, however, that such an example did not invalidate the desirability of moderate parliamentary reform at home.[49] As members of the established ranks of society they expected their social inferiors to accept in broad terms its existing structure—for the lower orders to do so was in their own interest as peace, law, order, and public tranquillity benefited all members of society. When they yearned for a pastoral society based on equitable landholdings, they did not argue for the class-oriented changes demanded by some of the new men; rather, their vision of an idyllic Eden was intended as a prophylactic against such an upheaval. Paine's proposals served as a catalyst, for the Commonwealthmen found the social implications of his philosophy alarming. Christopher Wyvill, one of the most cautious among the reformers but also a man of compassion committed to the principle of freedom of thought, strongly disapproved of the prosecution of Paine but feared that the extremists would take over the SCI. Wyvill found Paine's social views horrifying. Though he thought that Paine's offer of annuities to the poor from the estates of the rich would attract him much support among the lower orders, the combination of their anger and national distress on other accounts probably would be very destructive. Cartwright shared some of Wyvill's suspicions and worked hard to counteract Paine's republicanism, while Brand Hollis denied rumors that he saw *Rights of Man* prior to publication and reportedly refused Paine financial help when he was in difficulties.[50]

Their political objectives reflected these social concerns. Representation remained the key element in their thought, and although they differed on such matters as the extent of the franchise they remained moderate compared to the new men. In campaign tactics they preferred to attempt a junction with liberal parliamentarians rather than risk association with the artisans. Many, including Cartwright, Capel Lofft, and Brand Hollis, joined the Association of the Friends of the People, an aristocratic reform group whose main strength lay in the Foxite wing of the Whig party. The connection was an unhappy one for members of the society disapproved of the SCI in its new form and were uncomfortable with the LCS. Several, including Lord John Russell, withdrew in protest against Cartwright's presence in its ranks. In spite of their disagreements, old Commonwealthmen could agree that the principles of the English constitution were "admirably adapted to protect with equal justice the rights of the Peasant and the Peer" and that, as Wyvill put it, "a reformation temperate in its effect, & constitutional in its mode of accomplishment is the most likely way to prevent confusion; & of course to preserve our Constitution in all its parts."[51] For all the vehemence of their rhetoric, Price, Priestley, and other members of the unfortunately named Revolution Society (it commemorated the events of 1688) can still be placed among the moderates rather than with the new radicals. Their political credo (that all civil and political authority was derived from the people, that abuse of power justified resistance, and that the rights of the people including freedom of conscience, trial by jury, freedom of the press, and freedom of election) was restated with unusual vigor and frankness in Price's notorious *Discourse on the Love of Our Country* and aroused virulent hostility among the orthodox, but it contained nothing new, nor did it imply any extension of arguments that Commonwealthmen had held for generations. Propositions of this kind revolved around personal rights and did not require social change. The notable eccentric John Horne Tooke was forced to withdraw a motion to exclude peers from the Revolution Society, although not until after considerable altercation.[52]

Faced with conservative intransigence on one side and extreme radicalism on the other, the old radicals desperately needed an example of successful moderate reform. To find it they looked again to "the vast Plains of *America*, overspread with the peaceful Banners of triumphant Freedom."[53] Once again the United States provided a model of high moral conduct combined with political stability. Religion and morality, they believed, had taken deep root across the Atlantic. Already more advanced than England, America enjoyed the invaluable advantages of political, civil, and religious liberty and was led by men of humane and moderate character who had avoided the excesses of the French Revolution. These admirable social and personal qualities offered persuasive evidence that extremism and the Terror were avoidable, and pointed to an alternative path toward fulfillment of their objectives. In a vain attempt to persuade Pitt of the desirability of parliamentary reform, Wyvill argued that since liberty and equality in the United States had "produced the most happy tranquillity & good Order, it is evident that they are not principles necessarily destructive of the end for which Society was formed."[54] As Cartwright, who a decade earlier had stood in the vanguard of the reform movement and now occupied the middle ground without jettisoning any of his principles, remarked, the United States provided the established orders with a notable lesson "for teaching moderation in the exercise of power, and a sacred respect for the rights of the people."[55]

One obstacle to the deployment of America as a model of moderation was quickly removed. The old radicals found no indissoluble connection between the fundamental principles of American government and its republican institutions. Cartwright accepted the propriety of a government which included king and lords as well as commons. Wyvill found the notion of introducing a republic on American lines abhorrent, but still recognized the evident merits of the American political system and its manifest social virtues. Similarly, Price admired the United States Constitution but repudiated republicanism. Despite the accusations of his critics, Priestley still did not wish for a revolution to introduce republicanism into England even after spending several years in America and admiring the "wisdom and happiness of Republican governments."[56] As they had done in the past, so in the 1790s the Commonwealthmen saw America in the light of their own needs and principles and were discriminating in their application of the American model to English circumstances. In structural terms this increasingly meant following the Adams model in preference to the Pennsylvania model of a unicameral legislature because it seemed more appropriate to the social fabric of English society and provided a system of checks, though shortly before her death Catharine Macaulay told Washington that she had abandoned her preference for the American system in favor of the French unicameral model.[57]

In the work of the tireless Cartwright the function of America in the development of English radicalism can be most clearly observed. He had quickly established a reputation as one of the colonies' warmest friends in the 1770s, but at that time viewed America largely in the context of an imperial conflict. Like other radicals he conceived the United States as an asylum of liberty and though he discussed the Pennsylvania constitution at length, his use of it as a model was limited; for the most part he set it in the interstices of his own Anglocentric theory. By the end of the century his views had matured considerably, though their fundamentals remained constant. He saw America as a successful example of a reformed system of government and went beyond his previous position. This advance was possible because American political development, and particularly the federal Constitution of 1787, remained within the ideological tradition of commonwealth radicalism. He believed the United States Constitution shared the same roots as the pure English constitution and the case of America demonstrated that even if other constitutional orders were abolished, liberty, order, and good government might still be secure if a proper system of representation were intact. In this respect the independence of the United States was irrelevant, for "throwing off the English dominion, she changed the *other* English forms, as not essential; but she preserved *that* English form, on which political liberty absolutely depends."[58]

Some features of American practice were immediately attractive, and others were less obvious but went to the heart of English constitutionalism. Cartwright approved of the retention of English common law in the American states and cited the American militia as an instance of arming a nation on the ancient Saxon principle and the presidency as the nearest approximation to the Anglo-Saxon ideal; he also approved the American law of libel as derived from the Zenger case. These were not, however, central; what was fundamental was his conceptualization of the relationship between government and constitution. Here he was greatly influenced by the American model, and although he found much in the *Rights of Man* that was highly obnoxious, he was much impressed by Paine's formulation. Drawing on his American experience, Paine had distinguished between the functions of a constitution, which defined the basic laws and principles of the state, and of government, which operated under the general superintendence of the principles. Cartwright accepted this distinction and argued that the essential function of a constitution was to act as a law to hold the legislature to its duty as a trustee on behalf of the people, but to do no more. He disagreed with Paine's assertion that there was no such thing as an English constitution and insisted that it existed as a corpus of popular rights to which appeal could be made as in England in the seventeenth and in America in the eighteenth century when court despotism was unendurable.[59] By the end of the century Cartwright came to believe that this loose definition was inadequate and open to dispute; thereafter he devoted considerable energy to the propagation of a codified English constitution.

Cartwright's enthusiasm for a written constitution was fired partly by the example of the French constitution, but its original source was America. He lamented that Sir William Blackstone had failed to distinguish between laws and constitution in his *Commentaries*, but pointed out that he had composed his exposition of English law before the American Revolution. On that occasion, a people had systematically gone through the Lockean process of formulating a contractual structure of government; no similar attempt had been made before; and the Americans had been meticulous in distinguishing between the two forms of law, fundamental and municipal. As Cartwright put it, "The attention of mankind [was only] called up to the essential and eternal distinction between laws and constitutions, by the grand event on the theatre of *America*; where a people not 'tacitly', but 'expressly' drew up a constitution to be *a law to the legislature*, and to prevent the confusion, and the infinity of ill consequences resulting from a constitution being *undefined*."[60] In his judgment, a constitution should perform an appellate function by stating and enshrining the fundamental rights of the people (particularly those appertaining to representation) and providing a definitive criterion in instances of disagreement. Under such a system no unconstitutional legislation of any consequence could get on the statute book, and if any minor infringement occurred the offending legislation could be expunged speedily. Furthermore, the rigid separation of powers characteristic of the American constitutions, state as well as federal, prevented any conflict of interest in the minds of those who sought to serve two masters, the executive and the people, and would avert the reduction of English liberty brought about by the Triennial Act and parliamentary corruption. And there were benefits to be drawn from an intermediate body, the Senate, whose existence was dependent ultimately on the people, standing between the people and the executive.[61]

At the core of Cartwright's constitutional system was the principle of representation, and here again the American model had much to offer. Whatever the form of institution, no good government could exist without a sound and substantial representation because such representation was the essence of political liberty. Here, of course, was the nub of the debate among the various reformers of all shades and between them and their conservative critics. Cartwright firmly believed that concessions to the lower orders were necessary if an upheaval was to be averted. When men could see the improvement in representation on the

Continent following the original models of England and America, how could any Englishman wish to see his country's representation continue in its current morbid and paralyzed condition? When the advocates of an extension of the franchise attempted to argue their case, they were referred by critics such as Arthur Young to the unfortunate example of France. But, as Cartwright pointed out, there was an alternative example which could destroy the conservatives' argument. America had fifteen representative assemblies elected by a general suffrage which conferred on their communities "every blessing of good government; with *political liberty* in a degree of perfection never before attained on earth"; they demonstrated that representation based on personalty instead of property did not lead to anarchy, but was, if correctly understood, "the most complete specific against that popular phrenzy."[62]

Among the various systems of representation currently in operation, Cartwright believed the American system to be the most complete and so the most perfect. Although the suffrage was universal in only one or two states, political liberty was intended and understood to be universal; the ballot, which he had long advocated on the basis of Henry Laurens's reports of its success in South Carolina, was likewise almost universal. The system produced outstanding leaders such as Washington, and, just as the state legislatures were truly representative of their local communities, so Congress was truly representative of the states at large. In contrast, English elections were corrupt, expensive, and subject to influence; a county had little chance of securing the services of a representative of high quality. How long, Cartwright wondered in 1792, would Englishmen tolerate the shame of comparing their house of representatives with models as pure as those of America and France? Reform of the House of Commons was urgent or it would be necessary to say farewell to the liberty and former glory of the country. His arguments were ignored, and the desired reformation did not materialize. Four years later he declared, "It is high time we borrowed a leaf from the book of *American* practice."[63]

By the end of the century the United States and its revolution had become incorporated into the ideology of English radicalism. The image of America as a rich and fertile land, a haven for the victims of official persecution, and a model of political organization and conduct was still potent. Though men differed as to the emphasis they placed on various components in the American experience—Cartwright and the old radicals stressed its liberalism, the new men were attracted to its apparent egalitarianism—all could agree that it had relevance to their thought and argumentation. Necessarily and properly, radical ideology was molded primarily by domestic circumstances and requirements, but the example of overseas revolution was profoundly stimulating. Here America had a notable advantage, for the French Revolution was already speaking with a forked tongue. Some, especially among the new radicals, remained constant to their admiration for the French, but many, particularly among those who stood in the commonwealth tradition, were grievously disappointed at its degeneration. In contrast, there was no such disillusionment over America, and while the Alien and Sedition Acts dented optimism somewhat they did not destroy it. Cartwright in particular remained a warm friend to the United States until the end of his life; shortly before he died he was exchanging letters with Jefferson and offering his advice on the purchase of a library for the University of Virginia. At the same time he became far more radical and cited the American republic in support of his new arguments.[64] Nor was America forgotten by new generations of radicals. Jeremy Bentham, who had ridiculed the natural rights philosophy of the Declaration of Independence, came to see the United States as a successful example of the democratic ideal in operation. And although as the decades passed the memory of the Revolution dimmed, the example of the American present continued to encourage those who stood on the radical side of English politics.[65]

# 9

## Conclusion

The American Revolution was an event of far-reaching importance. The shot fired at Lexington was indeed heard round the world, and it produced not one echo but many. In the western hemisphere it brought forth a new nation. On the continent of Europe it contributed to the coming of another and yet more explosive revolution. For England it destroyed the most powerful empire of its day and forced a reexamination of many pressing questions; almost all sections of the nation were affected by it in one way or another, sooner or later, to a greater or lesser degree. It would have been strange if the greatest political crisis for many decades had had no importance for moderate radicals in the commonwealth tradition. Very properly the principal determinants of their ideology were located within the unique social structure and intellectual heritage of England itself, but they never ran in blinkers and were highly sensitive to any possible relevance for their own country of debates and conflicts elsewhere. In particular they were much concerned over the course of events in the western half of their transatlantic community. The same can be said to a lesser extent of the "new" or "artisan" radicals, though their concerns were in certain important respects different and they were often less cosmopolitan in their outlook.

Any assessment of the contribution made by the American Revolution to the processes of English radicalism is in good measure determined by the character of contemporary ideology. The old radicals attached the greatest importance to their theories of man, society, and government, though the commonwealth tradition was more a corpus of ideas and attitudes than a coherent and systematic philosophical schema and was sufficiently flexible to incorporate within its ranks men and women whose views were not fully consistent with one another. Two features of special note stand out. The Real Whigs adhered to abstract principles—natural rights and all that flowed from that central postulate—which were specifically intended to be of general rather than parochial application; second, they insisted on the need for practicability and the relevance of experience to the formulation of their public programs. This conjunction of empiricism to axiomatic propositions made them potentially men of broader outlook than their immediate situation might have dictated. In comparison, ideological considerations played a lesser part in the formulation of artisan radicalism and environmental factors a greater one. This is not to deny the importance of ideology to the new men (much of which was drawn from the same sources as that of the Commonwealthmen), but rather to suggest that the social pressures of an industrializing and urbanizing nation and the persecution of a reactionary government must be assigned primacy in the molding of their minds. And in spite of the reciprocal admiration that united them with the revolutionaries in France, the universalist elements in their intellectual system were necessarily subordinated to the requirements of local and immediate imperatives.

When it comes to considering the relationship between ideology and social class the advantage lay with the new radicals. In general the social attitudes of both groups were broadly consonant with those customary among their equals in society. Most Commonwealthmen were men of property or were closely associated with property owners, and in this respect they shared the values of a socially differentiated community. They had no desire to promote leveling since the strength and raison d'être of their political program was to be found in philosophical analysis and the observation of ministerial conduct rather than in a belief that the changing dynamics of the nation required a reordering of social relationships. Beyond this point the consonance obtaining between the values and objectives of commonwealth radicals and those of their fellows broke down, for the Real Whigs were unable to persuade them of the propriety, desirability, and safety of their proposals; they spoke for the middle orders of society, but their intended constituents resolutely ignored their call. Except for the Dissenters they could not persuasively claim to represent the political beliefs of their own class. For a time Christopher Wyvill, the most cautious and politically adept of the reformers, was able to carry his own county and several others under exceptional circumstances, but his temporary success hardly overturns the general proposition.

The new radicals were altogether more fortunate. As artisans and spokesmen for the lower orders they reflected that hostility toward their social superiors often found among the poor, and they enunciated a political platform which had a coherent correspondence to the social concerns of those for whom they claimed to speak. Here were men standing out on behalf of a new constituency, explicitly setting it off as distinct from other constituencies, and very directly claiming not only to be pursuing generalized political goals but to be promoting separate social interests. At the height of the new movement of the 1790s, groups such as the London Corresponding Society were able to attract the support of large numbers of their fellow artisans and, although their economic status in the community at large was low, their significance is well measured by the importance and size of the class they represented.

Yet more crucial for any evaluation is the degree of significance assigned to the eighteenth-century men in the long-term growth of the radical tradition. There is general agreement as to the role of artisan radicalism, for scholars accept it as marking the birth of an embryonic working-class movement. No longer would rioting remain the only overt means of expressing political opinion open to the lower orders; by announcing their support for "Wilkes and Liberty" and by joining the corresponding societies a quarter of a century later the artisans demonstrated their capacity for public analysis and sophisticated argument. But the contribution of commonwealth radicalism is usually denigrated, especially when it is inspected with the new movement still in mind, and it is frequently argued that the old radicals were a small group lacking in influence and of little importance.

This judgment is harsh and requires modification. The Commonwealthmen were certainly a small and heterodox minority; few sat in Parliament and none held office. Nevertheless, several were men of distinction in the intellectual life of the nation and some made important contributions to the deeper understanding of their particular subjects. More important, they all belonged to the broader political community outside the palace of Westminster and felt they were entitled to participate in the political process if only in the limited form of contributing to the formulation of public opinion. And the evidence of the pamphlet wars, periodical reviews, newspapers, official attitudes, and parliamentary debates supports them in their opinion. Nor, when considered as a group, were they obscure in the sense of being isolated from the mainstream of the country's social and political life. Such a charge could be fairly leveled against Sylas Neville, who is known only through the private remarks contained in his diary, and perhaps Matthew Robinson-Morris, though he was one of the few who actually sat in either house of Parliament. It could not be directed with justice against John Cartwright, John Fothergill, Richard Price, or Granville Sharp, to name only a few, for they enjoyed close if peripheral associations with the world of national politics. Furthermore, over the years, several radicals became national figures in their role as political activists. First came John Wilkes during the raging tempests over *North Briton 45* and the Middlesex election, then Price over *Civil Liberty* and later *The Love of Our Country*, Wyvill during the association campaigns, and in the early nineties, Joseph Priestley was incongruously coupled with Thomas Paine to become the twin objects of intense popular and official vilification. At the same time many other radicals acquired less hazardous reputations through the medium of pamphlets that were often widely read and commented upon.

Commonwealthmen as well as artisans made a substantial contribution to English historical development. Though they proved unable to persuade the country to follow them immediately on any major issue, they performed a useful function in the politics of their own day and a still more valuable role in the long-run growth of radicalism. Their immediate predecessors had been content to transmit the dogma of the Real Whig tradition; they had cherished it with love and zeal, but had allowed it to go stale and had made little contribution to its growth. During the age of the American

Revolution, however, the substance of English radicalism was reformulated and made ready for the debates and struggles of the nineteenth century. The nature of this change is strikingly evident in the appearance of new members in the ranks of the political nation, first at the time of "Wilkes and Liberty" and then in the closing decade of the century. Less obviously, a vital transformation was taking place in the character of radical ideology. Having inherited a tradition stemming from the bitter conflicts of the seventeenth century and the still more venerable doctrine of the ancient constitution, the radicals stood at the end of a long and rich inheritance. But they were also the precursors of a new line. By slowly shedding much of the superstructure of the old intellectual tradition and adding fresh proposals, they were making necessary preparations for the future. This process is most clearly apparent in the philosophy of new radicalism, for Thomas Paine ostentatiously claimed to have cut free from the historical justification of natural rights doctrine even though he and others drew much nourishment from the placenta of the commonwealth tradition. Beyond this he also elaborated the subterranean theme of social conflict inherent in earlier radical philosophy and reworked it for use as a theoretical footing for the working-class movement. By comparison, the old radicals were more modest. They passed on to their successors an ideology that demanded an extension of political, civil, and religious liberty without threatening the fabric of the constitution and the differentials of a hierarchical society. As loyal subjects, their goal was political reformation without impairment of social stability. Two modifications were crucial. First was the perception of Cartwright, John Jebb, and Thomas Brand Hollis that the poor had as much if not more of an interest in participating in the political process as the rich—a realization that led them to move away from the traditional concept of a franchise based on property toward one deriving from personalty. It is no accident that the recommendations of the Westminster Sub-Committee prefigured those of the Chartists more than fifty years later. Second was the demand for the dismantling of political discrimination based on confessional allegiance. In effect the old radicals modernized the commonwealth tradition without going to extremes and provided for later generations a liberal constitutionalism that offered a coherent alternative to the Benthamite omnicompetent state and socialism on the one side and conservative immobility on the other. The experience of the American Revolution contributed substantially to this transformation.

Radicals' comprehension of the Revolution operated at different levels and modulated during the course of time. Initially the Commonwealthmen were concerned for the domestic security and happiness of the colonies, but this brought them rapidly to an examination of the nature and premises of the imperial connection. During the middle 1770s they addressed themselves at great length to the problem of constructing a system that would be acceptable to both parties and consistent with the requirements of certain political principles. They were horrified by the war and profoundly alarmed by its implications for both England and America; this horror was scored deep and later reemerged as an element in the mythology of artisan radicalism in the 1790s. In particular they saw it as a consequence of political corruption and, in grander cosmological terms, as the product of Divine retribution for the country's moral decadence. At the same time the Commonwealthmen became aware of the potential relevance of the internal revolution to the millenarian hopes which formed a powerful strain in their moral and political philosophy. Increasingly they developed a deep interest in the processes of political change taking place within the American community and, in keeping with their original concern for the well-being of the colonies, they sustained an active superintending interest in the prosperity of the new republic after the consummation of independence. They drew from American experience many implications for the outside world, especially as the imperial crisis worsened and Britain's standing as a liberal community deteriorated. Both old and new radicals attached great importance to America's role as an asylum of liberty and came to visualize political developments in the United States as a model for England and other countries of the old world. They were, however, discriminating in the use they made of the American model for they were always careful to examine it in the context of their own particular needs and circumstances and had no compunction about discarding any components that had no obvious application. Always their interpretation was informed by their own ideology and social position (Commonwealthmen were especially concerned with the preservation of liberty and artisans with egalitarianism) and, to the old radicals, a strongly held belief in the existence of a single transatlantic community. Necessarily, the radicals' responses to the Revolution were far from simple, and though they seldom distinguished sufficiently clearly between them the various elements of their understanding frequently interacted upon one another. For analytical convenience, however, it remains useful to identify two general features of the Revolution: its character as a problem in imperial relations and its quality as a model in political behavior.

Commonwealthmen could agree with other sections of English opinion that the difficulties being encountered with the American colonies after 1763 posed fundamental questions concerning the nature and objectives of the British empire, but beyond this the consensus broke down. As the crisis worsened, orthodox opinion placed its faith in the operation of central authority. Though they shared conservatives' appreciation of the commercial and strategic importance of preserving the imperial connection, radicals rejected this solution since it ran counter to one of their major premises. Central to their theory of empire was an urgent desire to preserve both liberty and union. And if their various conciliatory proposals contained many defects—for their authors avoided many acute difficulties and slid over others and even the attractiveness of Cartwright's "dominion" proposals was superficial and misleading —they were not without merit. Always the radicals attempted to construct a system that would genuinely advance and preserve the interests of both parties and made valiant efforts to render political principles congruent with economic and strategic considerations. In so doing they were principally concerned with the high ground of political ethics, but they were also at pains to demonstrate the prudential wisdom of achieving an accommodation with the Americans. They, more than anyone else, realized that no policy had any hope of success unless it was acceptable to those leaders who were able to attract the support of the large body of their fellow colonists as distinct from the approbation of officials who exercised only a temporary legal authority. By comparison with the policies being pursued by the British government, the radical proposals were perceptive and practicable, for they were based on respect for American aspirations, included the possibility of meaningful concessions, and thus made feasible a negotiated settlement.

There was, nevertheless, a crucial incompatibility between the

reasoning of the American patriots and that of their English supporters. To the Americans the imperial crisis had rapidly become a
dispute over representation and then had been transfigured into a
fundamental conflict over the question of sovereignty. It was over
this issue that they fought especially after 1776; from 2 July,
America could be retained within the British empire only by coercion. Radical thinking suffered a temporary arrest halfway along
the chain of development. To the Englishmen the crisis long continued to revolve around the issue of representation because they
persisted in their belief that colonial rights could be fully preserved
within the overarching structure of the British empire. This disjunction between radical wishful thinking and American aspirations became yet sharper in 1776 since a corollary of the radicals'
desire to restore a harmonious and morally just union was that
initially they had little interest in American independence in the
sense that the Americans themselves had come to understand it. In
actuality they were attempting to attain an objective far more
difficult than those currently pursued by the British government
and the American colonists. Of the two concepts that lay at the
heart of their system—liberty and union—they were only willing
to concede primacy to liberty when they finally realized that
separation was inescapable. But once the radicals accepted the
point, it became essential that the United States should successfully
defend its independence in order that it might play its vital role as
an asylum of liberty.

After independence had been consummated a certain ambivalence underlay the radicals' feelings toward the United States.
They wished the United States well (of that there can be no doubt),
but the terms on which they offered their affection were never
entirely unambiguous. The tight interlocking of English and American society which had directed their attitudes toward the colonies
had been broken irreparably. But how, exactly, was the new relationship to be defined? To this question they could provide no
clear answer. On the one hand they saw the consequences of
American independence as virtually a political counterpart to commercial free trade—with the difference that they were more enthusiastic over independence. Liberty, they observed, was no longer
dependent on any particular political affiliation and, although
they initially regretted the severance of the formal association with

Britain, they believed that if it were enabled to flourish in one nation America's success would be of value to the rest of the world. But on the other hand loyalty to the notion of a single Anglo-American community refused to expire with the surrender at Yorktown or ratification of the peace treaty. And they remained firmly persuaded that the United States was operating within the context of their own political tradition. Figuratively and almost literally the radicals sought to have the best of both worlds.

Concern for American interests in the framework of an imperial conflict was laudable, but the radicals recognized that it was of limited importance. Rather like the attack on slavery, success would remove an evil but would not by itself produce any positive advance in the political circumstances of the remainder of mankind. Moreover, if they were to evaluate the Revolution only in the narrow context of a problem within an over-mighty empire, they would seem to be conceding the conservative case that it was only a colonial rebellion of no more than domestic significance. Like the Americans themselves, the Commonwealthmen looked for matters of greater import; and they found the task was not difficult. Military resistance to British armies was far from the sole component of the Revolution; there were also the process of establishing new governments and drafting constitutions in the states to replace the colonial charters and instructions. The American leaders were totally convinced that they were embarked on a venture which would have repercussions far transcending the immediate acts of resistance and independence, and their rhetoric proclaimed that their actions were intended to have universal as well as local significance. In England the radicals also placed their understanding of the Revolution on a higher and more expansive plane than was implicit in treating it as a crisis in imperial relations. At first they considered the domestic implications for Great Britain. This led them to the judgment that there was an integral and specific connection between events in America and those they could observe close at hand in England; a challenge addressed to liberty in the colonies was also a direct threat to liberty at home. In working out the ramifications of this proposition they concluded that America had a vital role to perform as a haven of refuge for immigrants and a still more important one as a prototype of a liberal state. While these responsibilities were expected to have general significance, they were also to have particular relevance for England.

For many radicals the imperial crisis, the bishopric campaign, and the domestic disputes associated particularly with John Wilkes became fused into three facets of a single crisis. Liberty, they firmly believed, was indivisible throughout the empire, and it appeared to stand at risk on both sides of the Atlantic simultaneously. Some had moved toward this conclusion a decade before the outbreak of war; others required more persuasion and were only reluctantly forced to concede the force of this thesis by what seemed to be the ineluctable progress of official policies. According to their understanding, firm evidence implied the existence of a coordinated conspiracy to establish tyranny in both England and America. As far as America is concerned the putative program is well known and requires no further exposition. In relation to liberty in England, the radical thesis suggested, briefly, that successive governments were seeking to reconstruct the imperial system in order to establish an authoritarian regime in the colonies as a means of providing the executive with an income that would enable it to outflank parliamentary control over revenue and so to undercut one of the most important elements in the representative system. And at home there were the general warrants affair, the St. George's Fields "massacre," the Middlesex election, and the acrimonious dispute over reporting parliamentary debates. Such argumentation undoubtedly failed to take a number of factors into proper consideration. Notably it postulated a new (but nonexistent) toryism and underestimated the administrative complexities inherent in any attempt to create a coherent imperial structure. On this latter point the program advocated in 1764 by Thomas Pownall, a man of liberal and even radical persuasion, is instructive in that it anticipated much that would shortly become official policy. Similarly it failed to comprehend the implications of radical alternatives for one of the bulwarks of English constitutionalism, the principle of parliamentary control of revenue (something George Grenville was aware of), and made insufficient allowance for differences of intention among the various ministers charged with responsibility for American affairs. It also failed to recognize that colonial resistance in 1766 and 1770 had secured three major reversals of British policy, thus demonstrating the effective limitations to government power. On the other hand, the radicals were more alarmed by the apparent determination of successive ministries to sidestep resistance by the introduction of fresh measures. They were concerned over Grenville's program of 1764–65, but relieved when the Rockingham administration repealed the Stamp Act in 1766. Had the development of policy terminated at that point all would have been well, but it did not. While Townshend's Revenue Act was abhorrent in itself, it was all the more horrifying in relation to what had gone before and what might be anticipated for the future. Still more was this so with the Coercive Acts of 1774 and the suppressive policies of following years. What was terrifying was not individual legislation, but the cumulation of successive measures, which suggested system and purpose.

Nor should the radicals' fears be dismissed as entirely chimerical. If the terms of analysis are changed by transferring attention away from the motivation behind official policies to the consequences that might flow from them, it becomes apparent that their hypothesis was not as absurd as it first seems. In the colonies the potential implications to be drawn from the establishment of an independent executive and a source of revenue free from the control of colonial assemblies were horrifying not only in theory but also in their potential actuality. Similarly it seems inherently improbable that as long as America retained its colonial status the church would have rested content with a bishop authorized to perform only spiritual duties. In England the years before 1775 saw an extension rather than a contraction of liberty (some of the greatest decisions in British legal history date from this period)— but it was not achieved by the operations of the executive, but in spite of them. The nation also was more sensitive to the libertarian implications of well-established practices than it had been in earlier years. This development should be assigned in good measure to the credit of the radicals, and the most appropriate comment is that an increased sensitivity was overdue. All in all, the falsity of the conspiratorial thesis does not entirely invalidate the arguments that were grounded in it.

Under such circumstances the suspicion that England was entering a period of irreversible decay led many radicals to a growing belief that America could and must offer to the cause of liberty an asylum that was no longer likely to be available in their own country. They interpreted the concept of an asylum of liberty in two related senses: as a haven for the victims of persecution in other countries and as a society in which the operation of a liberal system of government could flourish. Migration to the United States was an obvious and tangible expression of America's relationship to England and Europe, but was only of secondary importance to the old world for its reciprocal effect was negative rather than helpful. Emigration was of great benefit to the individuals concerned and to the growth of the United States but did nothing to improve the political environment of those societies the migrants left behind. As an asylum for the principle of liberty, however, America could perform a valuable reciprocal function. It was essential for all men that liberty should survive and flourish in some part of an otherwise hostile world, and in the sense that the experience of mankind is universal as well as particular it would offer an inspiration and encouragement to those elsewhere who were less fortunate. Such a function was normally diffuse rather than specific in operation, but it contained an implied corollary: that America could provide a model for emulation overseas and a demonstration of the empirical feasibility of liberal principles.

The need for a model was integral to the character of English radicalism. Commonwealthmen were sustained more by their intellectual tradition than by any close connection with the needs of a disaffected sector of society, but like contemporary British political philosophers in general they retained a strong respect for and dependence on the evidence of experience. This strain of empiricism led them to attach considerable relevance to the experience of contemporary societies. Besides, there was a quality of millenarian vision in their thought which eagerly predicted that with the spread of enlightened thought a new order of society might emerge in the not too distant future. The correspondence between empiricism and millenarianism was not easy, and their relationship to the situation in which the radicals found themselves was rendered still more difficult when the workings and judgments of Divine Providence were brought into account. All three factors led them to look outside their own country: and a natural focus for their attentions was America.

History, they believed, had a powerful instrumental function to perform in the analysis of the contemporary world. A profound sense of the unity and universality of the human experience obscured in their minds the distinction between the experience of the past and that of the present so that their sense of the differentness of the past was subordinated to their need for it to instruct and inform their understanding of the present. Hence their concern for the experience of the ancient world of Greece and Rome and rather more immediately with the fate of the Anglo-Saxon constitution and the triumphs and catastrophes of the seventeenth century. Priestley's *Lectures on History and General Policy* offer the most explicit instance of the importance of historical experience in the formulation of radical ideology, but in truth it pervaded their entire thought and argumentation. Unfortunately the record of the past seemed to give with one hand only to snatch away with the other. Much of the recent past seemed to indicate the possibility (and maybe even the probability) of human progress. But the evidence of the past seemed clear and unambiguous: the passage of man through the temporal world was subject to a continuing cycle of progress and retreat, rise and fall, optimism and disaster. Such a view might logically be supposed to lead to the conclusion that man and his societies were the hapless creatures of an inescapable fate.

This conclusion was totally unacceptable. It offended the radicals' sense of anticipation, drawn from the immediate past, theology, and the natural world, that human society was advancing toward new levels of social improvement. Priestley and others were busily engaged in sweeping away what they regarded as the corruptions of Christianity and believed that the same broom could be wielded through the house of politics. Not that the Commonwealthmen were exponents of a bland optimism and a vacuous belief in certain progress—their emancipation from the rigors of original sin and predestination had not misled them into this heresy—but they saw man as a more noble and self-directing creature than the cyclical theory would seem to allow. Yet they also argued that man remained subject to the superintendence and chastisement of his Creator, no matter how benevolent the Deity might be. God was more than the divine workman; He had an active role to play in the affairs of mankind. If hopes of amelioration were to be fulfilled, both dogma and historical experience made it plain that He required human behavior to conform to sacred law. In particular He was capable of visiting severe retribution on those men and nations who transgressed. Hence the radicals, many of whom were practicing Dissenters, felt deeply aware of the omnipresence of Divine Providence and saw the corruption of English political life and the disasters that flowed from it (notably the disintegration of the empire) in moral as well as political terms. Nor was this in any way coincidental, for social and political conduct was subject to judgment primarily according to moral criteria and only secondarily to political and prudential considerations.

The argument can, indeed, be taken further. Whatever the spiritual merits and demerits of eighteenth-century theology, it may be fairly said perhaps that it devoted more attention to the judgment of the mind than to the passions of the emotions. Many dissenting radicals seem instinctively to have transferred their emotional needs from the world of theology to that of politics. This transfer was independent of any obvious sectarian interest and was particularly apparent during the American Revolution; the horrific consequences of sin and eternal damnation had largely disappeared from the world of the spirit, but, they believed, the product of corruption, decay, and indifference was all too apparent in the world of contemporary politics. Their belief that the disasters of the Revolution were the form taken by the vengeance of Divine Providence and that the success of the morally pure Americans was the form taken by providential approval served powerfully to drive forward a belief in the urgency of a solution to the problem of empire and the desperate need for reform at home; only by these means could the political fabric of the country be restored to the path of virtuous behavior. It also reminded them that the path of progress was narrow and uncertain.

Two questions faced the radicals at this point. How could the country be morally reformed in such a way as to avert the imminent wrath of Divine Providence, and how could the cyclical rhythm of the rise and fall of successive societies be broken at a point that would permit the emergence of a uniquely new advance along the lines of unfettered improvement? Fundamentally the two questions were associated aspects of the same problem; this did not make them any the easier to answer, nor did it make the problem any less daunting. Worse still, although the issue was in essence moral and spiritual, its solution perforce had to be political, and at this point the spiritual heritage of English Dissent became conjoined to its political tradition and the immediate circumstances of radicalism. The substantive actualities of the problem were evident enough: they required empirical solutions that would be congruent with general moral and political principles rather than merely the needs of prudential considerations. Once again the radicals were led back to a reliance on the experience not only of their own generation but of past generations and other societies outside the immediate confines of Great Britain. External models would not provide all the answers to their problems, but they could prove extremely useful and greatly encouraging at a time of stress.

One such prototype already existed in the English past. However defective it might have been as a reconstruction of historical events, there can be no doubt that the Anglo-Saxon constitution exercised a powerful influence over the radical mind. Nor should it be patronizingly dismissed as a hopeless figment of the imagination and a demonstration of political naiveté. It had served for generations as a vehicle for liberal political ideals and had offered moral support and intellectual sustenance during the long decades when the processes of decay seemed triumphant. It also served a second important function, for belief in an ancient constitution ensured that radicalism would remain within the broad limits of English political custom: the radical objective need not be a fundamental upheaval in society after all, but rather its restoration to the customs of an earlier paradigm. Radicals of the age of the American Revolution were concerned principally with the extension (or restoration) and protection of political rights—an interest in abstract principles that no doubt was further encouraged by their primary devotion to the explorations of theology. They were not entirely indifferent to contemporary social problems, but accepted the hierarchical character of the society in which they lived; their grand cosmology, which centered on the relationship of man to his Creator, contributed to making them less aware than they might otherwise have been of the conflicts possible between one social class and another. Thus the Commonwealthmen occasionally grumbled at the power of the aristocracy but tolerated the House of Lords. Also, for better or worse, they accepted the legitimacy of the principal elements of eighteenth-century English constitutionalism such as monarchy coupled to a parliamentary system (dissenting hostility toward the privileges of the established church was a notable exception) and devoted their attention to matters which, in brief, were associated with representation. And here, of course, their concerns were reinforced by their interpretation of the imperial dispute as revolving around this very issue. Not even the commonwealth tradition drawn from the previous century could overturn this element of traditionalism, although it contributed powerful encouragement to demands for the extension of political rights and contained within it even more explosive seeds of social upheaval that would be exploited later by the new radicals.

But by the 1760s both the ancient constitution and the commonwealth traditions were getting somewhat worn out and threadbare—the former more than the latter. It is very apparent that the more sophisticated of the political theorists, in particular Priestley and Price, were rapidly emancipating themselves from the folk memory of the Anglo-Saxon tradition and were becoming less dependent on the formal canon of the seventeenth century; still more was this the case with Paine and the artisan radicals. Under such circumstances a new pattern was needed: one that would be fresher and would express itself in terms more germane to contemporary society and would add instrumental legitimacy to their normative values.

That model was the American experiment. It did not invalidate the earlier English models; rather, it reinforced and developed their value. Its potency lay to a considerable degree precisely in that it could be extrapolated from the English tradition. Moreover, in spite of the formal political separation initiated in the summer of 1776, the experiment was conducted within what the radicals always considered as a single community. The Revolution might have been a rare example of a provincial society seeking to lead its metropolitan state, but, although American society was recognized to be different from English in many important respects, radicals declined to accept that its experience should be regarded as exotic or foreign.

To a considerable degree the role of the Revolution in the development of English radicalism was dependent on the radicals' perception of the nature of American society. Their understanding of its character was often so tightly interwoven with their interpretation of the importance of the Revolution that at times the two were almost indistinguishable. Their vision was selective, and they made different uses of different elements. Regardless of America's defects, which included most notably its continued toleration of slavery, its society struck radicals as intellectually and culturally congenial. Dissenting radicals were embarrassed by seventeenth-century Puritans' reputation for religious persecution, but felt that the situation in their own day was very different and that the sins of earlier generations should not be visited on their successors. Perhaps more important, contemporary American communities seemed to be vigorously free from the corruption and moral degradation that were all too apparent on their own side of the Atlantic. In intellectual matters they compared American systems with their own and found them similar; in social terms they compared the generality of American society with that of England and found it more consonant with their hopes and desires for England than with the observable realities surrounding them.

Most radicals accepted American valuations of the positivist function of their Revolution as a "workshop of liberty." Naturally their response varied from person to person, just as the model itself changed considerably between 1776 and 1787. Generally it was weakest among those who were most willing to compromise with circumstances in the forlorn hope of achieving at least a modicum of reform; this was especially true of Wyvill. And in most respects the operation of the American model was held to have general rather than particular relevance and served as a fortifying rather than an innovative force.

One should not look too demandingly for recommendations that England should implement specific American practices, although there were certainly some. Major Cartwright made explicit reference to American examples when he urged the introduction of the secret ballot and later was much impressed by the separation between the constitutional structure and the legislative elements of government. He picked up what became the standard American practice of formulating written constitutions and demanded that a codified constitution be introduced in England. It is also clear that while he was in London, John Adams had extensive discussions on political affairs with his English friends and that their debates often revolved around the implications to be drawn from American experience. Most important of the topics was their discussion of the relative merits of a balanced or unitary legislature; here Adams was able to divert many radicals away from their inclination to follow the Pennsylvania model of a single-house assembly toward his own scheme of a divided structure.

Radicals were more concerned with the fundamental principles expressed in the new American governments than with the precise forms through which they were articulated. They were fully aware that there were important differences between the circumstances in America and those prevailing in England and that some institutions and practices workable in the United States were inappropriate in England. Two obvious examples are federalism and republicanism. The concept of federalism as it was maturing during the Revolution in America was beyond the intellectual grasp of radicals for they could not comprehend the relationship between the states and the central government; besides, there was no perceptible need for a federal system in Britain once the colonies had achieved their independence. Similarly, republicanism, defined as a nonmonarchical system, had no especial significance in the context of English reform. Among Commonwealthmen few even of those who openly proclaimed themselves to be republicans wished to see an end to the institution of monarchy, for while they might condemn it in theory and applaud its absence in America they also conceded its utility in the different circumstances prevailing in eighteenth-century England.

Instead they were greatly impressed by the Americans' apparent success in conjoining respect for equal individual rights with the requirements of viable and effective political authority. The key to this success lay in the complex mechanism of representation —and its lessons were applicable to England. The American experiment legitimated the vital move away from the system of property and interest-based representation toward the new principle of personalty without, to the relief of the Commonwealthmen, overturning the structural premises of contemporary society. It fortified legislative supremacy over the executive, thus apparently eliminating the debilitating effects of corruption, and it explicitly established the people as the constituent power and made the legislature responsible to them. The first example, the Pennsylvania constitution of 1776, proved to be misleading, but under the influence of Adams and the federal Constitution Real Whigs moved toward the model of a divided legislature confined in its authority and (ironically through the medium of Paine) to the principle of a written constitution drawing its power directly from the people and superior and antecedent to the authority of government. Liberty and constitutionalism: these were the principles that were strengthened in English radicalism by the model of American Revolutionary government. They provided strong armor against authoritarianism and later against the extremism and totalitarianism inherent in the example of the French Revolution. In contrast, however, the new radicals often deployed the American model to support an aggressive republicanism and the purist form of natural rights.

Another principle, equality, was also implied in the example of the American republic. The Commonwealthmen were reluctant to develop the concept of equality, even though it might have seemed a natural corollary of their own ideology. But the old radicals never stopped to examine the problems flowing from social inequality, nor did they fully realize that unless these issues were tackled their other liberal principles would be rendered null; in this respect they were incurably conservative. Accordingly, the social implications they drew from America and its Revolution were similarly cautious. They were greatly impressed by America's "comfortable mediocrity" and conceptualized the United States as a land of sturdy yeoman farmers. Such a model had little direct relevance to the circumstances of their own country, as they were well aware, and the manner in which they applied it to their own social thinking was, if anything, retrogressive. All radicals were especially struck by the absence of destitution in America, and men like Price made a particular point of the moral superiority of those areas away from the coast and towns. The image of a socially homogeneous, prosperous, and above all rural society encouraged the old radicals in their continuing affection for a preindustrial mythology of agrarianism. This, in turn, prevented them from addressing the increasingly acute problems of urban society in an age in which industrialization was advancing rapidly. Perhaps more important, it reinforced the Commonwealthmen's conception of the status of their own class in society by providing an intellectual defense against the pretensions of aristocracy above them while in effect dismissing the claims of those who stood below them. Paradoxically an inherently egalitarian if increasingly archaic social model immunized them against the revolutionary implications of their own theories. By such devices as these they were able to advance libertarian doctrines without destroying the position and authority of the middle ranks of society.

In one important instance the American Revolution created a unique prototype for which there was no counterpart in the English radical tradition. When Commonwealthmen considered the political economy they were able to refer to a ready-made example in the paradigm of the ancient constitution. In ecclesiastical matters there was no such long-established model, and yet Dissenters suffering from religious discrimination urgently needed one. Several were discovered in continental Europe during the second half of the eighteenth century, but none were as persuasive and influential in England as that offered by the extension of religious liberty in America. Before the war many Dissenters were impressed by the system of establishment coupled with toleration and public assistance that operated in several northern colonies and that Benjamin Franklin so devastatingly compared with English practice in his article "Toleration in Old and New England." Insofar as it went, the New England system formed a useful way station on the road to religious equality, but little more. During the war and the years immediately following it, however, many states moved still further toward relaxing religious restrictions and terminating discrimination based on confessional grounds. The many radicals who were also Dissenters were profoundly excited by this innovation. They had long argued the case for ending discrimination on theoretical grounds and their own record of loyalty to the House of Hanover, but to no avail. Now they could point to a specific example of the security of such a policy. In America the fetters on speculative thought had been removed, the various religious sects sat on terms of equality, and in many states the church was disestablished, and yet the fabric of society had resolutely not collapsed into chaos. The Dissenters were offered empirical validation of abstract propositions, a defense against the charges of the orthodox, and a strong prudential argument in favor of the secular benefits available from the implementation of religious freedom. They were encouraged to seek repeal of the Test and Corporation Acts, and though their opponents found the American example less persuasive then they did, it strengthened their confidence in the rectitude of their cause. No wonder that to many Dissenters the Virginia Statute for Religious Freedom was the most memorable document to emerge from the Revolution.

Although the dynamics of late eighteenth-century radicalism sprang principally from local circumstances and domestic traditions, America and its Revolution made a significant contribution to its development. Their central importance in the life of English radicalism lay in their function as an experiment to determine the operability of certain political principles. Radicals were steeped in the tradition of scientific experimentation and its theological counterpart, the search for the evidences of Christianity. Empirical validation of theoretical propositions was not only desirable; it was in a literal sense vital. In particular it was essential to discover whether the principles of liberty and a morally just society could exist and flourish in the distinctively favorable environment of the new world. If they could not, there was little hope of implementing or restoring them in the old world. But if the American experiment were successful it would be possible to proceed to the much more daunting task of promoting liberty in England and the almost infinitely more daunting task of introducing it on the continent of Europe. As far as England was concerned there was especial encouragement to be drawn from the American Revolution since a central premise of radical belief was that it belonged firmly within their own political tradition. Sensible men that they were, they took from it whatever was useful and discarded the remainder.

Nor should the importance of a model be denigrated. Over the years political ideology undergoes a continuing series of reformulations to meet the changing needs of successive generations. Models and precedents are essential in this process for the predictive act of imagination necessary to construct a theory of behavior and society appropriate to new circumstances is truly formidable. Even millenarians often need to rely on the past to justify their predictions. This was especially so with the old radicals, hence their intellectual dependence on the commonwealth and ancient constitution traditions; it was of less importance to the artisan radicals of the 1790s, and they accordingly paid less attention to the United States. By the middle of the eighteenth century these intellectual props were showing signs of being unable to bear the weight that was thrust upon them. Moreover, whatever its merits (which were considerable) the commonwealth tradition drawn from the debates of the seventeenth century was ultimately no more than an attractive theory; worse still, such attempts as had been made to introduce radical theory into the operation of English government had terminated in disaster with the restoration of Charles II. But English political thought attached great importance to the value of experience and empirical evidence. The ancient constitution only met this requirement inadequately and even when added to commonwealth ideology it could take the radicals so far but no farther. The American Revolution effectively updated and to a considerable extent supplanted the model of the Anglo-Saxon constitution and to a lesser extent the commonwealth tradition as well. By doing so it made a useful contribution to the modernization of radical thought and programs; this process was of considerable significance since it set the tone for the meliorist reform movements of the following century.

Although to set foot in the hazardous field of social comparisons between American revolutionaries and English radicals is to enter thickets dense in undergrowth and infested with hidden traps, a few tentative suggestions may be made. In view of the obvious differences between English and American society, and in particular the social complexity of the Revolutionary movement, any direct quantitative comparisons necessarily would be based on qualitative and subjective assessments. But the problem becomes simpler if the radical concept of a single community is taken as the point of reference and the revolutionaries are discussed not in terms of their own local society but in the context of a British imperial, transatlantic society. Once this is done the social similarities become striking. Perhaps the sharpest demonstration of the correspondence between the Americans and Englishmen can be found in the lives of those colonists who visited London before the war. Regardless of their status at home, the Americans mixed with members of the middling ranks of society, including several radicals, entered middle-class occupations (medicine, the law, and commerce) and enjoyed only moderate wealth. The Englishmen came from the same social circles, particularly from the ranks of the lower gentry and squirearchy and the urban professional and commercial classes. In social terms both groups resented the overweening dominance of the English aristocracy (though many of the Englishmen retained strong feelings of deference toward them) and believed that the political system should be reformed so as to allow greater influence to those ranks in society that held the greatest sense of moral and political virtue. In America emancipation led to independence; in England it came to a frustrating halt with the failure to achieve parliamentary reform.

In one vital respect the artisan radicals of the 1790s responded to the social implications of the American Revolution differently. The medium through which they observed the Revolution was similar—most of the intellectuals of the new radical movement were middle class by origin no matter how vehemently they pretended to be sans-culottes—but the conclusions they drew were sharply dissimilar. They too observed the relative lack of distinction in American society but used it to bolster an abrasive social egalitarianism. A petty bourgeois himself, Paine offered a vision of social as well as political reform which, though based on his own experience of America, took him far beyond the most advanced position adopted by the Commonwealthmen. Here was unconscious irony, for the new men drew their inferences from the same social structure, principles, and public conduct that were admired by the old radicals, not from the experience of American artisan radicalism of which they apparently knew little. Thus although there was an inherent disjunction between the dominant social character of the Revolutionary movement in America and the artisan movement in England, the new radicals were able to use the American model to support the development of a working-class ideology.

The American Revolution also had notable consequences for the position of commonwealth radicals as an interest group within the state. It is sometimes said that radicals, and particularly those who were Dissenters, were permanently alienated from English political life during these years. This judgment needs careful qualification. Radicals were unquestionably dismayed by what they regarded as incontrovertible evidence of accelerating corruption and moral decay. Their alarm became increasingly more acute after 1767 and reached its nadir of despair during the middle years of the war; they were also disappointed by their failures over subscription before the war, parliamentary reform in its closing stages, and repeal of the Test and Corporation Acts. But the conclusions they drew from their disillusionment were markedly different from those drawn by the colonists in the mid-seventies. In America disenchantment with British policies led seemingly inexorably to armed resistance, republicanism, and independence. In England it led to a reaffirmation of traditional principles. There was no violence or credible threat of violence, even on the pitiable scale of forging pikes as was discovered during the French Revolution. Radicals detested the use of force, but felt that it could be justified only by exceptional circumstances. Thus they condoned the actions of the patriots in America, just as they had assented to use of the army to suppress the rebellion of 1745 and were to approve of preparations against the possibility of a French invasion. But there was no possibility of rebellion at home during the War of Independence, nor was there any potential "revolutionary moment" in 1779. Rantings in *The Crisis* at the beginning of the war must be discounted as the rumblings of distant thunder; certainly they came to nothing. A second, more moderate possibility might have been a retreat into republicanism. In America this had proved fruitful; in England it was no more than a red herring. Both as a term to describe representative government based on the consent of the people and as an antimonarchical system it was irrelevant to English needs, as the radicals saw. Price, Priestley, and others insisted they were not republicans, and to apply the term to men like Sharp and Cartwright, whose principles were so closely related, is to demonstrate its absurdity. Unfortunately, however, the critics of radicalism and Dissent seized upon their support for the Americans as proof of their republicanism and disloyalty, and such charges—so unjustified but so easy to make—did grave damage to the cause of reform.

In actuality the behavior of the old radicals during the last quarter of the eighteenth century demonstrates that their intentions were the converse of those alleged by their opponents. Their conduct during the American Revolution and the repeal campaigns displayed a strong sense of loyalty to the state and an anxious desire to continue operating within its constitutional framework.

The only notable exception was Priestley's strident and ill-judged announcement that disestablishment was his ultimate objective. Otherwise the radicals' complaints against the contemporary political system were directed toward the corruption, distortion, and inequity of its current modus operandi, not against its principles. Indeed they were strengthened in their belief in its fundamental virtue, not disillusioned by newly revealed weaknesses. Possibly the radicals can be accused of offering loyalty on their own terms, that is, of requiring the state to conform to their own principles as the price for receiving their support. But what principles they were! Here were no demands for social and political upheaval. Instead they offered reaffirmation of the premises of the Glorious Revolution. And paradoxically, the success of the Americans in constructing a liberal system of government fortified their loyalty and dislike of republicanism. The American experience validated their system and confirmed their intention to continue working within the broad limits of English constitutionalism. It demonstrated that contemporary corruption was an aberration rather than a manifestation of a systematic defect, and it suggested that the path of melioristic reform remained open and attractive. Thus it was possible to implement political change and enjoy the benefits of stability simultaneously. One consequence was immediately seen with special clarity during the 1790s when the old radicals remained faithful to their traditional principles and in particular to the American model at a time when the French Revolution was disintegrating into bloodshed, chaos, reaction, and tyranny.

# Abbreviations

APS American Philosophical Society
BL British Library
DWL Dr. Williams's Library
GRO Gloucestershire Record Office
HSP Historical Society of Pennsylvania
LC Library of Congress
MHS Massachusetts Historical Society
NYHS New-York Historical Society
PRO Public Record Office

# Notes

INTRODUCTION

1. J. H. Plumb, *The Growth of Political Stability in England*, p. xviii.
2. See Douglas Hay et al., *Albion's Fatal Tree*.
3. The term "radical" was first used as a substantive noun in the late 1790s; it did not enter general currency until after 1819 (Elie Halévy, *The Growth of Philosophical Radicalism*, p. 261). Although anachronistic the reminder it offers of the connections between eighteenth-century reformers and those of later generations is salutary.
4. George Rudé, *Wilkes and Liberty*, p. 196.
5. Mercy Warren to Abigail Adams, 28 Jan. 1775, L. H. Butterfield et al., eds., *Adams Family Correspondence*, 1:182; Abigail Adams to John Adams, 30 July 1777, Charles Francis Adams, ed., *Familiar Letters of John Adams and His Wife Abigail Adams during the Revolution*, p. 286.
6. Dagobert D. Runes, ed., *Selected Writings of Benjamin Rush*, p. 325.
7. Thomas Jefferson to Edward Rutledge, 18 July 1788, Julian P. Boyd, ed., *The Papers of Thomas Jefferson*, 13:378.
8. George Washington to Jefferson, 1 Jan. 1788, ibid., 12:490; Jefferson to Adams, 12 Sept. 1821, Lester J. Cappon, ed., *The Adams-Jefferson Letters*, 2:575; James Madison, quoted in Adrienne Koch, *Power, Morals, and the Founding Fathers*, p. 105.
9. James Otis to anon., 18 July 1768, *Political Register* (London), Feb. 1769; [John Dickinson], *A New Essay on the Constitutional Power of Great Britain over the Colonies in America*, p. 62. Cf. H. Trevor Colbourn, *The Lamp of Experience*, pp. 115, 187.

CHAPTER 1

1. See Caroline Robbins, *The Eighteenth-Century Commonwealthman*, for a detailed exposition of the development of this form of radicalism. The "new" radicalism of the 1790s will be discussed in chapter 8.
2. Capel Lofft, *An Argument on the Nature of Party and Faction*, pp. 4, 6–7.
3. For general studies of reform during this period, see George Stead Veitch, *The Genesis of Parliamentary Reform*; H. W. C. Davis, *The Age of Grey and Peel*; S. Maccoby, *English Radicalism, 1762–1785*; Ian R. Christie, *Wilkes, Wyvill and Reform*, and John Cannon, *Parliamentary Reform 1640–1832*. For particular studies, see George Rudé, *Wilkes and Liberty*; Eugene Charlton Black, *The Association*; Anthony Lincoln, *Some Political and Social Ideas of English Dissent 1763–1800*; Richard Burgess Barlow, *Citizenship and Conscience*; and Ursula Henriques, *Religious Toleration in England 1787–1833*.

4. Almost all radicals were English; the few who were Scottish (such as James Burgh), Welsh (Richard Price), or Irish (John Jebb) by birth can be considered in an English context. Robbins, *Commonwealthman*, chapter 9, explores the network of radical friendships and associations.

5. Christie, *Wilkes, Wyvill and Reform*, p. 71.

6. Further biographical information can be found in Frances Dorothy Cartwright, *The Life and Correspondence of Major Cartwright*; Naomi Helen Churgin, "Major John Cartwright"; and John W. Osborne, *John Cartwright*.

7. John Adams to the Marquis de Lafayette, 31 Jan. 1786, Adams Papers microfilm, reel 113; all references to the Adams Papers are to the microfilm edition published by the Massachusetts Historical Society, Boston, which owns the originals. See Prince Hoare, *Memoirs of Granville Sharp*; and E. C. P. Lascelles, *Granville Sharp and the Freedom of Slaves in England*. Sharp's father had been an archdeacon and his grandfather the Williamite archbishop of York. He was a staunch Trinitarian, regarded Unitarianism as heretical, and approved the requirement that the clergy should subscribe to the Articles of Religion (Sharp to Robert Findlay, 16 March 1773, Granville Sharp Letter Book, fols. 99, 102). Sharp was also rabidly anti-Catholic, but sympathetic toward Protestant desires for relief.

8. See [Francis Blackburne], *Memoirs of Thomas Hollis, Esq.*; John Disney, *Memoirs of Thomas Brand Hollis, Esq.*; Caroline Robbins, "The Strenuous Whig, Thomas Hollis of Lincoln's Inn"; and Caroline Robbins, "Thomas Brand Hollis (1719–1804)."

9. See John Disney, ed., *The Works Theological and Medical, Political and Miscellaneous, of John Jebb MD, FRS, with Memoirs of the Life of the Author*.

10. See Carla Humphrey Hay, "Crusading Schoolmaster" (for Burgh); Lucy Martin Donnelly, "The Celebrated Mrs. Macaulay"; George Warren Gignilliat, Jr., *The Author of Sandford and Merton* (for Day); Alison Olson, *The Radical Duke* (for Richmond); Ghita Stanhope and G. P. Gooch, *The Life of Charles, Third Earl of Stanhope*; and Richard Watson, *Anecdotes of the Life of Richard Watson, Bishop of Landaff* [sic].

11. Roland Thomas, *Richard Price*, Carl B. Cone, *Torchbearer of Freedom*, and David O. Thomas, "Richard Price, 1723–91," for Price; [Joseph Priestley], *Memoirs of Dr. Joseph Priestley*, John Towill Rutt, *Life and Correspondence of Joseph Priestley*, and Anne Holt, *A Life of Joseph Priestley*, for the main themes of their subject's life.

12. Thomas Belsham, *Memoirs of the Late Reverend Theophilus Lindsey MA*.

13. Sharp knew several members of the royal family; his brother James owned a barge on the River Thames on which they entertained George III and others (including Lord North) to music (Sharp, MS Diary, 12, 29 Aug. 1777; 22, 24 Aug. 1778, Hardwicke MSS, box 56).

14. The analysis of English society presented in this and the two preceding paragraphs is based on Harold Perkin, *The Origins of Modern English Society*, chapter 2, esp. pp. 24–31, 37. See Asa Briggs, "The Language of 'Class' in Early Nineteenth-Century England," for the dangers of applying the term "class" in a modern sense in an eighteenth-century context.

15. *A Collection of the Letters which Have Been Addressed to the Volunteers of Ireland on the Subject of a Parliamentary Reform*, p. 80n.; Joseph Priestley, *Experiments and Observations on Different Kinds of Air and other Branches of Natural Philosophy Connected with the Subject*, 1:xli; Granville Sharp, *The Law of Retribution*, p. 6.

16. Brand Hollis to Mrs. Abigail Adams, 20 Dec. 1790, Adams Papers microfilm, reel 374.

17. This definition is based on David E. Apter, *The Politics of Modernization*, pp. 267, 314.

18. Thomas, "Richard Price," p. 45; Priestley, *The Importance and Extent of Free Inquiry in Matters of Religion*, pp. 5–6.

19. Granville Sharp, *A Declaration of the People's Natural Right to A Share in the Legislature*, p. 2; Richard Watson to the Duke of Grafton, 12 Oct. 1791, Watson, *Anecdotes*, 1:415; Christopher Wyvill, *A Defence of Dr. Price and the Reformers of England*, appendix, paper 4.

20. Richard Price, *Observations on the Nature of Civil Liberty, the Principles of Government and the Justice and Policy of the War with America*, p. 1; Cartwright to anon., 21 May 1775, Cartwright, *Life*, 1:59.

21. Price, *Civil Liberty*, p. 5.

22. Wyvill to William Pitt the Younger, 9 Feb. 1793, Chatham Papers, 112:247; John Cartwright, *American Independence the Interest and Glory of Great Britain*, p. 7; Cartwright, *Life*, 1:66.

23. Joseph Priestley, *An Essay on the First Principles of Government*, p. 11.

24. David Williams, *Lectures on Political Principles*, pp. 8–9.

25. Price, *Civil Liberty*, pp. 11–12, 3–6.

26. Cartwright, *Life*, 1:89; John Cartwright, *Take Your Choice!* pp. 21, 6–9; Robert Dodsley, "Three Dialogues Concerning Liberty," in Society for Constitutional Information, *Tracts Published and Distributed Gratis by the Society for Constitutional Information*, p. 4; Priestley, *First Principles of Government*, p. 41; Joseph Towers, *Tracts on Political and Other Subjects*, 2:202; John Cartwright, *A Letter from John Cartwright, Esq., to a Friend at Boston in the County of Lincoln*, pp. 23–24; Cartwright, *Take Your Choice!* p. 20.

27. [James Burgh], *Political Disquisitions*, 1:49; Joseph Priestley, *The Theological and Miscellaneous Works of Joseph Priestley*, 22:385; Priestley, *First Principles of Government*, pp. 21–22; Sharp, *People's Natural Right*, pp. 2–3; Sharp to Gamaliel Lloyd, Aug. 1795, box 28, pkt. D, Hardwicke MSS; Wyvill to Henry Joy, 22 Aug. 1783, *Letters to the Volunteers of Ireland*, pp. 26–27.

28. Cartwright, *Take Your Choice!* pp. 19–24; Cartwright, *Life*, 1:84–85. He explicitly rejected the extension of the franchise to women (*Legislative Rights of the Commonalty Vindicated*, pp. 46–47).

29. *Report of the Sub-Committee of Westminster Appointed April 12th 1780 . . .*, p. 4.

30. Cartwright, *American Independence*, p. 9; "Principles and Resolutions of the Constitutional Society at Cambridge" in Wyvill, *Defence of Price*, Appendix, paper 4; Burgh, *Political Disquisitions*, 1:3; Price, *Civil Liberty*, p. 6; Wyvill to Henry Joy, 22 Aug. 1783, *Letters to the Volunteers of Ireland*, pp. 22–23; Caleb Evans, *A Letter to the Rev. Mr. John Wesley Occasioned by His Calm Address to the American Colonies*, p. 11.

31. Sharp, *People's Natural Right*, p. xiv.

32. Cartwright, *Take Your Choice!* p. 6.

33. Ibid., p. 9.

34. [John Cartwright], *An Address to the Gentlemen Forming the Several Committees of the Associated Counties, Cities and Towns . . .*, p. ix.

35. Hoare, *Memoirs of Sharp*, p. 121; Robert Robinson, *A Political Catechism*, p. 34.

36. Robert, Viscount Molesworth, *The Principles of a Real Whig*, pp. 6–8. First printed as an introduction to Francis Hotoman's *Franco-Gallia* in 1721, Molesworth's remarks were later republished and offer a useful guide to commonwealth principles in the eighteenth century.

37. Sharp, *People's Natural Right*, p. 5.

38. Matthew Robinson-Morris, Baron Rokeby, to Elizabeth Montagu, 26 Nov. [1777], Montagu MSS; Sylas Neville, MS Diary, 21 Nov. 1767, quoted in Grayson McClure Ditchfield, "Some Aspects of Unitarianism and Radicalism 1760–1810," p. 49. But Mrs. Macaulay insisted she was no "bloody-minded Republican" (Donnelly, "Mrs Macaulay," p. 191).

39. Brand Hollis to John Adams, 5 Oct. 1787 and 28 May 1790, Adams Papers microfilm, reel 373; Robbins, *Commonwealthman*, p. 358; Basil Cozens-Hardy, ed., *The Diary of Sylas Neville, 1767–88*, pp. 15, 244–45.

40. Wyvill, *Defence of Price*, pp. v–vi; John Cartwright, *The People's Barrier against Undue Influence and Corruption*, p. v; Cartwright, *Life*, 1:192; Thomas Hollis to Andrew Eliot, summer 1767, transcript in "biographical account of Thomas Hollis," fol. 98, Jonathan Mayhew Papers; Burgh, *Political Disquisitions*, 1:9; Priestley, *First Principles of Government*, p. 22; Priestley, *Works*, 22:354, 358–59; Priestley, *Political Dialogues*, 34; Richard Price, *Observations on the Importance of the American Revolution and a Means of Making It a Benefit to the World*, p. 72n; Price to [William Smith, M.P.], 1 March 1790,

National Library of Wales. Zera S. Fink defines the term "republican" in the restricted sense used here in his study of the Commonwealthmen's seventeenth-century predecessors (*The Classical Republicans*, p. x).

41. Burgh, *Political Disquisitions*, 1:29.

42. Sharp, *People's Natural Right*, p. 5.

43. Burgh, *Political Disquisitions*, 1:406. Cf. Corinne Cornstock Weston, *English Constitutional Theory and the House of Lords*, pp. 143–59. Priestley and Cartwright later changed their view of the House of Lords.

44. Christie, *Wilkes, Wyvill and Reform*, pp. 72, 133–34; Sharp, Diary, 13 Feb. 1779, Sharp to Mr. Rogers, 31 March 1780, box G, Sharp 3, pkt. T, Hardwicke MSS.

45. Burgh, *Political Disquisitions*, 1:vi; Jebb to Lt. Col [William] Sharman, 14 Aug. 1783, *Letters to the Volunteers of Ireland*, p. 73.

46. See J. G. A. Pocock, *The Ancient Constitution and the Feudal Law*, and *Politics, Language and Time*; and Christopher Hill, *Puritanism and Revolution*.

47. The author has been persuasively identified as Obadiah Hulme (Robbins, *Commonwealthman*, p. 363).

48. [David Williams], *A Letter to the Body of Protestant Dissenters and to Protestant Ministers of All Denominations*, p. 4.

49. [Andrew Kippis], Review of *An Historical Essay on the English Constitution*, *Monthly Review* 44 (1771): 469–71; Cartwright, *American Independence*, p. 4. Granville Sharp called the system "frankpledge" and constantly advocated its introduction in both England and America (*A General Plan for Laying Out Towns and Townships on the Newly Acquired Lands in the East Indies, America, or Elsewhere*, pp. 10–13, and *An Account of the Constitutional Polity of Congregational Courts*, pp. 54–55, 191).

50. Catharine Macaulay to the Rev. Dr. Thomas Wilson, n.d., fols. 2–3, 125, 211–12, Catharine Macaulay Papers.

51. Cf. Robbins, *Commonwealthman*, p. 380.

52. Cartwright, *Take Your Choice!* pp. 17–18.

CHAPTER 2

1. For a general study of Atlantic society, see Michael Kraus, *The Atlantic Civilization*; it describes the wide range of elements that united Europe and America, but is largely concerned with the Anglo-American connection.

2. For a detailed description of American activities in England see William L. Sachse, *The Colonial American in Britain*, esp. pp. 178–90.

3. Leonard W. Labaree, "Benjamin Franklin's British Friendships," p. 423.

4. Robert E. Schofield, *The Lunar Society of Birmingham*, pp. 3, 17, 23–24, 38, 113.

5. David Williams, "Incidents in My Own Life," MS 2, 191, fols. 5–8, City of Cardiff Public Library; Franklin to Williams, 21 Feb. 1774, Benjamin Franklin Collection, Yale University.

6. Verner W. Crane, "The Club of Honest Whigs," pp. 216–26.

7. Labaree, "Franklin's British Friendships," p. 427; Carl B. Cone, *Torchbearer of Freedom*, pp. 63–65.

8. [Joseph Priestley], *Memoirs of Dr. Joseph Priestley*, p. 58.

9. Franklin to Brand Hollis, 5 Oct. 1783, Albert Henry Smyth, ed., *The Writings of Benjamin Franklin*, 9:103–5; Hollis to Mayhew, 19 June 1766, [Francis Blackburne], *Memoirs of Thomas Hollis, Esq.*, 1:335; James Burgh, *Political Disquisitions*, 2:277. For additional details of Franklin's associations, see Nicholas Hans, "Franklin, Jefferson and the English Radicals at the End of the Eighteenth Century," pp. 406–26.

10. Richard Henry Lee, *Life of Arthur Lee, LL.D.* 1:11–17, 52–55; George W. Connor, ed., *The Autobiography of Benjamin Rush*, pp. 54–55, 60–63.

11. Price to Charles Chauncy, 25 Feb. 1775, "The Letters of Richard Price," p. 279.

12. W. P. Cresson, *Francis Dana*, pp. 25–26; David Duncan Wallace, *The Life of Henry Laurens*, p. 185; Henry Marchant Papers and Diary (microfilm); George W. Gignilliat, Jr., *The Author of Sandford and Merton*, p. 123. Laurens's second visit to

London was less happy. He was captured en route for Holland in 1779 and spent three years as a prisoner in the Tower.

13. Benjamin Rush to Sharp, 1 May 1773, L. H. Butterfield, ed., *Letters of Benjamin Rush*, 1:80–81.

14. Baptists were less active as transatlantic correspondents, and when they did write their concerns were more circumscribed than those of other Dissenters. James Manning, president of Rhode Island College (later Brown University) began writing to a number of English Baptist ministers in about 1770. His correspondents included several men prominent within their own denomination such as Samuel Stennett, John Rylands, and particularly Caleb Evans of Bristol, but the subjects they discussed were almost always Baptist affairs and very seldom national politics. Even Manning's letters of 1776 made scarcely any reference to the Revolution (see James Manning Papers, Brown University Library).

15. Benjamin Vaughan to Franklin, 27 Jan. 1777, Franklin Papers, 5:36, APS. See Georgina Shipley to Franklin, 6 May 1781, ibid., 22:8; Franklin to Priestley, 3 Oct. 1775, Smyth, ed., *Writings*, 6:429–30, and 27 Jan. 1777, John Bigelow, ed., *The Complete Works of Benjamin Franklin*, 6:60–61.

16. See the collection of book-sale catalogues in the British Library.

17. [Thomas R. Adams], "The British Look at America during the Age of Samuel Johnson," p. ii. Much of the following paragraph is based on this catalogue; see the *Monthly Review* for additional studies published during these years.

18. Arthur John Hawkes, ed., *Lancashire Printed Books*, p. 123. Kalm's book was also published in London; it was the only overtly American book to be published in Lancashire before 1800.

19. Burnaby was an Anglican clergyman; he was conservative in his politics and opposed both the American cause during the Revolution and the granting of relief to Dissenters afterward.

20. Oldmixon's *British Empire* has recently been defended by Pat Rogers, "An Early Colonial Historian," pp. 113–23.

21. Fothergill to Lord Dartmouth, 12 [?] Jan. 1775, Betsy C. Corner and Christopher C. Booth, eds., *Chain of Friendship*, p. 436.

22. Thomas R. Adams, "The British Pamphlets of the American Revolution for 1774," p. 33. Adams's bibliography of Revolutionary tracts, *American Independence*, records many instances in which American political pamphlets were reprinted in England between 1764 and 1776. His "Preliminary Check List of British Pamphlets Relating to Affairs Concerning her Colonies in America, Printed 1764 through 1783," which he has very kindly permitted me to consult, has been of great assistance in this study; it will be published under the title *The American Controversy: A Bibliographical Study of the British Pamphlets Concerning the American Dispute, 1763–1783*.

23. The editor, Ralph Griffiths, was a Dissenter and possibly a Commonwealthman, and most of his colleagues shared his opinions. Their critical standards were high, but their political predispositions were often clear and evident in their reviews. See Benjamin Christie Nangle, *The Monthly Review: The First Series, 1749–1789*, p. ix.

24. *American Gazette* 1 (1768): title page.

25. *Monthly Review* 42 (1770): 153.

26. See Alvin R. Riggs, "Arthur Lee and the Radical Whigs," esp. chapter 1, for his activities as a publicist. His Junius Americanus letters may have been published in association with Stephen Sayre (see Sayre to S. Adams, 5 June 1770, Samuel Adams Papers).

27. Verner W. Crane, *Benjamin Franklin's Letters to the Press*, pp. xxvii, xxxiii–v.

28. Solomon Lutnick, *The American Revolution and the British Press*, pp. 20–22; Edward Dilly to John Dickinson, 28 Jan. 1775, Dickinson Papers; "Books printed for J. Almon," notice at end of brochure, *Speedily Will be Published a Map of the Middle British Colonies in North-America*, p. 4; John Almon, *Memoirs of a Late Eminent Bookseller*, p. 93.

29. John Lloyd to Almon, 21 Sept. 1775 and 9 Oct. 1776, Almon Correspondence, BL Add. MSS 20,733, fols. 67–68, 75; Samuel Wharton to Almon, 20 March 1779, ibid., fol.

141; Thomas Bradford to Almon, 20 March 1779, Almon, *Memoirs*, pp. 111–12; Ralph Izard to Almon, 16 Oct. 1777, fol. 60, Almon Correspondence.

30. *Monthly Review* 54 (1776): 501–2.

31. Vaughan to Franklin, 27 Jan. 1777, Franklin Papers, 5:36, APS; Crane, *Franklin's Letters*, pp. liii–liv.

32. For further details of the circulation of American pamphlets in England, especially among radicals, see my article, "An English Audience for American Revolutionary Pamphlets," *Historical Journal*, forthcoming.

33. Sons of Liberty of Boston to John Wilkes, 6 June 1768, William Palfrey to Wilkes, 21 Oct. 1769, James Bowdoin et al. to Wilkes, 23 March 1770, Wilkes Papers, BL Add. MSS 30,870, fols. 45, 212; 30,871, fols. 19–20. Palfrey asked Wilkes to pass a copy of Hutchinson's *Collection* to Mrs. Macaulay (Palfrey to Wilkes, 21 Oct. 1769 BL); Catharine Macaulay to the Town of Boston, 9 May 1770, and Charles Chauncy to Price, 22 March 1770, Boston Public Library.

34. Thomas Hollis, MS Diary, 6:169.

35. Ibid, 5:237. See Caroline Robbins, "The Strenuous Whig, Thomas Hollis of Lincoln's Inn," for further details of Hollis's activities.

36. Hollis, Diary, 5:149, 151; [Blackburne], *Memoirs of Hollis*, 1:400.

37. Hollis, Diary, 5:131, 135; 4:57; Franklin to Thomas Cushing, 7 July 1773, Colonial Office 5/118 fol. 61, PRO; Priestley to Franklin, 13 June 1772, Franklin Papers 3:103½, APS; Thomas Percival to Franklin, 21 June 1774, ibid., 4:21. Percival reported that he had distributed the tracts among leading citizens of the town and its vicinity and was confident they would make a significant impression. His optimism probably was misplaced as Manchester remained firmly loyal to the government.

38. Josiah Wedgwood to Thomas Bentley, 11 Dec. 1775, Wedgwood Papers.

39. Catalogue of Dr. Williams's Library, London, to which it was donated.

40. Nathaniel Lardner to Jonathan Mayhew, 18 July 1783, Jonathan Mayhew Papers; Hollis to Mayhew, 4 April 1764, Bernhard Knollenburg, ed., "Thomas Hollis and Jonathan Mayhew," pp. 144–45; Micaiah Towgood to Mayhew, 24 March 1764 and 5 April 1766, Jonathan Mayhew Papers; Catharine Macaulay to James Otis, 27 April 1769, "Warren-Adams Letters," *Collections of the Massachusetts Historical Society* 72 (1917): 7–8; Burgh, inscription on flyleaf of a copy of *Political Disquisitions* presented to John Adams, Boston Public Library, 2:vii (cf. Carla H. Hay, "Benjamin Franklin, James Burgh, and the Authorship of 'The Colonist's Advocate' Letters," pp. 119–22); Samuel Kenrick to James Wodrow, 2 April 1778, MS 24:157 fol. 59, Wodrow-Kenrick Correspondence; Fothergill to Lt. Col. Gilbert Ironside, 22 Dec. 1774, Corner and Booth, eds., *Chain of Friendship*, p. 430.

41. For example, Caleb Evans, *A Letter to the Rev. Mr. John Wesley Occasioned by His Calm Address to the American Colonies*, p. 21; Capel Lofft, *Observations on Mr. Wesley's Second Calm Address and Incidentally on Other Writings upon the American Question*, p. 86n.; Lee, *Life*, 1:189; Basil Cozens-Hardy, ed., *The Diary of Sylas Neville 1767–88*, pp. 244–45.

42. *Considerations upon This Question: What should be an Honest Englishman's Endeavour in the Present Controversy between Great Britain and the Colonies'*, p. 40.

43. [Joseph Priestley], *An Address to the Protestant Dissenters of All Denominations on the Approaching Election of Members of Parliament*, p. 5.

44. Jonathan Shipley, "A Sermon Preached before the Incorporated Society for the Propagation of the Gospel in Foreign Parts," *The Works of the Right Reverend Jonathan Shipley, D.D.*, 2:304.

45. [Blackburne], *Memoirs of Hollis*, 1:279.

46. The reputation of Jonathan Edwards, the greatest protagonist of the essentially Calvinist tradition of the Great Awakening, was largely confined to Scotland and the lesser of the English clergy (Thomas H. Johnson, *The Printed Writings of Jonathan Edwards, 1703–1758*, p. viii).

47. Richard Price, *A Preface to the Third Edition of the Treatise on Reversionary Payments*, pp. 27–28.

48. Ibid., pp. 28–29; Richard Price, *Observations on the Nature of Civil Liberty, the Principles of Government and the Justice Policy of the War with America*, p. 70.

49. Price, *Civil Liberty*, p. 70n.; Price, *Observations on the Importance of the American Revolution and the Means of Making It a Benefit to the World*, p. 69. Price may well have learned about Connecticut society through John Trumbull, the painter, whom he knew in London, and Jonathan Trumbull, the governor of the state, with whom he corresponded.

50. Richard Price, *Additional Observations on the Nature and Value of Civil Liberty and the War with America*, p. 25.

51. Price, *American Revolution*, pp. 77–78.

52. Sharp to Rush, 18 July 1775, John A. Woods, ed. "The Correspondence of Benjamin Rush and Granville Sharp 1773–1809," p. 16.

53. Price, *American Revolution*, pp. 75–76.

54. Joseph Priestley, *The Theological and Miscellaneous Works of Joseph Priestley*, 22:397–98.

55. Shipley, *Works*, 2:300.

56. Ibid., pp. 304–5.

57. [Matthew Robinson-Morris], *Considerations on the Measures Carrying on with Respect to the British Colonies in North America*, p. 135.

58. Price to Ezra Stiles, 2 Nov. 1773, Gratz Collection; Price, *Civil Liberty*, p. 98; Hollis, Diary, 6:168.

59. Price, *Civil Liberty*, p. 98.

60. Ibid.

61. Peter Gay, *Voltaire's Politics*, p. 42.

62. John Brooke, *King George III*, p. 75.

CHAPTER 3

1. Joseph Priestley, *An Address to the Protestant Dissenters of All Denominations on the Approaching Election of Members of Parliament*, p. 4.

2. The full story is told in Carl Bridenbaugh, *Mitre and Sceptre*, on which the following paragraphs are based. Although technically incorrect, the terms "Dissenter" and "Nonconformist" are applied to New England Congregationalists and Presbyterians since they are convenient and have the added advantage of indicating the relationship with their English counterparts.

3. Andrew Kippis, *A Vindication of the Protestant Dissenting Ministers with Regard to Their Late Application to Parliament*, p. 101.

4. Francis Blackburne, "A Critical Commentary on Archbishop Secker's Letter to the Right Honourable Horatio Walpole Concerning Bishops in America," pp. 48–49; Kippis, *Vindication*, p. 101.

5. Quoted in Bridenbaugh, *Mitre and Sceptre*, p. 259.

6. Micaiah Towgood to Mayhew, 5 April 1766, Jonathan Mayhew Papers. Towgood previously had written two pamphlets critical of the power of the Church of England which had been reprinted in America (Bridenbaugh, *Mitre and Sceptre*, pp. 140–41).

7. Thomas Pownall, Franklin's friend and sometime governor of Massachusetts whose *Administration of the Colonies* appeared in six editions between 1764 and 1777, is omitted from discussion here. He held advanced political opinions but remained outside the mainstream of radicalism. Similarly, the benevolence of his sentiments toward the colonists cannot be doubted, but he was particularly concerned with problems of imperial administration and argued for the establishment of a much stronger system of central control. Indeed, in his first edition he anticipated much that later became official policy, and he frequently supported the ministry during the crucial years of 1774 to 1775. When his patron ejected him from his seat at the general election of 1774, he was only returned to Parliament through the intercession of Lord North. Later, however, he warned of the need to recognize American independence. For Pownall's career see Caroline Robbins, *The Eighteenth Century Commonwealthman*, pp. 311–19; John A. Schutz, *Thomas Pownall*; G. H. Guttridge, "Thomas Pownall's *The Administration of the Colonies*"; John Shy,

"Thomas Pownall, Henry Ellis, and the Spectrum of Possibilities, 1763–1775," *Anglo-American Political Relations 1675–1775*, Alison Gilbert Olson and Richard Maxwell Brown, eds., pp. 161–81; Sir Lewis Namier and John Brooke, *The History of Parliament*, 1:371, 3:316–18.

8. [John Fothergill], *Considerations Relative to the North American Colonies*, pp. 16–28.

9. Fothergill to James Pemberton, 13 Feb. 1765, to the earl of Dartmouth, 29 Aug. 1765, to Pemberton, 8 April and 30 Sept. 1766, Betsy C. Corner and Christopher C. Booth, eds., *Chain of Friendship*, pp. 238–39, 248–49, 258–60, 269. Dartmouth was one of Fothergill's patients.

10. E.g., Theophilus Lindsey to the earl of Huntingdon, 4 Feb. 1776, Huntington Library.

11. In 1769, Priestley sent Franklin his best wishes "for the success of your laudable endeavours in the cause of *science, truth, justice, peace*, and, which comprehends them all, and everything valuable in human life, LIBERTY" (14 Feb. 1769, Leonard W. Labaree, William B. Willcox et al., eds., *The Papers of Benjamin Franklin*, 16:42).

12. Fred Junkin Hinkhouse, *The Preliminaries of the American Revolution as Seen in the English Press*, passim, esp. 51, 58–59, 141–42, 160, 182, 193–94; [John Adams], "Dissertation on the Canon and the Feudal Law," in [Thomas Hollis, ed.] *The True Sentiments of America*, p. 141.

13. [John Dickinson], *Letters from a Farmer in Pennsylvania to the Inhabitants of the British Colonies*, esp. pp. 3, 5, 7, 11–13, 16, 26, 47, 23–24; *Monthly Review* 39 (1768): 18–26.

14. Towgood to Mayhew, Dec. 1768, quoted in James Manning, *A Sketch of the Life and Writings of the Rev. Micaiah Towgood*, p. 68; Wilkes to the Sons of Liberty, 19 July 1768, Wilkes Papers, BL Add. MS 30, 879, fol. 46; John Cartwright, *American Independence the Interest and Glory of Great Britain*, pp. 5n., 70–71, appendix, p. 9, letter to Burke, p. 11; Granville Sharp, *A Declaration of the People's Natural Right to a Share in the Legislature*, p. 158n.; Caleb Evans, *A Letter to the Rev. Mr. John Welsey, Occasioned by His Calm Address to the American Colonies*, pp. 21–22; Capel Lofft, *Observations on Mr. Wesley's Second Calm Address and Incidentally on Other Writings upon the American Question*, p. 86n. Arthur Lee commented that the *Farmer's Letters* were widely read in London, but regretted that they were not having their intended effect on the ministry (A. Lee to R. H. Lee, 27 Dec. 1768, Lee Family Papers, microfilm edition, ed. Paul P. Hoffman, reel 1).

15. [Francis Blackburne], *Memoirs of Thomas Hollis, Esq.*, 1:59–60; Caroline Robbins, "The Strenuous Whig, Thomas Hollis of Lincoln's Inn," pp. 407–53, and "Library of Liberty," passim. For the reception of commonwealth ideology in the colonies see, in particular, Bernard Bailyn, *The Ideological Origins of the American Revolution*, pp. 34–54.

16. Hollis to Mayhew, 27 Oct. 1761, Bernhard Knollenberg, ed., "Thomas Hollis and Jonathan Mayhew: Their Correspondence," p. 124. Cf. Hollis to Eliot, 1 July 1768, "biographical account," fol. 107, Jonathan Mayhew Papers.

17. Benjamin Franklin, "Rules by which a Great Empire may be Reduced to a Small One," Adrienne Koch, ed., *The American Enlightenment*, p. 122; [John Adams], "Canon and Feudal Law," p. 141.

18. [Arthur Lee], *An Appeal to the Justice and Interests of the People of Great Britain, in the Present Disputes with America*, pp. 4–5.

19. Ibid., pp. 5–16.

20. *Monthly Review* 51 (1774): 148. Cf. Catharine Macaulay to James Otis, 27 April 1769, "Warren-Adams Letters," Massachusetts Historical Society, *Collections*, 72 (1917):7–8, and Brand Hollis to John Adams, 19 Oct. 1790, Adams Papers, microfilm reel 374.

21. Wedgwood to Bentley, 27 May 1767, Wedgwood Letters (microfilm transcript), Wedgwood Papers; Hollis to Eliot, 20 May [1768], "biographical account," fol. 106 Jonathan Mayhew Papers; Thomas Hollis, Diary, 5:172.

22. Joseph Priestley, *The Theological and Miscellaneous Works of Joseph Priestley*, 22:393.

23. Ibid., pp. 394–98; *Public Advertiser*, 4 Jan. 1770.

24. Wilkes to the Sons of Liberty of Boston, 19 July 1768, Wilkes Papers, BL Add. MS 30, 879, fol. 46; to John Horne Tooke, 14 June [1770], John Wilkes, John Horne Tooke et al., *The Controversial Letters of John Wilkes, Esq., the Rev. John Horne and Their Principal Adherents*, pp. 162–64; John Wilkes, *A Letter to His Grace the Duke of Grafton, First Commissioner of His Majesty's Treasury*, pp. 16–18; Rush to [?Jacob Rush], L. H. Butterfield, ed., *Letters of Benjamin Rush*, 1:72.

25. Alvin R. Riggs, "Arthur Lee," pp. 142–43, and A. Lee to R. H. Lee, 11 June 1771, quoted, ibid.; A. Lee to S. Adams, 14 June 1771, Samuel Adams Papers, vol. 1, New York Public Library; *Public Advertiser*, 25 July 1771, quoted in Ian R. Christie, *Wilkes, Wyvill and Reform*, p. 49; *Annual Register*, 16 March 1775, p. 99. The Adams cousins were sponsored by Lee and Sayre (Riggs, "Arthur Lee," p. 111).

26. Catharine Macaulay to the Town of Boston, 9 May 1770, Boston Public Library; Price to [Henry Marchant], 2 Nov. 1773, copy extract in Price to Ezra Stiles, Gratz Collection.

27. William Morgan, *Memoirs of the Life of the Rev. Richard Price*, pp. 50–51.

28. Catharine Macaulay to Marchant, Oct. 1774, Marchant Papers; Bernard Donoughue, *British Politics and the American Revolution*, pp. 127–61. Cf. Michael Kammen, "British and Imperial Interests in the Age of the American Revolution," *Anglo-American Political Relations*, ed. Olson and Brown, pp. 149–51.

29. Cartwright originally opposed the American cause but changed his mind after investigating the matter (Cartwright to Lord Howe, 6 Feb. 1776, Francis Dorothy Cartwright, *The Life and Correspondence of Major Cartwright*, 1:76).

30. Cartwright, *American Independence*, p. 6.

31. Ibid., pp. 54, 13, 63–64. Tucker based his arguments on economic self-interest rather than respect for any rights enjoyable by the colonists, whom he despised.

32. Ibid., pp. 65–67, 72, 30, 67–68.

33. Ibid., pp. 68, 27.

34. Anthony Benezet to Sharp, 14 May 1772, Prince Hoare, *Memoirs of Granville Sharp*, pp. 88–100; Sharp to Lord North, 18 Feb. 1772, box 28, pkt. O, Hardwicke MSS; Sharp to Benezet, 21 Aug. 1772, Granville Sharp Letterbook, fols. 58–69.

35. Sharp to Samuel Allinson, 28 July 1774, box 28, pkt. E, Hardwicke MSS; Rush to Sharp, 20 Sept. 1774, John A. Woods, ed., "The Correspondence of Benjamin Rush and Granville Sharp," p. 11; Sharp, Diary, 27 July 1774, to Rush, 27 July and to Allinson, 28 July 1774, box 28, pkt. E, Hardwicke MSS. Sharp warned his American correspondents that he regardẹd slavery as a serious impediment in the way of the colonists' attempts to justify their own rights.

36. Sharp to Rush, 21 Feb. 1774, box 28, pkt. E, Hardwicke MSS.

37. Sharp, *People's Natural Right*, pp. 44, 8–11, 227–29; Anne Pallister, *Magna Carta*, p. 64.

38. Thomas Blackburne to Jebb, 14 Oct. 1774, Letters of Francis Blackburne to Theophilus Lindsey, 12:52, fol. 101.

39. [Joseph Priestley], *Memoirs of Dr. Joseph Priestley*, p. 40; Priestley, *Address to the Protestant Dissenters of All Denominations*, pp. 10–15.

40. Christie, *Wilkes, Wyvill and Reform*, p. 53.

41. Verner W. Crane, *Benjamin Franklin's Letters to the Press*, pp. 286–87; Carla H. Hay, "Benjamin Franklin, James Burgh, and the Authorship of the 'Colonist's Advocate' Letters," pp. 119–22.

42. Namier and Brooke, *History of Parliament*, 1:75; *Annual Register* (1774), p. 152; Ian R. Christie, *Myth and Reality in Late-Eighteenth-Century British Politics and Other Papers*, pp. 244–60. Matthew Robinson-Morris was the anonymous author of a vigorous critique of government policy entitled *Considerations on the Measures Carrying on with Respect to the British Colonies in North America*, which went through three editions in London in 1774.

43. Obadiah Hulme, an obscure writer whose *Historical Essay on the English Constitution* had considerable influence on the formulation of domestic policy, was unique among radicals in arguing in support of virtual representation.

44. Lindsey to William Turner, 17 Nov. 1774, Letters to William Turner, 12:44, fol. 22.

45. Rush to Sharp, 1 Nov. 1774, Woods, ed., "Correspondence of Rush and Sharp," p. 14.

46. Josiah Quincy, Jr., to Abigail Quincy, 24 Nov. 1774, Josiah Quincy, Jr., Papers, QP 51, fol. 78.

47. "Journal of Josiah Quincy, Jun., During His Voyage and Residence in England from Sept. 28th. 1774 to March 3d, 1775," pp. 439–41, 443.

48. Quincy, "Journal," passim; Kippis, Joseph Jeffries, Matthew Towgood to Philip Furneaux, 22 Dec. 1774, Josiah Quincy, Jr., Papers, QP 51, fol. 87.

49. Lindsey to Turner, 17 Jan. 1775, Letters to William Turner, fol. 24.

50. Previously Mrs. Macaulay had declined to write on American affairs as she was too busy preparing her *History*; she also argued that "the general principles of the rights of man-kind inculcated in my great work, is of more advantage to them than the more suspected arguments framed for the service of a particular purpose" (Catharine Macaulay, *Loose Remarks on Certain Positions to be found in Mr Hobbes' Philosophical Rudiments of Government* . . . , p. 35).

51. Catharine Macaulay, *An Address to the People of England, Scotland and Ireland on the Present Important Crisis of Affairs*, pp. 2–6, 29.

52. Richard Price, "A Sketch of Proposals for Discharging the Public Debts, Securing Public Liberty, and Preserving the State" [late 1774 or early 1775], Shelburne Papers, 117:57; Price to Lord Chatham, 9 Feb. 1775, Chatham Papers, 5:209. Lindsey to Turner, 26 Jan. 1775, Letters to William Turner, fol. 25. Chatham recommended repeal of various acts offensive to the colonists and recognition of the Continental Congress; the crux was his insistence on the continuation of parliamentary sovereignty even though revenue was not to be raised by the colonial assemblies. Chatham also proposed withdrawal of the troops from Boston.

53. Price to Charles Chauncy, 25 Feb. 1775, "The Letters of Richard Price," p. 279.

54. R. Hingston Fox, *Dr. John Fothergill and His Friends*, pp. 328, 333, 343–44; Carl Van Doren, *Benjamin Franklin*, pp. 495–519; Fothergill to Lord Dartmouth, [6?] Feb. 1775, Corner and Booth, cds., *Chain of Friendship*, p. 442.

55. Ian R. Christie, *Crisis of Empire*, p. 95; Priestley, *Works*, 22:487; Jebb to a friend, 21 Nov. 1774, John Disney, ed., *The Works Theological, Medical, Political and Miscellaneous of John Jebb MD, FRS, with Memoirs of the Life of the Author*, 1:86.

56. *The Remembrancer* 1 (1775): 9, 10–11, 17–19, 21, 78–80; William Lee to Josiah Quincy, 12 April 1775, quoted in Pauline Maier, *From Resistance to Revolution*, p. 253n.

CHAPTER 4

1. A. Lee to S. Adams, 23 June 1773, Samuel Adams Papers, vol. 2.

2. Edward Dilly to John Dickinson, 7 March 1774, Dickinson Papers; Burgh, *Political Disquisitions*, 2:322.

3. John Cartwright, MS note in his *A Letter to Edmund Burke*, "Political Discourses," 1:28, bound and annotated collection of his published works, Houghton Library.

4. [John Cartwright], *American Independence the Interest and Glory of Great Britain*, pp. 58, 57n.; David Hartley, draft speech to the House of Commons, n.d., Hartley-Russell Papers, D/EHy 037 78a.

5. Fothergill to Pemberton, 17 March 1775, Betsy C. Corner and Christopher C. Booth, eds., *Chain of Friendship*, p. 446; Lettsom to Rush [summer 1775], Rush Papers, 28:45.

6. Jebb to Lindsey, 7 May 1775, Gratz Collection; Franklin to Priestley, 3 Oct. 1775, Albert Henry Smyth, ed., *The Writings of Benjamin Franklin*, 6:430.

7. Priestley to Franklin, 13 Feb. 1776, Franklin Papers, 4:79, APS. Six years later Price

assured Franklin that the club never met without drinking his health (Price to Franklin, 7 Jan. 1782, Franklin Papers–Bache Collection, APS).

8. The first issue of *The Crisis* was dated 21 Jan. 1775; the last, 12 Oct. 1776. Moore is identified by Paul Leicester Ford (*Bibliographer*, 1 [1902]: 140), and Thicknesse by a manuscript note in a set belonging to the Bodleian Library. For examples of attacks on George III, see pp. 15, 129–31, 208; and for incitement to armed resistance, see pp. 27, 78, 142, 180, 182, 244–46, 271, 319, 354. The question of a possible uprising in England is discussed at length by Pauline Maier in *From Resistance to Revolution*, pp. 246–63.

9. [David Williams], *Letters on Political Liberty*, p. 30; Kenrick to Wodrow, 30 Aug. 1775, Wodrow-Kenrick Correspondence, fol. 53. Josiah Quincy's judgment of November 1774 (formed during his fifteen-day journey from the Cornish port of Falmouth to London) that the people were as sympathetic to America as previously they had been hostile seems unduly optimistic (Quincy to Abigail Quincy, 24 Nov. 1774, Josiah Quincy, Jr., Papers, QP 51, fol. 78).

10. Cartwright, *American Independence*, p. 10; Richard Price, *Additional Observations on the Nature and Value of Civil Liberty and the War with America*, p. 32.

11. Cartwright, *American Independence*, p. 10.

12. Wedgwood to Bentley, 8 Jan. 1775, Wedgwood Letters (transcript microfilm), Wedgwood Papers.

13. Wedgwood to Bentley, 6 Feb. 1775, ibid. The "Dr. Roe" mentioned in Wedgwood's letter had been identified as John Roebuck, author of the progovernment tract *An Enquiry Whether the Guilt of Present Civil War Ought to be Imputed to Great Britain or America*, by Anne Finer (*American Letters in the Wedgwood Museum*, microfilm edition, p. 17.

14. Lindsey to Turner, 17 Jan. 1775, Letters to William Turner, fol. 24.

15. Lawrence Henry Gipson, *The British Empire before the American Revolution*, 12:288–93.

16. Solomon Lutnick, *The American Revolution and the British Press*, p. 52.

17. Home Office 55/7–8, PRO; Champion to Portland, 5 Oct. 1775, Portland Papers, PWF 2,718. The difference, he claimed, was that the government petition was signed by ex-Jacobite tradesmen and by many country gentry, whereas the signatories to his own petition were preponderant among the mercantile and trading interests.

18. Donald Read, *The English Provinces c. 1760–1960*, p. 10; John Alfred Langford, *A Century of Birmingham Life*, 1:214, 217, 228–30, 239–42; John Money, "Public Opinion in the West Midlands 1760–1793," pp. 305–14.

19. Fothergill to Pemberton, 26 Jan. 1775, Corner and Booth, eds., *Chain of Friendship*, p. 439; Dora Mae Clark, *British Opinion and the American Revolution*, p. 92.

20. Edmund Burke to the Marquess of Rockingham, [22]–23 Aug. 1775, Thomas W. Copeland et al., eds., *The Correspondence of Edmund Burke*, 3:190.

21. Ibid., p. 191.

22. Rockingham to Burke, 24 Sept. 1775, ibid., p. 215.

23. Anthony Lincoln, *Some Political and Social Ideas of English Dissent 1763–1800*, pp. 21–22; John Martin, *Familiar Dialogues Between Americanus and Britannicus*; Caleb Evans, *A Reply to the Rev. Mr. Fletcher's Vindication of Mr. Wesley's Calm Address to Our American Colonies*, p. 85; L. F. S. Ufton, ed., *The Diary and Selected Papers of Chief Justice William Smith*, 1:13; Sir Lewis Namier and John Brooke, *The History of Parliament*, 2:628–29.

24. Nehemiah Curnock, ed., *The Journal of the Rev. John Wesley, AM*, 6:84–85; Maldwyn Edwards, *After Wesley*, pp. 20–21. As yet the relationship of the Methodists to the Church of England was unsettled, and though they were no longer orthodox, they were not Dissenters in the fullest sense.

25. London Yearly Meeting to Philadelphia Yearly Meeting, 27 May 1776, London Yearly Meeting, Minutes, 16:279, and London Meeting for Sufferings, Minutes, 35:334–38, Friends' House Library; A. T. Gary, "The Political and Economic Relations of English and American Quakers (1750–1785)," p. 354.

26. Deposition of Captain Smyth, State Papers, Domestic, 17 June 1780, 37/20/276; [Judge] Davies [?] Barrington, to anon., 12 June 1780, SP 37/20/246. The papers relating

to the prosecution of Lord George Gordon do not refer to this (Treasury Solicitor's Papers 11/388 1212–14). Isaac Rogerson to Viscount Weymouth, 12 and 30 Aug. 1777, SP 37/12/116–17, all in PRO.

27. TS 11/24/62, 11/1079/5378–79, 5381–82, 5385–86, 5388–89, PRO. One of the accused, Henry Sampson Woodfall, retained Arthur Lee as his counsel, assuming he knew more about the subject (*The Trial (at Large) of John Horne, Esq . . .*, p. 15). The third issue of *The Crisis* had been condemned by both Houses of Parliament and burned by the public hangman.

28. *Further Proceedings on the Trial of John Horne Esq.*, p. 17; *The Trial (at Large) of John Horne, Esq.*, pp. 20–31.

29. TS 11/939, PRO; Maier, *Resistance to Revolution*, pp. 261–62.

30. [Granville Sharp], *An Address to the People of England*; Catharine Macaulay to Franklin, 8 Dec. 1777, Franklin Papers, 7:138, APS.

31. Fothergill to Pemberton, 26 Jan. 1775, Corner and Booth, eds., *Chain of Friendship*, p. 439; Savile, quoted in Read, *English Provinces*, p. 10.

32. Lord North, 18 April 1785, [William Cobbett, ed.], *The Parliamentary History of England from the Earliest Period to the Year 1803*, 25:457.

33. Ufton, ed. *The Diary and Selected Papers of William Smith*, 1:13; John Aiken et al., *General Biography*, 5:121; Priestley to Matthew Boulton, 8 Nov. 1775, Matthew Boulton Collection, p. 2, fol. 210; Frances Dorothy Cartwright, *The Life and Correspondence of Major Cartwright*, 1:72–81.

34. Sharp, Diary, 26 July 1775, box 56, Hardwicke MSS; Prince Hoare, *Memoirs of Granville Sharp*, pp. 128–29.

35. Thomas Day, *Fragment of an Original Letter on the Slavery of Negroes*, p. 33. Many other radicals, including Sharp and David Hartley in particular, found the incongruity between American principles and practices greatly distressing.

36. William Smith, *A Sermon on the Present Situation of American Affairs*, p. ii; Sharp to John Boddington, 26 Sept. 1775, Hoare, *Memoirs of Sharp*, p. 124; Fothergill to Pemberton, 23 Aug. 1775, Corner and Booth, eds., *Chain of Friendship*, p. 453; Price, Memorandum [1775], Richard Price Papers, APS; Cartwright, MS note dated April 1776 in *American Independence*, "Political Discourses," 1:n.p.

37. Sharp to Shute Barrington, bishop of Llandaff, 10 June 1775, box 28, pkt. D, Hardwicke MSS; Priestley to Savile, 28 Oct. 1775, Historical Manuscripts Commission, *Fifteenth Report Appendix*, pt 5: *The Manuscripts of the Right Honourable F. J. Savile Foljambe*, p. 149.

38. Enclosure in Fothergill to David Barclay, 8 Oct. 1775, Corner and Booth, eds., *Chain of Friendship*, pp. 481–88; John Wilkes, *The Speeches of John Wilkes . . . in the Parliament Appointed to Meet . . . the 29th day of November 1774 . . .*, 1:74; Capel Lofft, *A View of the Several Schemes with Respect to America*, pp. 24–39.

39. Turner to Lindsey, 6 Dec. 1775, MS letter inserted in John Towill Rutt, *Life and Correspondence of Joseph Priestley*, at 1:170, DWL MSS, 12:79–80.

40. Lindsey to Turner, Dec. 1775, Lindsey Correspondence, fol. 39, DW4; Kenrick to Wodrow, 29 Jan. 1776, Wodrow-Kenrick Correspondence, fol. 55.

41. Price originally suggested printing only five hundred copies of the first edition but Thomas Cadell, its publisher, suggested increasing the print run to one thousand copies when he learned that Price was willing to sign it (Price to William Adams, 14 Aug. 1776, Letters of Richard Price, GRO, D6/F140). Fourteen editions were printed in London alone in 1776, and within a few months more than fifty thousand copies had been sold (Carl B. Cone, *Torchbearer of Freedom*, pp. 77–78).

42. Priestley to Franklin, 13 Feb. 1776, Franklin Papers, 4:79, APS; Lindsey to Jebb, 17 Feb. 1776 in John Towill Rutt, *Life and Correspondence of Priestley*, 1:189n; Cartwright, *Life of Cartwright*, 1:116.

43. Wedgwood to Bentley, 21 and 24 Feb. 1776, Wedgwood Papers.

44. Kenrick to Wodrow, 29 Jan. 1776, *Monthly Review* 54 (1776): 225; Thomas Hardy, *Memoirs of Thomas Hardy*, pp. 8–9; City of London Common Council, Journal, 14 March 1776, 66:296. The Common Council was so anxious to honor Price immediately

that it voted to suspend a resolution of 1771 which required any motion proposing a grant of the freedom of the City to be adjourned until the next meeting for further consideration (ibid.).

45. Price, *Civil Liberty*, p. 32.

46. See above, chapter 1, for a brief discussion of Price's conception of liberty.

47. Price, *Civil Liberty*, pp. 6–7, 15.

48. Ibid., pp. 19–20, 24.

49. Ibid., pp. 34–36, 41, 48–51.

50. Ibid., pp. 57, 27.

51. Ibid., pp. 36–37, 48, 43–44.

52. Ibid., pp. 87–89, 94–96, 71–73, 74–87.

53. Ibid., pp. 8–9, 27.

54. Ibid., pp. 104–7.

55. Merrill Jensen, ed., *English Historical Documents: American Colonial Documents to 1776*, p. 867.

56. Lutnick, *American Revolution*, p. 75; *Lloyd's Evening Post*, 14 Aug. 1776; *Morning Chronicle*, 17 Aug. 1776; *Gazeteer*, 17 Aug. 1776; [U. S. Continental Congress], *Declaration of Independence*, broadsheet.

57. Ralph Izard to Claude Crespigny, 31 Aug. 1776, *Correspondence of Mr. Ralph Izard of South Carolina, From the Year 1774 to 1804*, 1:221–22; William Lee to C. W. F. Dumas, 10 Sept. 1776, and to Richard Henry Lee, 15 Oct. 1776, Worthington C. Ford, ed., *Letters of William Lee 1766–1783*, 1:183, 185.

58. *The Crisis*, pp. 527–31, 554–56; Wilkes, *Speeches of John Wilkes . . .* , 1:138; Lindsey to Turner, 6 Sept. 1776, Letters to William Turner, fol. 27; C. B. R. Kent, *English Radicals*, p. 90; *Monthly Review* 55 (1776): 345.

59. Price to William Adams, 14 Aug. 1776, Letters of Richard Price, GRO, D6/F140. Cf. Price to Adams, 10 Feb. 1778, ibid., "If the colonies are engaged to France as there is reason to fear, even a recognition of their independence would not recover them, or prevent a general war."

60. Catharine Macaulay to Marchant, June 1773, Marchant Papers.

61. Richard Watson, *The Principles of the REVOLUTION Vindicated*, pp. 18, 21–22; Kenrick to Wodrow, 29 Jan.–13 Feb. 1778, fol. 59, Wodrow-Kenrick Correspondence.

62. Newcome Cappe, *A Sermon Preached on the Thirteenth of December . . .* , pp. 28–29.

63. Wedgwood to Bentley, 29 Dec. 1777, Wedgwood Papers. Wedgwood had already found a distinctive medium for expressing his political opinions. Where some men expressed theirs in sermons, tracts, or speeches in the House of Commons, Wedgwood expressed his in clay. He informed Bentley in April 1777, "We have some good Doctr [sic] Franklins . . . out of the kiln today" and later the same year told him, "The Rattle-Snake is in hand. I think it will be best to keep such unchristian articles for PRIVATE TRADE" (Wedgwood to Bentley [14 Apr. 1777] and 8 Aug. 1777, Wedgwood Papers).

64. Fothergill to Franklin, [1778–80], Corner and Booth, eds., *Chain of Friendship*, pp. 477–80.

65. Lindsey to Turner, 4 Oct. 1778 and 22 July 1779, fols. 31, 34, Letters to William Turner.

66. Wilkes, *Speeches of John Wilkes*, 3:18.

67. Sharp, Diary, 14 March 1777, "fair copy of a draft" [to Dartmouth], March 1777, box 21, pkt. 5, both in Hardwicke MSS.

68. Sharp to the duke of Richmond, 11 Dec. 1777, box 28, pkt. D, ibid.

69. Cartwright to [Frances D. Cartwright], 24 March 1777, Cartwright, *Life of Cartwright*, 1:100; John Cartwright, *The Legislative Rights of the Commonalty Vindicated*, pp. 237–47. Some years later Cartwright put his proposals to Henry Laurens, the American statesman, after his release from the Tower of London. Laurens tactfully replied that it was probably better for the peace and happiness of mankind that such a union should not take place for it would give Britain such great influence as would upset the balance of power (Cartwright, *Life of Cartwright*, 1:60).

70. Price to Cadell, [?10] Jan. 1777, Bodleian MSS 25,435, fol. 19; Price, *Additional Observations on the Nature and Value of Civil Liberty and the War with America*, pp. 72–73.

71. Price, *Additional Observations*, pp. 77–82, 72–74, 89, viii–ix.

72. Price to Lee and Winthrop, 15 June 1777, "Letters of Richard Price," p. 311. Franklin, Lee, and John Adams to Price, 7 Dec. 1778, Benjamin Franklin Collection, Yale University; Lee to Price, 8 Dec. 1778, Richard Price Papers, APS; Price to Lee, 18 Jan. 1779, Boston Public Library.

73. David Hartley, "Draft speech to the House of Commons," n.d., Hartley-Russell Papers, D/EHy 78a; [Cobbett, ed.,], *Parliamentary History*, 17:1047–50.

74. Hartley, "Draft resolution for the House of Commons," endorsed 1777, Hartley-Russell Papers, D/EHy 037 7c. In Hartley's papers is a copy of a resolution of Congress dated 22 November 1777 declaring that any peace proposal that was inconsistent with American independence would be rejected (ibid., D/EHy 039 8); cf. Franklin to Hartley, 14 Oct. 1777 (Smyth, ed., *Writings of Franklin*, 7:68–72).

75. Hartley to Wyvill, 22 March 1780, Christopher Wyvill, *Political Papers*, 3:188–89; [Cobbett, ed.], *Parliamentary History*, 20:906–7. Hartley was defeated at the general election of 1780, reelected at a by-election in 1782, defeated again in 1784, and thereafter retired (Namier and Brooke, *History of Parliament* 2:593).

76. William Pulteney to Lord George Germain, 6 Dec. 1777, Historical Manuscripts Commission, *Report on the Manuscripts of Mrs. Stopford-Sackville*, 2:81–82; James Hutton to Germain, 25 Jan. 1778, ibid., p. 91–92; [John Jebb], *An Address to the Freeholders of Middlesex*, p. 17n; Capel Lofft, *An Argument on the Nature of Party and Faction*, p. 57.

77. London Common Council, Journal, 13 April 1780, 68:52; Yorkshire Committee Minute Book, vol. 2, 3 May 1780, Wyvill Papers, ZFW 7/2/2/2.

78. *General Advertiser*, 10 Oct. 1782. The Yorkshire Committee was also thinking wistfully along similar lines in April 1782 (Minute Book, vol. 2, 4 April 1782, Wyvill Papers).

79. Priestley to Franklin, 13 Feb. 1776 and 13 Dec. 1777, Franklin Papers, 4:79 and 7:145, APS; Priestley to Lord Shelburne, 20 March 1778, quoted in Anne Holt, *A Life of Joseph Priestley*, pp. 78–80.

80. Fothergill to Franklin, [1778–80], Cartwright to Portland, 22 Feb. and 31 March 1777, Portland Papers, PWF 2568–69; John Cartwright, *A Letter to the Earl of Abingdon*, pp. 38–39, 44, 45n.

81. John Wilkes, *The Speeches of Mr. Wilkes in the House of Commons*, pp. 299–300, 311; Price to Baron Johan Derck van der Capellen van der Poll, 28 May 1779, W. H. de Beaufort, ed., *Brieven van en aan Johan van der Capellen van der Poll*, p. 101.

82. Sharp, Diary, Jan., 17 Feb., 7 April 1778; Richmond does not seem to have given up the possibility of reunion at this stage; in May he tried to persuade a Virginian that it would be to America's advantage to accept a connection with England under the crown with proper safeguards (Sharp, Diary, 7 May 1778).

83. Sharp, "Memorandum for the Consideration of the Citizens of London," c. 1778, box 28, pkt. D; Sharp to John Hinchcliffe, bishop of Peterborough, 3 July 1781, ibid.; Diary, 23 June, 8, 10, 18, 19 Oct. 1781; Sharp to Oglethorpe, 26 Oct. 1781, box 54, Hardwicke MSS.

84. Horace Walpole, *Journal*, 2:482, 4 Dec. 1781, quoted in Henry Jephson, *The Platform*, 1:137. But they continued to hope for reunion (above, p. 107).

85. Jebb to Wyvill, 27 Sept. and 11 Dec. 1781, Wyvill MSS, ZFW 7/2/23/6,8; Westminster Committee, Minutes, 8, 10 Dec. 1781, BL Add. MSS 30,594, fols. 21–24; Price to Franklin, 7 Jan. 1782, Franklin Papers–Bache Collection, APS.

86. Thomas Day, *Reflections upon the Present State of England and the Independence of America*, pp. 7, 106; Vincent T. Harlow, *The Founding of the Second British Empire 1763–1793*, 1:231–34; Thomas Pownall to Franklin, July 1781 and 13 May 1782, Franklin Papers, 22:100, 25:70, APS; Thomas Pownall, *Two Memorials, Not Originally Intended for Publication and Now Published*, p. 7. Earlier Pownall had asked leave to bring

in a bill to the House of Commons empowering the king to make peace with America in the belief that a proper policy might bring about reconciliation ([Cobbett, ed.], *Parliamentary History*, 21:627, 24 May 1780).

87. Price to Franklin, 18 Nov. 1782, Franklin Papers–Bache Collection, APS.

88. Jebb, Speech at a General Meeting of the City of Westminster, 17 July 1782, Wyvill, *Papers*, 2:160–61.

89. [Andrew Kippis], *Considerations on the Provisional Treaty with America and the Preliminary Articles of Peace with France and Spain*, pp. 7–24, 30–31; See Harlow, *Second British Empire*, 1:461–78, 487–90, for Hartley's role in the peace negotiations.

90. Wyvill to Foljambe, 2 Jan. 1782, Wyvill Papers, ZFW 7/2/28/1; to Lord Mahon, 24 Aug. 1782, ibid., ZFW 7/2/27/9; to Hartley, 13 Sept. 1782, ibid., ZFW 7/2/26/7.

91. Weldon A. Brown, *Empire or Independence*, p. 141.

92. L. H. Butterfield, ed., *The Adams Papers*, 1:257.

CHAPTER 5

1. Ian R. Christie explodes much of the mythology surrounding the early years of George III's reign in his collection of articles published under the title *Myth and Reality in Late-Eighteenth-Century British Politics and Other Papers*, esp. chapters 1 and 7.

2. George Rudé, *Wilkes and Liberty*, pp. 179–84, 105. Rudé and Christie agree that the industrial unrest of the period was virtually independent of the political movement (Rudé, *Wilkes and Liberty*, pp. 103–4; Ian R. Christie, *Wilkes, Wyvill and Reform*, pp. 223–24).

3. Hollis was publicly urging reform in 1766 ([Francis Blackburne], *Memoirs of Thomas Hollis, Esq.*, 1:322); Christie, *Wilkes, Wyvill and Reform*, pp. 18–24; John Cannon, *Parliamentary Reform 1640–1832*, pp. 52–56.

4. Basil Cozens-Hardy, ed., *The Diary of Sylas Neville 1767–88*, pp. 61–62; Thomas Somerville, *My Own Life and Times 1741–1814*, p. 146; [Blackburne], *Memoirs of Hollis*, 1:289, 393; Priestley to Wilkes, n.d., Wilkes Papers, BL Add. MSS 30,877, fol. 66; Joseph Priestley, *The Theological and Miscellaneous Works of Joseph Priestley*, 22:486–87. Cartwright remarked to a friend, "I will agree with you in hanging Mr. Wilkes, if he can be *legally* tucked up; but no reflections, I beg of you, upon the cap of liberty" (Cartwright to anon., 4 Sept. 1775, Frances Dorothy Cartwright, *The Life and Correspondence of Major Cartwright*, 1:54).

5. William Palfrey to Wilkes, 21 Feb. 1769, Wilkes Papers, BL Add. MSS 30,870, fol. 114; Wilkes to Horne Tooke, 14 June [1770], John Wilkes, John Horne Tooke, et al., *The Controversial Letters of John Wilkes, Esq., the Rev. John Horne and Their Principal Adherents*, p. 164. Wedgwood had remarked some time earlier that "Mr. Grenville and his party seem determined to *Conquer England in America*," Wedgwood to Thomas Bentley, 20 May 1767, Wedgwood Letters (microfilm transcript), Wedgwood Papers. For the importance of the Wilkes affair in America, see Pauline Maier, "John Wilkes and American Disillusionment with Britain," pp. 373–95, and *From Resistance to Revolution*, esp. chapter 6.

6. James Burgh, "The Colonist's Advocate" letters in the *Public Advertiser*, 4 Jan. to 2 March 1770, and the "Constitutionalist" letters in the *Gazeteer and New Daily Advertiser*, 15 July 1769 to 25 May 1770; Priestley, *Works*, 22:361.

7. [Arthur Lee], *The Political Detection*, pp. 65–67. William Lee savagely attacked North as "a Tyrant from Principle, cunning, Treacherous & Persevering" in a letter to his brother Richard Henry Lee, 10 Sept. 1774, Lee Family Papers, microfilm ed., reel 2.

8. Stephen Sayre to Samuel Adams, 5 June 1770, Samuel Adams Papers.

9. Priestley, *Works*, 22:482–87, 496.

10. James Burgh, *Political Disquisitions*, 2:274–76; Price to Chatham, 9 Feb. 1775, Chatham Papers 53:209; Price to Chauncey, 25 Feb. 1775, "The Letters of Richard Price," p. 279; cf. Richard Price, *Observations on the Nature of Civil Liberty, The Principles of Government and the Justice and Policy of the War with America*, p. 102.

11. Brand Hollis to [Simeon Howard], 4 Jan. 1775, Boston Public Library; Catharine Macaulay, *Address to the People*, p. 24; John Cartwright, *Take Your Choice!* pp. xxi–xxii;

Willoughby Bertie, earl of Abingdon, *Thoughts on the Letter of Edmund Burke, Esq., to the Sheriffs of Bristol on the Affairs of America*, p. 60.

12. [Richard Goodenough], *The Constitutional Advocate*, pp. 4, 6–22, 25–27, 32–33, 42–43; *A Prospect of the Consequences of the Present Conduct of Great Britain towards America*, pp. 5–6; *The Case Stated on Philosophical Grounds Between Great Britain and Her Colonies*, pp. 120–21; "Constitutionalis," *Letters to the Electors and People of England Preparatory to the Approaching General Election*, pp. 6, 17–21.

13. [Blackburne], *Memoirs of Hollis*, 1:289; Price, "Sketch of Proposals," Shelburne Papers, 117:43; Cartwright, *American Independence, the Interest and Glory of Great Britain*, pp. iv, ix; Catharine Macaulay, *Address to the People*, p. 29.

14. Granville Sharp, *The Legal Means of Political Reformation*, p. 16; Richard Price, *A Sermon Delivered to a Congregation of Protestant Dissenters . . .*, pp. 27–28.

15. Rees David, *The Hypocritical Fast with its Design and Consequences*; Joshua Toulmin, *The American War Lamented*; Samuel Stennett, *National Calamities the Effect of Divine Displeasure*; Newcome Cappe, *A Sermon Preached on the Thirteenth of December . . .*, pp. 10–19; Ebenezer Radcliff, *A Sermon Preached at Walthamstow, December 13, 1776 . . .*, pp. 14–17.

16. Radcliffe, *Sermon*, p. 5, cf. Richard Price, *Observations on the Importance of the American Revolution and the Means of Making It a Benefit to the World*, p. 3.

17. Granville Sharp, *The Law of Retribution*, p. 252; Price, *Sermon*, pp. 16–17; Toulmin, *American War Lamented*, p. 12.

18. Price, *Sermon*, p. 26; note his comparison between English and American society at the beginning of the war (*Civil Liberty*, p. 98).

19. Cozens-Hardy, ed., *Diary of Neville*, p. 3.

20. *Gentleman's Magazine* 40 (1770): 312; Lindsey to Turner, 26 Jan. 1775, Letters of William Turner, fol. 25; Price to Chauncy, 25 Feb. 1775, "The Letters of Richard Price," p. 279.

21. Priestley, *Works*, 22:489–90.

22. Robinson-Morris, *Considerations on the Measures Carrying on with Respect to the British Colonies in North America*, pp. 134–45. He considered the Americans had excellent forms of government on somewhat the same lines as those of the ancient world.

23. Jebb to William Chambers, 16 July 1775, John Disney, ed., *The Works, Theological, Medical, Political and Miscellaneous of John Jebb MD, FRS, with Memoirs of the Life of the Author*, 1:148.

24. Price to van der Cappellen, 28 May 1779, W. H. de Beaufort, ed., *Brieven van en aan Johan Derck van der Cappellen van der Poll*, p. 101; Price, *Sermon*, pp. 1–17; Price to Arthur Lee, 18 Jan. 1779, Boston Public Library; Richard Price, *The General Introduction and Supplement to the Two Tracts on Civil Liberty . . .*, pp. xiv–xvi.

25. Thomas Day, *Reflections upon the Present State of England and the Independence of America*, pp. 105–6; Jebb to Wyvill, 27 Sept. 1781, Wyvill Papers, ZFW 7/2/23/6. Cf. Jebb's exultant eulogy to America: "O America! liberated, triumphant, independent, nurse of heroes, asylum sacred to suffering humanity!" ("To the Inhabitants of London and Westminster," 14 Aug. 1782, Disney, ed., *Works of Jebb*, 3:321); [Andrew Kippis], *Considerations on the Provisional Treaty with America*, pp. 7–24, 30–31.

26. Price to Franklin, 18 Nov. 1782, Franklin Papers–Bache Collection, APS.

27. Christie, *Wilkes, Wyvill and Reform*, p. 67; *The Crisis*, 21 Sept. 1776, pp. 554–56.

28. Price to Sharp, March 1780, box 54, Hardwicke MSS.

29. Herbert Butterfield, "The Yorkshire Association and the Crisis of 1779–80," p. 72.

30. Christie, *Wilkes, Wyvill and Reform*, p. 224; Cannon, *Parliamentary Reform*, p. 95.

31. Christie, *Wilkes, Wyvill and Reform*, pp. 72–77, 85–95, 99–106, 110–14.

32. Radicals had taken seven out of ten metropolitan seats in the general election of 1774 and nine out of twelve (including Surrey) in 1780 (George Rudé, *Hanoverian London*, pp. 170, 177).

33. Another of Sharp's more extreme proposals which produced no response was his suggestion that the county associations would never be respected by the government until

they were armed. In making this recommendation he was not urging military insurrection but declaring his belief in the putative ancient right of the people to bear arms and serve in a militia as a preferable alternative to the maintenance of a standing army (Sharp to Lord Carysfoot, 5 Dec. 1781, box 28, pkt. D, Hardwicke MSS). Taking his cue from Burgh's *Political Disquisitions*, he wished the counties, expressing the sense of the people through county courts, to elect, instruct, and supervise members of Parliament. His object was to ensure that government should be responsive to the people in the way that he believed it had been several centuries earlier; at no time did he act in a spirit of innovation, which he heartily mistrusted.

34. Rudé, *Hanoverian London*, p. 176; City of London Common Council Journal, 18 April 1780, 67:50; Christie, *Wilkes, Wyvill and Reform*, pp. 109–10.

35. Westminster Committee, Minutes, 2 Feb. 1780, BL Add. MSS 38, 593, fol. 1; Christie, *Wilkes, Wyvill and Reform*, pp. 82–83, 108–9.

36. Christie, *Wilkes, Wyvill and Reform*, pp. 77–79; Burgh, *Political Disquisitions*, 3:420–60; Herbert Butterfield, *George III, Lord North and the People 1779–80*, p. 192. Cartwright also approved Burgh's proposed grand association (*Take Your Choice!* p. 89).

37. Jebb to anon., 7 Aug. 1791, Disney, ed., *Works of Jebb*, 1:167. The similarity between the proposals recommended by Jebb and Sharp was not coincidental; Jebb had asked Sharp for information on his appointment to the subcommittee and requested copies of Sharp's circular letters to the petitioning counties (Jebb to Sharp, 13 March 1780, and n.d., box 28, pkt. D, Hardwicke MSS).

38. Christie, *Wilkes, Wyvill and Reform*, p. 91; Cannon, *Parliamentary Reform*, p. 80.

39. Cannon, *Parliamentary Reform*, pp. 93–97.

40. See Christie, *Wilkes, Wyvill and Reform*, p. 223.

41. Society for Constitutional Information (SCI), Minutes, TS 11/1133, fols. 1, 7, 11, 166, 168, PRO.

42. One or two dying spasms are recorded thereafter.

43. Petition of the Gentlemen, Clergy, and Freeholders of the County of York, 30 Dec. 1779, Christopher Wyvill, *Political Papers*, 1:7–8; resolution passed 28 March 1780, ibid., p. 163. Henry Duncombe, the Yorkshire Association's candidate at the 1780 general election, was typical in confining his criticism of the war to its economic effects (Speech at the County Meeting, 28 March 1780, ibid., p. 155).

44. *Form of Association Agreed to by the Committee of Sixty-One to be Recommended to the General Meeting of the County of York* (York, 1780), Wyvill Papers, ZFW 7/2/47/6.

45. Address of the Committee of Association for the County of York to the Electors of the Counties, Cities and Boroughs within the Kingdom of Great Britain [3 Jan. 1781], Yorkshire Committee Minutes, Wyvill Papers, ZFW 7/2/7/2. When in November 1779, Wyvill solicited support for his proposed county meeting only one of twenty-nine recorded replies mentioned America: William Constable declared, "This Nation soon will be inhabitable only for Merchants, Nabobs, Officers and Dependents on the nod of a Despot. A peace, or a truce, or a something with America . . . will open indeed an Asylum to the Inhabitants of Great Britain to which they must and will resort" (Wyvill, *Papers*, 3:144).

46. Watson, *Anecdotes of the Life of Richard Watson, Bishop of Landaff*, 1:126–28. The Cambridgeshire meeting, unlike those in Yorkshire, consisted of yeomen rather than gentry (ibid., p. 125).

47. Resolution of the County Meeting at York, 28 March 1780, Wyvill, *Papers*, 1:148–49.

48. Resolution of the County Meeting at Hertford, 17 April 1780, ibid., p. 187; Resolutions of the Dorset Association, 25 April 1780, Wyvill Papers, ZFW 7/2/18/11.

49. Butterfield, *George III, Lord North and the People*, p. 210. Wyvill claimed that the advocates of parliamentary reform were "without exception, zealous opponents of the American War." He was mistaken; Matthew Boulton, the Birmingham engineer, was one of those who had been hostile toward the Americans but was thought to be sympathetic to moderate reform (Wyvill to Franklin, 17 June 1785, Wyvill Papers, ZFW 7/2/51/38; Wyvill to Boulton, 31 Jan. 1785, W.3., fol. 250, Matthew Boulton Collection).

50. TS 11/1133, fol. 43, PRO.

51. Cartwright, *The People's Barrier*, pp. 45–46.

52. For example, Common Council Journal, 67:107, 268; 68:13; Westminster Committee Minutes, BL Add. MSS 38, 594 fols. 21–23, 32–33; Resolution of the Livery of London, 31 Jan. 1782, quoted in Granville Sharp, *The Claims of the People of England*, appendix, p. 3n.

53. Watson, *Anecdotes*, 1:137.

54. Memorial Containing Reasons for a Plan of Association . . . , 28 March 1780, Wyvill, *Papers*, 1:429.

55. [Thomas Day], *A Second Address to the Public from the Society for Constitutional Information*, p. 10.

56. Ibid., p. 11.

57. Ibid., pp. 11–21.

58. *General Advertiser*, 11 Sept. 1782; SCI Minutes, 18 Aug. 1790, TS 11/1133 fol. 26, PRO. The SCI considered a manuscript entitled "Answer to Mr. Galloway's Speeches," which was offered by Edward Bridgen, but took no action. Presumably this was the group of articles Adams sent for publication to Edmund Jennings in Brussels and which were sent on to a friend in England (L. H. Butterfield, ed., *The Adams Papers*, 3:89n). They were principally concerned with the diplomatic and economic aspects of American independence.

59. Butterfield, *George III, Lord North and the People*, p. 209.

60. *Public Advertiser*, 4 Dec. 1779.

61. *A Solemn Appeal to the Good Sense of the Nation*, pp. 2–9.

62. SCI Minutes, 1 April 1785, TS 11/961 fol. 100, PRO; Yorkshire Committee Minutes, 21 Jan. 1780, Wyvill Papers, ZFW 7/2/2/1; Westminster Committee, Minutes, BL Add. MSS 38, 593, fol. 28; Resolutions of the General Meeting for the County of Gloucester, 18 April 1780, printed broadsheet (Gloucester, 1780), D1356, GRO.

63. Charles James Fox to Sir Robert Smyth, 11 Feb. 1780, quoted in N. C. Phillips, "Edmund Burke and the County Movement, 1779–1780," p. 271.

64. Cartwright, *People's Barrier*, pp. 74–75.

65. Wyvill to Henry Joy, 22 Aug. 1783, *A Collection of the Letters Which have been Addressed to the Volunteers of Ireland on the Subject of a Parliamentary Reform*, p. 21.

66. [Day], *Second Address*, p. 7.

67. This conceptualization is based on David E. Apter, *The Politics of Modernization*, pp. 236–37.

68. Benjamin Vaughan to the earl of Shelburne, 27 Dec. 1782, Benjamin Vaughan Papers; Fothergill to Franklin, 25 Oct. 1780; Betsy C. Corner and Christopher C. Booth, eds., *Chain of Friendship*, pp. 498–99; Abingdon, *Thoughts on the Letter of Edmund Burke*, pp. 27–28, 34–39.

69. Christie, *Wilkes, Wyvill and Reform*, pp. 73, 78–79.

70. Cartwright to W. Sharman, 26 Aug. 1783, *Letters to the Volunteers of Ireland*, p. 102. He regarded the suffrage requirements as no more than the product of inveterate prejudice since some were worth less than ten shillings sterling a year (ibid., pp. 102–3).

71. Ibid., pp. 101–2.

72. Wyvill to Joy, Price to Sharman, 7 Aug. 1783, *Letters to the Volunteers of Ireland*, pp. 32, 83–84. Although addressing his remarks to Irish circumstances in particular, it is clear that Wyvill considered them as having general application.

73. Cartwright, *The Legislative Rights of the Commonalty Vindicated*, pp. 181–83. He attributed the wisdom of the constitution to Franklin.

74. Cartwright, *People's Barrier*, p. 64n. For Thomas Paine's deployment of early American constitutionalism in an English context, see chapter 8.

75. Sharp to Rush, 18 July 1775, box 28, pkt. E, Hardwicke MSS.

76. Price to Arthur Lee, 18 Jan. 1779, Miscellaneous MSS, Boston Public Library; Abingdon, *Thoughts on the Letter of Edmund Burke*, pp. 53–54.

CHAPTER 6

1. Shipley to Franklin, 27 Nov. 1785, John Bigelow, ed., *The Complete Works of Benjamin Franklin*, 9:280–81. Shipley, whose country home was in Hampshire, was the only friend to meet Franklin at Southampton.

2. Franklin to Price, 16 Aug. 1784, ibid., pp. 46–48; Franklin to Hartley, 27 Oct. 1785, and to Shipley, 24 Feb. 1786, Albert Henry Smyth, ed., *The Writings of Benjamin Franklin*, 9:472–73, 489.

3. Wedgwood to Franklin, 29 Feb. 1788, Benjamin Franklin Papers, 36:28, APS. Franklin replied that the cameos had made a great impact on the friends among whom he had distributed them (Franklin to Wedgwood, 15 May 1788, Benjamin Franklin Collection, Yale University).

4. Sharp to Franklin, 17 June and 29 Oct. 1785, Franklin Papers, 33:138, 230, APS.

5. Rush to Price, 26 Nov. 1785, Peters Papers, 9:81. Peters was a prominent politician who shortly became speaker of the Pennsylvania assembly.

6. Charles R. Ritcheson, "The London Press and the First Decade of American Independence, 1783–93," pp. 93–98.

7. Dilly to Rush, 26 June 1783 and 2 Dec. 1786, L. H. Butterfield, "The American Interests of the Firm of E. and C. Dilly, with Their Letters to Benjamin Rush, 1770–1795," pp. 314, 327.

8. John Adams to Timothy Dwight, 4 April 1786, Adams Papers microfilm, reel 113.

9. John Adams to John Jay, 15 Dec. 1795, ibid., reel 112.

10. Mrs. Abigail Adams to John Quincy Adams, 12 Sept. 1785, ibid., reel 365. In 1784, William Pitt paid Stockdale "for various pamphlets and publications" £228-18-6 (Chatham Papers 8/229, quoted in A. Aspinall, *Politics and the Press*, p. 166). Almon had an arrangement "to keep his paper in the interest service of the Portland whigs" (MS note, John Almon Papers, 1:15).

11. L. H. Butterfield, ed., *The Adams Papers*, 3:189n.; John Adams to David Ramsay, 1 Aug. 1786, Adams microfilm, reel 113; Priestley to Lindsey, 25 Nov. 1790, 12:12, Joseph Priestley Letters, DWL.

12. Charles Dilly to John Adams, 3 Feb. 1790, Adams Papers microfilm, reel 373. Gordon had been unable to obtain sufficient subscriptions for his book to be published by Brown and Brown in Providence (Brown and Brown to William Gordon, 13 April 1786, Brown Family Papers).

13. John Adams to Joel Barlow, 4 April 1786, Adams Papers microfilm, reel 113; Dwight to Adams, *ante* 31 March 1786, ibid., reel 367; Day to Price, 8 April 1786, "Letters of Richard Price," pp. 339–41; Price to Barlow, 4 Feb. 1787, Joel Barlow Papers, Houghton Library, and 24 March 1788, Joel Barlow Papers, Pequot Library, Yale University. Barlow sent a poem to Day through Price as an intermediary in 1787 (Barlow to Day, 14 June 1787, Huntington MSS, HM 27051).

14. [Leman Thomas Rede], *Bibliotheca Americana*, p. 14.

15. *Monthly Review* 66 (1782): 401–5; 67 (1782): 140–46, 273–77.

16. Brand Hollis to Adams, 16 June 1787, Adams Papers microfilm, reel 370; Price to Noah Webster, 2 Aug. 1785, Webster Papers.

17. Ezra Stiles, "The United States Elevated to Glory and Honour" [1783], in John W. Thornton, ed., *The Pulpit of the American Revolution*, p. 454.

18. Stennett to Manning, 14 May 1783, James Manning Papers.

19. Williams to Franklin, 14 Feb. 1783, Franklin Papers, 27:109, APS.

20. Brand Hollis to Willard, 15 Aug. and 2 Sept. 1783, "Letters of Joseph Willard," pp. 612–13; Price to Willard, 15 May 1783 and 14 March 1784, ibid., pp. 611–12, 616; Price to Rush, 26 June 1783, Rush Papers; Price to Franklin, 6 April 1784, Benjamin Franklin Papers, 31:140, APS; Price to Marchant, 6 Oct. 1783, Marchant Papers; Richard Price, *Observations on the Importance of the American Revolution and the Means of Making It a Benefit to the World*, pp. 2–3, 5–6.

21. Cartwright to John Quincy Adams, 4 June 1817, Frances Dorothy Cartwright, *The Life and Correspondence of Major Cartwright*, 2:133.

22. SCI to John Lathrop, 30 [sic] Feb. 1784, TS 11/961 fol. 58, PRO. The letter was

drafted by Joseph Towers, ibid., fol. 56. Cf. [John Baynes], *A Third Address from the Society for Constitutional Information to the People of Great Britain and Ireland*, pp. 18–21, for the society's pride in its opposition to the war.

23. TS 11/961, fols. 119, 139, 164, PRO. Much of the society's original zest had gone by the mid-1780s, and its attention was directed particularly to the issue of freedom of the press associated with the prosecution of the dean of St. Asaph for seditious libel (Eugene Charlton Black, *The Association*, pp. 197–200).

24. Jonathan Trumbull, Sr., to Price, 1 Dec. 1783, Jonathan Trumbull, Sr., Papers.

25. Wyvill to Franklin, 17 June 1785, Wyvill Papers, ZFW 7/2/51/3; [Robinson-Morris], *The Dangerous Situation of England*, pp. 87–88; Price to Jonathan Trumbull, Sr., 8 Oct. 1784, Jonathan Trumbull, Sr. Papers.

26. Sharp to Franklin, 17 June 1785, Franklin Papers, 33:138, APS; Lindsey to Adams, 23 Feb. 1787, Adams Papers microfilm, reel 369; Robinson-Morris to Adams, 27 Feb. 1786, ibid., reel 367 (Adams tactfully replied, "The Americans are indeed Englishmen, and will continue such in language & sentiments, & manners whether they are allowed to be friends or Compelled to be Ennemies [sic] of those other Englishmen who inhabit these Islands, Great Britain, and Ireland" [to Robinson-Morris, 2 March 1786, ibid., reel 113]); Priestley, *Familiar Letters Addressed to the Inhabitants of Birmingham*, p. 35.

27. John Rippon to Manning, 1 May 1784, Manning Papers.

28. Jebb to a friend in Paris, Sept. 1783, John Disney, ed., *The Works Theological, Medical, Political and Miscellaneous of John Jebb, MD, FRS, with Memoirs of the Life of the Author*, 1:188–89; Brand Hollis to Samuel Williams, 31 March 1784, Huntington MSS, HM 22592; Brand Hollis to Franklin, 28 June 1785, Franklin Papers, 33:152, APS; Brand Hollis to Adams, 22 Oct. 1786, Adams Papers microfilm, reel 369.

29. Pownall to Charles Thompson, 9 May 1783, U.S. Continental Congress, Miscellany, vol. 2.

30. Thomas Pownall, *A Memorial Addressed to the Sovereigns of America*, pp. iii, 9, 129.

31. Price, *American Revolution*, pp. 3–4, 2.

32. George Walker, *The Doctrine of a Providence . . .* , p. 26.

33. Sharp to Franklin, 29 Oct. 1785, SPG Misc. MSS, 8:192. Cf. Price, *American Revolution*, pp. 3, 7.

34. Price to Franklin, 10 March 1783, Franklin Collection, Yale; Disney, ed., *Works of Jebb*, 1:195; Wyvill to Sir Watts Horton, 30 April 1784, Wyvill Papers, ZFW 7/2/42/14; Price to Shelburne, 21 Jan. 1789, Misc. MSS, APS; Brand Hollis to Franklin, 28 June 1785, to Adams [1–8 Jan. 1788], Adams Papers microfilm, reel 371; Robinson-Morris to Elizabeth Montague, 22 Dec. 1789, Montague MSS; Price to Franklin, 6 April 1784, Benjamin Franklin Papers, 31:140, APS.

35. Sharp to anon., box 21, pkt. 6, Hardwicke MSS; Price to John Jay, 9 July 1785, John Jay Papers.

36. Thomas Day, *A Dialogue Between a Justice of the Peace and a Farmer*, pp. 47–48; Day to Walter Pollard, 1 Aug. 1785, BL Add. MSS 35, 655, fol. 253.

37. Sharp to Rush, 4 Aug. 1783, and to Brook Watson, 16 Aug. 1784, box 28, pkt. E, Hardwicke MSS; Rush to Sharp, 29 Nov. 1783, 27 April 1784, John A. Woods, ed., "The Correspondence of Benjamin Rush and Granville Sharp 1773–1809," pp. 20, 22.

38. Price to Willard, 23 July 1784, "Letters of Joseph Willard," p. 618.

39. Price, *American Revolution*, p. 85.

40. Franklin to Price, 17 Feb. 1785, "Letters of Richard Price," p. 325. Price to Franklin, 21 March 1785, Franklin Papers–Bache Collection, APS. William Bingham, among others, was more pessimistic than Franklin (to Price, 1 Dec. 1786, Richard Price Papers, MHS).

41. Price to Jefferson, 21 March 1785, Julian P. Boyd, ed., *The Papers of Thomas Jefferson*, 7:52–54; Price to Franklin, 5[?] Nov. 1785, Franklin Papers, 33:237, APS.

42. [William Cobbett, ed.], *The Parliamentary History of England from the Earliest Period to the Year 1803*, 21:627; Pownall to Franklin, July 1781, Franklin Papers, 22:100,

APS; Thomas Pownall, *Two Memorials Not Originally Intended for Publication, Now Published*, p. 7.

43. Thomas Pownall, *A Memorial Addressed to the Sovereigns of America*, pp. 15, 80–86, 93.

44. Price, *American Revolution*, p. 20; Carl B. Cone, *Torchbearer of Freedom*, pp. 111–12.

45. Price, *American Revolution*, pp. 64–65.

46. Ibid., pp. 74–76.

47. Ibid., pp. 66–67, 14–18.

48. Ibid., pp. 9–13, 18.

49. Cone, *Torchbearer*, pp. 112–23.

50. Price, *American Revolution*, pp. 15–16.

51. Ibid., p. 17.

52. Sharp to Franklin, 17 June 1785, Benjamin Franklin Papers, 33:138, APS.

53. Granville Sharp, *A General Plan for Laying Out Towns and Townships on the Newly Acquired Lands in the East Indies, America, or Elsewhere*, pp. 10–13; Granville Sharp, *An Account of the Constitutional Polity of Congregational Courts*, pp. 54–55, 191.

54. Sharp to a friend of the Abbé Mably, 30 Dec. 1784, Granville Sharp Papers, NYHS; Commonplace Book E, pp. 36–38, box 56, Hardwicke MSS.

55. Sharp to Franklin, 17 June 1785, Benjamin Franklin Papers, 33:138, APS.

56. Sharp to Manning, 21 Feb. 1785, box 28, pkt. E, Hardwicke MSS.

57. John Adams to Gordon, 26 June 1785, Adams Papers microfilm, reel 107.

58. John Adams to Jay, 3 Dec. 1785, ibid., reel 366.

59. Mrs. Abigail Adams to Charles Storer, 22 May 1787, John Adams to Philip Mazzei, 15 Dec. 1785, ibid., reels 113, 368.

60. John Adams to Elbridge Gerry, 15 July 1785, to the president of Congress, 14 Dec. 1783, to Jay, 3 Dec. 1785, ibid., reels 107, 366.

61. John Adams to Jay, 14 Feb. 1788, ibid., reel 112. Jefferson also was uncomfortable on his trip to England. In 1786 he reported that both town and country fell short of his expectations during a two-month visit; moreover, "That nation hate us, their ministers hate us, and their Kings, more than all other men" (to John Page, 4 May 1786, Boyd, ed., *Papers of Jefferson*, 9:446).

62. John Adams to Mercy Warren, 13 Dec. 1785, Adams Papers microfilm, reel 113.

63. Miss Abigail Adams to John Quincy Adams, 5 Dec. 1785, 6 Feb. 1786, ibid., reel 366; Edward Bridgen to John Adams, 1 Nov. 1783, ibid., reel 361 (cf. Jebb to John Adams, 27 Nov. 1783: "It is much to be wished that the friends of Civil and Religious Liberty held a more frequent and more enlarged intercourse with each other" [ibid.]). Adams made no reference to attending the society's meeting in his autobiographical letters in the *Boston Patriot*, 17 Feb. 1812 (quoted in Butterfield, ed., *Adams Papers*, 3:149–54). Lindsey met Adams by chance at Jebb's house and found him "a grave but agreeable character, not talkative but not shy or dark" (Lindsey to Turner, 6 Nov. 1783, Letters to William Turner, fol. 40).

64. "List of Visits" [1785], Butterfield, ed., *Adams Papers*, 3:178–80; entry, 7 Aug. 1786, ibid., p. 210; John Adams to Jefferson, 25 June 1813, Lester J. Cappon, ed., *The Adams-Jefferson Letters*, 2:234.

65. John Adams to Stockdale, 31 Jan. 1784, Adams Papers microfilm, reel 107.

66. Miss Abigail Adams to John Quincy Adams, 31 July and [26 Aug. to 13 Sept.] 1785, ibid., reel 365; Price to John Adams, 2 March 1786, ibid., reel 367; John Adams to Samuel Adams, 15 Aug. 1785, ibid., reel 111; Robinson-Morris to John Adams [25 April 1786], ibid., reel 367. Adams told Price, "There are few portions of my life that I recollect with more entire satisfaction than the hours I spent at Hackney under your ministry, and in private society, and conversation with you at other places" (to Price, 29 May 1789, Letters of John Adams, HSP).

67. John Adams to Jebb, 21 Aug. 1785, Adams Papers microfilm, reel 107. See Mrs. Adams to John Quincy Adams, 6 May 1787, "The subject [the *Defence*] has been long contemplated, and was in that respect no sudden work" (ibid., reel 370).

68. Brand Hollis to John Adams, 27 Jan. 1787, ibid., reel 369.

69. Jebb to John Adams, 13 Sept. 1785, ibid., reel 365; Adams to Jebb, 21 Aug., 10 and 26 Sept. 1785, ibid., reel 107. Jebb earlier had sent a political manuscript to Franklin, but it did not apparently lead to any discussion (Vaughan to Franklin, 12 May 1780, Franklin Papers, 3:593, LC).

70. John Adams to Jebb, 25 and 26 Sept. 1785, Adams Papers microfilm, reel 107.

71. Price to Franklin, 12 July 1784, Franklin Papers, 32:55, APS; Price to [A. Lee], 4 Feb. 1787, Houghton Autograph File; SCI Minutes, 2, 23 Feb., 30 March, 20 April 1787, TS 11/961 fols. 156–57, 159–60, PRO; Robinson-Morris to [William Smith], 14 March 1787, Adams Papers microfilm, reel 369; Monthly Review 76 (1787): 394; Lindsey to John Adams, 23 Feb. 1787, Adams Papers microfilm, reel 369; Catharine Macaulay told Mercy Warren in March that she had not yet had time to read it (Catharine Macaulay to Mercy Warren, 6 March 1787, "Warren–Adams Letters," 73:284). Horne Tooke may have read it (MS note by Horne Tooke in his Diversions of Purley, BL copy, opposite 1:101).

72. John Adams, A Defence of the Constitutions of Government of the United States of America, 1:i, xv–xviii. For Adams's alarm at the state of American affairs, see John R. Howe, The Changing Political Thought of John Adams, pp. 122–32.

73. Sharp, MS "Remarks on Adams's Defence of the Constitutions of the United States," box 21, pkt. C, Hardwicke MSS; copy of a letter to an American Gentleman, n.d., ibid., box 28, pkt. E. He also insisted on the absolute necessity that the "two first Foundations of Law (Natural and Revealed Religion)" should be maintained as the basis of all legislative and judicial proceedings (copy of a letter to an American Gentleman, n.d., ibid., box 28, pkt. E).

74. Priestley, Familiar Letters, pp. 11–21; Priestley to John Adams, 20 Dec. 1791, Adams Papers microfilm, reel 375. Two volumes of an earlier set had been destroyed in the Birmingham riots (Priestley to John Adams, 20 Dec. 1791); Price to [A. Lee], 4 Feb. 1787, and to William Bingham, n.d., printed in Massachusetts Centinel, 30 June 1787; Price to Adams, 5 March 1789, Adams Papers microfilm, reel 372.

75. Brand Hollis to John Adams, 27 Jan., 15 Feb., 15 Oct. 1787, Adams Papers microfilm, reel 370; 22 June 1794, ibid., reel 377.

76. For a discussion of Adams's reading, see H. Trevor Colbourn, The Lamp of Experience, chapter 5, esp. p. 86.

77. Jefferson to Price, 1 Feb. 1785, "Letters of Richard Price," p. 326; Rush to Price, 22 April 1786, ibid., p. 341.

78. Price to Willard, 22 Jan. 1787, "Letters of Joseph Willard," pp. 625–26; to [A. Lee], 4 Feb. 1787, Houghton Autograph File.

79. Price to Franklin, 26 Sept. 1787, Bigelow, ed., Works, 9:412; Price to Willard, 10 Oct. 1787, "Letters of Joseph Willard," p. 527; Price to Franklin, Dec. 1788, Franklin Papers 36:110, APS; Price to John Adams, 5 March 1787, Adams Papers microfilm, reel 372, and 1 Feb. 1790, ibid., reel 373.

80. Brand Hollis to John Adams, 4 Nov. 1787, Adams Papers microfilm, reel 371. Brand Hollis arranged for it to be printed in the country papers (to Willard, 30 Jan. 1788, "Letters of Joseph Willard," p. 628).

81. Brand Hollis to Willard, 30 Jan. 1788, "Letters of Joseph Willard," p. 628; Hollis to John Adams, 4 Nov. 1787, and 19 Oct. 1790, Adams Papers microfilm, reel 374.

82. Sharp to Franklin, 10 Jan. 1788, Sharp Papers, NYHS; Sharp to William Knox, 16 June 1790, box 28, pkt. E, Hardwicke MSS; Sharp to the governor of Sierra Leone, 14 Feb. 1797, Sharp Papers, NYHS.

83. Catharine Macaulay to Mercy Warren, Nov. 1787, and 29 Oct. 1788, "Warren–Adams Letters," pp. 73, 299, 303–5. She made a long tour of the United States in 1784–85, culminating in a visit to George Washington at Mount Vernon. Apparently she agreed with him that the powers of Congress were inadequate, but there is very little other information concerning the tour (Lucy Martin Donnelly, "The Celebrated Mrs. Macaulay," p. 194).

84. Catharine Macaulay to George Washington, 30 Oct. 1789, George Washington Papers, 244:96.

85. Joseph Priestley, *Lectures on History and General Policy*, p. 309; Joseph Priestley, *Letters to the Right Honourable Edmund Burke, Occasioned by His Reflections on the Revolution in France*, p. 8n. The *Lectures* were a published version of lectures originally given at the Warrington Academy before the war. For Thomas Paine's deployment of the federal Constitution in England, see chapter 8.

86. Lindsey to John Adams, 30 Oct. 1787, Adams Papers microfilm, reel 370; William Belsham, *Memoirs of the Reign of George III*, 3:199.

87. Priestley, *Familiar Letters*, p. 35 (later he moved from this position); John Cartwright, *The English Constitution Produced and Illustrated*, p. 248.

88. Wyvill, *A Defence of Dr. Price and the Reformers of England*, p. 68; Wyvill, *Political Papers*, 2:620. Franklin's friend David Williams also suspected that the United States would probably owe its tranquillity to its situation rather than to any particular wisdom in its Constitution (*Lectures on Political Principles*, p. 274).

89. Richard Price, *Additional Observations on the Nature and Value of Civil Liberty and the War with America*, pp. 8–9; Richard Price, *The Evidence for a Future Period of Improvement in the State of Mankind, with the Means and Duty of Promoting It*, p. 30. Cf. Price to [William Smith, M.P.?], 1 March 1790, National Library of Wales.

90. Priestley, *Lectures*, p. 14.

CHAPTER 7
1. Joseph Priestley, *The Theological and Miscellaneous Works of Joseph Priestley*, 15:12; Joseph Priestley, *Experiments and Observations on Different Kinds of Air and Other Branches of Natural Philosophy Connected with the Subject*, 1:xxxiii.

2. Jebb, "In a private book," John Disney, ed., *The Works Theological, Medical, Political and Miscellaneous of John Jebb, MD, FRS, with Memoirs of the Life of the Author*, 1:189; Wyvill to William Smith, 3 June 1808, William Smith Papers; Sharp to Joseph Reed, 7 Feb. 1785, box 28, pkt. E, Hardwicke MSS.

3. Robert Robinson, "Plan of Lectures on Nonconformity," *Miscellaneous Works of Robert Robertson*, 2:248; Joseph Priestley, *An Address to Protestant Dissenters of All Denominations on the Approaching Election of Members of Parliament*, p. 3.

4. Anthony Lincoln, *Some Political and Social Ideas of English Dissent 1763–1800*, pp. 14–16.

5. Body of Protestant Dissenting Ministers of the Three Denominations In and About the Cities of London and Westminster, Minutes, 2:155, 38:105.

6. The nature of Dissenters' political disabilities is discussed in N. C. Hunt, *Two Early Political Associations*, pp. 120–29.

7. The Conventicle and Five Mile Acts were repealed in 1812, and the Test and Corporation Acts in 1828. Other penal laws, including part of the Act of Supremacy of 1559, were repealed in 1844 and 1846.

8. Sir William Holdsworth, *A History of English Law*, 12:714n.; Sir William Blackstone, *Commentaries on the Laws of England*, 4:49–54.

9. The support given to William Pitt by Dissenters at the general election of 1784 had insufficient political importance to require him to curry favor with them.

10. For recent studies see Richard Burgess Barlow, *Citizenship and Conscience*, which examines the condition of religious toleration in the eighteenth century with particular reference to the Dissenters' campaigns for relief, and Ursula Henriques, *Religious Toleration in England, 1787–1833*, which discusses the same topics more briefly and goes on to set them in a broader context.

11. See Lincoln, *English Dissent*, pp. 249–51, and Henriques, *Religious Toleration*, p. 82.

12. Jonathan Mayhew, "A Discourse Concerning Unlimited Submission and Nonresistance to the Higher Powers," Bernard Bailyn, ed., *Pamphlets of the American Revolution, 1750–1776*, 1:215; Alan Heimert, *Religion and the American Mind*, p. 361.

13. Daniel Neal, *The History of New-England*, 1:ii–iii, 31–42.

14. Jonathan Mayhew, *Observations on the Charter and Conduct of the Society for the Propagation of the Gospel in Foreign Parts*, pp. 34–35.

15. Neal, *History*, 2:254. He did not, however, make much more of the question of religious liberty.

16. [Ebenezer Radcliff], *Two Letters Addressed to the Right Rev. Prelates, Who a Second Time Rejected the Dissenters' Bill*, p. 21; [Francis Blackburne], ed., *A Collection of Letters and Essays in Favour of Public Liberty*, 3:67, 217.

17. [Robert Robinson], *Arcana*, pp. 49–50; [John Palmer], *Free Remarks on A Sermon . . .* , p. 39; [Caleb Fleming], *Three Letters Concerning Systematic Taste*, pp. 22–23. Cf. *The Present State of the British Empire in Europe, America, Africa and Asia*, pp. 299–300; *Monthly Review* 38 (1768): 113.

18. Ezra Stiles, of Newport, R.I., described the position in New England in a letter to Furneaux dated 20 Nov. 1772 (draft, Stiles Papers).

19. Franklin, "Toleration in Old and New England," John Bigelow, ed., *The Complete Works of Benjamin Franklin*, 4:466–78.

20. Price to Chatham, 13 May 1772, Chatham Papers, 53:211; Priestley to Franklin, 13 June 1772, Franklin Papers, 3:103½ [sic], APS; [Radcliff], *Two Letters*, pp. 117–23.

21. Priestley, "A Letter of Advice to Those Dissenters Who Conducted the Application to Parliament for Relief from Certain Penal Laws," *Works*, 22:454; Priestley, "An Essay on the First Principles of Government," ibid., pp. 91.

22. Samuel Adams, *An Oration Delivered at the State-House in Philadelphia to a Very Numerous Audience . . .*, pp. 34–35; John Witherspoon, *The Dominion of Providence Over the Passions of Men*, p. 29.

23. Jebb to Chambers, 16 July 1775, Disney, ed., *Works of Jebb*, 1:96; Watson to Jebb, 11 Oct. 1777, Richard Watson, *Anecdotes of the Life of Richard Watson, Bishop of Landaff*, 1:104; Shipley, "A Speech, etc. etc., on the Bill for Repealing the Penal Laws Against Protestant Dissenters in the Year 1779," Jonathan Shipley, *The Works of the Right Reverend Jonathan Shipley, D.D.*, 2:240.

24. Joseph Priestley, *A Free Address to Those Who Have Petitioned for the Repeal of the Late Act of Parliament in Favour of the Roman Catholics*, pp. 11–12, 23–24; *Monthly Review* 62 (1780): 196–97.

25. Richard Price, *The General Introduction and Supplement to the Two Tracts on Civil Liberty, the War with America, and the Finances of the Kingdom*, pp. xiv–xv.

26. Jebb to Wyvill, 27 Sept. 1781, Wyvill Papers, ZFW 7/2/23/6.

27. Richard Price, *Observations on the Importance of the American Revolution and the Means of Making It a Benefit to the World*, pp. 46, 48, 34.

28. One consequence of the disestablishment of the Anglican church in America was that the official organizations of English Dissent ceased to take much interest in the affairs of their American coreligionists. The Deputies made no reference to the American war; their correspondence lapsed on its outbreak and was not resumed after it was over. Even the foundation of an American episcopate in the 1780s failed to stimulate any response. The reason was simple: Dissenters disliked episcopacy on theological grounds, but objected to it only as a component in the alliance between church and state. Once the danger of an association between the spiritual power of bishops and the temporal power of the state had evaporated, they were fully prepared to acquiesce in the foundation of an American bishopric, for it posed no threat to the position of nonepiscopalians. Indeed, Price found the first two bishops to be worthy and liberal (Price to Franklin, 26 Jan. 1787, Benjamin Franklin Papers, 35:10, APS).

29. Franklin to Price, 9 Oct. 1780, Bigelow, ed., *Works*, 7:13. The Quaker John Fothergill had been impressed by the liberality of the new Massachusetts constitution in permitting affirmation as a qualification for office (Fothergill to Franklin, 25 Oct. 1780, Betsy C. Corner and Christopher C. Booth, eds., *Chain of Friendship*, p. 498).

30. L. H. Butterfield, ed., *The Adams Papers*, 3:197; Brand Hollis to Willard, 4 July 1786; "Letters of Joseph Willard," p. 622; *Chelmsford Gazette*, 14 July 1786; John Disney, "Memoir of Jebb," in *Works of Jebb*, 1:100n. (Disney also printed a long extract from an ordination sermon by Barnard of Salem, Mass., ibid., p. 96n.); Price to Rush, 30 July 1786, Rush Papers.

31. Price to Rush, 30 July 1786, Rush Papers.

32. *An Act for Establishing Religious Freedom, Passed in the Assembly of Virginia in the Beginning of the Year 1786*, introduction by R. P[rice] (London, 1786). Price's text was

an edited version of Jefferson's conflation of his original bill and the final statute (Julian P. Boyd, ed., *The Papers of Thomas Jefferson*, 2:552–53).

33. Boyd, ed., *Papers of Jefferson*, 1:544–50; James Madison to William Bradford, 9 May and 28 July 1775, William T. Hutchinson and William M. E. Rachal, eds., *The Papers of James Madison*, 1:145, 160, 162n.

34. Price to A. Lee, 4 Feb. 1787, Houghton Autograph File.

35. Barlow, *Citizenship and Conscience*, pp. 221–23; Henriques, *Religious Toleration*, pp. 57–58.

36. SCI Minutes, 3 and 4 Nov. 1786, TS 11/961, fols. 151–52, PRO (the statute was probably sent by Price himself); *Gentleman's Magazine* 57 (1787): 74–75; *St. James's Chronicle*, 20–22 March 1787. A motion that it should be printed among the papers of the SCI was rejected, presumably because the society usually confined itself to matters concerning parliamentary reform. The evidence connecting the Virginia statute with the decision to supplicate for repeal is circumstantial; it is also as strong as other evidence offered to explain the timing of the decision.

37. Henriques, *Religious Toleration*, pp. 58–59.

38. For example, John Moore, archbishop of Canterbury, explicitly cited Price's *American Revolution* in his MS, "Answer to the Case of the Dissenters in 1787" and Notes, Arch P/A Moore, 17, Protestant Dissenters, fols. 14–16; [Samuel Horsley], *A Review of the Case of the Protestant Dissenters*, p. 31; [Spencer Madan], *A Letter to Dr. Priestley*, . . . , p. 26; "An Ecclesiastic," *A Scourge for the Dissenters*, pp. 36–39, 44–47. One of the Dissenters' most adamant opponents in previous Commons debates, the high churchman Sir Roger Newdigate, constantly referred to the alleged intolerance of New England (Lindsey to William Tayleur, 10 March 1774, Letters of Theophilus Lindsey, vol. 3, Unitarian College).

39. Minutes of the Committee Appointed to Conduct the Application to Parliament for the Repeal of the Corporation and Test Acts, MS 3084, 1:1–3, Guildhall Library, London. *The Case of the Protestant Dissenters in Relation to the Corporation and Test Acts*.

40. A provincial minister expressed the importance of the evidence of experience when he replied to the charge of a group of Anglican clergy that if the Dissenters were admitted to office they would overthrow the church and substitute their own tenets. He argued, "Happily for us, the present aera, the most enlightened in the history of man, enables us to oppose to an imaginary evil, and an argument founded on conjecture, the instruction of examples and the evidence of fact. Whatever apprehensions, real or pretended may be formed in the minds, either of the interested or the timid, of danger arising to the establishment from admitting Dissenters into offices of trust, the experience of Scotland, Ireland, America, France, Germany and Holland, is an answer to them all" (J. Smith, *Some Remarks on the Resolutions Which Were Formed at a Meeting of the Archdeaconry of Chester . . .* , p. 39). For a general discussion of the Dissenters' arguments, see Henriques, *Religious Toleration*, pp. 82–95.

41. C. L. [presumably Capel Lofft] to the editor, 4 March [1787], *Gentleman's Magazine* 57 (1787): 237–40; *The Case of Protestant Dissenters*.

42. Vaughan to John Adams, 21 March 1787, Adams microfilm, reel 369; John Adams to Price, 8 April 1785, ibid., reel 107; Brand Hollis to John Adams, 29 March 1790, ibid., reel 373. Among those members of the Repeal Committee certainly known to Adams were Brand Hollis, William Smith, M.P., Joseph Paice, Matthew Towgood, and Sir John Sinclair; he also knew Andrew Kippis, who assisted in preparing the *Case* for distribution.

43. Samuel Heywood to William Russell, 25 Nov. 1789, H.O. 42/19, PRO. [Samuel Heywood], *The Right of Protest Dissenters to A Compleat Toleration Asserted*, pp. 108–9. Cf. William Paley, *The Principles of Moral and Political Philosophy*, pp. 538, 566.

44. Thomas Sherlock, *A Vindication of the Corporation and Test Acts*, reprinted in 1787 and 1790 under the title *Bishop Sherlock's Arguments Against the Repeal of the Corporation and Test Acts*, Henriques, *Religious Toleration*, p. 73.

45. Heywood, *Right of Protestant Dissenters*, p. 222.

46. Ibid.

47. Ibid., pp. 223–26. The extracts were taken from Vaughan's edition of Franklin's *Political, Miscellaneous, and Philosophical Pieces*, pp. 74–79.

48. Heywood, *Right of Protestant Dissenters*, pp. 226–27.

49. Henriques, *Religious Toleration*, pp. 60, 63, 65.

50. For example, Henry Beaufoy, *The Substance of a Speech of March 26, 1787*, p. 43: "The Church has a right to her *establishment*, and the *Dissenters* have a right to a *compleat toleration*."

51. *Debate in the House of Commons on Mr. Beaufoy's Motion* . . ., pp. 70, 90, also quoted in Henriques, *Religious Toleration*, p. 90.

52. [Charles James Fox], *Two Speeches, Delivered in the House of Commons on Tuesday the 2nd of March, 1790*, pp. 40–41.

53. [William Cobbett, ed.], *The Parliamentary History of England from the Earliest Period to the Year 1803*, 26:413–14.

54. Caleb Evans to James Manning, 22 Feb. 1790, James Manning Papers.

55. *Extracts from Books and Other Small Pieces*, pp. 28–31, printed by order of the Committee of the Seven Congregations of the Three Denominations of Protestant Dissenters.

56. [Benjamin Vaughan ed.], *A Collection of Testimonies in Favour of Religious Liberty in the Case of the Dissenters, Catholics, and Jews.*

57. *A Letter to the Public Meeting of the Friends to the Repeal of the Test and Corporation Acts*, appendix, p. 15. They added that they were also encouraged by the success of the French friends of freedom.

58. Priestley, *Works*, 8:5.

59. Price to Mirabeau, 4 July 1789, Misc. MSS Collection, APS. Price had been delighted with the provision for separating religion from the state incorporated in the federal Constitution (Price to Franklin, Dec. 1788, Franklin Papers, 36:100, APS).

60. Joseph Priestley, *A Letter to the Right Honourable William Pitt* . . ., pp. 16, 35–36; Priestley, *Lectures on History and General Policy*, pp. 449–51.

61. Joseph Priestley, *Familiar Letters Addressed to the Inhabitants of Birmingham*, pp. 73–74.

62. Joseph Priestley, *Letters to the Right Honourable Edmund Burke, Occasioned by His Reflections on the Revolution in France*, p. 208.

63. Ibid., p. 128.

64. Ibid., p. 143. Priestley's belief that not religious belief but the advancement of one sect to a position of favored monopoly caused discord and jealousy was given added poignancy by his experience during the Birmingham "church and state" riots. In America the various sects lived in harmony.

65. Ibid., p. 139.

66. Christopher Wyvill, *Intolerance the Disgrace of Christians*, pp. 56–58; David Bogue and James Bennett, *History of Dissenters from the Revolution in 1688 to the Year 1808*, 4:155; Thomas Belsham, *Memoirs of the Late Reverend Theophilus Lindsey MA*, p. 238.

67. Bogue and Bennett, *History of Dissenters*, 4:148.

CHAPTER 8

1. Priestley, *Letters to the Right Honourable Edmund Burke, Occasioned by His Reflections on the Revolution in France*, p. 142. Cf. Price to Maton de la Cour, 1 July 1789, Richard Price Papers, APS; John Cartwright to the president of the Committee of the Constitution of the States General, 18 Aug. 1789, Frances Dorothy Cartwright, *The Life and Correspondence of Major Cartwright*, 1:182; Theophilus Lindsey to William Frend, 14 Nov. 1789, Add. MSS 7886, William Frend Correspondence; Thomas Brand Hollis to John Adams, 29 Oct. 1790, Adams Papers microfilm, reel 374; Granville Sharp to the Marquis de Lafayette, 2 Aug. 1789, transcript in the possession of Dr. John A. Woods, Hardwicke MSS; Catharine Macaulay to George Washington, 1 March 1791, George Washington Papers, 249:75.

2. Gwyn A. Williams, *Artisans and Sans-Culottes*, pp. 3, 58.

3. For general studies of the radical movement of these years, see George Stead Veitch, *The Genesis of Parliamentary Reform*; P. A. Brown, *The French Revolution in English*

*History*; S. Maccoby, *English Radicalism, 1786–1832*; Eugene Charlton Black, *The Association*; W. A. L. Seaman, "British Democratic Societies in the Period of the French Revolution"; E. P. Thompson, *The Making of the English Working Class*; Williams, *Artisans*; James Walvin, "English Democratic Societies and Popular Radicalism 1791–1800"; John Cannon, *Parliamentary Reform 1640–1832*; and Carl B. Cone, *The English Jacobins*.

4. Williams, *Artisans*, pp. 58–60; Thomas Hardy to the Manchester Constitutional Society, 1 April 1792, TS 11/959/3505/2, PRO.

5. Jeremiah Batley to Wyvill, 14 April 1792, Wyvill Papers, ZFW 7/271/2; Birmingham Society for Constitutional Information, printed broadsheet, TS 11/953, PRO; Williams, *Artisans*, p. 63.

6. *To The Inhabitants of Manchester*, broadsheet, TS 11/959/3505/2, PRO; *To the Parliament and People of Great Britain, An Explicit Declaration of the Principles and Views of the London Corresponding Society*, TS 11/541/1755, PRO; MS "Address of the London Corresponding Society to the Other Societies in Great Britain United for the Obtaining of reform in Parliament," London, 29 Nov. 1792, TS 11/952/3496, PRO.

7. Report of a dinner of the SCI, 29 April [1793], TS 11/966/B, PRO.

8. John Thelwall to Allum, 13 Feb. 1794, TS 11/965, PRO; "Abstract of the Account of the Proceedings of the L.C.S. and of Thelwall's Lectures from the 21st Feby to the 2d of May 1794," ibid.; Thompson, *Working Class*, pp. 157–60.

9. Williams, *Artisans*, pp. 108–90; Thompson, *Working Class*, pp. 161–62; London Corresponding Society, *To the Parliament and People of Great Britain*, TS 11/541/1755, PRO. Evans was one of the last secretaries of the LCS but his views were far from typical. Cf. SCI Minutes, 15 Dec. 1792, TS 11/966A, PRO; The society disclaimed any wish to effect a change in the present system "by violence and public commotion."

10. Thomas Hardy, *Memoirs of Thomas Hardy*, pp. 12, 102, 23; Joseph Gerrald, *A Convention the Only Means of Saving Us from Ruin*, pp. 88–89; [Thomas Spence, ed.], *One Pennyworth of Pig's Meat*; *The Manual of Liberty*, passim. Cf. *Address of the British Convention Assembled at Edinburgh, November 19, 1793, to the People of Great Britain*, pp. 15–16, 4–6, 10–11; [Henry Yorke], *These Are the Times That Try Men's Souls!* p. 31.

11. Brand Hollis to Adams, 22 June 1794, Adams Papers microfilm, reel 377; Sharp, *Diary*, March 21, 1795.

12. Elhanan Winchester, *An Oration on the Discovery of America*, pp. 26–29.

13. Hardy, *Memoirs*, p. 57n.; John Francis, MS Journal 1792, 3:77, 117–18, Codex Brown 7, John Carter Brown Library; Gerrald, *Convention*, p. 74.

14. "Pamphlets published by J. Smith," advertisement in *Assassination of the King*; Wesley Frank Craven, *Legend of the Founding Fathers*, p. 61n.; Stockdale to Adams, 16 March 1793, Adams Papers microfilm, reel 376. Adams's tract was quoted by the prosecution at Paine's trial, *The Trial at Large of Thomas Paine for a Libel in the Second Part of Rights of Man*, p. 9. Cf. Thomas Brigges to Wyvill, 29 May 1798, Wyvill Papers, ZFW 7/2/121/9, for the circulation of American papers in Yorkshire.

15. Jeremy Belknap, broadside dated 22 Dec. 1796, Belknap Papers. Price warned Jedediah Morse of the same problem but arranged for the booksellers to sell a number of copies of his *American Geography* (Price to Morse, 18 May 1789 and 29 March 1790, Gratz Collection).

16. Price to Adams, 1 Feb. 1790, Adams Papers microfilm, reel 373; Price to the Comte de Mirabeau, 2–4 July 1789, Misc. MSS, APS. Cf. Price to [William?] Smith, 28 July 1789, Coxe Papers; Richard Price, *A Discourse on the Love of Our Country*, p. 50.

17. Joseph Priestley, *The Theological and Miscellaneous Works of Joseph Priestley*, 19:416; Brand Hollis to Wyvill, 3 Oct. 1791, Wyvill Papers, ZFW 7/2/65/1.

18. Revolution Society to the Societe des Amis de la Constitution a Poitiers, 31 Jan. 1792, *The Correspondence of the Revolution Society in London . . .*, p. 261.

19. LCS to SCI, 11 Oct. 1792, TS 11/966/C; Minutes of SCI, 12 Oct. 1792, ibid., PRO; T. B. Howell, ed., *A Collection of State Trials and Proceedings for High Treason and Other Crimes and Misdemeanors from the Earliest Period to the Year 1803*, 24:313; William Godwin, *An Enquiry Concerning Political Justice* 1:203–4, 223–25; [Charles Pigott], *The Jockey Club*, 1:181.

20. Champion was one of Wedgwood's unsuccessful competitors; he emigrated to South Carolina in 1784 and was very happy. See William Bingham's remark that there was a general enthusiasm for emigration and William Smith's comment that there was unease in London at the number of emigrants to the United States in 1784 (Bingham to Thomas Willing, 30 July 1783, Bingham Papers, HSP; L. F. S. Ufton, ed., *The Diary and Selected Papers of Chief Justice William Smith 1784–1793*, 1:82).

21. Lindsey to Samuel Shore, 16 Aug. 1781, Lindsey Correspondence, 12:57, fol. 5, DWL; Priestley to William Withering, 15 April 1793, Priestley Letters 67419, p. 43, Birmingham Reference Library; Gamaliel Lloyd to Wyvill, 19 April 1793, Wyvill Papers, ZFW 7/2/79/6; Lindsey to Joseph Chadwick, 17 Dec. 1793, DWL 12:80 at p. 208; Lindsey to Tayleur, 30 June 1794, Letters of Theophilus Lindsey, vol. 3, Unitarian College; Brand Hollis to John Adams, 22 June 1794, Adams Papers microfilm, reel 377; Williams, *Artisans*, p. 80; Lindsey to Tayleur, 10 March 1795, Letters of Theophilus Lindsey, vol. 3, Unitarian College. Priestley told Morse that his *American Geography* contributed to the widespread desire to emigrate (to Morse, 24 Aug. 1793, Misc. Papers, NYHS).

22. Hardy, *Memoirs*, p. 58; Gilbert Wakefield to Thomas Russell, 17 July 1794, BL Add. MSS 44, 992, fol. 86; Thomas Fysshe Palmer to James Smitton, 20 July [1793], Howell and Jones, *State Trials*, 23:325. Palmer intended to emigrate to America after completion of his term at Botany Bay (Lindsey to Tayleur, 19 April 1793, Letters of Theophilus Lindsey, vol. 3, Unitarian College); unfortunately he died before he could return home.

23. C. B. Jewson, *The Jacobin City*, p. 59.

24. Seaman, "British Democratic Societies," p. 360; LCS Original Journal or Minute Book, Place Papers, BL Add. MSS 27, 812, fol. 26.

25. "Abstract of the Proceedings of the L.C.S. and Thelwall's Lectures"; Gerrald, *Convention*, p. 21; A Member of the Birmingham Constitutional Society, *A Letter to the English Nation*, p. 3.

26. Joel Barlow, *Advice to the Privileged Orders in the Several States of Europe*, pp. 19, 30, 34–36.

27. Barlow to Hardy, 6 Oct. 1792, TS 11/953, to the LCS, 5 Oct. 1792, TS 11/965, PRO; Journal of the LCS, 11 Oct. 1792, BL Add. MSS 28, 811, fol. 23; Barlow to the Society of Constitutional Whigs, Independents and Friends of the People, 6 Oct. 1792, Barlow Papers, Pequot Library, Yale University; Barlow to the SCI, 4 Oct. 1792, TS 11/952/3496, PRO.

28. SCI Minutes, TS 11/962, fols. 51–52, 114, 116–17, Examination of John Frost by the Privy Council, 31 May 1794, TS 11/963, p. 464, PRO. At one point the address declared, "The sparks of Liberty, preserved in England for ages, like the coruscations of the Northern Aurora, served but to shew the darkness visible in the rest of Europe; the lustre of the American Republics, like an effulgent Morning, arose with increasing vigour, but still too distant to enlighten our hemisphere, till the splendour of the French revolution burst forth upon the nations in the full fervour of a meridian sun, and displayed in the midst of the European world the practical result of principles which philosophy had sought in the shade of speculation, and which experience must everywhere confirm."

29. Thompson, *Working Class*, p. 94.

30. Thomas Paine, *Rights of Man*, ed. Henry Collins, pp. 63, 87–95.

31. Ibid., p. 166.

32. SCI Minutes, TS 11/961, fol. 223, PRO.

33. Thomas Paine, *Rights of Man, Part the Second*, p. 1.

34. Ibid., p. 2.

35. Ibid., pp. 2–3, 12–13, 30, 33. Cf. Thomas Paine, *Address to the Republic of France*, p. 8.

36. Paine, *Rights of Man, Part the Second*, pp. 40–45.

37. Ibid., pp. 50–58, 163–64.

38. Manchester Constitutional Society to the SCI, 13 March 1792, and Sheffield Constitutional Society, broadsheet, 14 March 1792, TS 11/962, fols. 52, 53; Resolutions of the United Constitutional Societies of Norwich, 24 March 1792, Norwich Revolution

Society to the SCI, 26 April 1792, TS 11/952/3496; SCI Minutes, 18 May and 6 July 1792, TS 11/966C; SCI to Paine [1792], TS 11/953; Thomas Penton to Chamberlayne and White, 17 Dec. 1792, TS 11/954, PRO. Richard Gimbel, *Thomas Paine*, pp. 92–93; SCI draft resolution [15 June 1792], TS 11/951/3495.

39. A Member of the Birmingham Constitutional Society, *Letter to the English Nation*, p. 7; Gerrald, *Convention*, pp. 22–23; MS Notebook endorsed "King v. Yorke," n.d., TS 11/959/3505/1, PRO.

40. [John Thelwall], *The Natural and Constitutional Right of Britons to Annual Parliaments, Universal Suffrage, and the Freedom of Popular Association*, pp. 82–85; John Thelwall, *The Rights of Nature*, pp. 84–85.

41. Gerrald, *Convention*, p. 73.

42. MS Notebook, King v. Yorke, TS 11/959/3505/1, PRO.

43. Spence, ed., *Pig's Meat*, 2:283.

44. Thomas Cooper, *A Reply to Mr. Burke's Invective against Mr. Cooper and Mr. Watt*, pp. 21, 24–27; [Charles Pigott], *A Political Dictionary*, p. 148.

45. William Belcher, *Precious Morsels*, p. 148.

46. John Oswald, *Review of the Constitution of Great Britain*, p. 45; [William Vaughan], *A Catechism of Man*, pp. 16, 17, 20; Letter in *The Patriot* (Sheffield), 3:28–29; Felix Vaughan, speaking in defense of Daniel Isaac Eaton, in Howell and Jones, *State Trials*, 22:811.

47. MS Notebook, King v. Yorke, TS 11/959/3505/1, PRO.

48. John Thelwall, *Sober Reflections on the Seditious and Inflammatory Letter of the Right Hon. Edmund Burke to a Noble Lord*, pp. 26–27.

49. Wyvill to Pitt, 9 Feb. 1793, Chatham Papers, 192:247; Priestley to William Withering, 15 April 1793, Birmingham Reference Library; Lindsey to Tayleur, 10 April and 29 Sept. 1794, Letters of Theophilus Lindsey, vol. 3, Unitarian College; Sharp to Rush, 25 March 1794, Rush Papers, 28:99; Brand Hollis to Wyvill, 9 June 1796, Wyvill Papers; Cartwright, *Life of Cartwright*, 1:185.

50. Wyvill to Batley, 4 April 1792, Wyvill Papers, ZFW 7/3/71/1; Cartwright, *Life of Cartwright*, 1:192; Brand Hollis to Adams, 18 Feb. 1793, Adams Papers microfilm, reel 376; Francis, *Journal*, 1:43–44.

51. P. A. Brunsdon, "The Association of the Friends of the People, 1792–1796," pp. 251–52; [Society of the Friends of the People], *Proceedings of the Society of the Friends of the People*, pp. 33, 48–49; Cannon, *Parliamentary Reform*, p. 123; Association of the Friends of the People to the LCS, 28 Dec. 1792, TS 11/956, PRO; Wyvill to Brand Hollis, 13 March 1794, Wyvill Papers, ZFW 7/2/91/3. One of the society's prominent members, Philip Francis, referred to the example of mild government in America while arguing against universal suffrage, but its committee advised the LCS "Carefully to avoid mixing Foreign Politics with our domestic concerns" (private pamphlet, no title, begins "On the Eight of March, 1794 . . ." [London, 1794], p. 8; Association of the Friends of the People, to LCS, 28 Dec. 1792).

52. Christopher Wyvill, *A Defence of Dr. Price and the Reformers of England*, pp. 70–72; *The Correspondence of the Revolution Society*, p. 2; Price, *A Discourse on the Love of Our Country*, passim; Lindsey to Tayleur, 10 Nov. 1790, Letters of Theophilus Lindsey, vol. 3. Unitarian College, John Adams approved of Price's discourse: he would not have welcomed sentiments challenging the fabric of society (Adams to Price, 19 April 1790, Letters of John Adams, fol. 19).

53. Capel Lofft, *Remarks on the Letter of the Rt Hon Edmund Burke, Concerning The Revolution in France . . .*, p. 55.

54. Sharp to Wyvill, 4 Aug. 1794, Wyvill Papers, ZFW 7/2/88/25; Priestley, *Works*, 19:416, and *A Discourse to the Supporters of the New College at Hackney*, p. 5; Christopher Wyvill, *The Case of the Rev. C. Wyvill Respecting the Right Honorable William Pitt*, pp. 74–77; Wyvill to Fox, 12 July 1799, Christopher Wyvill, *Political Papers*, 6:34; Wyvill to Pitt, 9 Feb. 1793, Chatham Papers, 192:247.

55. John Cartwright, *A Letter from John Cartwright Esq. to a Friend at Boston in the County of Lincoln*, pp. 27–28.

56. John Cartwright, *The Constitutional Defence of England, Internal and External*, pp. 4, 65; Wyvill to Batley, 4 April 1792 Wyvill Papers, ZFW 7/2/71/1; Wyvill, *Defence of Price*, pp. 62, 70, 72, 75; [Joseph Priestley], *Political Dialogues*, p. 2; Priestley to Lindsey, 11 July 1803, Priestley Letters, DWL, 12:13. Sharp continued to advocate frankpledge as suitable for America (Sharp to Rufus King, 28 June 1797, box 50, Hardwicke MSS).

57. Price to Adams, 1 Feb. 1790, Adams Papers microfilm, reel 373; Catharine Macaulay to Washington, June 1790, George Washington Papers, 246:118.

58. John Cartwright, *The English Constitution Produced and Illustrated*, pp. 88, 248; and *The Constitutional Defence of England*, pp. 49–51.

59. See the following works by John Cartwright: *An Appeal, Civil and Military, on the Subject of the English Constitution*, pp. 265–66; *Consitutional Defence*, p. 146; *The English Constitution Produced and Illustrated*, p. 216; *A Letter to the Duke of Newcastle*, pp. 100–101; *Six Letters to the Marquis of Tavistock, on Reform of the Commons House of Parliament*, p. 25.

60. John Cartwright, *The Comparison: In Which Mock Reforms, Half Reform and Constitutional Reform are Considered*, p. 18; *Appeal, Civil and Military*, p. 23. Cf. *English Constitution*, p. 29.

61. Cartwright, *Appeal, Civil and Military*, pp. 29, 41; *Appeal on the Subject of the English Constitution*, p. 51; *The Commonwealth in Danger*, p. cxxxiv. Toward the end of his life Cartwright felt that even the American states had failed completely to separate their constitutions and their laws (*English Constitution Produced*, pp. 82–83).

62. Cartwright, *Constitutional Defence*, pp. 52–53, 40–41; *Letter to Newcastle*, p. 127; *Appeal on the Subject of the English Constitution*, p. 9; *Commonwealth in Danger*, pp. lxxxix–xc. He warned that Franklin's instructions for reducing the size of the empire could be adapted to become excellent "Rules for Rooting our Royalty and Nobility from Great Britain" (*Letter to Newcastle*, p. 127).

63. Cartwright, *Constitutional Defence*, pp. 51–52, 111n.; *Commonwealth in Danger*, p. 91n.; *Appeal, Civil and Military*, p. 266; *Letter to Newcastle*, pp. 92–94.

64. Cartwright, *The English Constitution Produced and Illustrated*, pp. 216–20, 249.

65. For studies of America and nineteenth-century radicals, see Frank Thistlethwaite, *America and the Atlantic Community*; David Paul Crook, *American Democracy in English Politics, 1815–1850*; G. D. Lillibridge, *Beacon of Freedom*.

# Bibliography

## PRIMARY SOURCES

MANUSCRIPTS

*Great Britain*

ABERYSTWYTH
   *National Library of Wales*
William Dillwyn Diary
Richard Price Letter

BIRMINGHAM
   *Birmingham Assay Office*
Matthew Boulton Collection
   *Birmingham Reference Library*
Inventory of the House and Goods of Dr. Joseph Priestley which were
   destroyed during the Riots at Birmingham, 1791
Priestley Letters
Letters from Joseph Priestley to Josiah Wedgwood (photocopies)

CAMBRIDGE
   *Cambridge University Library*
William Frend Correspondence
Priestley Letters

CARDIFF
*Cardiff Public Library*
David Williams, Autobiography "Incidents in my own life"

EDINBURGH
*National Library of Scotland*
Meredith Letters

GLOUCESTER
*Gloucester Public Library*
Josiah Tucker Papers
*Gloucestershire Record Office*
Gloucestershire Committee for Parliamentary Reform: Minute Book
Hardwicke Manuscripts (from Hardwicke Court, Gloucestershire)
Richard Price Letters

KEELE
*Keele University Library*
Wedgwood Papers

LIVERPOOL
*Liverpool Public Library*
Miscellaneous Letters of John Cartwright
Miscellaneous Letters of Richard Price
Miscellaneous Letters of Joseph Priestley

LONDON
*British and Foreign Bible Society*
Granville Sharp Letters
*British Library (formerly British Museum)*
Additional Manuscripts:
    Almon Correspondence
    Correspondence of Thomas Day and Walter Pollard
    Letter of Thomas Day to Erasmus Darwin
    Holland House Papers (C. J. Fox Papers)
    Letters of Thomas Hollis to William Taylor How
    Place Papers
    Price Letters
    Priestley Letters
    Register of a Pamphlet Club at Ely
    Russell Papers
    Strahan Papers

Westminister Committee Minutes
Caleb Whitefoord Correspondence
Wilkes Papers
King's Manuscripts:
    Franklin Letters
    *City of London, Guildhall Library*
Deputies of Protestant Dissenters: Minutes, vols. 2 and 3
Deputies of Protestant Dissenters: Minutes of the Committee Appointed to Conduct the Application to Parliament for the Repeal of the Corporation and Test Acts
    *Corporation of London Record Office*
City of London Common Council: Journal, vols. 66–68.
Committee of Common Council for Corresponding with other Committees of Counties, Cities, and Boroughs: Minutes
Committee of the Livery of London Appointed to Correspond: Minutes
Common Hall Book
Small MS Box 23
    *Dr. Williams's Library*
Body of Protestant Dissenting Ministers of the Three Denominations in and about the Cities of London and Westminster: Minute Books
Correspondence between Francis Blackburne and John Wiche
Letters of Archdeacon Francis Blackburne to Theophilus Lindsey
Letters of Joshua Toulmin to John Sturch
Letters to William Turner
Lindsey Correspondence
Odgers Manuscripts
Joseph Priestley Letters
Letters from Joseph Priestley to Theophilus Lindsey and Thomas Belsham
Manuscript Letters in John Towill Rutt, ed., *The Life and Correspondence of Joseph Priestley*: 12:79–80.
Robert Millar Papers
Letters of Richard Price
The Wodrow-Kenrick Correspondence
    *Friends' House Library*
Official Manuscript Records and Correspondence of the Society of Friends
    *Lambeth Palace Library*
Secker Papers
Arch P/A More 17
Society for the Propagation of the Gospel Miscellaneous, vols. 8 and 15

*Public Record Office*
Chatham Papers
Colonial Office 5
Home Office 42 and 55
State Papers, Domestic: George III
Treasury Solicitor's Papers
*University College*
Sharp MSS: Kenrick Papers

MANCHESTER
*Unitarian College*
Letters of Theophilus Lindsey

NORTHALLERTON
*North Yorkshire Record Office*
Wyvill Papers

NOTTINGHAM
*Nottingham University Library*
Portland Papers

OXFORD
*Bodleian Library*
Letters of Richard Price and Joseph Priestley
Letters to Ralph Griffiths
*Monthly Review* (MS notes by Ralph Griffiths)

READING
*Berkshire Record Office*
Hartley-Russell Papers

SHEFFIELD
*Sheffield City Library*
Wentworth-Woodhouse Muniments:
Edmund Burke Papers
Fitzwilliam Papers
Rockingham Papers

STAFFORD
*William Salt Library*
Dartmouth Papers

WARRINGTON
*Warrington Municipal Library*
Joseph Priestley Papers

YORK
*York Minster Library*
Granville Sharp Letter Book

*United States*

ANN ARBOR, MICH.
*William L. Clements Library, University of Michigan*
Shelburne Papers

BOSTON, MASS.
*Boston Public Library*
Miscellaneous Manuscripts
*Boston University Library*
Jonathan Mayhew Papers
*Massachusetts Historical Society*
The Adams Papers (microfilm edition)
Belknap Papers
Bowdoin-Temple Papers
Gerry Papers
Thomas Hollis Papers
Richard Price Papers
Josiah Quincy, Jr., Papers
Smith Carter Collection
Waterston Collection

CAMBRIDGE, MASS.
*Houghton Library, Harvard University*
Arthur Lee Papers
Autograph File
Joel Barlow Papers
John Cartwright, "Political Discourses"
Thomas Hollis Diary
Thomas Hollis-Timothy Hollis Correspondence
Miscellaneous Letters

CHARLOTTESVILLE, VA.
*University of Virginia*
Francis Walker Gilmore Papers
Lee Family Papers

DURHAM, N.C.
*Duke University Library*
John Cartwright Letters
William Smith Letters
William Wilberforce Letters

HARTFORD, CONN.
*Connecticut Historical Society*
Jonathan Trumbull, Sr., Papers

NEW HAVEN, CONN.
*Yale University*
Sir Joseph Banks Papers
Joel Barlow Papers, Pequot Library
Benjamin Franklin Collection
Stiles Papers
Miscellaneous Papers

NEW YORK, N.Y.
*Columbia University Library*
John Jay Papers
*New-York Historical Society*
John Almon Papers
Catharine Macaulay Papers
Joseph Reed Papers
Granville Sharp Papers
Miscellaneous Papers
*New York Public Library*
Samuel Adams Papers
Henry Laurens, MS Journal of Voyage, Capture, and Confinement, 1781
Webster Papers
Miscellaneous Papers

PHILADELPHIA, PA.
*American Philosophical Society*
Benjamin Franklin Papers
Franklin Papers-Bache Collection

Benjamin Vaughan Papers
Joseph Priestley Papers
Madiera Vaughan Collection
Richard Price Papers
Miscellaneous Manuscripts Collection
*Historical Society of Pennsylvania and Library Company of Philadelphia*
Letters of John Adams
Bingham Papers
Coxe Papers: Tench Coxe Section
Dickinson Papers
Dreer Collection
Etting Papers
Gratz Collection
Pemberton Papers
Peters Papers
Rush Papers
Miscellaneous Papers
*University of Pennsylvania*
Franklin Papers

PROVIDENCE, R.I.
*Brown University Library*
James Manning Papers
*John Carter Brown Library*
Brown Family Papers
Clarendon Papers on America
John Francis, MS Journal, 1792
*Rhode Island Historical Society*
Marchant Papers
Henry Marchant Diary (microfilm)

SAN MARINO, CALIF.
*Henry E. Huntington Library*
Cadell and Davies Papers
Montagu Papers
W. Hutton, MS "Narrative of the Dreadful Riots in Birmingham, July 14th, 1789"
Miscellaneous Papers

WORCESTER, MASS.
*American Antiquarian Society*
Curwen Papers

WASHINGTON, D.C.
  *Library of Congress*
Benjamin Franklin Papers
Thomas Jefferson Papers
George Washington Papers
Personal Papers—Miscellany
United States Continental Congress—Miscellany

MICROFILMS

American Letters in the Wedgwood Museum, Barlaston, Staffordshire. Anne Finer, ed. East Ardsley, Yorkshire: Micromethods, 1970.
*Lee Family Papers 1742–1795.* Paul P. Hoffman, ed. Charlottesville, Va.: University of Virginia, 1966.
*The Papers of Henry Laurens in the South Carolina Historical Society.* Philip M. Hamer, ed. Charleston, S.C.: South Carolina Historical Society, 1966.

## PRINTED PRIMARY WORKS

PRINTED DOCUMENTS, CORRESPONDENCE, PAPERS

*An Abstract of the History and Proceedings of the Revolution Society in London.* London, 1789.
Adams, Charles Francis, ed. *Familiar Letters of John Adams and His Wife Abigail Adams during the Revolution.* New York, 1876.
————. *The Works of John Adams.* 10 vols. Boston, 1850–56.
Beaufort, W. H. de., ed. *Brieven van en aan Johan Derck van der Cappellen van der Poll.* Utrecht, 1879.
Bigelow, John, ed. *The Complete Works of Benjamin Franklin.* 10 vols. New York, 1887–88.
Boyd, Julian P., ed. *The Papers of Thomas Jefferson.* 19 vols. to date. Princeton, N.J.: Princeton University Press, 1950–.
Butterfield, L. H. "The American Interests of the Firm of E. and C. Dilly, With Their Letters to Benjamin Rush, 1770–1795." *The Papers of the Bibliographical Society of America* 45 (1951): 283–332.
————, ed. *The Adams Papers: The Diary and Autobiography of John Adams.* 4 vols. Cambridge, Mass.: Belknap Press, 1961–.
————, ed. *Letters of Benjamin Rush.* 2 vols. Princeton, N.J.: Princeton University Press, 1951.
————, et al., eds. *Adams Family Correspondence.* 4 vols. to date. Cambridge, Mass.: Belknap Press, 1963–.
Cappon, Lester J., ed. *The Adams-Jefferson Letters.* 2 vols. Chapel Hill, N.C.: University of North Carolina Press, 1959.

Cobban, Alfred, ed. *The Debate on the French Revolution: 1789–1800.* London: Nicholas Kaye, 1950.

Copeland, Thomas W., et al., eds. *The Correspondence of Edmund Burke.* 9 vols. to date. Chicago: University of Chicago Press, 1958–.

Corner, Betsy C. and Booth, Christopher C., eds. *Chain of Friendship: Selected Letters of Dr. John Fothergill of London, 1735–1780.* Cambridge, Mass.: Belknap Press, 1971.

Corner, George, ed. *The Autobiography of Benjamin Rush.* Princeton, N.J.: Princeton University Press, 1948.

*Correspondence of Mr. Ralph Izard of South Carolina, From the Year 1774 to 1804.* Vol. 1. New York, 1844.

*The Correspondence of the Late John Wilkes.* 5 vols. London, 1805.

*The Correspondence of the Revolution Society in London, With the National Assembly and With Various Societies of Liberty in France and England.* London, 1792.

*The Correspondence of the Right Honourable Sir John Sinclair, Bart.* 2 vols. in 1. London, 1831.

Costin, W. C., and Watson, J. Steven. *The Law and Working of the Constitution: Documents 1660–1914.* Vol. 1. London: Adam and Charles Black, 1952.

Cozens-Hardy, Basil, ed. *The Diary of Sylas Neville 1767–88.* London: Oxford University Press, 1950.

Curnock, Nehemiah, ed. *The Journal of the Rev. John Wesley, AM.* Vol. 6. Standard ed. London: Epworth Press, 1938.

Cushing, Harry Alonzo, ed. *The Writings of Samuel Adams.* 4 vols. New York: Octagon Books, 1968.

Elliot, Jonathan, ed. *The Debates in the Several State Conventions on the Adoption of the Federal Constitution.* 5 vols. in 2. Philadelphia: Lippincott, 1941.

Elsey, George M., ed. "John Wilkes and William Palfrey." *Publications of the Colonial Society of Massachusetts* 34 (1943): 411–28.

Finer, Ann, and Savage, George, eds. *The Selected Letters of Josiah Wedgwood.* London: Cory Adams and Mackay, 1965.

Fitzmaurice, Lord. *Life of William Earl of Shelburne, afterwards First Marquess of Lansdowne.* 2 vols. 2d rev. ed. London: Macmillan, 1912.

Fitzpatrick, John C., ed. *The Diaries of George Washington, 1748–1799.* 4 vols. Boston and New York: Houghton Mifflin, 1925.

———. *The Writings of George Washington.* 39 vols. Washington, D.C.: U.S. Government Printing Office, 1931–44.

Ford, Worthington C., ed. "The Letters of William Gordon." *Proceedings of the Massachusetts Historical Society* 63 (1931): 303–613.

———. *Letters of William Lee 1766–1783*. 3 vols. New York, 1891.

Guttridge, G. H., ed. *The American Correspondence of a Bristol Merchant 1766–1776*. University of California Publications in History, 22 (1934): 1–72.

Hewins, W. A. S., ed. *The Whitefoord Papers*. Oxford, 1898.

Historical Manuscripts Commission. *Eleventh Report, Appendix, Part V. The Manuscripts of the Earl of Dartmouth*. London, 1887.

———. *Fourteenth Report, Appendix, Part X: The Manuscripts of the Earl of Dartmouth*. Vol. 2. London, 1895.

———. *Fifteenth Report, Appendix, Part I. The Manuscripts of the Earl of Dartmouth*. Vol. 8. London, 1896.

———. *Fifteenth Report, Appendix, Part V: The Manuscripts of the Right Honourable F. J. Savile Foljambe*. London, 1897.

———. *Report on the Manuscripts of Mrs. Stopford-Sackville*. 2 vols. London: His Majesty's Stationery Office, 1904–10.

Hoffman, Ross J. S. *Edmund Burke, New York Agent*. Philadelphia: American Philosophical Society, 1956.

Hutchinson, William T., and Rachal, William M. E., eds. *The Papers of James Madison*. 4 vols. to date. Chicago: University of Chicago Press, 1962–.

Jensen, Merrill, ed. *English Historical Documents. Vol. X: American Colonial Documents to 1776*. London: Eyre and Spottiswoode, 1955.

"Journal of Josiah Quincy, Jun. During his Voyage and Residence in England from September 28th 1774, to March 3, 1775." *Proceedings of the Massachusetts Historical Society* 50 (1916–17): 433–71.

Knollenberg, Bernhard, ed. "Thomas Hollis and Jonathan Mayhew: Their Correspondence, 1759–1766." *Proceedings of the Massachusetts Historical Society* 69 (1956): 102–93.

Koch, Adrienne, ed. *The American Enlightenment*. New York: George Braziller, 1965.

Koch, Adrienne, and Peden, William, eds. *The Life and Selected Writings of Thomas Jefferson*. New York: Modern Library, 1944.

Labaree, Leonard W.; Willcox, William B.; et al., eds. *The Papers of Benjamin Franklin*. 19 vols. to date. New Haven, Conn.: Yale University Press, 1959–.

Lee, Richard Henry. *Life of Arthur Lee, Ll.D.* 2 vols. in 1. Boston, 1829.

"Letters from Andrew Eliot to Thomas Hollis." *Collections of the Massachusetts Historical Society*, 4th ser., 4 (1958): 398–461.

"Letters of Joseph Willard." *Proceedings of the Massachusetts Historical Society* 43 (1910): 609–44.

"The Letters of Richard Price." *Proceedings of the Massachusetts Historical Society* 17 (1903): 262–378.

"Letters to Josiah Quincy Jr." *Proceedings of the Massachusetts Historical Society* 50 (1916–17): 471–96.

McLachlan, H., ed. *Letters of Theophilus Lindsey*. Manchester: Manchester University Press, 1920.

———, ed. "More Letters of Theophilus Lindsey. *Transactions of the Unitarian Historical Society* 3 (1923–26): 361–77.

Runes, Dagobert D., ed. *The Selected Writings of Benjamin Rush*. New York: Philosophical Library, 1947.

Rutland, Robert A., ed. *The Papers of George Mason*. 3 vols. Chapel Hill, N.C.: University of North Carolina Press, 1970.

Rutt, John Towill. *Life and Correspondence of Joseph Priestley*. 2 vols. London, 1831.

Schuyler, Robert Livingston, ed. *Josiah Tucker*. New York: Columbia University Press, 1931.

Smyth, Albert Henry, ed. *The Writings of Benjamin Franklin*. 10 vols. New York: Macmillan, 1905–7.

Sprigge, Timothy L. S., ed. *The Correspondence of Jeremy Bentham*. Vol. 1. London: Athlone Press, 1968.

Steuart, A. Francis, ed. *The Last Journals of Horace Walpole during the Reign of George III from 1771–1783*. 2 vols. London: John Lane, 1910.

Todd, Charles Burr. *Life and Letters of Joel Barlow, LL.D.* New York, 1886.

Ufton, L. F. S., ed. *The Diary and Selected Papers of Chief Justice William Smith 1784–1793*. 2 vols. Toronto: Champlain Society, 1963.

"Warren-Adams Letters." *Collections of the Massachusetts Historical Society* 72–73 (1917 and 1925).

Williams, E. Neville, ed. *The Eighteenth Century Constitution 1688–1815: Documents and Commentary*. Cambridge: Cambridge University Press, 1960.

Woods, John A., ed. "The Correspondence of Benjamin Rush and Granville Sharp 1773–1809." *Journal of American Studies* 1 (1967): 1–38.

Wyvill, Christopher. *The Correspondence of the Rev. C. Wyvill with the Right Honourable William Pitt*. Part I. 2d ed. Newcastle, 1796.

———. *Political Papers: Chiefly Respecting the Attempt of the County of York and Other Considerable Districts, Commenced in 1779 and Continued during Several Subsequent Years to Effect a Reformation of the Parliament of Great Britain*. 6 vols. York, 1794–1802.

NEWSPAPERS AND MAGAZINES

[Almon, John], ed. *The Remembrancer*. 17 vols. London, 1776–84.

[Kearsley, George], ed. *American Gazette*. London, 1768–69.

*The Crisis.* London, 1775–76.

*Chelmsford Chronicle.*

[Stockdale, John], ed. *The Debates and Proceedings of the House of Commons.*

*Gazeteer and New Daily Advertiser.*

*General Advertiser.*

*Gentleman's Magazine.*

*London Magazine.*

*London Review.*

*Massachusetts Centinel.*

*The Monthly Review.*

*The North Briton.*

*Pennsylvania Gazette.*

*The Parliamentary Register.*

*Public Advertiser.*

Spence, Thomas, ed. *One Pennyworth of Pig's Meat.* 3 vols. London, 1794.

MISCELLANEOUS

Almon, John. *Speedily Will be Published a Map of the Middle British Colonies in North-America. . . .* [London, 1776].

Belsham, W[illiam]. *Memoirs of the Reign of George III. To the Session of Parliament Ending AD 1793.* 4 vols. London, 1795.

[Bent, William]. *A General Catalogue of Books in all Languages Arts, and Sciences, that have been Printed in Great Britain and Published in London, Since the Year MDCC to the Present Time.* London, 1779.

Blackstone, Sir William. *Commentaries on the Laws of England.* 4 vols. 14th ed. London, 1803.

Bogue, David, and Bennett, James. *History of Dissenters, from the Revolution in 1688 to the Year 1808.* 4 vols. London, 1809.

Carver, J[onathan]. *Travels Through the Interior Parts of North America in the Years 1766, 1767 and 1768.* 3d ed. London, 1781.

*A Catalogue of Books, Written by Joseph Priestley, LL.D. FRS and Printed for J. Johnson Bookseller.* London, 1804.

*A Catalogue of the Books Belonging to the Birmingham Library.* Birmingham, 1795.

*A Catalogue of the Very Elegant Classical and Critical Library of the Late Rev. Gilbert Wakefield, AM.* London, 1802.

*A Catalogue of the Very Valuable Library of the Late John Wilkes, Esq. MP.* [London, 1802].

*A Cataloge* [sic] *of Tracts* [belonging to Catharine Macaulay]. np., 1790.

[Cobbett, William], ed. *The Parliamentary History of England from the Earliest Period to the Year 1803*. 36 vols. London, 1814–16.

[Disney, John]. *An Arranged Catalogue of the Several Publications Which have Appeared, Relating to the Enlargement of the Toleration of Protestant-Dissenting-Ministers and the Repeal of the Corporation and Test Acts*. London, 1790.

Howell, T. B., ed. *A Collection of State Trials and Proceedings for High Treason and Other Crimes and Misdemeanors from the Earliest Period to the Year 1803*. Vols. 20–26. London, 1814–17.

Kalm, Petr. *Travels into North America*. 3 vols. Warrington, Lancashire, 1770–71.

Macaulay, Catharine. *The History of England from the Accession of James I to the Revolution*. 8 vols. London, 1763–83.

Neal, Daniel. *The History of New-England*. 2 vols. 2d ed. London, 1747.

————. *The History of the Puritans*. 2 vols. 2d ed. London, 1744.

Paley, William. *The Principles of Moral and Political Philosophy*. London, 1785.

[Rede, Leman Thomas]. *Bibliotheca Americana*. London, 1789.

CONTEMPORARY BIOGRAPHIES

Aikin, John, et al. *General Biography*. 10 vols. London, 1799–1815.

Aikin, Lucy. *Memoir of John Aikin, MD*. 2 vols. London, 1823.

[Almon, John]. *Anecdotes of the Life of the Right Honourable William Pitt, Earl of Chatham*. 3 vols. 3d ed. London, 1793.

————. *Memoirs of a Late Eminent Bookseller*. London, 1790.

Belsham, Thomas. *Memoirs of the Late Reverend Theophilus Lindsey MA*. London, 1812.

Binns, John. *Recollections of the Life of John Binns*. Philadelphia, 1854.

[Blackburne, Francis]. *Memoirs of Thomas Hollis, Esq*. 2 vols. London, 1780.

Brydges, Samuel Egerton. *A Brief Character of Matthew Lord Rokeby*. London, 1817.

Cappe, Catherine. *Memoirs of the Late Rev. Newcome Cappe*. York, 1820.

Cartwright, Frances Dorothy. *The Life and Correspondence of Major Cartwright*. 2 vols. London, 1826.

Disney, John. *Memoirs of Thomas Brand-Hollis Esq*. London, 1808.

Dyer, George. *Memoirs of the Life and Writings of Robert Robinson*. London, 1796.

*Gerrald: A Fragment*. London, [1796].

Hardy, Thomas. *Memoir of Thomas Hardy*. London, 1832.

Hoare, Prince. *Memoirs of Granville Sharp*. London, 1820.

[Keir, James]. *An Account of the Life and Writings of Thomas Day, Esq.* London, 1791.

Le Breton, Anna Letitia. *Memoir of Mrs. Barbauld.* London, 1874.

Lettsom, John Coakley. *Memoirs of John Fothergill MD.* 4th ed. London, 1786.

————. *Recollections of Dr. Rush.* London, 1815.

Manning, James. *A Sketch of the Life and Writings of the Rev. Micaiah Towgood.* Exeter, 1792.

[Martin, John]. *Some Account of the Writings of the Rev. John Martin.* London, 1797.

[Meadley, G. M.]. *Memoirs of Mrs. Jebb.* [London, 1812?].

*A Memoir of John Cartwright, the Reformer.* London, 1831.

*Memoirs of the Life and Writings of Thomas Percival MD.* London, 1807.

Morgan, William. *Memoirs of the Life of the Rev. Richard Price.* London, 1815.

Pettigrew, Thomas Joseph. *Memoirs of the Life and Writings of the Late John Coakley Lettsom.* 3 vols. London, 1817.

Powell, G. H., ed. *Reminiscences and Table Talk of Samuel Rogers.* London, 1903.

[Priestley, Joseph]. *Memoirs of Dr. Joseph Priestley.* London, 1904.

Somerville, Thomas. *My Own Life and Times, 1741–1814.* Edinburgh, 1861.

Mrs. Thelwall. *The Life of John Thelwall.* Vol. 1. London, 1837.

Watson, Richard. *Anecdotes of the Life of Richard Watson, Bishop of Landaff* [sic]. 2 vols. 2d ed. London, 1818.

AMERICAN TRACTS

Adams, Amos. *A Concise, Historical View of the Difficulties, Hardships and Perils which Attended the Planting and Progressive Improvement of New-England.* London, 1770.

Adams, John. *A Defence of the Constitutions of Government of the United States of America.* 3 vols. London, 1787–88.

————, ed. *A Collection of State-Papers Relative to the First Acknowledgement of the Sovereignty of the United States of America. And the Reception of Their Minister Plenipotentiary by Their High Mightinesses the States General of the United Netherlands.* London, 1782.

Adams, John Quincy. *An Oration, Pronounced July 4th 1793, at the Request of the Inhabitants of the Town of Boston in Commemoration of the Anniversary of American Independence.* Boston, 1793.

Adams, Samuel. *An Oration Delivered at the State-House in Philadelphia*

*to a Very Numerous Audience; on Thursday the 1st of August, 1776.*
London, 1776.

*Additional Observations to a Short Narrative of the Horrid Massacre in Boston.* [London, 1770].

*Additions to Common Sense.* London, 1776.

*An Appeal to the World: Or A Vindication of the Town of Boston, From Many False and Malicious Aspersions Contained in Certain Letters and Memorials Written by Governor Bernard, General Gage, Commodore Hood, The Commissioners of the American Board of Customs and Others, and By Them Respectively Transmitted to the British Ministry.* London, 1770.

*Authentic Account of the Proceedings of the Congress Held at New-York, in MDCCLXV, on the Subject of the American Stamp Act.* [London], 1767.

Bailyn, Bernard, ed. *Pamphlets of the American Revolution 1750–1776.* Vol. 1. Cambridge, Mass.: Belknap Press, 1965.

Barlow, Joel. *Advice to the Privileged Orders in the Several States of Europe.* London, 1792.

―――. *The Conspiracy of Kings.* London, 1792.

―――. *A Letter to the National Convention of France.* London, 1792.

―――. *The Vision of Columbus.* London, 1787.

Bland, Richard. *An Enquiry into the Rights of the British Colonies.* London, 1769.

Chauncy, Charles. *The Appeal to the Public Answered in Behalf of the Non-Episcopal Churches in America.* Boston, 1768.

―――. *A Discourse on "The Good News From a Far Country."* London, 1767.

―――. *A Letter to a Friend.* London, 1768.

―――. *A Reply to Dr Chandler's "Appeal Defended."* Boston, 1770.

Crèvecoeur, J. Hector St. John. *Letters From an American Farmer.* London, 1782.

[John Dickinson], *The Late Regulations Respecting the British Colonies on the Continent of America Considered.* London, 1766.

[―――]. *Letters from a Farmer in Pennsylvania to the Inhabitants of the British Colonies.* London, 1768.

[―――]. *A New Essay on the Constitutional Power of Great-Britain over the Colonies in America.* London, 1774.

Douglass, William. *A Summary, Historical and Political, of the First Planting, Progressive Improvements and Present State of the British Settlements in North-America.* 2 vols. London, 1755.

Duché, Jacob. *The Duty of Standing Fast in Our Sprirtual and Temporal Liberties.* London, 1775.

[Dulany, Daniel]. *Considerations on the Propriety of Imposing Taxes in the British Colonies for the Purpose of Raising A Revenue by Act of Parliament*. 2d ed. London, 1766.

Eliot, Andrew. *A Sermon Preached Before His Excellency Francis Bernard, Esq*. Boston, 1765.

[Franklin, Benjamin]. *The Causes of the Present Distractions in America Explained*. London, 1774.

―――. *Philosophical and Miscellaneous Papers*. Edited by Benjamin Vaughan. London, 1787.

―――. *Political, Miscellaneous, and Philosophical Pieces*. Edited by Benjamin Vaughan. London, 1779.

―――. *Two Tracts: Information to Those Who Would Remove to America. And, Remarks Concerning the Savages of North America*. 2d ed. London, 1784.

[Gordon, William]. *Proposals for Printing by Subscription, in Four Volumes Octavo in Good Type, on the Best Paper to be Delivered, Neatly Bound in Calf and Lettered, to Subscribers at Six Dollars and Two Thirds, the History of the Rise, Progress and Conclusion of the American Revolution*. Broadside. [Boston, 1785].

[Hollis, Thomas], ed. *The True Sentiments of America*. London, 1768.

Jefferson, Thomas. *A Summary View of the Rights of British America*. 2d ed. London, 1774.

Lathrop, John. *Innocent Blood Crying to God from the Streets of Boston*. London, 1770.

[Lee, Arthur]. *An Appeal to the Justice and Interests of the People of Great Britain, in the Present Disputes with America*. London, 1775.

[―――]. *An Appeal to the Justice and Interests of the People of Great Britain, in the Present Disputes with America*. 4th ed. London & Newcastle, 1776.

[―――]. *The Political Detection*. London, 1770.

[―――]. *A Second Appeal to the Justice and Interests of the People on the Measures Respecting America*. London, 1775.

[―――]. *A Speech, Intended to Have Been Delivered in the House of Commons, in Support of the Petition from the General Congress at Philadelphia*. London, 1775.

[―――]. *A True State of the Proceedings in the Parliament of Great Britain, and in the Province of Massachusetts Bay, Relative to the Giving and Granting the Money of the People of that Province, and of All America, in the House of Commons in Which They are Not Represented*. London, 1774.

*A Letter to the Right Honourable The Earl of Hillsborough, of the Present Situation of Affairs in America*. London, 1769.

*Letters from General Washington to Several of His Friends in the Year 1776.* London, 1777.

*Letters to the Ministry From Governor Bernard, General Gage, and Commodore Hood.* London, [1769].

*Letters to the Right Honorable the Earl of Hillsborough From Governor Bernard, General Gage and the Honourable His Majesty's Council for the Province of Massachusetts-Bay.* London, 1769.

*A Manual of Religious Liberty.* London, 1767.

Mayhew, Jonathan. *Observations on the Charter and Conduct of the Society for the Propagation of the Gospel in Foreign Parts.* London, 1763.

————. *The Snare Broken.* [London, 1766].

[Murray, William Vans]. *Political Sketches.* London, 1787.

*Observations on Several Acts of Parliament, Passed in the Fourth Sixth and Seventh Years of His Present Majesty's Reign.* London, 1770.

Otis, James. *A Vindication of the British Colonies.* London, 1769.

Paine, Thomas. *A Letter Addressed to the Abbé Raynal on the Affairs of North America.* London, 1782.

————. *Thoughts on the Peace and the Probable Advantages Thereof to the United States of America.* London, 1783.

————, and Chalmers, Joseph. *Common Sense and Plain Truth.* London, 1776.

Quincy, Josiah. *Observations on the Act of Parliament Commonly Called the Boston Port-Bill.* London, 1774.

[Rush, Benjamin]. *Considerations Upon the Present Test-Law of Pennsylvania.* Philadelphia, 1784.

[Sayre, Stephen]. *The Englishman Deceived.* London, 1768.

*A Short Narrative of the Horrid Massacre in Boston Perpetrated in the Evening of the Fifth Day of March 1770.* London, 1770.

Smith, William. *An Oration in Memory of General Montgomery.* London, 1776.

————. *A Sermon on the Present Situation of American Affairs.* London, 1775.

Thornton, John Wingate, ed. *The Pulpit of the American Revolution.* 2d ed. Boston, 1876.

[Trumbull, John]. *McFingal: A Modern Epic Poem.* London, 1776.

[Trumbull, Jonathan]. *An Address of His Excellency Governor Trumbull to the General Assembly.* New London, Conn., 1783.

[U.S. Continental Congress]. *A Clear Idea of the Genuine and Uncorrupted British Constitution: In an Address to the Inhabitants of the Province of Quebec.* [London, 1774?].

[————]. *The Declaration by the Representatives of the United Colo-*

*nies of North America Now Met in General Congress at Philadelphia*
*Setting Forth the Causes and Necessity of Taking Up Arms*. London,
1775.
[_____]. *The Declaration of Independence*. London, 1776.
Winchester, Elhanan. *A Century Sermon on the Glorious Revolution*.
London, 1788.
_____. *An Oration on the Discovery of America*. London, 1792.
Witherspoon, John. *An Address to the Natives of Scotland Residing in
America*. London, 1778.
_____ . *The Dominion of Providence Over the Passions of Men*. London, 1778.
Zubly, John Joachim. *The Law of Liberty*. London, 1775.


ENGLISH POLITICAL TRACTS

*Address and Declaration of the Society of Constitutional Whigs, Inde-
pendents, and Friends of the People United for Obtaining Equal Lib-
erty by a Parliamentary Reform*. [London, 1792].
*Address of the Bristol Constitutional Society for a Parliamentary Reform
to the People of Great-Britain*. [Bristol], 1794.
*The Address of the British Convention Assembled at Edinburgh,
November 19, 1793, to the People of Great Britain*. London, [1793].
*An Address to the People of Great Britain*. London, 1779.
[Almon, John]. *An Address to the Interior Cabinet*. London, 1782.
_____ , ed. *An Asylum for Fugitive Pieces in Prose and Verse, Not in
Any Other Collection, With Several Pieces Never Before Published*. 4
vols. London, 1785–98.
[_____], ed. *A Collection of Tracts on the Subjects of Taking the
British Colonies in America and Regulating Their Trade*. 4 vols. London, 1773.
[_____]. *Free Parliaments*. London, 1783.
_____ . *The Revolution in MDCCLXXXII Impartially Considered*.
London, 1782.
*America: An Ode*. London, 1776.
Andrews, John. *An Essay on Republican Principles*. London, 1783.
_____ . *History of the War with America, France, Spain and Holland*. 4
vols. London, 1785.
Anglo-Saxon. *The Duty of a Freeman, Addressed to the Electors of Great
Britain*. [London], 1780.
*Assassination of the King*. [London, 1794].
*An Authentic Account of the Riots in Birmingham on the 14th, 15th,
16th and 17th Days of July, 1791*. [Birmingham, 1791].
[Bacon, Anthony]. *A Short Address to the Government, the Merchants,*

Manufacturers, and the Colonists in America, and the Sugar Islands on the Present States of Affairs. London, 1775.

Bancroft, Edward. *Remarks on the Review of the Controversy Between Great Britain and Her Colonies*. London, 1769.

[Baynes, John]. *A Third Address from the Society for Constitutional Information to the People of Great Britain and Ireland*. [London, 1785].

Belcher, William. *Precious Morsels*. [London? 1795].

Belsham, William. *An Examination of an Appeal from the New to the Old Whigs*. London, 1782.

———. *Essays Philosophical and Moral, Historical and Literary*. 2d ed. 2 vols. London, 1799.

Bertie, Willoughby, earl of Abingdon. *Thoughts on the Letter of Edmund Burke, Esq., to the Sheriffs of Bristol on the Affairs of America*. 6th ed. Oxford, [1777].

Birmingham Society for Constitutional Information. [*Address, Declaration, Rules and Orders*], Birmingham, 1792.

[Blackburne, Francis], ed. *A Collection of Letters and Essays in Favour of Public Liberty*. 3 vols. London, 1774.

———. "A Critical Commentary on Archbishop Secker's Letter to the Right Honorable Horatio Walpole Concerning Bishops in America." *The Works, Theological and Miscellaneous of Francis Blackburne*. Vol. 2. Cambridge, 1805.

Boothby, Sir Brooke. *A Letter to the Right Honourable Edmund Burke*. 2 vols. London, 1791.

[Burgh, James]. *Crito*. 2 vols. London, 1766–67.

[———]. *Political Disquisitions*. 3 vols. London, 1774–75.

Burke, Edmund. *Speeches and Letters on American Affairs*. Edited by Peter McKevitt. London: Dent, 1908.

———. *Thoughts on the Cause of the Present Discontents*. London, 1770.

Burke, William. *An Account of the European Settlements in America*. London, 1757.

Cappe, Newcome. *A Sermon Preached on Friday the Fourth of February MDCCLXXX the Late Day of National Humiliation to a Congregation of Protestant-Dissenters, in Saint-Savior Gate York*. York, 1780.

———. *A Sermon Preached on the Eighth of February 1782, a Day of National Humiliation and Again (by the Assistant Minister) on Wednesday the 25th of Feb.* [sic] *1795 the Late Day of National Humiliation to a Congregation of Protestant Dissenters in St. Savior Gate, York*. York, [1795].

———. *A Sermon Preached on the Thirteenth of December, the Late Day of National Humiliation, to a Congregation of Protestant Dissenters in Saint-Saviour-Gate, York*. York, 1776.

————. *A Sermon Preached on the Thirteenth of December the Late Day of National Humiliation, to a Congregation of Protestant Dissenters in Saint-Saviour-Gate, York.* 2d ed. London, 1778.

————. *A Sermon Preached on Thursday the Twenty-Ninth of July MDCCLXXXIV the Late Day of National Thanksgiving to a Congregation of Protestant Dissenters in Saint Savior Gate, York.* York, 1784.

————. *A Sermon Preached on Wednesday the 21st of February MDCLXXXI the Late Day of National Humiliation to a Congregation of Protestant Dissenters in Saint Savior Gate, York.* York, 1781.

[Cartwright, Edmund]. *The Prince of Peace and Other Poems.* London, 1779.

Cartwright, John. *An Account of the Proceedings at the Meeting of the Freeholders of Nottinghamshire Held at Newark, March 8th, 1785.* Nottingham, [1785].

[————]. *An Address to the Gentlemen Forming the Several Committees of the Associated Counties, Cities and Towns for Supporting the Petitions for Redress of Grievances, and against the Unconstitutional Influence of the Crown over Parliament.* London, 1780.

[————]. *American Independence the Interest and Glory of Great Britain.* London, 1774.

————. *American Independence The Interest and Glory of Great Britain.* A new edition. London, 1775.

————. *An Appeal, Civil and Military, on the Subject of the English Constitution.* 2d ed. London, 1799.

————. *An Appeal on the Subject of the English Constitution.* Boston, Lincs., [1797?].

————. *A Bill of Rights and Liberties or An Act for a Constitutional Reform of Parliament.* London, 1817.

————. *The Commonwealth in Danger.* London, 1795.

————. *The Comparison: In Which Mock Reform, Half Reform, and Constitutional Reform are Considered.* London, 1810.

————. *The Constitutional Defence of England, Internal and External.* London, 1796.

————. *The English Constitution Produced and Illustrated.* London, 1823.

————. *Give Us Our Rights!* London, [1782].

————. *The Legislative Rights of the Commonalty Vindicated.* London, 1777.

[————]. *A Letter from John Cartwright Esq. to a Friend at Boston in the County of Lincoln.* London, 1793.

[————]. *A Letter to Edmund Burke, Esq.; Controverting the Princi-*

ples of American Government, Laid Down in his Lately Published Speech on American Taxation Delivered in the House of Commons on the 19th of April 1774. London, 1774.

————. A Letter to the Duke of Newcastle. London, 1792.

————. A Letter to the Earl of Abingdon. London, 1778.

[————]. The Memorial of Common-Sense upon the Present Crisis Between Great-Britain and America. London, 1778.

[————]. The People's Barrier against Undue Influence and Corruption. 2d ed. London, 1780.

————. Six Letters to the Marquis of Tavistock, on Reform of the Commons House of Parliament. London, 1812.

————. The State of the Nation. Harlow, Essex, 1805.

————. Take Your Choice! London, 1776.

Case of Great Britian and America. 2d ed. London, 1769.

The Case Stated on Philosophical Grounds Between Great Britain and Her Colonies. London, 1777.

[Cawthorne, Joseph]. A Plan of Reconciliation with America. London, 1782.

Champion, Richard. Comparative Reflections on the Past and Present Political Commercial and Civil State of Great Britain. London, 1787.

The Charters of the British Colonies in America. London, [1774].

Citizen of London. The Rights and Duties of Man. London, [1792].

A Collection of Papers, Addresses, Songs, Etc. Printed on All Sides during the Contest for Representatives in Parliament for the Borough of Liverpool. Liverpool, 1780.

A Collection of the Letters Which have been Addressed to the Volunteers of Ireland on the Subject of a Parliamentary Reform. London, 1783.

A Conciliatory Address to the People of Great Britain and of the Colonies in the Present Important Crisis. London, 1775.

Considerations on the Policy, Commerce and Circumstances of the Kingdom. London, 1771.

Considerations on the Political and Commercial Circumstances of Great Britain and Ireland. London, 1787.

Considerations upon This Question, What Should Be an Honest Englishman's Endeavor in this Present Controversy between Great-Britain and the Colonies? London [1775].

"Constitutionalis." Letters to the Electors and People of England, Preparatory to the Approaching General Election. London, 1780.

Cooper, Thomas. A Reply to Mr. Burke's Invective against Mr. Cooper, and Mr. Watt, in the House of Commons on the 30th of April, 1792. London, 1792.

Copy of a Declaration and Articles Subscribed by the Members of Administration. London, 1789.

[Crowley, Thomas]. *Dissertations on the Grand Dispute Between Great Britain and America*. London, 1774.

D., W. *A Second Answer to Mr. John Wesley*. London, 1775.

[Dalrymple, Alexander]. *Considerations on the Present State of Affairs Between England and America*. London, 1778.

[Dalrymple, Sir John]. *The Address of People of Great-Britain to the Inhabitants of America*. London, 1775.

David, Rees. *The Hypocritical Fast with its Design and Consequences*. Norwich, 1781.

[Day, Thomas]. *The Desolation of America*. London, 1777.

[_____]. *The Devoted Legions: A Poem*. London, 1776.

_____ . *A Dialogue Between a Justice of the Peace and a Farmer*. 3d ed. London, 1786.

_____ . *Fragment of an Original Letter on the Slavery of the Negroes*. London, 1784.

_____ . *Reflections upon the Present State of England and the Independence of America*. 5th ed. London, 1783.

[_____]. *A Second Address to the Public from the Society for Constitutional Information*. London, 1780.

_____ . *Two Speeches of Thomas Day Esq. at the General Meetings of the Counties of Cambridge and Essex, Held March 25, and April 25, 1780*. [London], 1780.

*The Derby Address*. [London, 1793].

Disney, John. *The Progressive Improvement of Civil Liberty*. London, 1792.

_____ . *A Sermon Preached in the Parish Church of Swinderby in the County of Lincoln; on Friday, February the 8th, 1782 Being the Day Appointed by His Majesty's Proclamation, for A General Fast*. London, 1782.

[Eardley-Wilmot, John]. *A Short Defence of the Opposition*. London, 1778.

*An Earnest Invitation to the Friends of the Established Church, to Join with Several of Their Brethren, Clergy and Laity, in London, in Setting Apart One Hour of Every Week for Prayer and Supplication during the Present Troublesome Times*. London, 1779.

An Elector. *An Address to the Electors of Southwark*. 2d ed. London, [1794?].

*English Liberty: Being a Collection of Interesting Tracts from the Year 1762 to 1769*. London, [1769].

*An Enquiry Whether the Absolute Independence of America is Not to be Preferred to Her Partial Dependence as Most Agreeable to the Real Interests of Great Britain*. London, [1776?].

[Erskine, Thomas]. *The Speech of the Hon. Thomas Erskine at a Meeting of the Friends to the Liberty of the Press at Free-Mason's Tavern, Dec. 22, 1792*. London, 1792.

*An Essay on Parliament and the Causes of Unequal Representation*. London, 1793.

*An Essay on the Interests of Britain, in Regard to America*. London, 1780.

*Essays Commercial and Political on the Real and Relative Interests of Imperial and Dependent States, particularly Those of Great Britain and Her Dependencies*. Newcastle, 1777.

Evans, Caleb. *British Freedom Realised*. Bristol, [1788].

[_____]. *A Letter to the Rev. Mr. John Wesley, Occasioned By His Calm Address to the American Colonies*. Bristol, 1775.

_____. *Political Sophistry Detected*. Bristol, 1776.

_____. *The Remembrance of Former Days*. 3d ed. Bristol, [1778].

_____. *A Reply to the Rev. Mr. Fletcher's Vindication of Mr. Wesley's Calm Address to Our American Colonies*. Bristol, [1776].

[Fothergill, John]. *Considerations Relative to the North American Colonies*. London, 1765.

*Four Letters from the Country Gentleman on the Subject of the Petitions*. London, 1780.

Freeth, John. *The Political Songster*. Birmingham, 1790.

A Friend to Both Countries. *America Vindicated from the High Charge of Ingratitude and Rebellion*. Devizes, Wilts., 1774.

A Friend to Great Britain. *Address to the Rulers of the State*. London, 1778.

*A Full and Faithful Report of the Debates in Both Houses of Parliament, on Monday the 17th of February and Friday the 21st of February, 1783 on the Articles of Peace*. London, [1783].

*Further Proceedings on the Trial of John Horne Esq*. London, 1777.

Gerrald, Joseph. *A Convention the Only Means of Saving Us from Ruin*. London, 1793.

_____. *The Defence of Joseph Gerrald on a Charge of Sedition Before the High Court of Justiciary at Edinburgh*. London, 1794.

*Give Us Our Rights!* London, n.d.

A Gloucestershire Freeholder. *The Crisis*. London, 1780.

Godwin, William. *An Enquiry Concerning Political Justice*. 2 vols. London, 1793.

[Goodenough, Richard]. *The Constitutional Advocate*. London, 1776.

*The Gulf of Ruin, or a Quick Reform. Which Will You Choose*. London, 1795.

Hartley, David. *Argument on the French Revolution*. Bath, Som., 1794.

————. *Letters on the American War.* 6th ed. London, 1779.

Holcroft, Thomas. *A Letter to the Right Honourable William Windham on the Intemperance and Dangerous Tendency of His Public Conduct.* London, 1795.

Horne Tooke, John. *The Diversions of Purley.* 2 vols. 2d ed. London, 1797.

[Hulme, Obadiah]. *An Historical Essay on the English Constitution.* London, 1771.

Hutchinson, Benjamin. *A Sermon.* London, 1778.

Ibbetson, James. *A Dissertation on the National Assemblies under the Saxon and Norman Governments.* London, 1781.

*The Independent Freeholders Letter to the People of England, upon the One Thing Needful At This Final Crisis.* London, [1775?].

*An Inquiry Into the Policy of the Penal Laws Affecting the Popish Inhabitants of Ireland.* London, 1775.

[Jackson, Richard]. *An Historical Review of the Constitution and Government of Pennsylvania.* London, 1759.

[Jebb, Ann]. *Two Penny-Worth of Truth for a Penny.* London, 1793.

Jebb, John. *An Address to the Freeholders of Middlesex.* London, 1779.

————. *The Works Theological, Medical, Political and Miscellaneous of John Jebb, MD, FRS, with Memoirs of the Life of the Author.* Edited by John Disney. 3 vols. London, 1787.

Jones, William. *An Inquiry into the Legal Mode of Suppressing Riots.* 2d ed. London, 1782.

Joyce, Jeremiah. *A Sermon Preached on Sunday, February the 23rd, 1794.* London, 1794.

*Junius.* 2 vols. [London], 1772.

[Keld, Christopher]. *An Essay on the Polity of England.* London, 1785.

Kippis, Andrew. *An Address Delivered at the Interment of the Late Rev. Dr. Richard Price on 26th of April, 1791.* London, 1791.

————. *Considerations on the Provisional Treaty with America and Preliminary Articles of Peace with France and Spain.* London, 1783.

————. *A Sermon Preached at the Old Jewry, on the Fourth of November, 1788, Before the Society for Commemorating the Glorious Revolution.* London, 1788.

*Letters from a Country Gentleman to a Member of Parliament, on the Present State of the Nation.* 4th ed. London, 1789.

*Letters from His Excellency George Washington, President of the United States of America to Sir John Sinclair, Bart MP on Agricultural, and Other Interesting Topics.* London, 1800.

*Letters on the Present State of England and America.* London, 1794.

Lofft, Capel. *An Argument on the Nature of Party and Faction*. London, 1780.

―――――. *Observations on Mr. Wesley's Second Calm Address, and Incidentally on Other Writings upon the American Question*. London, 1777.

―――――. *Remarks on the Letter of the Rt Hon Edmund Burke, Concerning the Revolution in France, and on the Proceedings in Certain Societies in London, Relative to That Event*. London, 1790.

[―――――]. *A Summary of a Treatise by Major Cartwright Entitled the People's Barrier Against Undue Influence*. [London, 1782].

[―――――]. *A View of the Several Schemes with Respect to America*. London, 1775.

London Corresponding Society. *Address from the London Corresponding Society to the Inhabitants of Great Britain on the Subject of a Parliamentary Reform*. London, 1792.

―――――. *Address to the People of Great Britain and Ireland*. [London, 1794].

―――――. *The Report of the Committee of Constitution of the London Corresponding Society*. [London], n.d.

―――――. *A Vindication of the London Corresponding Society*. London, [1794?].

Longley, John. *An Essay toward Forming a More Complete Representation of Great Britain*. London, 1795.

Mably, Gabriel Bonnot de, Abbé. *Remarks Concerning the Government and the Laws of the United States of America*. London, 1784.

Macaulay [Graham], Catharine. *An Address to the People of England, Scotland, and Ireland on the Present Important Crisis of Affairs*. Bath, Som., 1775.

―――――. *Loose Remarks on Certain Positions to be Found in Mr Hobbes' Philosophical Rudiments of Government and Society with a Short Sketch of a Democratical Form of Government in a Letter to Signior Paoli*. 2d ed. London, 1769.

―――――. *Observations on a Pamphlet Entitled Thoughts on the Causes of the Present Discontents*. London, 1770.

[―――――]. *Observations on the Reflections of the Right Hon. Edmund Burke on the Revolution in France, in a Letter to the Right Hon. The Earl of Stanhope*. London, 1790.

*The Manual of Liberty*. London, 1795.

Martin, John. *Familiar Dialogues Between Americanus and Britannicus*. London, 1776.

―――――. *A Review of Some Things Pertaining to Civil Government*. London, 1791.

Mauduit, Israel. "A Hand Bill Advocating American Independence." *Winnowings in American History*. Edited by Paul Leicester Ford. Brooklyn, 1890.

A Member. *An Account of the Proceedings of the British Convention*. London, [1794?].

[A Member of Parliament]. *An Examination into the Conduct of the Present Administration from the Year 1774 to the Year 1778, and a Plan of Accommodation with America*. London, 1778.

Member of the Birmingham Constitutional Society. *A Letter to the English Nation*. [Leeds, 1793].

Molesworth, Robert, Viscount. *The Principles of a Real Whig*. London, 1775.

Murray, James. *The Finishing Stroke to Mr Wesley's Calm Address to the People of England*. Newcastle upon Tyne, 1778.

―――― . *An Impartial History of the Present War in America*. 2 vols. London, [1778].

―――― . *Sermons for the General Fast Day*. London, 1781.

―――― . *Sermons to Asses, to Doctors in Divinity, to Lords Spiritual, and to Ministers of State*. London, 1819.

Nedham, Marchamont. *The Excellence of a Free State*. Edited by Richard Barron. London, 1767.

Northcote, Rev. Thomas. *The Constitution of England*. London, 1783.

―――― . *Observations on the Natural and Civil Rights of Mankind the Prerogatives of Princes, and of the Powers of Government*. London, 1781.

O'Bierne, Thomas Lewis. *A Short History of the Last Session of Parliament. With Remarks*. London, 1780.

[O'Bryan, Denis]. *A Defence of the Right Honorable The Earl of Shelburne from the Reproaches of His Numerous Enemies in a Letter to Sir George Savile, Bart*. 6th ed. London, 1783.

An Old Fashioned Independent Whig. *Thoughts on the Present County Petitions*. [London], 1780.

An Old Whig. *The Present State of the British Constitution, Deduced from Facts*. London, 1793.

Oswald, John. *Review of the Constitution of Great Britain*. 3d ed. [London? 1793?].

Paine, Thomas. *Address and Declaration of the Friends of Universal Peace and Liberty Held at the Thatched House Tavern St. James's Street*. [London, 1791].

―――― . *Address to the Republic of France*. London, [1792].

―――― . *The Age of Reason*. London, 1795.

————. *Agrarian Justice, Opposed to Agrarian Law, and to Agrarian Monopoly*. London, 1797.

————. *The Decline and Fall of the English System of Finance*. 3d ed. London, 1796.

————. *Dissertation on First-Principles of Government*. London, 1795.

————. *Letter Addressed to the Addressers on the Late Proclamation*. London, 1792.

————. *Letter from Thomas Paine to George Washington*. London, 1797.

————. *Letter of Thomas Paine to the People of France*. London, 1792.

————. *A Letter to George Washington on the Subject of the Late Treaty Concluded Between Great Britain and the United States of America*. London, 1797.

————. *Letter to Mr Secretary Dundas*. [London, 1791].

————. *A Letter to the Earl of Shelburne on His Speech July 10, 1782, Respecting the Acknowledgement of American Independence*. London, 1783.

————. *Rights of Man*. London, 1791.

————. *Rights of Man: Part the Second*. London, 1792.

————. *Rights of Man*. Edited by Henry Collins. Harmonsworth, Middx.: Penguin Books, 1969.

————. *The Writings of Thomas Paine*. Edited by Moncure Daniel Conway. 4 vols. New York and London, 1894–96.

*The Patriot: Containing a Declaration in Support of the Constitution; the Present State of the Representation; and the Means of Obtaining a Parliamentary Reform*. London, 1793.

Percival, Thomas. *The Works, Literary, Moral and Medical of Thomas Percival, MD*. New ed. 4 vols. London, 1807.

Perry, Sampson. *Oppression!!!: The Appeal of Captain Perry (Late Editor of the Argus) to the People of England*. London, 1795.

[Pigott, Charles]. *The Female Jockey Club*. London, 1794.

[————]. *The Jockey Club*. London, 1792.

————. *Persecution. The Case of Charles Pigott*. London, 1793.

————. *A Political Dictionary*. London, 1795.

[Pitt, William], Earl of Chatham. *Plan Offered by the Earl of Chatham, to the House of Lords Entitled "A Provisional Act" which was Rejected, and not Suffered to Lie upon the Table*. London, 1775.

*Political Reveries and Utopian Schemes for the Welfare of Great Britain and Ireland*. London, 1780.

Pownall, Thomas. *The Administration of the Colonies*. 4th ed. London, 1768.

————. *A Memorial Addressed to the Sovereigns of America*. London, 1783.

————. *Two Memorials, Not Originally Intended for Publication, Now Published*. London, 1782.

*The Present State of the British Empire in Europe, America, Africa and Asia*. London, 1768.

Price, Richard. *Additional Observations on the Nature and Value of Civil Liberty and the War with America*. 2d ed. London, 1777.

————. *Britain's Happiness and the Proper Improvement of It*. London, 1759.

————. *A Discourse Addressed to a Congregation at Hackney on February 21st 1781 Being the Day Appointed for a Public Fast*. London, 1781.

————. *A Discourse on the Love of Our Country*. 2d ed. London, 1789.

————. *The Evidence for a Future Period of Improvement in the State of Mankind, with the Means and Duty of Promoting it*. London, 1787.

————. *The General Introduction and Supplement to the Two Tracts on Civil Liberty, the War with America, and the Finances of the Kingdom*. London, 1778.

————. *Observations on the Importance of the American Revolution, and the Means of Making It a Benefit to the World*. London, 1785.

————. *Observations on the Nature of Civil Liberty, the Principles of Government, and the Justice and Policy of the War with America*. 3d ed. London, 1776.

————. *A Preface to the Third Edition of the Treatise on Reversionary Payments*. London, 1773.

————. *A Sermon Delivered to a Congregation of Protestant Dissenters, at Hackney, on the 10th of February Last, Being a Day Appointed for a General Fast*. London, 1779.

[Priestley, Joseph]. *An Address to the Protestant Dissenters of all Denominations on the Approaching Election of Members of Parliament, with Respect to the State of Public Liberty in General, and of American Affairs in Particular*. London, 1774.

————. *An Address to the Subscribers to the Birmingham Library on the Subject of Mr Cooke's Motion, to Restrict the Committee in the Choice of Books with a View to Exclude Controversial Divinity*. Birmingham, 1787.

————. *An Appeal to the Public on the Subject of the Riots in Birmingham*. Dublin, 1792.

————. *A Discourse on the Occasion of the Death of Dr. Price*. London, 1791.

————. *A Discourse to the Supporters of the New College at Hackney*. London, 1791.

_____ . *An Essay on a Course of Liberal Education for Civil and Active Life*. [London], 1765.

_____ . *An Essay on the First Principles of Government*. London, 1768.

_____ . *An Essay on the First Principles of Government*. 2d ed. London, 1771.

_____ . *Experiments and Observations on Different Kinds of Air and Other Branches of Natural Philosophy Connected with the Subject*. 3 vols. Birmingham, 1790.

_____ . *Extracts from Dr Priestley's Works Read in Court at the Last Warwick Assizes*. Birmingham, 1792.

_____ . *A Free Address to Those Who have Petitioned for the Repeal of the Late Act of Parliament in Favour of the Roman Catholics*. London, 1780.

_____ . *Lectures on History and General Policy*. Birmingham, 1788.

_____ . *Lectures on History and General Policy*. New ed. London, 1826.

_____ . *Letters to the Inhabitants of Northumberland and Its Neighbourhood on Subjects Interesting to the Author and to Them*. 2 pts. Northumberland [Pa.], 1799.

_____ . *Letters to the Right Honourable Edmund Burke, Occasioned by His Reflections on the Revolution in France*. Birmingham, 1791.

_____ . *Political Dialogues*. London, 1791.

_____ . *The Present State of Europe Compared with Ancient Prophesies*. London, 1794.

_____ . *The Theological and Miscellaneous Works of Joseph Priestley*. Edited by John Towill Rutt. 25 vols. London, 1817–31.

Proby, John Joshua, Earl Carysfort. *Copy of a Letter from the Right Honourable Lord Carysfort to the Huntingdonshire Committee*. [London, 1780].

*Proceedings of the Friends to the Liberty of the Press*. London, 1793.

*A Prospect of the Consequences of the Present Conduct of Great Britain towards America*. London, 1776.

[Pulteney, William]. *Thoughts on the Present State of Affairs with America, and the Means of Conciliation*. London, 1778.

Radcliff, Ebenezer. *A Sermon Preached at Walthamstow, December 13, 1776, Being the Day Appointed for a General Fast*. London, 1776.

Raynal, Guilliaume Thomas François. *The Revolution of America*. London, 1781.

_____ . *The Sentiments of a Foreigner on the Disputes of Great Britain with America*. Philadelphia, 1775.

*Reformers No Rioters*. London, [1794].

*The Reply of a Gentleman in a Select Society, upon the Important Contest Between Great Britain and America*. London, 1775.

A *Report of the Proceedings of the Committee of Association Appointed at the Adjourned General Meeting of the County of York, Held on the 28th Day of March, 1780.* York, 1783.

*Report of the Sub-Committee of Westminster Appointed April 12th 1780 to Take into Consideration All Such Matters Relative to the Election of Members of Parliament as May Promote the Purposes of the Present Association.* London, 1780.

*The Repository.* 2 vols. London, 1771.

*The Repository.* 2 vols. London, 1788.

*The Resolutions of the First Meeting of the Friends to the Liberty of the Press, December 19th, 1792.* London, 1793.

*A Review of the Laws of the United States of North America, the British Provinces, and West India Islands.* London, 1790.

*A Review of the Present Administration.* London, 1774.

Robinson, Robert. *Miscellaneous Works of Robert Robinson.* 4 vols. London, 1807.

_____ . *A Political Catechism.* 3d ed. London, 1784.

[Robinson-Morris, Matthew, Baron Rokeby]. *Considerations on the Measures Carrying on with Respect to the British Colonies in North America.* London, [1775?].

[_____]. *The Dangerous Situation of England.* 2d ed. London, 1786.

[_____]. *Peace the Best Policy.* London, 1777.

[Roebuck, John]. *An Enquiry Whether the Guilt of the Present Civil War in America Ought to be Imputed to Great Britain or America.* London, 1776.

[Rous, George]. *The Power of the Crown to Establish Peace by Yielding Independence to Revolted Colonies.* [London, 1781?].

*A Serious Lecture Delivered at Sheffield; February 28, 1794 Being the Day Appointed for a General Fast; to Which are Added Hymn and Resolutions.* London, 1794.

*A Sermon Preached in a Country Church on Friday, the 13th of December, 1776, the Day Appointed for a General Fast.* London, 1776.

Sharp, Granville, *An Account of the Ancient Division of the English Nation.* London, 1784.

_____ . *An Account of the Constitutional Polity of Congregational Courts.* 2d ed. London, 1786.

[_____]. *An Address to the People of England; Being the Protest of a Private Person Against Every Suspension of Law that is Liable to Injure or Endanger Personal Security.* London, 1778.

_____ . *A Circular Letter to the Several Petitioning Counties Cities and Towns.* London, 1780.

————. *The Claims of the People of England*. 4th ed. London, 1782.

————. *A Declaration of the People's Natural Right to a Share in the Legislature*. London, 1774.

————. *A Defence of the Ancient, Legal and Constitutional Right of the People to Elect Representatives for Every Session of Parliament*. 3d ed. London, 1780.

————. *A General Plan for Laying Out Towns and Townships on the Newly Acquired Lands in the East Indies, America, or Elsewhere*. [London], 1794.

————. *The Just Limitation of Slavery in the Laws of God*. London, 1776.

————. *The Law of Liberty or Royal Law*. London, 1776.

————. *The Law of Passive Obedience*. [London, 1776].

————. *The Law of Retribution*. London, 1776.

————. *The Legal Means of Political Reformation*. 7th ed. [London, 1780].

————. *Remarks on Several Very Important Prophesies*. 2d ed. London, 1775.

————. *A Tract on the Law of Nature*. London, 1777.

————. *Tracts Concerning the Ancient and Only True Legal Means of National Defence by a Free Militia*. 3d ed. London, 1782.

[Shipley, Jonathan]. *A Speech Intended to Have Been Spoken on the Bill for Altering the Charters of the Colony of Massachusetts Bay*. London, 1774.

————. *The Works of the Right Reverend Jonathan Shipley, D.D*. 2 vols. London, 1792.

*A Short History of the Administration during the Summer Recess of Parliament*. London, 1779.

*A Short View of the History of the Colony of Massachusetts Bay with Respect to Their Original Charter and Constitution*. London, 1769.

Sinclair, John. *Lucubrations during a Short Recess Containing a Plan for a More Equal Representation of the People*. 2d ed. London, 1783.

Society for Constitutional Information. [*Tracts*]. London, 1781.

————. *Tracts Published and Distributed Gratis by the Society for Constitutional Information*. London, 1783.

Society of the Friends of the People. *Authentic Copy of a Petition Praying for a Reform in Parliament Presented to the House of Commons by Charles Grey Esq. on Monday, 6th May 1793*. [London, 1793].

————. "On the Eight of March 1794 . . ." London, 1794.

————. *Petition of the Friends of the People*. London, 1793.

————. *Proceedings of the Society of the People; Associated for the Purpose of Obtaining a Parliamentary Reform in the Year 1792*. London, 1793.

————. *The State of the Representation of England, Scotland and Wales*. London, [1793].

A *Solemn Appeal to the Citizens of Great Britain and Ireland upon the Present Emergency*. London, 1788.

A *Solemn Appeal to the Good Sense of the Nation*. London, 1783.

[Spence, Thomas]. *The Important Trial of Thomas Spence, for a Political Pamphlet Intitled "The Restorer of Society to its Natural State" on May 27, 1801, at Westminster Hall, Before Lord Kenyon and a Special Jury*. 2d ed. [London, 1801].

————. *The Meridian Sun of Liberty*. London, 1796.

Stanhope, Earl. *The Speech of Earl Stanhope in the House of Peers, on His Motion to Acknowledge the French Republic*. London, 1794.

Stennett, Samuel. *National Calamities the Effect of Divine Displeasure*. London, [1781].

A *Supplement to the Trial of Thomas Paine*. London, 1793.

Symonds, John. *Remarks upon the Essay Intitled "The History of the Colonization of the Free States of Antiquity" Applied to the Present Contest Between Great Britain and Her American Colonies*. London, 1778.

[Thelwall, John]. *The Natural and Constitutional Right of Britons to Annual Parliaments, Universal Suffrage, and the Freedom of Popular Association*. London, 1799.

————. *Political Lectures*. London, 1795.

————. *The Rights of Nature against the Usurpation of Establishments*. London, 1796.

————. *Sober Reflections on the Seditious and Inflammatory Letter of the Right Hon. Edmund Burke to a Noble Lord*. London, 1796.

————. *The Speech of John Thelwall at the General Meeting of the Friends of Parliamentary Reform, Called by the London Corresponding Society and Held in the Neighbourhood of Copenhagen-House*. 3d ed. London, [1795].

————. *The Speech of John Thelwall at the Second Meeting of the London Corresponding Society and Other Friends of Reform Held at Copenhagen-House, on Thursday, November 12, 1795*. London, 1795.

*Thoughts on National Insanity*. London, 1797.

[Toplady, Augustus]. *An Old Fox Tarr'd and Feather'd*. London, 1775.

Toulmin, Joshua. *The American War Lamented: A Sermon Preached at Taunton, February the 18th and 25th, 1776*. London, 1776.

Towers, John. *A Friendly Dialogue Between Theophilus and Philadelphus*. London, 1776.

Towers, Joseph. *Tracts on Political and Other Subjects.* 3 vols. London, 1796.

*The Trial (at large) of John Horne, Esq., upon an Information Filed Ex Officio, by His Majesty's Attorney General, for a Libel.* London, 1777.

*The Trial at Large of Thomas Paine for a Libel in the Second Part of Rights of Man Dec. 18. 1792.* London, [1792].

*The Trial of Thomas Muir . . . For Sedition.* New ed. London, [1793].

*The Trial of Wm Winterbotham Assistant Preacher at How's Lane Meeting, Plymouth Before the Hon. Baron Perryn and a Special Jury at Exeter; on the 25 of July 1793 for Seditious Words Charged to have been Uttered in Two Sermons Preached on the 5th and 18th of November, 1792.* 2d ed. London, 1794.

Turner, William. *The Whole Service as Performed in the Congregation of Protestant Dissenters at Wakefield on Friday, December 13, 1776, Being the Day Appointed for a General Fast.* Wakefield, 1777.

[Vaughan, William]. *The Catechism of Man.* London, [1794?].

Wakefield, Gilbert. *A Reply to Thomas Paine's Second Part of the Age of Reason.* London, 1795.

————. *A Sermon Preached at Richmond in Surry [sic] on July 29th 1784, the Day Appointed for a General Thanksgiving on Account of the Peace.* London, 1784.

Walker, George. *The Doctrine of a Providence, Illustrated and Applied in a Sermon Preached to a Congregation of Protestant Dissenters, at Nottingham, July 29th, 1784, Being the Day Appointed for a General Thanksgiving, on the Conclusion of the Late Destructive War.* London, 1784.

————. *The Duty and Character of a National Soldier.* London, 1779.

————. *A Sermon Preached to a Congregation of Protestant Dissenters at Nottingham, December 13th 1776; Being the Day Appointed for a General Fast.* London, 1777.

————. *A Sermon Preached to a Congregation of Protestant Dissenters at Nottingham, February 27th 1778; Being the Day Appointed for a General Fast.* London, 1778.

————. *Substance of the Speech of the Rev. Mr Walker at the General Meeting of the County of Nottingham Held at Mansfield on Monday the 28th of February 1780.* [London], 1780.

Watson, Richard. *The Principles of the REVOLUTION Vindicated.* 2d ed. Cambridge, 1776.

————. *Sermons on Public Occasions and Tracts on Religious Subjects.* Cambridge, 1788.

Wesley, John. *A Calm Address to Our American Colonies.* London, 1775.

———. *Reflections on the Rise and Progress of the American Rebellion.* London, 1780.

[Wheelock, Matthew]. *Reflections Moral and Political on Great Britain and Her Colonies.* London, 1770.

*The Whole Proceedings on the Trial of an Information Exhibited Ex Officio by the King's Attorney-General Against Thomas Paine for a Libel upon the Revolution and Settlement of the Crown and Regal Government as by Law Established; and Also upon the Bill of Rights, the Legislature, Government, Laws, and Parliament of this Kingdom, and upon the King.* London, 1793.

Wilkes, John. *A Collection of All Mr Wilkes's Addresses to the Gentlemen, Clergy and Freeholders of the County of Middlesex.* London, 1769.

———. *A Letter to His Grace the Duke of Grafton, First Commissioner of His Majesty's Treasury.* 4th ed. London, 1767.

———. *The Speech of the Right Hon. John Wilkes, Esq. Lord Mayor of the City of London, in the House of Commons on Wednesday, February 8, 1775, Relative to the American Taxation Bills.* London, 1775.

———. *The Speeches of John Wilkes . . . in the Parliament Appointed to Meet . . . the 29th Day of November 1774. . . .* 3 vols. London, 1777.

———. *The Speeches of Mr. Wilkes in the House of Commons.* [London], 1786.

Wilkes, John; Horne Tooke, John; et al. *The Controversial Letters of John Wilkes, Esq., the Rev. John Horne and Their Principal Adherents.* London, 1771.

Williams, David. *Egeria.* London, 1803.

———. *Essays on Public Worship, Patriotism, and Projects of Reformation.* London, 1773.

———. *Lectures on Political Principles.* London, 1789.

———. *Lessons to a Young Prince, on the Present Disposition in Europe to a General Revolution.* London, 1790.

———. *Letters on Political Liberty.* London, 1782.

[Williams, David]. *A Letter to the Body of Protestant Dissenters and to Protestant Dissenting Ministers of All Denominations.* London, 1777.

———. *The Nature and Extent of Intellectual Liberty in a Letter to Sir George Savile. Bart.* London, 1778.

———. *A Plan of Association on Constitutional Principles for the Parishes Tithings Hundreds and Counties of Great Britain.* London, 1780.

———. *Unanimity in All Parts of the British Commonwealth Necessary to its Preservation Interest and Happiness.* London, 1778.

[Williamson, Hugh]. *The Plea of the Colonies on the Charges Brought Against them by Lord M[ansfield] and Others in a Letter to His Lordship*. London, 1775.

Wollstonecraft, Mary. *A Vindication of the Rights of Man*. London, 1790.

———. *Vindication of the Rights of Woman*. London, 1792.

[Wraxall, Sir Nathaniel]. *A Short Review of the Political State of Great-Britain at the Commencement of the Year 1787*. London, 1787.

Wyvill, Christopher. *The Case of the Rev. C. Wyvill Respecting the Right Honourable William Pitt*. London, 1796.

———. *A Defence of Dr. Price and the Reformers of England*. London, 1792.

———. *The Secession from Parliament Vindicated*. 3d ed. York, 1800.

Yorke, Henry. *These Are the Times That Try Mens Souls!* London, 1793.

———. *Thoughts on Civil Government*. London, 1794.

*The Yorkshire Question*. London, n.d.


ENGLISH RELIGIOUS LIBERTY PAMPHLETS

*Address to the Protestant Dissenters of England and Wales*. [London, 1792].

[Aikin, John]. *An Address to the Dissidents of England on Their Late Defeat*. London, 1790.

[———]. *The Spirit of the Constitution and that of the Church of England Compared*. London, 1790.

*An Appeal to the Candor, Magnanimity, and Justice of Those in Power, to Relieve from Severe and Opprobrious Severities and Penalties, a Great Number of Their Fellow Subjects, Who Will Give Every Security and Testimony of Their Fidelity and Attachment to the Present Establishment, Which Does Not Oblige Them to Violate the Rights of Conscience*. London, 1787.

*An Appeal to the Common Sense, and Common Honesty, of Every Inhabitant of Birmingham, Respecting the Passages Extracted from the Preface to Dr. Priestley's Letters to the Rev. Edward Burn and Sent to the Bishops, and Members of the House of Commons, Previous to the Debate on the Repeal of the Corporation and Test Acts*. Birmingham, [1790?].

[Barbauld, Anna Letitia]. *An Address to the Opposers of the Repeal of the Corporation and Test Acts*. 2d ed. London, 1790.

[Barrington, Shute]. *Letter the First Addressed to the Delegates from the Several Congregations of Protestant Dissenters Who Met at Devizes on September 14, 1789*. 2d ed. Salisbury, Wilts., 1790.

Barron, Richard, ed. *The Pillars of Priestcraft and Orthodoxy Shaken*. 2 vols. London, 1752.

Bealey, Joseph. *Observations upon the Rev. Mr Owen's Sermon, Preached in the Parish Church at Warrington, on the Thirtieth of January, MDCCXC.* Warrington, [1790].

Beaufoy, Henry. *The Substance of a Speech Delivered by Henry Beaufoy, Esq., in the House of Commons 28th March, 1787, on His Motion for the Repeal of the Test and Corporation Acts.* London, 1787.

Beilby, Samuel. *A Sermon on Religious Toleration Preached in the Church of Bowness upon Windermere, Westmorland.* York, 1790.

Belsham, Thomas. *The Importance of Truth, and the Duty of Making an Open Profession of It.* London, 1790.

Berington, Joseph. *An Address to the Protestant Dissenters.* 2d ed. Birmingham, 1787.

————. *The Rights of Dissenters from the Established Church, in Relation, Principally, to English Catholics.* Birmingham, 1789.

*Bishop Hoadly's Refutation of Bishop Sherlock's Arguments Against a Repeal of the Test and Corporation Acts.* Birmingham, [1787?].

*Bishop Sherlock's Arguments Against a Repeal of the Corporation and Test Acts.* London, 1787.

*Bishop Sherlock's Arguments Against a Repeal of the Corporation and Test Acts.* Oxford, 1790.

Blackburne, Francis. *Proposals for an Application to Parliament for Relief in the Matter of Subscription to the Liturgy and Thirty-Nine Articles of the Established Church of England.* London, 1771.

[————]. *Reflections on the Fate of a Petition for Relief in the Matter of Subscription Offered to the Honourable House of Commons, February 6th, 1772.* London, 1772.

[Bogue, David]. *Reasons for Seeking a Repeal of the Corporation and Test Acts, Submitted to the Consideration of the Candid and Impartial.* London, 1790.

Bradberry, David. *A Letter to Edward Jeffries, Esq. Chairman of the Committee, Appointed by the Deputies of the Three Denominations of Protestant Dissenters, to Carry into Effect a Resolution of the Said Deputies to Apply to Parliament, for a Repeal of the Corporation and Test Acts, So Far as They Concern Protestant Dissenters.* London, 1789.

Brand, John. *Political Observations on the Test Act.* n.p., 1790.

*Brief State of the Controversy Respecting the Corporation and Test Acts.* [London, 1790].

Bristow, W. *Cursory Reflections on the Policy, Justice and Expediency of Repealing the Test and Corporation Acts Addressed to the Nation.* London, 1790.

Burnaby, Andrew. *Two Charges Delivered to the Clergy of the Archdeaconry of Leicester, in the Years 1786 and 1787*. London, 1787.

*The Case of the Protestant Dissenters in Relation to the Corporation and Test Acts*. London, 1787.

*The Case of the Protestant Dissenters in Relation to the Laws by Which the Sacramental Test is Imposed*. [London, 1789].

Catlow, Samuel. *An Address to the Dissenters on the State of Their Political and Civil Liberty, as Subjects of Great Britain*. Bradford, Yorks., 1788.

Colebrooke, Sir George, Bart. *A Letter to a Nobleman*. London, 1790.

Cornish, —. *A Letter to the Right Reverend the Lord Bishop of Carlisle Containing a Few Remarks on Some Passages of his Lordship's Pamphlet, Intitled "Considerations on the Propriety of Requiring a Subscription to Articles of Faith."* London, 1777.

*A Country Curate's Observations on the Advertisement (in the Morning Herald of Thursday January 28th 1790) from the Leeds Clergy Relative to the Test Act. Etc.* New ed. London, [1790].

Courtenay, John. *Philosophical Reflections on the Late Revolution in France, and the Conduct of the Dissenters in England*. 2d ed. London, 1790.

Croft, George. *The Test Laws Defended*. Birmingham, 1790.

*Dean Swift's Tracts on the Repeal of the Test Act, Written and First Published in Ireland in the Years 1731–2*. London, 1790.

*The Debate in the House of Commons on Mr. Beaufoy's Motion for the Repeal of Such Parts of the Test and Corporation Acts as Affect the Protestant Dissenters*. London, 1789.

*Debate on the Repeal of the Test and Corporation Act, in the House of Commons, March 28th, 1787*. London, 1787.

*A Dialogue Between Bishop Hoadly and Bishop Sherlock, on the Corporation and Test Acts*. London, 1790.

[Disney, John]. *An Address to the Bishops; Upon the Subject of a Late Letter from One of Their Lordships to Certain Clergy in His Diocese*. London, 1790.

An Ecclesiastic. *A Scourge for the Dissenters*. London, 1790.

Englefield, Sir Henry C., Bart. *A Letter to the Author of the Review of the Case of the Protestant Dissenters*. London, 1790.

*Extracts from Books and Other Small Pieces; in Favour of Religious Liberty and the Rights of Dissenters*. 2 vols. Birmingham, 1789–90.

*Facts Submitted to the Consideration of the Friends to Civil and Religious Liberty, but More Particularly Addressed to the Protestant Dissenters of England and Wales*. London, [c. 1789].

Fawcett, Benjamin. *The Encouraging Prospect that Religious Liberty will be Enlarged*. Shrewsbury, Salop., 1773.

Fell, John. *A Fourth Letter to the Rev. Mr Pickard on Genuine Protestantism*. London, 1775.

———. *Genuine Protestantism*. London, 1773.

[Fleming, Caleb]. *An Apology for a Protestant Dissent from a National-Church, or Civil Establishment of Religion*. London, 1755.

[———]. *Civil Establishments in Religion, a Ground of Infidelity*. London, 1767.

[———]. *The Claims of the Church of England Seriously Examined*. London, 1764.

[———]. *Delays Dangerous. No Tomorrow for the Repeal of the Test and Corporation Acts*. London, 1739.

[———]. *The Equality of Christians in the Province of Religion*. London, 1760.

[———]. *A Letter from a Protestant Dissenting Minister, to the Clergy of the Church of England, Occasioned by the Alarming Growth of Popery in This Kingdom*. London, 1768.

[———]. *A Letter to the Revd. Dr Cobden*. London, 1738.

[———]. *The Palladium of Great Britain and Ireland*. London, 1762.

[———]. *Three Letters Concerning Systematic Taste*. London, 1755.

Fownes, Joseph. *An Enquiry into the Principles of Toleration*. London, 1772.

[Fox, Charles James]. *Two Speeches, Delivered in the House of Commons on Tuesday the 2d of March, 1790, by the Right Honourable Charles James Fox, in Support of His Motion for a Repeal of the Corporation and Test Acts*. London, 1790.

*A Full and Fair Discussion of the Pretensions of the Dissenters to the Repeal of the Sacramental Test*. 1733. Reprint. Oxford, 1790.

Furneaux, Philip. *An Essay on Toleration*. London, 1773.

[Geddes, Alexander]. *Letter to a Member of Parliament on the Case of the Protestant Dissenters and the Expediency of a General Repeal of All Penal Statutes that Regard Religious Opinions*. London, 1787.

[———] . *Letter to the R. R.* [sic] *The Archbishops and Bishops of England; Pointing Out the Only Sure Means of Preserving the Church from the Dangers that Now Threaten Her*. London, 1790.

Gibbons, Thomas. *Objections Against the Application to the Legislature for Relief for Protestants Dissenting Ministers and Dissenting Tutors and Schoolmasters Dispassionately Considered and Obviated*. London, 1773.

*Half an Hour's Conversation, Between a Churchman and a Dissenter, on the Subject of the Test Laws: In Which Propriety of Repealing Them is Plainly Demonstrated*. London, [1789].

[Heywood, Samuel]. *The Right of Protestant Dissenters to a Compleat Toleration Asserted*. London, 1787.

[_____]. *The Right of the Protestant Dissenters to a Compleat Toleration Asserted*. 2d ed. London, 1789.

[_____]. *The Right of Protestant Dissenters to a Compleat Toleration Asserted*. 3d ed., corrected. London, 1790.

[_____]. *High Church Politics*. London, 1792.

"H." *Hints Respectfully Addressed to the Members of the House of Commons on the Subject of the Test Laws, and Recommended to the Candid Attention of Every Member of the Church of England*. Broadsheet. Worcestershire, 1790.

Hobson, John. *A Series of Remarks upon a Sermon Preached at St Philip's Church, in Birmingham, on Sunday Jan. 3, 1790; Entitled "The Test Laws Defended" by George Croft, D.D.* Birmingham, [1790].

[Horne, George]. *Observations on the Case of the Protestant Dissenters with Reference to the Corporation and Test Acts*. Oxford, 1790.

[Horsley, Samuel]. *A Review of the Case of the Protestant Dissenters; with Reference to the Corporation and Test Acts*. London, 1790.

*Jack and Martin; a Poetical Dialogue on the Proposed Repeal of the Test-Act*. Hereford, 1790.

[Jebb, John]. *A Letter to Sir William Meredith upon the Subject of Subscription to the Liturgy and Thirty-Nine Articles of the Church of England*. London, 1772.

Keate, William. *A Free Examination of Dr Price's and Dr Priestley's Sermons*. London, 1790.

_____. *Quotation Against Quotation or Cursory Observations on Dr Priestley's Letters to the Inhabitants of Birmingham*. London, 1790.

Kippis, Andrew. *A Sermon Preached at the Old Jewry, on Wednesday the 26th of April 1786, on Occasion of a New Academical Institution, Among Protestant Dissenters, for the Education of Their Ministers and Youth*. London, 1786.

_____. *A Vindication of the Protestant Dissenting Ministers with Regard to Their Late Application to Parliament*. 2d ed. London, 1773.

[Law, Edmund]. *Considerations on the Propriety of Requiring a Subscription to Articles of Faith*. 2d ed. London, 1774.

*A Letter to a Friend on the Test Act*. London, 1790.

*A Letter to Earl Stanhope on the Subject of the Test, as Objected to in a Pamphlet Recommended by His Lordship*. Oxford, 1789.

*A Letter to the Bishops on the Application of the Protestant Dissenters, to Parliament, for a Repeal of the Corporation and Test Acts*. London, 1789.

A *Letter to the People Called Quakers, on the Probable Consequences to Them of a Repeal of the Corporation and Test Acts.* London, 1790.

A *Letter to the Public Meeting of the Friends to the Repeal of the Test and Corporation Acts at the London Tavern on February the 13th, 1790.* London, 1790.

Lettsom, John Coakley. *Reflections on Religious Persecution.* London, 1799.

Lindsey, Theophilus. *Vindiciae Priestleianae.* London, 1788.

Lofft, Capel. *An History of the Corporation and Test Acts.* 2d ed. London, 1790.

[_____]. *A Vindication of the Short History of the Corporation and Test Acts.* London, 1790.

A *Look to the Last Century, or, the Dissenters Weighed in Their Own Scales.* London, 1790.

[Madan, Spencer]. *A Letter to Doctor Priestley, in Consequence of His "Familiar Letters Addressed to the Inhabitants of the Town of Birmingham, Etc."* Birmingham, [1790].

_____. *The Principal Claims of the Dissenters Considered.* Birmingham, [1790].

Martin, John. *A Speech on the Repeal of Such Parts of the Test and Corporation Acts as Affect Conscientious Dissenters.* London, 1790.

[Mather, Cotton]. *A Letter of Advice to the Churches of the Non-Conformists in the English Nation: Endeavouring Their Satisfaction in that Point, Who are the True Church of England?* London, 1700.

Mauduit, Israel. *The Case of the Dissenting Ministers.* 3d ed. London, 1772.

Milton, John. *A Treatise of Civil Power in Ecclesiastical Causes: Shewing That it is Not Lawful for Any Power on Earth to Compel in Matters of Religion.* London, 1790.

"Nott, John" (pseud. ie. John Morfitt?). *Very Familiar Letters Addressed to Dr Priestley, in Answer to His Familiar Letters to the Inhabitants of Birmingham.* 2d ed. Birmingham, 1790.

*Observations on Doctor Price's Revolution Sermon.* . . . London, 1790.

*Observations on the Conduct of the Protestant Dissenters.* 3d ed. London, 1790.

[Palmer, John]. *Free Remarks in a Sermon Entitled "The Requisition of Subscription to the Thirty Nine Articles and Liturgy of the Church of England not Inconsistent with Christian Liberty: To Which are Prefixed, Reasons Against Subscribing a Petition to Parliament for the Abolition of Such Subscription."* London, 1772.

_____. *A Letter to Dr Balguy, on the Subject of His Charge Delivered to the Archdeaconry of Winchester, in the Year 1772.* London, 1773.

Palmer, Samuel. *A Vindication of the Modern Dissenters Against the Aspersions of the Rev. William Hawkins, M.A. in his Bampton-Lecture Sermons, and the Right Reverend Author of a Review of the Case of the Protestant Dissenters; with Reference to the Corporation and Test Acts.* London, 1790.

Price, Richard. *Four Dissertations.* London, 1768.

————. *Sermons on the Christian Doctrine as Received by the Different Denominations of Christians.* London, 1787.

[————], ed. *An Act for Establishing Religious Freedom, Passed in the Assembly of Virginia, in the Beginning of the Year 1786.* London, 1786.

Priestley, Joseph. *The Conduct to be Observed by Dissenters in Order to Procure the Repeal of the Corporation and Test Acts.* Birmingham, [1789].

————. *Considerations on Church-Authority.* London, 1769.

————. *Familiar Letters Addressed to the Inhabitants of Birmingham.* Birmingham, [1790].

————. *Familiar Letters Addressed to the Inhabitants of Birmingham.* 2d ed. Birmingham, 1790.

————. *A Free Address to the Protestant Dissenters, as Such.* 3d ed. Birmingham, 1788.

[————]. *A Free Address to Those Who Have Petitioned for the Repeal of the Late Act of Parliament in Favour of the Roman Catholics.* London, 1780.

————. *A General History of the Christian Church, From the Fall of the Western Empire to the Present Time.* 4 vols. Northumberland, Pa., 1802–3.

————. *The Importance and Extent of Free Inquiry in Matters of Religion.* Birmingham, 1785.

————. *A Letter of Advice to Those Dissenters Who Conduct the Application to Parliament for Relief from Certain Penal Laws.* London, 1773.

————. *A Letter to the Right Honourable William Pitt, First Lord of the Treasury, and Chancellor of the Exchequer; on the Subjects of Toleration and Church Establishments.* London, 1787.

————. *Letters to the Author of "Remarks on Several Late Publications Relative to the Dissenters," in a Letter to Dr Priestley.* London, 1770.

————. *The Proper Constitution of a Christian Church, Considered in a Sermon Preached at the New Meeting in Birmingham, November 3, 1782.* Birmingham, 1782.

————. *Remarks on some Paragraphs in the Fourth Volume of Dr Blackstone's Commentaries on the Laws of England, Relating to the Dissenters.* London, 1769.

————. *The Use of Christianity, Especially in Difficult Times.* London, 1794.

————. *A View of the Principles and Conduct of the Protestant Dissenters with Respect to the Civil and Ecclesiastical Constitution of England.* London, 1769.

*Proceedings Respecting the Application to Parliament for the Repeal of the Test Laws.* [London], 1790.

*Public Documents Declaratory of the Principles of the Protestant Dissenters.* Birmingham, 1790.

Radcliff, Ebenezer. *A Sermon Preached to a Congregation of Protestant Dissenters at Crutched-Friars.* London, 1772.

[————]. *Two Letters Addressed to the Right Rev. Prelates, Who a Second Time Rejected the Dissenters' Bill.* London, 1773.

Robinson, Anthony. *A Short History of the Persecution of Christians by Jews Heathens and Christians.* Carlisle, Cumbs., [1793].

[Robinson, Robert]. *Arcana: Or the Principles of the Late Petitioners to Parliament for Relief in the Matter of Subscription.* Cambridge, 1774.

————. *The General Doctrine of Toleration Applied to the Particular Case of Free Communion.* Cambridge, 1781.

[Sharp, Richard]. *A Letter to the Public Meeting of the Friends to the Repeal of the Test and Corporation Acts at the London Tavern, Feb 13, 1790 from a Lay Dissenter.* Birmingham, [1790].

[Sherlock, Thomas]. *The History of the Test Act.* London, 1732. Reprint. Oxford, 1790.

*A Short Reply to the Speech Intended to be Spoken by the Right Hon. Charles James Fox, in Favour of the Repeal of the Test and Corporation Acts.* London, 1790.

*A Sketch of the History and Proceedings of the Deputies Appointed to Protect the Civil Rights of the Protestant Dissenters.* London, 1813.

Smith, J. *Some Remarks on the Resolutions Which Were Formed at a Meeting of the Archdeaconry of Chester, Held at the City of Chester, on Monday, the 15th Day of February, 1790.* Liverpool, 1790.

*Some Strictures on a Late Publication Entitled Reasons for Seeking a Repeal of the Corporation and Test Acts.* London, [1790].

*The Speeches of Lord North, on a Motion for a Repeal of the Corporation and Test Acts, as Delivered in the House of Commons, Wednesday, March 28, 1787 and Friday, May 8 1789.* London, 1790.

[Stennett, Samuel]. *Considerations on the Propriety of Protestant Dissenting Ministers' Acceding to a Declaration of Their Belief in the Holy Scriptures.* London, 1779.

*A Summary of the Laws Relating to Subscriptions, etc.* London, 1771.

*Test Against Test, or a View of the Measures Proposed in the Resolutions of the Dissenters, to Remove All Tests by Imposing One of Their Own upon Every Candidate for a Seat in the House of Commons, at the Next General Election*. London, [1790].

Toulmin, Joshua. *Letters to the Rev. John Sturges MA in Answer to His Considerations on the Present State of the Church Establishment*. London, 1782.

————. *A Letter to the Bishops on the Application of the Protestant Dissenters, to Parliament for a Repeal of the Corporation and Test Acts*. London, 1789.

————. *Two Letters on the Late Application to Parliament by the Protestant Dissenting Ministers*. London, 1774.

[Towgood, Micaiah]. *A Calm and Plain Answer to the Enquiry, Why Are You a Dissenter from the Church of England*. London, 1772.

[————]. *A Dissent from the Church of England Fully Justified*. 6th ed. London, 1779.

[————]. *Serious and Free Thoughts on the Present State of the Church and of Religion*. 4th ed. London, 1774.

[Trist, Jeremiah]. *Historical Memoirs of Religious Dissension*. London, 1790.

[Vaughan, Benjamin], ed. *A Collection of Testimonies in Favour of Religious Liberty in the Case of the Dissenters, Catholics, and Jews*. London, 1790.

Wakefield, Gilbert. *An Address to the Inhabitants of Nottingham Occasioned by a Letter Lately Sent to the Mayor, and Some Other Members of the Corporation of That Town*. New ed. London, 1789.

————. *Cursory Reflections, Occasioned by the Present Meetings in Opposition to the Claims of the Dissenters and the Repeal of the Corporation and Test Acts*. Birmingham, [1790].

Walker, George. *The Dissenters' Plea*. Birmingham, n.d.

Wilton, Samuel. *An Apology for the Renewal of an Application to Parliament by the Protestant Dissenting Ministers*. London, 1773.

————. *A Review of Some of the Articles of the Church of England, to Which a Subscription is Required of Protestant Dissenting Ministers*. London, 1774.

Wyvill, Christopher. *Intolerance the Disgrace of Christians*. 2d ed. London, 1809.

[————]. *A More Extended Discussion in Favour of Liberty of Conscience Recommended by the Rev. Christopher Wyvill*. London, 1808.

————. *A Sermon Preached on the Parish Church of Kelvedon at the Visitation of the Rev. Dr Powell, on Tuesday, June 2d, 1772*. London, 1772.

————. *Thoughts on Our Articles of Religion with Respect to Their Supposed Utility to the State*. 3d ed. London, 1773.

SECONDARY WORKS

Adams, Thomas R. *American Independence: The Growth of an Idea.* Providence, R.I.: Brown University Press, 1965.

[————]. "The British Look at America during the Age of Samuel Johnson: An Exhibition of Books, Maps and Prints." Typescript. Providence, R.I.: John Carter Brown Library, 1971.

————. "The British Pamphlets of the American Revolution for 1774: A Progress Report." *Proceedings of the Massachusetts Historical Society* 81 (1969): 31–103.

Agnew, John Philip. *Richard Price and the American Revolution.* Urbana, Ill.: University of Illinois, 1949.

Aldridge, Alfred Owen. *Man of Reason.* London: The Cresset Press, 1960.

Altick, Richard D. *The English Common Reader.* Chicago: University of Chicago Press, 1957.

Apter, David E. *The Politics of Modernization.* Chicago and London: University of Chicago Press, 1965.

Arendt, Hannah. *On Revolution.* New York: Viking Press, 1963.

Aspinall, Arthur. *Politics and the Press, c. 1780–1850.* London: Horne and Van Thal, 1949.

Aspinwall, Bernard. "William Smith, MP, 1756–1835." M.A. thesis, University of Manchester, 1962.

Bailyn, Bernard. *The Ideological Origins of the American Revolution.* Cambridge, Mass.: Belknap Press, 1967.

Bargar, B. D. *Lord Dartmouth and the American Revolution.* Columbia, S.C.: University of South Carolina Press, 1965.

Barlow, Richard Burgess. *Citizenship and Conscience.* Philadelphia: University of Pennsylvania Press, 1962.

Bebb, E. D. *Nonconformity and Social and Economic Life 1660–1800.* London: Epworth Press, 1935.

Best, G. F. A. *Temporal Pillars.* Cambridge: Cambridge University Press, 1964.

Black, Eugene Charlton. *The Association.* Cambridge, Mass.: Harvard University Press, 1963.

Bleackley, Horace. *Life of John Wilkes.* London: John Lane, The Bodley Head, 1917.

Bolam, C. Gordon, et al. *The English Presbyterians.* London: George Allen & Unwin, 1968.

Bowyer, T. H. *A Bibliographical Examination of the Earliest Editions of the Letters of Junius.* Charlottesville, Va.: University of Virginia Press, 1957.

Bragg, Mary Jane. "American News in English Periodicals 1783–1800." *Huntington Library Quarterly* 8 (1944–45): 393–403.

Bridenbaugh, Carl. *Mitre and Sceptre*. New York: Oxford University Press, 1962.

Briggs, Asa. "The Language of 'Class' in Early Nineteenth-Century England." In *Essays in Social History*, edited by M. W. Flinn and T. C. Smout, pp. 154–77. Oxford: Clarendon Press, 1974.

Brooke, John. *King George III*. London: Constable, 1972.

Brown, Philip Anthony. *The French Revolution in English History*. London: Frank Cass, 1945.

Brown, Weldon A. *Empire or Independence*. University, La.: Louisiana State University Press, 1941.

Brunhouse, Robert L. "David Ramsay's Publication Problems 1784–1808." *The Papers of the Bibliographical Society of America* 39 (1945): 51–67.

Brunsdon, P. A. "The Association of the Friends of the People, 1792–1796." M.A. thesis, University of Manchester, 1961.

Butterfield, Herbert. *George III, Lord North and the People 1779–80*. London: Bell, 1949.

———. "The Yorkshire Association and the Crisis of 1779–80." *Transactions of the Royal Historical Society*, 4th ser. 29 (1947): 69–91.

Cannon, John. *Parliamentary Reform 1640–1832*. Cambridge: Cambridge University Press, 1973.

Carlson, C. Lennart. *The First Magazine: A History of the Gentleman's Magazine*. Providence, R.I.: Brown University Press, 1938.

*Catalogue of the John Adams Library in the Public Library of the City of Boston*. Boston: The Trustees (of the Boston Public Library), 1917.

Cestre, Charles. *John Thelwall*. London: Swan Sonneuschein, 1906.

Christie, Ian R. *Crisis of Empire*. London: Edward Arnold, 1966.

———. *The End of North's Ministry 1780–1782*. London: Macmillan, 1958.

———. *Myth and Reality in Late-Eighteenth-Century British Politics and Other Papers*. London: Macmillan, 1970.

———. *Wilkes, Wyvill and Reform*. London: Macmillan, 1962.

Churgin, Naomi Helen. "Major John Cartwright: A Study in Radical Parliamentary Reform, 1774–1824." Ph.D. dissertation, Columbia University, 1963.

Clark, Dora Mae. *British Opinion and the American Revolution*. New Haven: Yale University Press, 1930.

Cochrane, J. A. *Dr. Johnson's Printer: The Life of William Strahan*. London: Routledge & Kegan Paul, 1964.

Colbourn, H. Trevor. *The Lamp of Experience*. Chapel Hill, N.C.: University of North Carolina Press, 1965.

Collins, Henry. "The London Corresponding Society." In *Democracy and the Labour Movement*, edited by John Saville, pp. 103–34. London: Lawrence & Wishart, 1954.

Cone, Carl B. *Burke and the Nature of Politics*. Vol. I: *The Age of the American Revolution*. Lexington, Ky.: University of Kentucky Press, 1957.

———. *The English Jacobins*. New York: Scribner, 1968.

———. *Torchbearer of Freedom*. Lexington, Ky.: University of Kentucky Press, 1952.

Conway, Moncure Daniel. *The Life of Thomas Paine*. 2 vols. New York and London, 1892.

Cragg, Gerald R. *Reason and Authority in the Eighteenth Century*. Cambridge: Cambridge University Press, 1964.

Crane, Verner W. *Benjamin Franklin and a Rising People*. Boston: Little Brown, 1954.

———. "The Club of Honest Whigs: Friends of Science and Liberty." *William and Mary Quarterly*, 3d ser. 23 (1966): 210–33.

Craven, Wesley Frank. *The Legend of the Founding Fathers*. New York: New York University Press, 1956.

Cresson, W. P. *Francis Dana*. New York: Lincoln MacVeagh, 1930.

Crook, David Paul. *American Democracy in English Politics, 1815–1850*. Oxford: Clarendon Press, 1965.

Crook, Donald E. *A Bibliography of Joseph Priestley 1733–1804*. London: The Library Association, 1966.

Dana, Richard Henry. "Francis Dana." *Publications of the Cambridge* [Mass.] *Historical Society* 3 (1908): 56–78.

Davidson, Philip. *Propaganda and the American Revolution 1763–1783*. Chapel Hill, N.C.: University of North Carolina Press, 1941.

Davis, H. W. C. *The Age of Grey and Peel*. Oxford: Oxford University Press, 1929.

Dinwiddy, J. R. *Christopher Wyvill and Reform 1790–1820*. York: St. Anthony's Press, 1971.

Ditchfield, Grayson McClure. "Some Aspects of Unitarianism and Radicalism 1760–1810." Ph.D. dissertation, University of Cambridge, 1968.

Donnelly, Lucy Martin. "The Celebrated Mrs Macaulay." *William and Mary Quarterly*, 3d ser. 6 (1949): 173–207.

Donoughue, Bernard. *British Politics and the American Revolution: The Path to War, 1773–1775*. London: Macmillan, 1964.

Edwards, Maldwyn. *After Wesley*. London: Epworth Press, 1935.

Fink, Zera S. *The Classical Republicans*. Evanston, Ill.: Northwestern University, 1945.

Foord, Archibald S. *His Majesty's Opposition 1714–1830*. Oxford: Clarendon Press, 1964.

Fox, R. Hingston. *Dr. John Fothergill and His Friends*. London: Macmillan, 1919.

Gary, A. T. "The Political and Economic Relations of English and American Quakers (1750–1785)." D.Phil. thesis, University of Oxford, 1935.

Gay, Peter. "The Enlightenment." In *Comparative Approach to American History*, edited by C. Vann Woodward, pp. 37–49. [Washington, D.C.]: U.S. Information Service, 1968.

―――. *Voltaire's Politics: The Poet as Realist*. Princeton, N.J.: Princeton University Press, 1959.

Gegenheimer, Albert Frank. *William Smith*. Philadelphia: University of Pennsylvania Press, 1943.

Gibbs, F. W. *Joseph Priestley: Adventurer in Science and Champion of Truth*. London: Nelson, 1965.

Gignilliat, George Warren, Jr. *The Author of Sandford and Merton: A Life of Thomas Day, Esq.* New York: Columbia University Press, 1932.

Gimbel, Richard. *Thomas Paine: A Bibliographical Check-list of Common Sense with an Account of Its Publication*. New Haven, Conn.: Yale University Press, 1956.

Gipson, Lawrence Henry. *The British Empire before the American Revolution*. 15 vols. New York: Alfred Knopf, 1958–70.

Guttridge, George Herbert. *David Hartley, M.P.: An Advocate of Conciliation 1774–1783*. University of California Publications in History, 14 (1926): 231–340.

―――. *English Whiggism and the American Revolution*. Berkeley and Los Angeles: University of California Press, 1963.

―――. "Thomas Pownall's *The Administrations of the Colonies*: The Six Editions." *William and Mary Quarterly*, 3d ser. 26 (1969): 31–46.

Halevy, Elie. *The Growth of Philosophic Radicalism*. Boston: Beacon Press, 1955.

Hall, Walter Phelps. *British Radicalism 1791–1797*. New York: Columbia University Press, 1912.

Handlin, Oscar, and Handlin, Mary F. "James Burgh and American Revolutionary Theory." *Proceedings of the Massachusetts Historical Society* 73 (1961): 38–57.

Hans, Nicholas. "Franklin, Jefferson and the English Radicals at the End of the Eighteenth Century." *Proceedings of the American Philosophical Society* 98 (1954): 406–26.

Harastzi, Zoltan. *John Adams and the Prophets of Progress*. Cambridge, Mass.: Harvard University Press, 1952.

———. "John Adams on Dr. Priestley." *More Books* 10 (1935): 301–18.

Harlan, Robert Dale. "William Strahan: Eighteenth Century London Printer and Publisher." Ph.D. dissertation, University of Michigan, 1960.

Harlow, Vincent T. *The Founding of the Second British Empire 1763–1793*. Vol. 1. London: Longmans Green, 1952.

Hawkes, Arthur John, ed. *Lancashire Printed Books*. Wigan: Public Libraries Committee, 1925.

Hay, Carla H. "Benjamin Franklin, James Burgh, and the Authorship of 'The Colonist's Advocate' Letters." *William and Mary Quarterly*, 3d ser. 32 (1975): 111–24.

———. "Crusading Schoolmaster: James Burgh, 1714–1775." Ph.D. dissertation, University of Kentucky, 1972.

Hay, Douglas; Linebaugh, Peter; Rule, John G.; Thompson, E. P.; and Winslow, Cal. *Albion's Fatal Tree*. London: Allen Lane, 1975.

Heimert, Alan. *Religion and the American Mind*. Cambridge, Mass.: Harvard University Press, 1966.

Hendrick, Burton J. *The Lees of Virginia*. Boston: Little Brown, 1935.

Henriques, Ursula. *Religious Toleration in England, 1787–1833*. London: Routledge & Kegan Paul, 1961.

Hernlund, Patricia. "William Strahan's Ledgers: Standard Charges for Printing, 1738–1785." *Studies in Bibliography* 20 (1967): 89–112.

Hill, Christopher. *Puritanism and Revolution*. London: Secker and Warburg, 1958.

Hinkhouse, Fred Junkin. *The Preliminaries of the American Revolution as Seen in the English Press, 1763–1775*. New York: Columbia University Press, 1926.

Hobsbawn, E. J. "The Social Function of the Past: Some Questions." *Past and Present*, no. 55 (1972): 3–17.

Holdsworth, Sir William. *A History of English Law*. 16 vols. London: Methuen/Sweet Maxwell, 1903–66.

Holmes, Geoffrey, ed. *Britain After the Glorious Revolution: 1689–1714*. London: Macmillan, 1969.

Holt, Anne. *A Life of Joseph Priestley*. London: Oxford University Press, 1931.

Howe, John R., Jr. *The Changing Political Thought of John Adams*. Princeton, N.J.: Princeton University Press, 1966.

Hughes, Graham W. *With Freedom Fired*. London: Carey Kingsgate Press, 1955.

Hunt, N. C. *Two Early Political Associations*. Oxford: Clarendon Press, 1961.

Jameson, J. Franklin. *The American Revolution Considered as a Social Movement*. Boston: Beacon Press, 1956.

Jarrett, J. D. "The Bowood Circle, 1780–1793." B.Litt. thesis, University of Oxford, 1955.

Jensen, Merrill. *The New Nation*. New York: Vintage Books, 1965.

Jephson, Henry. *The Platform*. 2 vols. London, 1892.

Jewson, C. B. *The Jacobin City*. Glasgow and London: Blackie, 1975.

Jeyes, S. H. *The Russells of Birmingham in the French Revolution and in America 1791–1814*. London: George Allen, 1911.

Johnson, Thomas H. *The Printed Writings of Jonathan Edwards 1703–1758: A Bibliography*. Princeton, N.J.: Princeton University Press, 1940.

Jones, E. Alfred. *American Members of the Inns of Court*. London: St. Catherine Press, 1924.

Jones, R. Tudur. *Congregationalism in England 1662–1962*. London: Independent Press Ltd., 1962.

Jones, Rufus M. *The Quakers in the American Colonies*. London: Macmillan, 1911.

Kaufman, Paul. "A Bookseller's Record of Eighteenth-Century Book Clubs." *The Library*, 5th ser. 15 (1960): 278–87.

———. *Borrowings from the Bristol Library 1773–1784*. Charlottesville, Va.: Bibliographical Society of the University of Virginia, 1960.

———. "English Book Clubs and Their Role in Social History." *Libri* 14 (1964): 1–31.

Keir, David Lindsay. *The Constitutional History of Modern Britain since 1485*. 6th ed. London: Adam and Charles Black, 1961.

Knight, Frida. *The Strange Case of Thomas Walker*. London: Lawrence and Wishart, 1957.

———. *University Rebel: The Life of William Frend (1757–1841)*. London: Gollancz, 1971.

Knorr, Klaus E. *British Colonial Theories 1570–1850*. London: Frank Cass, 1963.

Koch, Adrienne. *Power, Morals, and the Founding Fathers*. Ithaca, N.Y.: Cornell University Press, 1961.

Kraus, Michael. *The Atlantic Civilization: Eighteenth Century Origins*. Ithaca, N.Y.: Cornell University Press, 1949.

Labaree, Benjamin W. "The Idea of American Independence: The British View, 1774–1776." *Proceedings of the Massachusetts Historical Society* 82 (1971): 3–20.

Labaree, Leonard W. "Benjamin Franklin's British Friendships."

*Proceedings of the American Philosophical Society* 108 (1964): 423–28.

Langford, John Alfred. *A Century of Birmingham Life*. Vol. 1. Birmingham, 1868.

Lascelles, E. C. P. *Granville Sharp and the Freedom of Slaves in England*. London: Oxford University Press, 1928.

Leslie, Margaret Evelyn. "The Social and Political Thought of Joseph Priestley." Ph.D. dissertation, University of Cambridge, 1966.

Lillibridge, G. D. *Beacon of Freedom: The Impact of American Democracy upon Great Britain, 1830–1870*. [Philadelphia]: University of Pennsylvania Press, 1955.

Lincoln, Anthony. *Some Political and Social Ideas of English Dissent 1763–1800*. Cambridge: Cambridge University Press, 1938.

Loveland, Clara O. *The Critical Years*. Greenwich, Conn.: Seabury Press, 1956.

Lutnick, Solomon. *The American Revolution and the British Press*. Columbia, Mo.: University of Missouri Press, 1967.

Maccoby, S. *English Radicalism, 1762–1785*. London: George Allen & Unwin, 1955.

———. *English Radicalism, 1786–1832*. London: George Allen & Unwin, 1955.

McLachlan, H. *English Education under the Test Acts*. Manchester: Manchester University Press, 1931.

Magnus, Sir Philip. *Edmund Burke*. London: John Murray, 1939.

Maier, Pauline. *From Resistance to Revolution*. London: Routledge and Kegan Paul, 1973.

———. "John Wilkes and American Disillusionment with Britain." *William and Mary Quarterly*, 3d ser. 20 (1963): 373–95.

Manning, Bernard Lord. *The Protestant Dissenting Deputies*. Cambridge: Cambridge University Press, 1952.

Mesick, Jane Louise. *The English Traveller in America 1785–1835*. New York: Columbia University Press, 1922.

Meteyard, Eliza. *The Life of Josiah Wedgwood*. 2 vols. London, 1865–66.

Miller, Victor Clyde. *Joel Barlow: Revolutionist, London, 1791–92*. Hamburg: n.p., 1932.

Money, John. "Public Opinion in the West Midlands 1760–1793." Ph.D. dissertation, University of Cambridge, 1967.

Mullett, Charles F. "English Imperial Thinking: 1764–1783." *Political Science Quarterly* 45 (1930): 549–79.

Namier, Sir Lewis, and Brooke, John. *The History of Parliament: The*

*House of Commons 1754–1790.* 3 vols. London: Her Majesty's Stationery Office, 1964.

Nangle, Benjamin Christie. *The Monthly Review: First Series 1749–1789.* Oxford: Clarendon Press, 1934.

_____. *The Monthly Review: Second Series 1790–1815.* Oxford: Clarendon Press, 1955.

Nelson, William H. *The American Tory.* Oxford: Oxford University Press, 1961.

Norman, E. R. *The Conscience of the State in North America.* Cambridge: Cambridge University Press, 1968.

Norris, John. *Shelburne and Reform.* London: Macmillan, 1963.

O'Gorman, F. *The Whig Party and the French Revolution.* London: Macmillan, 1967.

Olmstead, Clifton E. *History of Religion in the United States.* Englewood Cliffs, N.J.: Prentice Hall, 1960.

Olson, Alison Gilbert. *The Radical Duke.* London: Oxford University Press, 1961.

_____, and Brown, Richard Maxwell, eds. *Anglo-American Political Relations, 1675–1775.* New Brunswick, N.J.: Rutgers University Press, 1970.

Osborne, John W. *John Cartwright.* Cambridge: Cambridge University Press, 1972.

Pallister, Anne. *Magna Carta: The Heritage of Liberty.* Oxford: Clarendon Press, 1971.

Palmer, Robert R. *The Age of the Democratic Revolution.* Vol. 1. Princeton, N.J.: Princeton University Press, 1959.

_____. "The Revolution." In *A Comparative Approach to American History.* Edited by C. Vann Woodward, pp. 51–66. [Washington, D.C.]: U.S. Information Service, 1968.

Perkin, Harold. *The Origins of Modern English Society 1780–1880.* London: Routledge and Kegan Paul, 1969.

Phillips, N. C. "Edmund Burke and the County Movement 1779–1780." *English Historical Review* 76 (1961): 254–78.

Pittman, R. Carter. Review of "Sources of Our Liberties." *Virginia Magazine of History and Biography* 68 (1960): 109–12.

Plumb, J. H. *The Growth of Political Stability in England 1675–1725.* London: Macmillan, 1967.

_____, and Dearing, Vinton A. *Some Aspects of Eighteenth-Century England.* Los Angeles: William Andrews Clark Memorial Library, 1971.

Pocock, J. G. A. *The Ancient Constitution and the Feudal Law.* New York: Norton, 1967.

———. "Burke and the Ancient Constitution—A Problem in the History of Ideas." *The Historical Journal* 3 (1960): 125–43.

———. *Politics, Language and Time.* London: Methuen, 1972.

Pole, J. R. *Political Representation in England and the Origins of the American Republic.* London: Macmillan, 1966.

Rea, Robert R. *The English Press in Politics 1760–1774.* Lincoln, Neb.: University of Nebraska Press, 1963.

———. "John Almon: Bookseller to John Wilkes." *Indiana Quarterly for Bookmen* 4 (1948): 20–28.

Read, Donald. *The English Provinces c. 1760–1960.* London: Edward Arnold, 1964.

Riggs, Alvin Richard. "Arthur Lee and the Radical Whigs, 1768–1776." Ph.D. dissertation, Yale University, 1967.

Ritcheson, Charles R. *British Politics and the American Revolution.* Norman, Okla.: University of Oklahoma Press, 1954.

———. "The London Press and the First Decade of American Independence, 1783–93." *Journal of British Studies* 2 (1963): 88–109.

Robbins, Caroline. *The Eighteenth Century Commonwealthman.* Cambridge, Mass.: Harvard University Press, 1959.

———. "Honest Heretic: Joseph Priestley in America, 1794–1804." *Proceedings of the American Philosophical Society* 106 (1962): 60–76.

———. "Library of Liberty—Assembled for Harvard College by Thomas Hollis of Lincoln's Inn." *Harvard Library Bulletin* 5 (1951): 5–23, 181–96.

———. "The Strenuous Whig, Thomas Hollis of Lincoln's Inn." *William and Mary Quarterly,* 3d ser. 7 (1950): 407–53.

———. "Thomas Brand Hollis (1719–1804): English Admirer of Franklin and Intimate of John Adams." *Proceedings of the American Philosophical Society* 97 (1953):239–47.

Robson, Eric. *The American Revolution.* London: Batchworth Press, 1955.

Rogers, Pat. "An Early Colonial Historian: John Oldmixon and *The British Empire in America.*" *Journal of American Studies* 7 (1973): 113–23.

Rose, R. B. "The Priestley Riots of 1791." *Past and Present,* no. 18 (1960): 68–88.

Rudé, George. *Hanoverian London: 1714–1808.* London: Secker and Warburg, 1971.

———. "John Wilkes and the Re-Birth of British Radicalism." *Political Science* [New Zealand] 14 (1962): 11–29.

_____. *Paris and London in the Eighteenth Century*. London: Collins, 1974.

_____. *Wilkes and Liberty*. Oxford: Clarendon Press, 1962.

Sachse, William L. *The Colonial American in Britain*. Madison, Wisc.: University of Wisconsin Press, 1956.

Schofield, Robert E. *The Lunar Society of Birmingham*. Oxford: Clarendon Press, 1963.

Schutz, John A. *Thomas Pownall: British Defender of American Liberty*. Glendale, Calif.: The Arthur H. Clark Company, 1951.

Seaman, William Alban Lewis. "British Democratic Societies in the Period of the French Revolution." Ph.D. dissertation, University of London, 1954.

Sherman, Stuart C. "Leman Thomas Rede's *Bibliotheca Americana*." *William and Mary Quarterly*, 3d ser. 4 (1947): 332–49.

Smith, Page. *John Adams*. 2 vols. Garden City, N.Y.: Doubleday, 1962.

Spiller, Robert E. *The American in England during the First Half Century of Independence*. New York: Henry Holt, 1926.

Stanhope, Ghita, and Gooch, G. P. *The Life of Charles, Third Earl Stanhope*. London: Longmans Green, 1914.

Stephen, Sir Leslie. *History of English Thought in the Eighteenth Century*. 2 vols. 3d ed. London: Smith, Elder, 1902.

Stephens, W. B., ed. *A History of the County of Warwick*. Vol. 7: *The City of Birmingham*. London: Oxford University Press, 1964.

Stromberg, Roland N. *Religious Liberalism in Eighteenth Century England*. London: Oxford University Press, 1954.

Sutherland, Lucy S. *The City of London and the Opposition to Government 1768–1774*. London: Athlone Press, 1959.

_____. "The City of London in Eighteenth-Century Politics." In *Essays Presented to Sir Lewis Namier*. Edited by Richard Pares and A. J. P. Taylor. London: Macmillan, 1956.

Sweet, William Warren. *Religion in the Development of American Culture 1765–1840*. Gloucester, Mass.: Peter Smith, 1963.

_____. *The Story of Religion in America*. New York: Harper, 1930.

Sykes, Norman. *Church and State in England in the XVIIIth Century*. Cambridge: Cambridge University Press, 1934.

Tate, Thad W. "The Social Contract in America, 1774–1787: Revolutionary Theory as a Conservative Instrument." *William and Mary Quarterly*, 3d ser. 22 (1965): 375–91.

Thistlethwaite, Frank. *America and the Atlantic Community*. New York: Harper and Row, 1963.

Thomas, David Oswald. "The Political Philosophy of Richard Price." Ph.D. dissertation, University of London, 1956.

————. "Richard Price, 1723–91." *Transactions of the Honourable Society of Cymmrodorian*, Session 1971, pt. I, 45–46.

Thomas, P. D. G. *The House of Commons in the Eighteenth Century*. Oxford: Clarendon Press, 1971.

Thomas, Roland. *Richard Price*. London: Oxford University Press, 1924.

Thompson, E. P. *The Making of the English Working Class*. New York: Vintage, 1966.

Tolles, Frederick B. *Quakers and the Atlantic Culture*. New York: Macmillan, 1960.

Underwood, A. C.; and Rushbrooke, J. H. *A History of the English Baptists*. London: Carey Kingsgate Press Ltd., 1947.

Van Alstyne, Richard W. "Europe, the Rockingham Whigs, and the War for American Independence: Some Documents." *Huntington Library Quarterly* 25 (1961): 1–28.

————. "Parliamentary Supremacy Versus Independence: Notes and Documents." *Huntington Library Quarterly* 26 (1963): 201–33.

Van Doren, Carl. *Benjamin Franklin*. New York: Viking Press, 1938.

Veitch, George Stead. *The Genesis of Parliamentary Reform*. London: Constable, 1913.

"A View of English Nonconformity in 1773." *Congregational Historical Society Transactions* 5 (1911–12): 205–22, 261–77, 372–85.

Wallace, David Duncan. *The Life of Henry Laurens*. New York: G. P. Putnam's, 1915.

Walvin, James. "English Democratic Societies and Popular Radicalism, 1791–1800." D.Phil. dissertation, University of York, 1969.

Watson, J. Steven. *The Reign of George III 1760–1815*. Oxford: Clarendon Press, 1960.

Watson, Winslow C. *Men and Times of the Revolution, or Memoirs of Elkanah Watson*. New York, 1856.

Wead, Eunice. "British Public Opinion of the Peace with America in 1782." *American Historical Review* 34 (1929): 513–31.

Webb, R. K. *The British Working Class Reader 1790–1848*. London: George Allen & Unwin, 1955.

Welford, Richard. *Men of Mark 'Twixt Tyne and Tweed*. 3 vols. London and Newcastle, 1895.

Werkmeister, Lucyle. *The London Daily Press 1772–1792*. Lincoln, Neb.: University of Nebraska Press, 1963.

Weston, Corinne Comstock. *English Constitutional Theory and the House of Lords, 1556–1832*. London: Routledge and Kegan Paul, 1965.

Whiteman, Anne, et al., eds. *Statesmen, Scholars and Merchants*. Oxford: Oxford University Press, 1973.

Wilbur, Earl Morse. *A History of Unitarianism in Transylvania, England, and America*. Cambridge, Mass.: Harvard University Press, 1952.

Willey, Basil. *The Eighteenth-Century Background*. Harmondsworth, Middx.: Penguin Books, 1962.

Williams, Gwyn A. *Artisans and Sans-Culottes*. London: Edward Arnold, 1968.

Wolf, Edwin. *Benjamin Franklin's Political Miscellaneous and Philosophical Pieces, 1779*. n.p., 1950.

Wood, Gordon S. *The Creation of the American Republic, 1776–1787*. Chapel Hill, N.C.: University of North Carolina Press, 1969.

Yarborough, Minnie Clare. *John Horne Tooke*. New York: Columbia University Press, 1926.

————. "John Horne Tooke: Champion of the American Colonists." *South Atlantic Quarterly* 35 (1936): 374–92.

# Index

Associated counties, 4, 8, 114, 131–33, 134–35, 138, 142, 162
Association of Friends of the People, 226, 235
Avery, Benjamin, 33

## B

Baptists, 86, 151–52, 191, 192, 273 (n. 14)
Barclay, David, 79
Barlow, Joel, 155–56, 221, 225–26, 296 (n. 28)
Baron, Richard, 22
Barré, Isaac, 31, 78, 133
Beaufoy, Henry, 209
Belknap, Jeremy, 156, 221–22
Belsham, William, 184
Benezet, Anthony, 33, 44, 73
Benson, George, 33
Bentham, Jeremy, xiv, 241, 246–47
Bentley, Thomas, 10, 29, 43, 84, 92
Bertie, Willoughby, earl of Abingdon. See Abingdon, earl of
Beverley, Robert: History . . . of Virginia, 37
Bewdley, 85
Bingham, William, 152, 154
Binns, John, 224
Birmingham, 85, 210, 212, 218, 223
Birmingham Society for Constitutional Information, 218
Blackburne, Francis, 11, 55, 67, 75, 201
Blackburne, Thomas, 75
Blackstone, William, 74, 193, 238–39
Bland, Richard, 39
Boston Massacre, 38–39, 42, 66, 118
Boston Tea Party, xvii, 58, 66–67, 68, 70, 75, 82–83, 120
Boulton, Matthew, 29, 89, 285 (n. 49)
Bradford, Thomas, 41
Brand Hollis, Thomas, xv, 5, 7–8, 11, 14, 20, 22, 155, 157, 162, 179, 222, 235; imperial crisis, 77, 121; American friends, 78, 152, 173, 220; parliamentary reform, 134–35, 136, 138, 246; American model, 160, 175, 178–79, 181–82, 204; and new radicals, 220, 226, 235
Bristol, 76, 85, 86, 87, 223
Burgh, James, 8, 19, 22, 119, 121; Political Disquisitions, 8, 22, 75, 76, 134, 145–46, 284 (n. 33); and Franklin, 30, 31, 65; imperial crisis, 65, 75, 82
Burgoyne, John, 107
Burke, Edmund, 31, 76, 86, 113, 130–31, 133, 172, 213, 223, 226, 227, 228
Burke, William: An Account of the European Settlements in America, 36
Burnaby, Andrew: Travels through the Middle Settlements . . ., 36, 273 (n. 19)
Bute, John Stuart, earl of, 115, 120

## C

Cadell, Thomas, 155
Cambridge Constitutional Society, 16
Camden, earl of, 62
Cappe, Newcome, 10, 101, 123
Caribs of St. Vincent, 27
Cartwright, John, xv, 5, 6, 10, 11–12, 62, 84, 90, 138, 146, 158, 220, 235, 245, 283 (n. 4); ideology, 16, 17, 18, 19–20, 22, 23, 25, 72, 265, 286 (n. 70); English constitution, 20, 25, 72, 184, 238–39; imperial crisis, 54, 68, 70–72, 76, 82–83, 97, 248; American Independence, 70, 84, 91, 92, 103; American society, 70; American independence, 71, 74, 99, 100–101, 108; War of Independence, 89, 112, 130, 138, 237; hopes for reconciliation, 103–4, 105, 281 (n. 35); parliamentary reform, 103, 105, 130, 135, 136, 138, 240, 246; Anglo-American crisis, 121–22; English decadence, 123; American model, 142–143, 146, 147–48, 184, 236, 237–40, 241, 258
Case Stated on Philosophical Grounds, The, 122
Catholics, 189, 190, 192, 196, 201
Chamberlayne and White (Treasury solicitors), 231
Chambers, William, 126
Champion, Richard, 85, 223
Chatham, earl of. See Pitt, William
Chauncy, Charles, 33, 38, 125, 151, 198
Church of England, xiii, 188–89, 190, 195, 196, 197, 206, 207, 208, 212–13, 214
Civil war, 24
Clerical relief, 192, 201
Club of Honest Whigs, 30, 83
Club of 13, 29
Coercive Acts, 58, 66, 75, 76, 79, 80, 98, 118, 121, 252
Collinson, Peter, 29
Colonial agents, 68
Commonwealthmen: American society, xi, xvi, 27, 37, 44–50, 70, 76, 124, 156–57, 163–65, 236; War of Independence, xii, xvii, xviii, xx, 3, 33, 40–41, 50, 80, 81–113, 114, 122–23, 127, 128, 136, 137, 138, 139–40, 141, 150, 265; political ideology, xv, xvi, 3, 4, 5, 12–24, 25, 28, 77, 122, 144, 149, 163, 166, 170–71, 174, 243, 246, 253–55; universalism, xvi, 13–14, 151; American friends and correspondents, xvi, 28–34, 59, 151–53, 220, 221; transatlantic community, xvi, 27–28, 34–35, 70, 76, 81–82, 125, 159–60, 242, 248, 257, 263–64; American pamphlets and

America, xxi–xxii, 224, 225, 226, 228–30, 231–34, 242, 247, 260, 264

New England, xix, 33, 36–37, 45–46, 47, 54, 62, 78, 119, 125, 177, 197, 198–99, 200, 208, 261

New York, 164

Noorthouck, John, 39–40, 62, 64

Norman Yoke, 24

North, Frederick, Lord, 66, 67, 68, 73, 76, 78, 81, 89, 102, 107, 108, 109, 112, 122, 128, 130, 162, 172, 205, 275 (n. 7)

*North Briton, The,* 115, 245

Norwich, 123, 218, 224, 230

### O

Olive Branch Petition, 90

Oswald, John, 233

Otis, James, xix, 38, 43, 44

### P

Paine, Thomas, xiv, 8, 22, 135, 145, 154, 217, 221, 245, 246, 260; *Rights of Man,* xiv, xxii, 226–31, 235, 238; *Common Sense,* 39, 41, 44, 226, 231

Paley, William, 207–8

Palmer, Thomas Fysshe, 224

Paoli, Pasquale, 27

Paris, Treaty of, 150, 250

Parliament, xiii, 7, 13, 23, 51, 52, 57–80 passim, 95, 97, 98, 103, 105, 115, 116, 122, 135, 138, 141, 147, 193, 195; House of Commons, xiii, 9, 19, 21, 22, 23, 51, 68, 79, 80, 84, 91, 103, 105, 116, 118, 122, 131, 134, 148, 209, 210, 214, 237, 240; House of Lords, xiii, 9, 19, 21, 22, 23, 98, 121, 200, 237, 256

Parliamentary opposition, 68–69, 79, 80, 85, 90–91, 101, 115, 133, 154, 172, 235

Parliamentary reform, 4, 5–9, 13, 23, 24, 58, 106, 107, 110–11, 114, 117, 118, 129, 130, 131–49, 163, 187, 236

Pemberton, James, 59

Pennsylvania, 32, 37, 39, 40, 154, 164, 221, 223, 230, 232; religious model, 199, 200, 202, 203, 212

Pennsylvania: Constitution, xxi, 147–48, 169–70, 171, 175, 176, 179, 184, 230, 237, 259, 260

Percival, Thomas, 29, 43, 274 (n. 37)

Peters, Richard, 153

Philadelphia Convention, 151, 171, 180, 187, 230

Pigott, Charles, 223

Pitt, William, earl of Chatham, 60, 62, 68, 79, 90, 108, 113, 122, 200, 278 (n. 52)

Pitt, William, the younger, xxii, 114, 135, 162, 205, 206, 209–10, 211, 216, 236, 291 (n. 9)

Pownall, Thomas, 109–10, 160–61, 165, 166, 174, 251, 275 (n. 7), 282 (n. 86)

Presbyterians, 191, 192

Price, Richard, xv, 9–10, 15, 54, 88, 117, 153, 155, 157, 159, 191, 192, 220, 232, 245, 257, 280 (n. 44); social status, 11–12; ideology, 13, 16, 17–18, 22, 93–94, 184–86, 225, 235–36, 265; religious liberty, 18, 206; American friends and correspondents, 30–31, 32, 33, 78, 104, 151, 152, 153, 159, 173; receives American tracts, 42; *Observations on the Nature of Civil Liberty . . .,* 46, 81, 91–98, 245, 280 (n. 41); *The Importance of the American Revolution,* 46, 165–68, 176, 228; view of American society, 46–49, 50, 96, 124, 164, 166, 260; English decadence, 50, 122, 123; imperial crisis, 54, 67, 79; America as asylum, 66, 124–25, 126; War of Independence, 80, 83, 104, 109, 111, 130; imperial theory, 93–98; American independence, 96–97, 99, 100–101, 104, 108, 109–10, 127, 281 (n. 59); hopes for reconciliation, 99, 104, 106, 281 (n. 59); refuses U.S. citizenship, 104–5; America as model, 126, 127, 146, 148, 157, 161, 162, 178, 179, 181, 185; parliamentary reform, 130; economic relations with U.S., 164–65; advice to U.S., 166–68, 180, 202, 222; U.S. Constitution, 181; American religious model, 201–2, 204, 205, 294 (n. 59); American and French Revolutions, 222; *Discourse on the Love of Our Country,* 225, 235, 245

Priestley, Joseph, xv, 9–10, 15, 92, 117, 121, 155, 160, 188, 191, 192, 205, 245, 257; social status, 11, 30; ideology, 13, 17, 19, 22, 178, 235–36, 237, 265; American friends, 30, 75, 78, 152, 173, 178; American society, 45; imperial crisis, 53, 64–65, 75, 76; War of Independence, 80, 83, 89; and parliamentary opposition, 90–91, 112; American independence, 107–8; threat to English liberty, 119, 120–21; America as model, 126, 178, 183–84, 186; American religious model, 200, 211–13; religious liberty, 206; religious establishments, 211–14, 223, 266; French Revolution, 216–17, 222; church and state riots, 223

Progress, 26, 49, 157–58, 160, 161, 162–63, 254–55

Protestant Association, 201

Protestant Dissenting Deputies, 55, 194, 196, 205–6, 292 (n. 28)

Providence, Divine: in Commonwealth ideology, 15, 161–62, 253, 254–56; and empire, 72–73; War of Independence, 91, 101–2; American model, 113, 157; punishes England, 123–24, 125, 127, 247